Semantic Web Services Challenge
Results from the First Year

T0180537

SEMANTIC WEB AND BEYOND
Computing for Human Experience

Series Editors:

Ramesh Jain
University of California, Irvine
http://ngs.ics.uci.edu/

Amit Sheth
University of Georgia
http://lsdis.cs.uga.edu/~amit

As computing becomes ubiquitous and pervasive, computing is increasingly becoming an extension of human, modifying or enhancing human experience. Today's car reacts to human perception of danger with a series of computers participating in how to handle the vehicle for human command and environmental conditions. Proliferating sensors help with observations, decision making as well as sensory modifications. The emergent semantic web will lead to machine understanding of data and help exploit heterogeneous, multi-source digital media. Emerging applications in situation monitoring and entertainment applications are resulting in development of experiential environments.

SEMANTIC WEB AND BEYOND
Computing for Human Experience
addresses the following goals:

➢ brings together forward looking research and technology that will shape our world more intimately than ever before as computing becomes an extension of human experience;
➢ covers all aspects of computing that is very closely tied to human perception, understanding and experience;
➢ brings together computing that deal with semantics, perception and experience;
➢ serves as the platform for exchange of both practical technologies and far reaching research.

AdditionalTitles in the Series:

Ontology Management: Semantic Web, Semantic Web Services, and Business Applications edited by Martin Hepp, Pieter De Leenheer, Aldo de Moor, York Sure; ISBN: 978-0-387-69899-1
The Semantic Web:Real-World Applications from Industry edited by Jorge Cardoso, Martin Hepp, Miltiadis Lytras; ISBN: 978-0-387-48530-0
Social Networks and the Semantic Web by Peter Mika; ISBN: 978-0-387-71000-6
Ontology Alignment: Bridging the Semantic Gap by Marc Ehrig, ISBN: 0-387-32805-X
Semantic Web Services: Processes and Applications edited by Jorge Cardoso, Amit P. Sheth, ISBN 0-387-30239-5
Canadian Semantic Web edited by Mamadou T. Koné., Daniel Lemire; ISBN: 0-387-29815-0
Semantic Management of Middleware by Daniel Oberle; ISBN: 0-387-27630-0

Additional information about this series can be obtained from
http://www.springer.com   ISSN: 1559-7474

Semantic Web Services Challenge
Results from the First Year

Edited by

Charles Petrie
Stanford University
Stanford, CA, USA

Tiziana Margaria
University of Potsdam
Potsdam, Germany

Holger Lausen
Michal Zaremba
University of Innsbruck
Innsbruck, Austria

 Springer

Editors:

Charles Petrie
Stanford University
Computer Science Dept.
353 Serra Mall
Stanford, CA 94305-9020
petrie@stanford.edu

Holger Lausen
Semantics Technology Institute (STI)
University of Innsbruck ICT
Technologie Park
Technikerstraße 21a
6020 Innsbruck Austria
mail@holgerlausen.net

Tiziana Margaria
Chair *Service and Software Engineering*
Institute for Informatics
University Potsdam
August-Bebel-Str.89 – Haus 4
D-14482 Potsdam, Germany
margaria@cs.uni-potsdam.de

Michal Zaremba
Semantics Technology Institute (STI)
University of Innsbruck ICT
Technologie Park
Technikerstraße 21a
6020 Innsbruck Austria
michal.zaremba@sti2.at

ISBN-13: 978-1-4419-4440-5   e-ISBN-13: 978-0-387-72496-6

Foreword by James A. Hendler

Back in 2001, I published a paper called "Agents and the Semantic Web," [1] which outlined a vision of how the then-new Semantic Web technologies being explored at DARPA could be used as a mechanism for connecting descriptions of software to the dynamic content engines of the Web - essentially, outlining the idea that what we now call Web services could be tied to semantics and ontologies. The paper has become one of my more highly cited ones, but really it was more of a vision paper than a technological prescription. Luckily for those people interested, Sheila McIlraith and her colleagues published a paper in that same issue [2] (which has been even more highly cited) which outlined a technical approach for Semantic Web Services, the name by which this area has come to be known.

In the years since, Semantic Web Services have become an increasingly important part of Semantic Web research. This work has essentially co-evolved with the growing importance of service-oriented architectures (SOAs), to the industrial computing sector, providing a set of interesting, and realistic, challenges to researchers. The area has thrived on a combination of research funding for universities, especially from the EU's framework 6 and framework 7 programs, and industrial support within corporate laboratories. In fact, since the coining of the term in 2001, a Google Scholar search on "semantic web services" now finds over 8,000 publications that discuss some aspect of this integration of semantics and Web services, a staggering amount of research in such a short amount of time.

However, this growth in interest in the area, and the wide swath of research it engendered, also led to significant confusion over, well, what was it really all good for? Could the addition of Semantics really increase the capabilities of Web Services? Could the theoretical results from the research labs be transitioned into workable and scalable systems? Could the techniques of the researchers be made to work with the commercial languages - SOAP, WSDL, BPEL, etc. - being used in the real world? Finding papers that showed clean results on toy problems was easy, but finding practicable technologies that could be used in real world applications required more effort.

In short, we had an odd situation. With Service-Oriented Computing becoming more and more important as a means of software engineering for distributed systems, the Semantic Web community was finding it hard and harder to explain what it was able to do or to compare the many competing approaches that were being developed. The many different approaches could not easily be reconciled on purely theoretical grounds, rather, an empirical means of evaluating their capabilities with standard testbeds was clearly needed.

Starting in the middle of this decade, a set of workshops was held to explore this issue. Researchers who felt their work was reaching a capability level that could lead to transition came together to explore how they could develop testbeds that could compare and contrast the various approaches to mediation, composition and choreography, and discover of Web Services that were being proposed. The idea of a Semantic Web Services Challenge was born, and in 2006 the first workshop to include the challenge was held. In the following year, a series of these meetings were held around the world, and a number of systems were tested. This book is the result - the first collection to pull together these results and to allow readers to evaluate the results. Whether they are professionals, interested in using this information to help shape investments in technology, or students, looking for up to date information on the application of semantics to Web Services, readers will find this book to contain a wealth of information.

Since the early days of the Semantic Web, I have often been asked to give talks about emerging trends and capabilities. I must confess that in the past two years, I have avoided discussion of Semantic Web Services due to the very confusion I mentioned earlier. However, the question I've been asked most often is "what is the status of Semantic Web Services?" and until now, I didn't really have very good answers. Thus, I am indebted to the editor of this book for all the work he has done in helping to create and run the challenge, and now in making sure that the results are documented in this book. It'll be nice to put this topic back in my talks!

Professor James A. Hendler
Rensselaer Polytechnic Institute, NY, USA
August 11, 2008

References

1. James A. Hendler: Agents and the Semantic Web. In 16(2):30-37, IEEE Intelligent Systems (2001)
2. Sheila A. McIlraith, Tran Cao Son, and Honglei Zeng: Semantic Web Services. In 16(2):46-53, IEEE Intelligent Systems (2001)

Foreword by Michael L. Brodie

This book documents lessons learned in the first year of the Semantic Web Services Challenge - the first significant step towards the creation of a set of benchmarks and processes by which to define and measure the performance and correctness of semantic web services at web-scale. The Semantic Web Services Challenge is at an early stage in the development of semantic web services benchmarks for the Web of services, similar to that of the Database Derby in mid-1980s for relational databases. As with relational databases and the Web of documents, the Web of services will have an enormous impact on our increasingly digital lives that in turn will become increasingly dependent on the underlying technologies including semantic web services. Unlike relational databases, the Web of services posses, as does each Next Generation of Computing, qualitatively greater challenges in defining and achieving performance and correctness. The lessons told in this book are not only guides down that path, they will be the tales told of the origins of the Web of services, just as today we tell tales of Ted Codd and origins of relational databases and of Jim Gray and the origins of relational benchmarks.

Let me try to put this book in an historical perspective and tell you why this topic is important and challenging.

In our increasingly digital world the Web has become an integral part of our professional and personal lives. "Just Google it!" can be heard from Anchorage to Zambia, from executives in boardrooms to 13 year olds in grade schools, to grannies in kitchens. We are constantly amazed at the Web, the largest man-made artifact ever created, with over 30 billion Web pages - 5 pages for every man, woman, and child on the planet. More information is added to the Web yearly than has been created in the preceding 5,000 years and will grow by a factor of six from 2007 to 2010 with more than 11 billion searches each month, almost double the world's population. While the size and the growth of the Web constantly amaze us, what may be more striking is the impact of the Web on our world.

Given the significance and size of the Web, how readily can we find what we need? A search for my name produces 227,000 pages. A search for my company produces 98 million pages. While the first entries are often what I want, how would an automated process select the correct one for a specific purpose? This imprecision prohibits current web search technology for automated business interactions. The Semantic Web vision is to augment web resources with meta-data to improve web search and facilitate automated interactions between web resources.

Service-orientation is emerging as the paradigm of the Next-Generation of computing. Happily, it will take some time - time to figure out what we are doing. With its origins in the 1970s in abstract data types, objects, and containers, the notion of a service - an interoperable, composable, reusable, and remotely invokable function - will evolve, mature, and persist. So services are not Johnnie-come-latelys. The typically overblown estimates of new technology adoption and growth are far from reality for services in 2007, a year that marked the first significant adoption of services since their introduction in 2000. In 2008, 1,000 services is considered large even for very large enterprises. Converting the major systems of a large enterprise might result in 1 million services of which less than 50% would be published externally resulting in a Web of services two orders of magnitude larger than the Web of documents.

As web and service technologies evolve, the web will move from a Web of documents to a Web of functional and data services in which a web page may contain 5 to 10 services. Services will move the web from the surface web, information available to current web browsers, to the deep web, information and services in databases and systems that underlie current web pages. The deep web is estimated to be 500 times larger than the surface web.

The move from the surface Web of documents to a deep Web of services not only increases the search space by a factor of 500, it also leads to a qualitatively new form of computing. The scale pushes the web beyond the size and complexity that can be dealt with by humans. The Web of services requires a services automation solution in which services interact without human intervention. The vision is for services to achieve a goal by discovering services that meet a requirement and negotiate the use of that service or even adaptation of the service or composition with other services that collectively meet the requirement. The Semantic Web Services vision is to enhance web services with meta-data to enable automated service discovery, selection, negotiation, mediation, adaptation, composition, invocation, and monitoring.

As we enter the Web of services we face two great challenges - scale and automation. While these challenges are familiar, the scale and complexity of this new computing environment make these problems qualitatively different from past computing environments. Scale poses challenges of performance while automation poses challenges of correctness.

In the past, performance issues were primarily addressed with hardware and systems engineering solutions. While these are still fruitful, we are now looking to software for solutions. Augmenting web services with semantics is a software solution emerging from the Semantic Technologies community, a community with little experience in engineering solutions especially at web-scale. Indeed few communities have experience with web-scale computing. Hence, the semantic web services space is novel in many ways and may require more sophisticated measures of engineering as well as of performance and correctness.

It is easy to envisage services interacting dynamically to discover other services with which to negotiate, adapt, and compose, and then to invoke to achieve a requirement. It is quite another matter to specify correctness in this context, let alone achieve it in implementations.

Almost three decades ago, the Next Generation of Computing, at the time, faced similar challenges. In the early 1980's the projected scale of relational databases was unimaginable, and like the Web of documents far exceeded its projections. As with our current Web of services we are facing unimaginable scale and complexity with novel, unproven technology and with few benchmarks. Now, as then, we require efficient, scalable solutions to problems for which we lack definitions of correctness. But this time we do not control the architecture, which is both distributed and emergent. We require objective means of testing whether the new technology solutions meets realistic performance and correctness requirements. We want to encourage innovation via competition amongst possible solutions, and the development of an objective basis of appropriate measures against which to compare them, and the standardization of accepted solutions. In addition to providing benchmarks for emerging technologies, we want to provide a focal point for such engineering challenges, discussions, and achievements where well-defined industrial problems can be used to drive and test technology solutions. Ideally semantic web services benchmarks will contribute to the development and acceptance of semantic technologies just as relational benchmarks did for relational technology.

In the early 1980's several database benchmark activities emerged as candidates against which to measure the performance and correctness of emerging relational database technologies. One of the earliest candidates, The Database Derby, run by an emerging database magazine, was run as a series of workshops at database conferences. The importance and need for an objective database benchmark lead to the definition of the "DebitCredit" benchmark [1] by Jim Gray and 24 academic and industrial co-authors. By 1988 eight companies formed the Transaction Processing Performance Council (TPC) [2]. Since then, TPC has defined benchmarks with which to measure the performance and correctness of DBMSs and methodologies by which they are conducted, fairly and objectively. TPC benchmarks have been used to define requirements for emerging workloads such as for e-commerce, decision support, application servers, and web services.

Let me conclude with a projection and a challenge to consider as you read this book. Each Next Generation of Computing needs benchmarks - for the web services era as for the database era. Next Generation challenges will always be at a greater scale and complexity than those of the previous generation. However, the Web of services poses qualitatively greater unknowns and opportunities than did the database era. The relational model of 1970 is largely in tact today. Relational database benchmarks evolved with dramatically new workloads prompting radically new hardware, engineering, and systems technologies, all within the bounds of the relational data model.

There is no such constraining model for web services. While the lack of a single model permits opportunities for other computational and informational models, it also opens the space for engineering and technology solutions. Are there multiple computational models for web services that require multiple benchmarks? Is the Semantic Web Services Challenge the entrance to a wide but single path to the future or to a myriad of paths to parallel but distinct computational futures?

Michael L. Brodie
Chief Scientist Verizon
Cambridge, MA, USA
August 19, 2008.

References

1. A Measure of Transaction Processing Power, Datamation, April 1, 1985.
2. http://tpc.org/

Preface

This "first year" book addresses results of the the SWS Challenge through the November 2007 workshop at Stanford University (USA). The first workshop was held at Stanford in March of 2006, setting up the organization and the drafting the methodology. The subsequent workshops were functioning evaluations: at Budva (Montenegro), Athens (USA), Innsbruck (Austria), and again at Stanford.

This series of workshops has provided a forum for discussion based on a common application. The Challenge focuses on the use of semantic annotations: participants are provided with semantics in the form of natural language text that they can formalize and use in their technologies. Being a challenge rather than a contest, workshop participants mutually evaluate and learn from each others' approaches.

In this book, the focus is on the understanding of the technical issues in the proposed solutions, and of their tradeoffs. Therefore, solution chapters that describe in depth the technologies of the participant teams are complemented by other chapters containing pairwise comparisons of solutions. A full list of the workshops in the ongoing initiative is available at the SWS Challenge wiki[1].

There have been further results, and teams, in 2007 and 2008 and we invite new teams to participate in any of the coming workshops announced on the Challenge wiki as well to join the W3C SWS Challenge Testbed Incubator during 2008.

We are grateful for the continual and substantial support from Professor Dieter Fensel of the Semantic Technologies Institute Innsbruck and Professor Michael Genesereth of the Stanford Logic Group. This book reflects the major efforts of all the technology contributors and the STII and Potsdam staff, including Omair Shafiq and Christian Winkler, who not only supported the SWS Challenge directly, but who did the final composition of this book in LaTeX.

August 2008,

Charles Petrie
Tiziana Margaria
Michal Zaremba
Holger Lausen

---

[1] $http://sws-challenge.org/$

Contents

Part V Lessons Learned

List of Figures

1

Introduction to the First Year of the Semantic Web Services Challenge

Charles Petrie

Stanford Logic Group, California, USA `petrie@stanford.edu`

Summary. The Semantic Web Services Challenge is an initiative that includes a set of workshops in which participants present papers on how they have solved some set of benchmark problems in mediating, discovering, and composing web services. The claims are verified by capturing the messages exchanged with the Challenge testbed, and also by code inspection by workshop participants. Technology certifications are stated publicly on the Challenge wiki. Experience thus far shows that even simple problems are much harder to actually solve than is suggested by papers in venues that do not so verify such claims.

1.1 SWS Challenge Mission and Organization

Service-Oriented Computing is one of the most promising software engineering trends for future distributed systems. Adopted by major industry players and supported by many standardization efforts, Web services is the premiere technology of the service-oriented paradigm, promising to foster reuse and to ease the implementation of loosely-coupled distributed applications. However, there are several serious issues that must be addressed before this potential can be reached. And there is a serious issue with the current scientific methodology that should be considered.

The original web was designed for human use: web-based services are presented in easy-to-read and use web pages designed for humans that understand some natural language. Computers can use them only if they have been carefully programmed to "read" each individual web page, the format of which varies for each page. Web services are designed for computer interoperability: a web service has no presentation page in a natural language but rather a web page that describes the service in a common machine-readable format.

Web services are appealing especially in the area of enterprise application integration, because of the vision of thousands of services, which can be composed to implement desired processes and achieve desired goals as needed. This vision is especially important as enterprises become increasingly interconnected. However, today, the discovery and composition of such services is done manually. Even though the format of the web service descriptions is common, the meaning of the terms and how they can be used still requires some agreement among the programmers.

This cannot scale and indeed offers little advantage over previous IT methods, other than allowing all such work to be done with a common toolset (XML[1] and web protocols), instead of having to learn particular complex proprietary systems.

Semantic technology may help here, by lifting service-oriented applications to a new level of adaptability and robustness. By using semantic annotations to describe services and resources, the tasks of service discovery, selection, negotiation, and binding could be automated.

Currently there are many different approaches to semantic Web service descriptions and many frameworks built around them, yet a common understanding, evaluation scheme, and testbed to compare and classify these frameworks in terms of their abilities and shortcomings is still missing.

This is an opportunity. Since there are many possibilities for semantically annotating services, it is an open question still, which are best for which purposes. In general, the question is what annotation is sufficient for service discovery and composition, and is also easy to maintain in the face of inevitable change.

The purpose of the ongoing *Semantic Web Service (SWS) Challenge* is precisely to develop this common understanding of various technologies intended to facilitate the automation of mediation, choreography and discovery for Web Services using semantic annotations. This explores trade-offs among existing approaches, reveals the strengths and weaknesses of the proposed approaches as well as which aspects of the problem space are not yet covered. Furthermore, the Challenge is a certification service that offers an independent verification that the claimed technologies actually work.

The SWS Challenge provides a set of problems and web services to participants. The participants must semantically annotate the web services so as to solve the problems. Unlike academic papers, the participants are not allowed to modify the services and problems to suit their technologies. The solution code and claims are peer-reviewed in workshops.

1.2 Scope of the Challenge and this Book

This "first year" book addresses results of the the SWS Challenge through the November 2007 workshop at Stanford University (USA). The first workshop was held at Stanford in March of 2006 but was only an organizing workshop. The next workshops were functioning evaluations: at Budva (Montenegro), Athens (USA), Innsbruck (Austria), and again at Stanford. A full list of the workshops in the ongoing initiative is available at the SWS Challenge wiki[2].

This series of workshops of the SWS Challenge has provided a forum for discussion based on a common application. The Challenge focuses on the use of semantic annotations: participants are provided with semantics in the form of natural language text that they can formalize and use in their technologies. Being a challenge rather

---

[1] $http://www.w3.org/XML/$

[2] $http://sws-challenge.org/$

than a contest, workshop participants mutually evaluate and learn from each others' approaches.

The Challenge has participating groups from industry and academia developing software components and/or intelligent agents able to automate mediation, choreography and discovery processes between Web services. All approaches and participants are invited. Though "Semantic" is in the title of this Challenge, we invite non-semantic approaches to participate and we attempt to evenly evaluate all submissions in our methodology.

"Semantics" is really a hypothesis that certain technologies largely derived from logic-based ontologies would be more easily maintainable than would code written with more traditional methods. The chief idea of the technologies is that there is some common reference for various web service descriptions that can be used to relate one to another. Logic-based ontologies are the most common way to do this, though some simpler methods may turn out to be the most useful and practical.

This "maintainable hypothesis" is testable and falsifiable. The Challenge is designed to do so, though the evaluation methodology is itself a research project and the Challenge is the place where we experiment.

The SWS Challenge has another main purpose. There are many workshops and conferences today. If a researcher has something to publish, he can find a venue. And when publishing in a complex area such as service discovery and composition, it is very difficult if not impossible to verify the claims of the paper. But without verification, and reproducibility, there is no, or little, science.

The SWS Challenge addresses this major issue within the scope of web services. The Challenge certifies that claims of functionality have been verified, by actual testing and peer-review of the code. We hope that other workshops and conferences will move in this direction as it is important for the credibility of at least web services science.

Though we address this topic more in "Lessons Learned", it is important to note that though the Challenge problems seem simple, every team has found them to be extremely challenging. Experience with the Challenge makes for strong skepticism about the unverified claims of most papers published in this field today.

1.3 Related Initiatives

The SWS Challenge complements other initiatives that have similar missions.

First, there is a conference that is not on web services but with a similar mission: The Repeatability Experiment of SIGMOD 2008[3]. However, the SIGMOD methodology required that the organizers be able to run the code of the participants. We do not do this. The Challenge requires that the participants access the testbed web services and send and receive some correct sequence of messages (or discover the correct services.) In the workshop, we only require that the already demonstrated

---

[3] $http$: $www.sigmod.org/sigmod/record/issues/0803/p39.open$ — $repeatability.pdf$

functionality be demonstrable, and that the participants be able to inspect the code. At the same time, in line with the principles of the Challenge methodology (in the next section), we ask the participants to share as much code as possible that might be usefully reusable by other participants.

The SWS Challenge initiative is specifically designed to develop a standard methodology and testbed for the evaluation of Semantic Web Services technologies. We are currently focused on web services described in WSDL[4], in order to be as industrially relevant as possible in such a setting.

We are interested in web services in general. By "web service", we mean the definition developed in the Dagstuhl Seminar on Service Oriented Computing [2]: roughly a service with a description of how to use it presented in some widely-supported format (such as XML) and reachable via some standard Internet protocol (such as HTTP[5]). Such services need not be WSDL and we remain open to developing scenarios in other technologies that fit this description. But currently, the Challenge and related contests are based upon WSDL services.

There is also the associated W3C SWS Challenge Testbed Incubator which has issued a report[6] about the evaluation methodology developed within the SWS Challenge.

The activity next most closely related to the SWS Challenge is the S3 Contest on Semantic Service Selection[7]. However, the SWS Challenge and the S3 contest are working in different parts of the research space. The S3 Contest is a competition that measures the speed and precision of retrieval algorithms in performing discovery tasks and declares winners each year. Moreover, the contest requires commitment to a specific semantic formalism. Most of the existing services have been described in OWL-S[8]. The SWS Challenge is interested in comparing the effectiveness of different formalisms for different problems. The S3 contest does have different kinds of problem sets and, in 2008, is including the SAWSDL[9] specification for annotating WSDL, which does not commit to a specific semantic formalism.

The organizers agree that the two initiatives are related and both should be explored. In fact, the cross-referencing between both events on their web sites and inter-linkage of other activities (e.g., common use of test services) has been agreed between organizers. This is described more in Chapter 17.

The IEEE Web Services Challenge (WSC) has changed over the years to become closer to the SWS Challenge. At first, this was a strictly syntactic-based contest. The latest 2008 workshop[10] has been announced as focusing on the use of semantics to compose web services. However, this newest version of this contest still differs from the the SWS Challenge in significant ways.

---

[4] $http://www.w3.org/TR/wsdl20/$

[5] $http://www.w3.org/Protocols/$

[6] $http://www.w3.org/2005/Incubator/swsc/XGR - SWSC - 20080331/$

[7] $http://www - ags.dfki.uni - sb.de/ \sim klusch/s3/$

[8] $http://www.w3.org/Submission/OWL - S$

[9] $http://www.w3.org/2002/ws/sawsdl/$

[10] $http://cec2008.cs.georgetown.edu/wsc08/$

First,like the S3 contest, the WSC is a contest with two winners, rather than a certification of functionality on particular tasks. One winner is based upon speed, and another is based upon a judgement about the elegance of the architecture. Second, this contest does not test the efficacy of different approaches to semantics but only the efficacy of different composition algorithms using OWL-S. Third, there is no attempt to make various industrially-relevant scenarios that include discovery as well as composition.

Both the S3 and the WSC are contests with well-defined metrics because they are focused on more narrow problem sets with selected semantic formalisms. The SWS Challenge is both more ambitious and difficult to evaluate. We now describe the difficulties of attempting to evaluate, from a software engineering perspective, various approaches without predetermining a formalism. Indeed, development of this evaluation methodology has turned into something of a research experiment itself.

1.4 SWS Challenge Evaluation Methodology

At the SWS workshops, the approaches are presented and demonstrated, but also the code is jointly reviewed. The common applications have helped to foster a profound mutual understanding of each other's technology and the collaborative discussion of the profiles of the various approaches. The participants have evolved an evaluation scheme that classifies the functionality and the agility offered by the various approaches, and applied it to the participating technologies.

The SWS Challenge is an evaluation of functionality rather than performance. We are not interested in how fast a particular piece of code works. We are interested not in the speed of the code but in programmer productivity. For a given change in the emerging era of Service-Oriented Architectures, how hard will it be for programmers to make changes in an increasingly flexible and dynamic IT environment? This Challenge seeks to understand the advantages and tradeoffs, wrt. this question, of various programming approaches.

There is no "winner" in these challenges, though one can look at the results of each workshop and see which team has so far solved the most problems with what level of difficulty. This Challenge is intended to be an objective certification of approaches to the problems of semantic technologies, with an emphasis on industrial problems in order to make the technologies relevant.

Therefore the SWS Challenge is taking a software engineering approach to evaluating Semantic Web Services [3]. The working hypothesis of the semantic technology community is that a semantic approach will allow a given change to be made with less difficulty than with traditional coding techniques. This is essentially a software engineering claim. Thus we allow "all comers" to participate. If it develops that a particular coding technique manages the problem changes of the challenge scenarios better than a semantic approach, this will also be be valuable information for the semantic community.

In the Challenge methodology, teams validate their solution to problems by having their system send correct messages to the web services in the SWS Challenge infrastructure. At the workshops, teams present papers about their approach with claims about the ease of changing from one problem to another. Then we peer-review these claims and agree upon an evaluation of the approach, as well as certifying the technology problem level.

The problems are specified in English, other than the WSDL descriptions associated with the test services. We challenge the participating teams to develop their own semantic annotation formalisms that are sufficient to solve the problems. Additionally, we analyse the general difficulty in moving from solving one problem level or sub-level to another.

This is why we use standards such as RosettaNet PIP3A4[11] and WSDL and make our scenarios at least similar to industrial problems. It is also why we insist that submissions actually solve the problems by sending correct messages to the Challenge web services for each scenario. It is easy to make claims in academic papers that such-and-such a problem has been solved. It turns out to be much more difficult in practice, as our teams have discovered, to make such approaches actually work. Our slogan is "no participation without invocation". In order to be evaluated on a problem level, the submission must have demonstrated the correct exchange of messages with the corresponding Challenge web services, or in cases where this is not feasible, the claim must be demonstrable and verifiable by the SWS Challenge community.

The specifics of the current methodology have evolved over time and are the subject of the W3C SWS Challenge Testbed Incubator Methodology Report. Though this book reports the developments of only the first year, the evaluation methodology has, and continues, to evolve. But this report cites principles that summarize the discussion above:

- We do not pre-suppose what technologies are best but rather evaluate them and certify the results as a result of solving common problems.
- We evaluate both the ability to solve a problem and the developer effort in responding to a problem change.
- We are less interested in program speed than in correctness of program behavior and the degree of programmer productivity.
- We are interested in learning trade-offs among technologies and which formalisms are successful in which contexts.
- The evaluation results should be simple but useful to people deciding among technologies, especially within industry.
- The evaluation exercises should also result in reusable principles and code that can be swapped among the participants and help to evolve "best-of-breed" technologies: particularly ontologies.
- The problems and their syntactic specifications should be as industrially-relevant as possible.

We do not describe the methodology in much more detail here but refer the reader to the W3C report or the Challenge Wiki because the methodology continues to

---

[11] $http://www.rosettanet.org/PIP3A4$

evolve, and because there is more discussion in "Lessons Learned". However, there are a few issues worth noting.

In addition to the goal of scientific verification, the Challenge has an additional goal: to understand how easy the participant's technology is to change in the face of a changing problem. The fundamental idea is to give the participants problems that are variations of those already solved.

Initially, we tried a code freeze and then presented the participants with scenario variations one time shortly before the workshop to see if they could solve them in a limited time as a way of judging the ease of change of the technologies. We found people had difficulty with the way we were doing code freezes, and we were getting new participants for whom these variations were no longer new as they had been published. We experimented with changing the methodology and as of the last workshop in 2008 at Karlsruhe, we will require an upload of code at some point, and a commitment to work on a "surprise" variation, which will then be released privately to each agreeing participant, but which will not be made public. Participants received a "plus" mark by their verification check on the published certification matrices if they can solve the surprise problem by presentation time in the workshop.

It should also be noted that we have not yet developed scenarios that require semantic unification across ontologies: all of the scenarios allow the participants to use a ontology common to their own application. Currently, this is for two reasons. One is that, as previously explained, we do not wish to force a particular technology upon the participants. Therefore, we will not give them two ontologies in any given format. We are interested in this problem however and are exploring whether we can find some neutral expression of two ontologies the participants might be required to express in their own formalisms, and unify. A surprise problem will be extremely meaningful in this case.

Also, at least one of the organizers, Petrie, while supporting scientific research in this area, is doubtful that ontology unification is compatible with our emphasis on industrial problems. Petrie rather believes that most service discovery and composition in industry in the near future will take place in homogeneous environments[4].

1.5 SWS Challenge Problem Scenarios

The problems being solved by the teams are business scenarios divided into major problem levels with sub-problem variations. The first major problem level consists of developing a mediator that allows a hypothetical company, Moon, to have its legacy web services to conform to a RosettaNet purchase order (PO) standard that is being used by a customer, Blue. We then change the web services, the protocol, and the order in consecutive variations.

In particular, we have presented two broad areas of problem scenarios:

- The *mediation* type of scenarios concern making a legacy order management system interoperable with external systems that use a simplified version of the RosettaNet PIP3A4 specifications.

- The *discovery* type of scenarios concern
  - the dynamic discovery, selection, binding, and invocation of the most appropriate shipment service for a set of given shipment requests; and
  - the selections of components from different suppliers and catalogs in order to configure a computer, with different preferences and conditions.

Subsequent problem levels involve increasingly difficult web service discovery and composition scenarios. In the larger supply chain setting, teams should process the order from the company, mediating the PO process, order the right parts from the suppliers, the suppliers should ship the parts, and the company should ship to the customer the completed order, with associated "paperwork". The computer configuration scenarios are also planned to be extended and some of the elements of these scenarios are also planned to be included into the larger supply chain setting. The basic scenario problems are described in Chapter 2.

We expect the scenarios to grow in number of services and overall complexity. Indeed, we believe that the results of the Challenge are likely to be really meaningful when we have linked together many of the individual scenarios into a super supply chain scenario involving multiple customers, suppliers, and shippers together with the Moon company, and the discovery scenarios involve sufficient number of services that blind search among them makes the problem intractable. However, we must of necessity grow the scenarios and services incrementally, with the help of the participants. This also allows the participants to make progress without being presented with an overwhelming scenario at the start.

1.6 Overview of Technologies

In the first year of the SWS Challenge, we have had six (6) teams participating. The other chapters in this paper describes the contributions of these teams, but one, in more detail. Here we give an overview that will help the reader with an overall perspective.

- DIANE (Universität Jena) is a method for automated service matchmaking, selection, binding and invocation.

- WebML/Webratio (Politecnico di Milano/CeFRIEL) uses a combination of software engineering and F-logic.

- jABC/jETI (Universität Dortmund/Universität Potsdam) jABC/jETI is based upon a modeling of composition of software components using finite state automata. This team provided first a software engineering approach to the mediation scenario, and later a declarative approach for automatic generation of the Mediator workflow via Linear Time Logic (LTL)-guided synthesis.
- METEOR-S (Wright State University) uses SAWSDL + AI-Planning + Data Mediation.

- WSMX/WSMO (DERI) is a semantic approach based upon abstract state machines.

- Swashup (IBM) was a purely engineering approach using Ruby on Rails.

The precise current results of all current and past teams can always be found in the SWS Challenge Wiki. It should be noted here that the three teams of Politecnico di Milano/Cefriel, DERI, and Jena currently have solved the most problems in both the mediation and discovery scenarios. The IBM approach was near to solving the first level of the mediation problem but had not done so as of the publication time of this book, and so is not included as a chapter in this book. We now give an overview of the technical approaches to the scenarios of these six teams that will inform the reader of the subsequent chapters.

The five of them were ranked according to the evaluation criteria (the IBM approach was not evaluated), and indeed they showed very different approaches. This book covers the following, listed from very to less declarative approaches.

- METEOR-S achieved nearly full automation (Chapter 6), as did an approach based on automatic generation of the workflows from semantics-enhanced LTL specifications (Chapter 7). Both of these have solve the first mediation problem.
- Three approaches combined partially automatic generation and partially automatic adaptation, but in different subproblems:
  - The WSMO/WSMX approach uses a generic (abstract) state machine for the flow, thus having an advantage on the process adaptation level. This approach has been very successful on the mediation problems but is also, along with DIANE, one of the most successful approaches to solving the discovery problems.
  - The WebML/Webratio uses generic import/export mechanisms from the WSDL and a partial generation of the processes, that ease the adaptation of them. This hybrid approach has been very successful in solving both discovery and mediation problems.
  - The fundamental jABC/jETI approach provides automatic generation of *ad hoc* components from the published WSDL descriptions into its own service components (called SIBs). One advantage of this system has been minimal effort to otherwise semantically annotate the services. Ease of software construction and maintenance is achieved by manual graphical construction of the service logic. This approach has been shown capable of solving both mediation and discovery problems with fairly easy adaptation effort by the user.
- The DIANE (and SWE-ET) light-weight ontology approach is oriented primarily (almost exclusively) towards discovery, thus the mediation solution falls outside the specific profile. The mediation problem was solved traditionally by providing specific adapters to the RosettaNet messages and to the Moon system, and a process logic written in BPEL. The adaptation required for mediation is described further in the DIANE chapter.

1.7 Organization of the Book

In addition to this introduction, the last chapter contains observations and insights into the issues of conducting such an ambitious evaluation initiative as this one. Our understanding of how to conduct such an evaluation continues to evolve and we invite the participation of new contributors.

In terms of understanding the Challenge content, a discussion of the problem scenarios directly follows this introduction. A scan of this chapter will be very helpful for the reader in understanding the technical solutions to these problems and what they really mean. This chapter should also serve as a reference for detailed reading of the solution chapters.

The solution chapters describe the technologies of the participant teams and are organized into two parts, corresponding to the two main types of scenarios: Mediation and Discovery. Within each part, we have two further divisions: individual solutions and pairwise comparison of solutions.

The latter are not pair-wise complete, largely because each of these comparison chapters involved a great deal of joint analysis by teams working with different technologies, and because the teams had to agree on the analysis. However, exactly for those reasons, these comparison chapters will be particularly valuable to readers attempting to understand the technical issues and solutions.

An overview of these solution chapters follows:

- Part I: Mediation
  - *Mediation individual Solutions*
    - · WSMO/WSMX
    - · WebML/Webratio
    - · jABC/jETI
    - · METEOR-S
    - · LTL-guided synthesis of the Mediator in jABC
  - *Mediation solution comparisons*
    - · WSMO/WSMX vs. WebML/Webratio
    - · WebML/Webratio vs. jABC/jETI

- Part II: Discovery
  - *Discovery Individual Solutions*
    - · WSMO/WSMX
    - · Glue/Webratio
    - · Diane
    - · jABC/miAamics
  - *Discovery solutions comparisons*
    - · Service Discovery with SWE-ET and DIANE
    - · WSMO/WSMX - jABC/miAamics
    - · DIANE - jABC/miAamics

1.8 The Challenge is Open

Finally we would emphasize that the SWS Challenge is open, both to participation and to the submission of new scenario problems. Some of the scenarios can be "stand alone" and others will refine and extend the "Blue Moon" customer/company/supplier/shipper scenario. Eventually, this scenario should include the company fulfilling the customer order using a supply chain composed of the best suppliers and shippers for the specific customer order.

Our mission is to supply not only a large useful "sandbox" for testing semantic web service approaches, but also a *de facto* standard for certifying such technologies, as well as furthering an academic understanding of the benefits and trade-offs of these approaches. The chapters in this book are the first results from this understanding as they include comparisons of approaches.

There have been further results, and teams, in 2007 and 2008 and we invite new teams to participate in any of the coming workshops announced on the Challenge wiki as well join the W3C SWS Challenge Testbed Incubator during 2008.

References

1. T. Margaria: The Semantic Web Services Challenge: Tackling Complexity at the Orchestration Level. Invited paper ICECCS 2008 (13th IEEE Intern. Conf. on Engineering of Complex Computer Systems) EEE CS Press, pp 183-189, April 2008, Belfast, UK.
2. Heiko Ludwig and Charles Petrie: 05462 Session Summary – "Cross Cutting Concerns. Service Oriented Computing (SOC), Dagstuhl Seminar Proceedings, ISSN 1862-4405, Dagstuhl, Germany.
3. Charles Petrie: It's the programming, stupid IEEE Internet Computing, Vol. May-June (2006).
4. Charles Petrie and Christoph Bussler, The Myth of Open Web Services: Rise of the Service Parks. IEEE Internet Computing In IEEE Intelligent Systems, page 80-82, vol. May-June (2008).

2

SWS Challenge Scenarios

Holger Lausen, Ulrich Küster, Charles Petrie, Michal Zaremba, and Srdjan
Komazec

[1] Semantic Technology Institute Innsbruck, University of Innsbruck, Technikerstr. 21, 6020
Innsbruck, Austria, firstname.lastname@sti2.at
[2] Institute of Computer Science, Friedrich-Schiller-University Jena, 07743 Jena, Germany,
ukuester@informatik.uni-jena.de
[3] Computer Science Dept. University of Stanford, Gates Building, Stanford, CA
94305-9020, USA petrie@stanford.edu

Summary. The Semantic Web Service Challenge defines problem scenarios that serve as
the basis for the certification and comparison of approaches participating in the challenge.
These scenarios are classified in two broad types: Mediation and Discovery. The first primarily
address aspects of data and process mediation whereas the latter focus on problems around
automated service discovery. Currently, there are two main scenarios in each type which are
described in detail in this chapter.

2.1 Introduction

In this chapter, we discuss the rationale for the existing scenarios and give an
overview of them that will inform the reader about the problems solved by the various technologies covered in other chapters of this book. What is most important for
the reader to understand is that each of these scenarios is supported by real web services, not changeable by the participants, in a testbed; and that solving each of the
scenario problems requires really parsing the WSDL of these services and correctly
sending and processing messages to these services as required by the scenarios.

Instead of having a single giant scenario, we choose to have several problems on
different levels, which ideally build one upon the other. The rationale is that it is easier for people to attempt individual small problems rather than one large one. And,
as described elsewhere in this book, the individual problems have proved very challenging. However, some set of these problems will eventually be used to form one
large supply-chain problem that may more adequately test the software engineering
aspects of the technologies evaluated.

In addition, it has always been the intention of the challenge organizers to provide
problems that are as close to industrial reality as practical, rather than the very simple
travel agent or book order examples usually covered in academic papers. The Challenge participants have found even these simple problems, using industrial standards

and fixed real services, not designed by the paper authors, to be surprisingly challenging, which we conclude is of significant benefit to the development of semantic web service technology and science.

There are two broad types of problems, which we have classified as "mediation" and "discovery". Problem scenarios in the former pushes more on service orchestration, but some of the scenarios in discovery do as well. The first mediation problem is centering around process and data mediation during a purchase order process. The discovery basic scenario is about discovering shipment providers given specific constraints such as destination country, weight, etc. Subsequent organizers and participants have together developed an enhanced discovery scenario as well as an orchestration scenario. In this section we familiarize the reader with the basic details of the scenarios. These details are intended to help understanding the solutions presented in subsequent chapters.

2.2 The Mediation Scenarios

After deciding that the mediation types of scenarios should fundamentally include mediating a purchase order between various systems we started looking closer at currently used solutions. We identified three industrial standards that could potentially be used to derive a problem scenario:

- EDIFACT[4] is the United Nations/Electronic Data Interchange For Administration, Commerce, and Transport (UN/EDIFACT). It is a plain text format for data exchange developed by the United Nations.
- ebXML[5] is sponsored by sponsored by OASIS and UN/CEFACT and commonly known as e-business XML. ebXML is a family of XML based standards whose mission is to provide an open, XML-based infrastructure that enables the global use of electronic business information in an interoperable, secure, and consistent manner by all trading partners.
- RosettaNet[6] is a non-profit consortium aimed at establishing standard processes for the sharing of business information (B2B). The standard is based on XML and defines message guidelines, business processes interface and implementation frameworks for interactions between companies.

As EDIFACT is based on plain text messages, we decided not to take it as basis since this would push too many low level data transformation issues to the participants. In opposite to the two XML based standards no parsers and other tools could be used. The choice between ebXML and RosettaNet was taken on the base of available documentation. Since only the RosettaNet messages and protocols are freely and easily accessible we decided to use RosettaNet.

---

[4] http://www.unece.org/trade/untdid/welcome.htm
[5] http://www.ebxml.org/
[6] http://www.rosettanet.org/

In the mediation scenario we focus on interoperability problems of existing systems. The aim is to show how semantic Web technologies can help to overcome the need for manual development of mediation systems.

In our initial scenario description we provide relevant information about the systems involved in two forms: using current Web Service description (WSDL) and natural language text annotations. Using current state-of-the-art technologies a programmer has to interpret the information given and to code components that overcome the heterogeneity between the different systems. In the SWS-Challenge participants are asked to extend the syntactic descriptions in a way that their algorithms/systems can perform the necessary translation tasks in a semi or fully automatic manner.

We focused on the scenario of purchasing goods using a simplified version of the RosettaNet specification. While the external interfaces must follow the RosettaNet specification, internally Moon uses a propriety legacy system in which data model and message exchange patterns differ from those of RosettaNet. Participants shall basically enable Moon to "talk RosettaNet" and implement the Purchase Order receiving role part of the interaction described in the RosettaNet PIP 3A4.

There are three main components taking part in the process are depicted in Figure 2.1:

- Company Blue, which is a customer (service requester) ordering products,
- Mediator, which is a piece of technology providing automatic or semi-automatic mediation for the Moon company
- Legacy System of the Moon Company. While the external interfaces must follow the RosettaNet specification, internally Moon uses a propriety legacy system in which data model and message exchange patterns differ from those of RosettaNet.

The Moon legacy systems and the customer Web Services (Blue) are provided by the challenge organizers and can not be altered (although their description may be semantically enriched). The sketch of the mediator shall be implemented by the participants.

In the mediation scenario, Moon uses two backend systems to manage its order processing, namely a Customer Relationship Management system (CRM) and an Order Management System (OMS). The challenge testbed provides access to both systems through public Web Services described using WSDL. In the scenario Moon wants to exchange purchase order messages with its client company called Blue using the RosettaNet PIP 3A4 specification.

In order to address the integration of Blue and Moon services, the participating groups are encouraged to use Semantic Web Service technology to facilitate conversation between all systems, to mediate between the PIP 3A4 and the XML schema used by Moon, as well as to ensure that the message exchange between all parties is correctly choreographed. In particular,

- Data mediation is involved in mapping the Blue RosettaNet PIP 3A4 message to the messages of the Moon back-end systems.

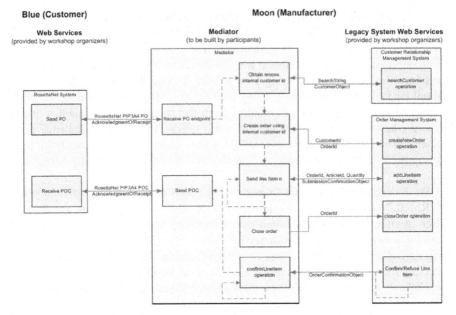

Fig. 2.1. Purchase Order Process Mediation

- Process mediation is involved in mapping of message exchanges defined by the RosettaNet PIP 3A4 process to those defined in the WSDL of the Moon back-end systems.

The messages used in the challenge are simplified versions of the original specification. To describe context of messages we provide simplified PIP3A4 as RosettaNet XML Schemas. Within the RosettaNet PIP3A4 specification the information is given using a DTD. We have converted this DTD to XML Schema and removed some fields to make the message less complex. Tag names, their meaning and structure have not been changed. The PIP 3A4 enables a buyer to issue a purchase order and to obtain a response from the provider that acknowledges which of the purchase order product line items are accepted, rejected, or pending.

A purchase process is initiated by the buyer when it sends the Purchase Order message to the endpoint exposed by a mediator (this one has to be provided by challenge participants). The Purchase Order message must be synchronously confirmed by an Acknowledgement of Receipt message. The original RosettaNet specification allows 24 hours for confirmation of the Purchase Order Action. We changed it and for the sake of practicability, the Purchase Order Confirmation should be issued no later than 5 minutes since the Mediator has received Purchase Order.

RosettaNet messages contain no specific information about products, but refer only to a global unique product identifier. For the purpose of the challenge we provide a list of products, which can be ordered from Moon. We recognize that a pure identifier remains quite meaningless from the perspective of Semantic Web. Nevertheless we decided not to change existing specification.

In the RosettaNet standard a purchase order is sent using just a single message, however, in order for Moon to be able to process an order, several steps have to be made. The overall ordering process of Legacy System is more complex that the one defined by RosettaNet protocol and the Mediator must take care of this. This process is illustrated in Figure 2.2

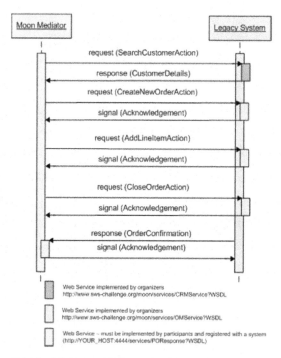

Fig. 2.2. The Mediation PO Scenario: Legacy System Interaction

First, the Mediator must communicate with the Legacy Customer Relationship Management (CRM) System to obtain relevant customer details. With the data from the CRM system the mediator can assess if the order is eligible, i.e. if the customer is known and authorized to do business with. As a next step a new order must be created with the Legacy Order Management System. Now individual line items can be added to the order created. Once all the line items have been submitted, the order has to be closed. Finally the Order Management System sends a response back containing the products that are on stock and can be delivered. Challenge participants must provide an endpoint for their mediators to which this response can be sent.

Finally the mediator must aggregate all the information received and send it back to the originating party using the Purchase Order Confirmation message of the RosettaNet standard.

2.2.1 Production Management Mediation Scenario

In the second phase of the challenge a Production Management (PM) system has been added. With the Production Management system products that are not on stock can be scheduled for production. This means that the mediator needs to perform an additional step, i.e. to enquiry the production costs and completion dates for every item that is not on stock and confirm production for those where the constraints fit those specified in the original Purchase Order. Figure 2.3 depicts this extended scenario.

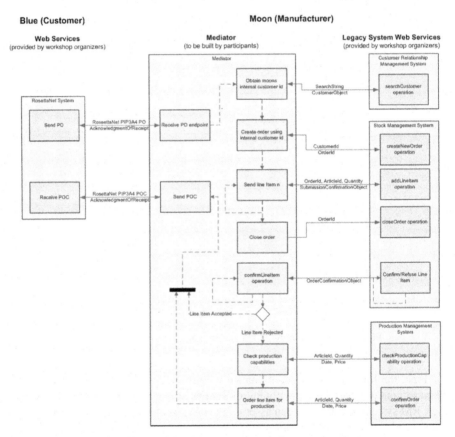

Fig. 2.3. Production Management Mediation Scenario

Unless some item of an order is not on stock, the workflow carried out by the mediator is identical to the first version of the mediation scenario. When an item is not on stock, the mediator must communicate with the legacy Production Management system to enquire whether and to what conditions a production of an item is possible.

The Production Management system provides the relevant information on estimated production date and price. If this information meets initial expectations of the customer as specified in the RosettaNet message, the product should be ordered. Beside the addition of the Production Management system the RosettaNet schema has been extended. The extended version of the RosettaNet schema provides the possibility to define a shipment address at the line item level. If present, this address should be used instead the one defined at the purchase order level.

The changes in the scenario have been added with the intention to determine how difficult it is to adapt the solutions to changing requirements. Or whether - in the best case - the systems are able to adopt to the new environment without change to the actual implementation, but purely by adding (semantic) annotations to the services. However, as explained in Chapters 1 and 17, our methodology has evolved so that these have become another set of problems to be solved and it is the so-called "surprise" problems that test problem adaptation.

2.2.2 Payment Scenario

The Payment Scenario aims at covering yet another aspect of the comprehensive SWS problem landscape. The emphasis the scenario is Web Service orchestrations. Although positioned as a type of mediation scenario it especially challenges the orchestration problem solving capability domain of technologies used by participants.

After decision was made that the scenario will be in area of orchestrating various services in order to initiate purchase order payment existing solutions coming from financial market were evaluated. Unfortunately, RosettaNet used in preceding scenario does not provide support for communication with financial institutions (e.g. banks) in order to conclude purchase order with a payment. After some time spent in research it was identified that the gap between RossettaNet enabled systems and financial institutions could be bridged with a solution relying on ISO 20022 UNIversal Financial Industry (UNIFI) message scheme standard[7]. It is supported by major players in financial market (e.g. SWIFT[8] and TWIST[9]) and it provides common development platform for exchanging and processing financial messages encoded in a standardized XML. The standard covers wide range of possible cases found in respective domain (like Cash management, Payments Clearing and Settlement, Securities management, Trade Services, etc). Among them, especially interesting for the scenario, was Payments Initiation[10] case describing set of messages used to initiate and manage funds transfer between debtor (or customer) and creditor (or seller). This scenario uses simplified versions of messages than the messages provided in original specification. All message definitions are given as appropriate XML Schemas.

As in the mediation scenario there are three main components participating in the conduction of payment initiation as depicted in Figure 2.4:

---

[7] http://www.iso20022.org

[8] http://www.swift.com

[9] http://www.twiststandards.org

[10] http://www.iso20022.org/index.cfm?item_id=59950

- Company Blue, which intends to pay for ordered goods,
- Integrator, which is a piece of technology providing capability to orchestrate a number of services on behalf of Blue company, and
- Moon Company, offering interface to retrieve creditor data (e.g. bank account number) needed to successfully complete payment initiation.

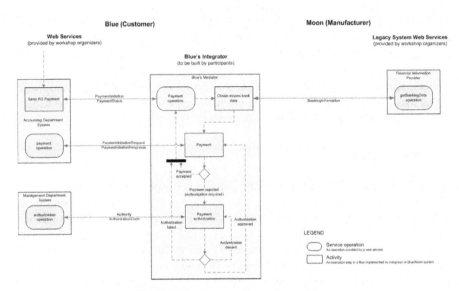

Fig. 2.4. The Payment Scenario overview

The scenario description starts where the mediation purchase order problem ends, i.e. after reception of acknowledgment for a purchase order initiated by Blue. The intention of Blue to pay for the approved purchase order results in a payment instruction message sent to its Accounting Department system (i.e. Accounting Department service). The payment instruction must be completed with necessary data (Blue's and Moon's addresses, bank accounts and identifiers, purchase order amount) coming from various sources (e.g. Moon's Financial Information Provider service). Under certain circumstances payment instruction must be authorized by Blue's Management Department system (i.e. Management Department service). After payment instruction has been dispatched customer expects to receive a payment status report from its Accounting Department system. A solution should play the role of Blue's integrator concerned with the proper orchestration of before mentioned services.

The conditions governing Integrator's need to consult Management Department system for payment authorization are based on the *threshold* amount. If the requested payment amount is below *threshold* there is no need for communication with the Management department, thus payment initiation orchestration can skip this step. Otherwise, Accounting Department will reject payment instruction, unless accompanied with an optional authorization code obtained by making a request to the

Management Department service. The request must designate an Authority (i.e. a Blue employee) capable of approving or denying payment requests up to the specified amount. This system returns either an authorization code (after which payment initiation messages can be completed and provided to the Accounting Department) or a denial code. If a denial code is returned, the service may be questioned again, but not with the same Authority as in previous call. Furthermore, Blue has a policy that the least senior Authority, as determined by the amount of money up to which an authorization could be made, should be requested first.

As in the case of the mediation scenario the challenge organizers provide a set of services which can not be altered by participants but which descriptions can be semantically enriched by participants. All services representing Blue and Moon systems are publicly accessible and described by accompanying WSDLs. It is expected that the Integrator component will be implemented by the participants.

To illustrate the scenario we will assume that the *threshold* amount is 2 €000, and that we have two authorities, Jackie Brown (authorizes amounts up to 5 €000), and Cathy Johnson (authorizes amounts up to 1 €0000). Furthermore, in order to achieve compact description of service invocations we will annotate Blue's Accounting Department service as AD, Blue's Management Department service as MD and Moon's Financial Information Provider service as FIP.

Payment amount below *threshold*

In the case of payment amount below *threshold* there is no need to request payment authorization from MD, thus the Integrator can directly invoke AD service after successful compilation of the payment initiation message. Correct invocation sequence orchestrated by the Integrator should be FIP → AD.

Payment amount above *threshold*

A payment amount greater than *threshold* adds additional step in expected orchestration, i.e. the Integrator must consult MD to authorize payment initiation. If we assume that payment amount is 3 €000 than expected invocation sequence could be FIP → AD → MD → AD (FIP is contacted to gather Moon's financial data, AD refused to initiate payment because payment amount is above *threshold* and an authorization code is missing, MD is contacted with Jackie Brown as least senior designated authority who approves payment and gives authorization code, and AD is contacted again with all necessary data needed to complete payment initiation). The expected service invocation sequence could also be FIP → AD → MD → MD → AD (if Jackie Brown as least senior authority refuses to give payment initiation approval the Integrator is contacting MD again but with Cathy Johnson as the next authority in hierarchy which decides to authorize payment).

2.3 The Discovery Scenarios

The discovery scenarios are independent of the integration/mediation problem. The integration problem can be solved with current syntactic technologies, however it shall be shown how semantic annotation can be used to make this task easier and more flexible. The discovery scenarios - service providers have to be located, selected and invoked dynamically - are more visionary scenarios, since in present business scenarios this task always involves a human in the loop. Two complementary scenarios have been defined, one concerned with shipping of packages, the second dealing with requests to purchase computer hardware.

2.3.1 Shipping Discovery Scenario

The first discovery scenario defines five shipping services (described via their WSDL and natural language documentations). It presents a set of increasingly complex shipping requests. Given a request, a suitable shipper needs to be discovered and invoked. Thus, participants have to create (semantic) descriptions for the available shippers and the given shipping requests such that the discovery and invocation task can be performed by an automated autonomous agent.

Shipping services are characterized by the following properties:

- Operation range: Shippers operate worldwide or in a set of listed countries or continents.
- Package limitations: Shippers define maximum bounds on the dimensions and the weight of packages. Additionally the notion of a dimensional weight is used: Packages with a low weight, but big dimensions need to use the dimensional weight (computed from the dimensions of the package) instead of the actual weight.
- Price: Four shippers statically specify the price as rules how to compute the price of a package depending on shipping location and package dimensions or weight. One shipper requires to dynamically call a Web Service endpoint to gather the current price providing the same information. Thus for goals specifying an upper price limit for the shipping operation, this service could not be discovered by exploiting static descriptions alone, but required dynamic negotiation during the discovery process.
- Package collection: Shippers offer collection of packages and define various constraints on the minimum or maximum advance notice for collection or the total length of the collection interval.
- Shipping time: Shippers specify rules about the maximum shipping time depending on the location of the shipment and the time of the pickup.

Predefined shipping requests specify a required shipping operation, characterized by concrete pickup and delivery addresses as well as concrete package dimensions and weight. The more complex goals additionally specify a maximum price for the shipping operation or constraints regarding the maximum shipping time. During discovery, participants have to filter unsuitable shippers, automatically choose a suitable one and invoke it by calling the corresponding Web Service endpoint. Since the shipper do not use a common XML-Schema for their messages, participants also have to deal with issues of data mediation to create the properly formatted messages.

One advanced goal requests sending two packages instead of one. Since none of the shippers support multiple packages, this goal has to be mapped to multiple invocations of the same or different shippers.

Similar to the mediation scenario we provided implementations of all shipping services. The implementation behavior is to be used in case of ambiguity in the textual descriptions. With an invocation of one of the corresponding Web Services an order is triggered which allows the organizer to automatically verify if a particular solution has chosen the right shipment provider.

To illustrate the scenario we present the details of one shipper and a sample goal.

Racer

The rates are composed of a flat fee and a fee per pound different for every continent: Europe($41/$6.75), Asia($47.5/$7.15), North America($26.25/$4.15), Rates for South America like North America, Rates for Oceania like Asia. Furthermore for each collection order $12.50 are added! Racer ships to 46 countries which are listed in its interface specification (WSDL file) The maximum package weight is 70lbs. Racer requires at least a pick-up interval of 120 minutes for collection and the latest possible collection time is 8pm. If a package is collected by 6pm, it is shipped in 2 business days within a country and 3 business days internationally.

Example Goal

One package with dimensions 40/24/10 (l/w/h) (in inch) weighing 40 pounds shall be shipped from an address in California to an address in Bristol, UK. As we can see Racer is one of the shipment providers that match. Others must be excluded since the dimensional weight is either exceeding the specified limits or they are not shipping to the UK.

2.3.2 Hardware Purchasing Scenario

In the second discovery scenario, a customer wants to buy computer hardware with fairly clear requirements on the products to buy. We will provide some examples below. Additionally, three services (called Bargainer, Hawker, and Rummage) are defined, which sell products. Each of the services offers an endpoint that allows to inquire about the products (and their detailed properties) currently on stock. Like in the first scenario, the task is to select the right service and invoke it with the right input parameters to purchase the products that best match the customer's expectations. The hardware purchasing scenario was designed to extend the shipping scenario along three dimensions of difficulty.

- Currently, the available services offer 19 products all together which are identified by a global product id (GTIN). Clearly more realistic services offer way more different products. It may or may not be feasible to specify all different options and all the product details in the offer description(s). Solutions to the scenario should indicate how they attempt to address this issue in more realistic scenarios with hundreds of products available. For the future, it is planned to extend the scenario in this direction.

- Some requests contain competing preferences as is usual for realistic matchmaking: price should be as low as possible, processor power, hard disk drive size and memory size should be as big as possible. The scenario request definitions clearly define rankings among such competing preferences. The semantic task is to represent these ranking rules clearly and execute them.
- The scenario requests involves increasingly difficult requirements of basic service composition:
  1. Uncorrelated composition: Some requests ask for several products that may or may not need to be purchased from different providers. Thus, a single request needs to be mapped to multiple invocations of the same or different services.
  2. Correlated composition: Some requests ask for several products but not all possible pairings of requested products are compatible to each others. Making a choice for one product may limit the choices for the remaining products to purchase or even make it impossible to fulfil the goal.
  3. Composition with global optimization goal: Some requests ask for several products with global optimization goals and constraints. A power minimum or a price maximum are examples of constraints that should not be violated for the total order. Therefore, like in the previous case, products can not be chosen independently of each other.

Example Goals

We illustrate the scenario by two exemplary goals.

Goal B2

Purchase a 13 inch Apple MacBook with a 2.0 GHz Intel Core Duo processor. It should have at least 1 GB RAM and at least 100 GB HDD. The price should be around $ 1500, at the very most $ 1800. If the white version is significantly cheaper than the black one (at least $ 100) buy the white one, otherwise buy the black version.

The resulting preferred solution is a white MacBook for $ 1449 by Bargainer. Another, albeit less preferred, solution is a black MacBook for $ 1699 by Rummage.

Goal C4

Purchase a 13 inch Apple MacBook with at least 2.0 GHz Intel Duo Core Processor, 512 MB RAM and 80 GB HDD. Additionally buy a web cam for notebooks with a resolution of at least VGA (640*480) and a 13 inch notebook sleeve. The total price must not exceed $ 1750. As long as the price limit is satisfied, choose the better product: The processor power of the notebook is most important to me. Besides that I rather need more RAM than a bigger HDD. If possible prefer webcams with a higher resolution.

The resulting solutions are as follows: The MacBook can be purchased by Hawker or Bargainer (preferred since better product). The products offered by Rummage either have not enough processor power or are too expensive after the web cam is added. The web cam needs to be purchased from Rummage since other web cam offers either do not specify a resolution or the specified resolution is too low. Hawker is the only service that offers sleeves.

2.3.3 Status and Future of the Discovery Scenarios

As of now there are two comprehensive scenarios related to service discovery and matchmaking. The first, original scenario, involves the discovery of an appropriate shipment service out of five offers, each with different peculiarities regarding price, supported locations, maximum package weight, constraints on the pickup time and the speed of delivery. A second scenario deals with purchasing computer hardware from a set of available vendors. The task is to determine which combination of products suits the needs of the client best and then to invoke the various vendor services properly to purchase the desired products.

Based on a hierarchy of increasingly difficult given goals for both scenarios (i.e. shipping and purchasing requests), submitted solutions are evaluated by determining the the problem levels that they are able to solve. For the first discovery scenario the problem levels are as follows:

1. discovery based on location,
2. discovery with arithmetic price and weight computations,
3. discovery including request for quote,
4. discovery including sending multiple packages (which had to be resolved to multiple service invocations), and
5. discovery with temporal semantics, i.e. pickup times and required speed of delivery.

The problem levels for the second discovery scenario have been defined as follows:

1. discovery based on clear product specifications,
2. discovery including (competing) preferences (like as cheap as possible),
3. discovery for multiple products that must be resolved to multiple service invocations,
4. discovery for multiple correlated products (like a notebook and a compatible docking station),
5. discovery for multiple products with a global optimization goal (e.g. overall minimal price), and
6. discovery for multiple products with a global optimization goal and preferences.

Submissions for new goals and also completely new scenarios that extend the coverage of the complete problem space are encouraged any time. Such submissions will be evaluated by the challenge organizers to become part of the official SWS-Challenge test bed.

For the near future, two extensions to the scenarios are already planned. On the one hand we will add goals that require automated unit conversion to either of the discovery scenarios. This might e.g. be done by mixing products with a price stated in Dollars with products with a price stated in Euro in the purchasing scenario. Participants will have to detect that prices are given in different currencies and develop means to deal with this, e.g. by automatically invoking a currency conversion service during service matchmaking. This will be one further step towards really adaptable systems.

On the other hand we are currently working to include a realistic number of products into the supplier scenario. We are investigating whether it is possible to exploit the Amazon E-Commerce service to gather the necessary amount of realistic product data. Including a large number of products into the scenario will have major implications on the solutions. First, creating meaningful descriptions will become much more difficult. A broad generic description in the sense of "this service sells electronic products" will be of little use during discovery. On the other hand it might not be feasible to explicitly list all available products within a description for various reasons (privacy, dynamicity, . . .). Thus participants will have to balance their solution somewhere between these extremes, decide on the amount of statically encoded information versus the amount of information being dynamically gathered, and provide means how to integrate dynamic information into service descriptions and service matchmaking algorithms.

The first of the two planned extensions is targeted at increasing the complexity of the discovery problems at the process and reasoning level. Solutions being able to still tackle the problems will have proven an even higher level of adaptability to homogeneous environments.

The second extension is complementary and increases the complexity with respect to the amount of information that needs to be processed and finally taken advantage of during discovery. Both extensions combined are aiming at making the discovery scenarios even more realistic than they already are, thereby underlining the goal of the SWS-Challenge to provide industrial level application scenarios.

2.4 Summary

The above described scenarios provide the current set of challenge problems. They are intended as common ground to discuss semantic (and other) Web Service solutions. By providing implementations to every scenario we want to ensure that solutions are close to the real world. More over different solutions become comparable with respect to the set of features supported for a particular scenario.

Finally we want to emphasize that the SWS-Challenge is open, not only to participation but also to the submission of new scenarios that extend the current coverage of problems.

Such scenarios can be "stand alone" or refine and extend the "Blue Moon" customer/company/supplier/shipper scenario. Eventually, this scenario should include the company fulfilling the customer order using a supply chain composed of the best suppliers and shippers for the specific customer order.

Part I

Mediation Individual Solutions

3

Mediation using WSMO, WSML and WSMX

Tomas Vitvar[1], Maciej Zaremba[2], Matthew Moran[2], and Adrian Mocan[1]

[1] The Semantics Technology Institute Innsbruck, University of Innsbruck, Austria,
`firstname.lastname@sti2.at`
[2] Digital Enterprise Research Institute, National University of Ireland, Galway, Ireland,
`firstname.lastname@deri.org`

Summary. This chapter presents DERI's solution to solving SWS Challenge mediation scenario.We demonstrate our approach building upon an established Semantic Web Service Framework to facilitate interoperability within the execution of heterogeneous services that support both the RosettaNet standard and proprietary information models.

3.1 Introduction

Inter-enterprise integration is an essential requirement for today's successful business. With the aim of overcoming heterogeneity, various technologies and standards for the definition of languages, vocabularies and integration patterns are being developed. For example, RosettaNet defines standardised Partner Interface Processes (PIPs), which include standard inter-company choreographies (e.g. PIP3A4 Request Purchase Order (PO)), and the structure and semantics of business messages. Although such standards certainly enable B2B integration, they still suffer from several drawbacks. All partners must agree to use the same standard and often the rigid configuration of standards makes them difficult to adapt to local business needs. On the other hand, the adoption of Service Oriented Architectures (SOA) for B2B integration is becoming a defacto standard approach. However, today's SOA technologies only provide a partial solution to interoperability, mainly through unified technological environments, while generic and scalable solutions are still in their infancy. In particular, message level interoperability is often hardwired in business processes using traditional XSLT approaches, and process level interoperability is often maintained through manual configuration of workflows. In order to address these drawbacks, the extension of SOA with semantics offers a scalable integration, more adaptive to changes in business requirements.

In this chapter we describe a generic conceptual model for execution of heterogenous business services that is able to resolve a wide range of interoperability issues. On the use case scenario from the SWS Challenge and based on the underlying technologies of Semantic Web services and B2B standards we also show how business services can be modeled and how the execution model is implemented.

3.1.1 Chapter Overview

In Section 3.2 we describe a generic execution model based on the formal definitions of service's information and behavioral semantics. In Section 3.3 we describe the implementation of the model based on the technology of the Web Service Modeling Ontology (WSMO), the Web Service Modeling Language (WSML) and the Web Service Execution Environment (WSMX). In addition, we use a business process and corresponding messages defined by the RosettaNet B2B standard. In section 3.3.2 we present a case scenario and its architecture which we use as a running example throughout the chapter while in section 3.3.3 we describe how services can be modeled using the WSMO framework. Section 10.3.4 describes the evaluation of our solution and in sections 4.4 and 6.7 we indicate related work and conclude the chapter.

3.2 Execution Model

In [3], we define two phases of the semantic web service integration process, namely *late-binding phase* and *execution phase*. The late-binding phase allows binding a user request (goal) and a set of services through semi-automation of the *service life-cycle*. We call this phase late-binding because the binding of the goal and business services is not known a priori (during modeling) and can be performed in a semi-automated way on-the-fly. On the other hand, execution phase allows for the invocation and conversation of services with resolving interoperability issues between heterogeneous services where necessary.

In order to enable automation in the web service integration process, the agent needs to operate on semantic descriptions of services. For this purpose four types of service semantics, namely *information, functional, behavioral*, and *non-functional*, are usually exploited by various semantic service models (see e.g. [14] for definitions of those semantics). In this section we demonstrate how information and behavioral semantics facilitate the execution phase of the web service integration process and how the data and process mediation is applied within that process.

3.2.1 Definitions

Information Semantics

Information Semantics is the formal definition of some domain knowledge used by the service in its *input* and *output* messages. We define the information semantics as an ontology:

$$O = (C, R, E, I) \tag{3.1}$$

with a set of classes (unary predicates) C, a set of relations (binary and higher-arity predicates) R, a set of explicit instances of C and R called E (extensional definition), and a set of axioms called I (intensional definition) that describe how new instances are inferred.

Behavioral Semantics

Behavioral Semantics is a description of the public and the private behavior of a service. For our work we only use the public behavior (called choreography[3]) as a description of a protocol which must be followed by a client in order to invoke the service. We describe a choreography as a public process, i.e. from the service point view, all the messages are sent in to the service from the network and all the messages are sent from the service out to the network. We define the choreography X (read: chi) of the service using the Abstract State Machine (ASM) as [14]

$$X = (\Sigma, L), \tag{3.2}$$

where $\Sigma \subseteq (\{x\} \cup C \cup R \cup E)$ is the signature of symbols, i.e. variable names $\{x\}$ or identifiers of elements from C, R, E of some information semantics O; and L is a set of rules. Further, we distinguish dynamic symbols denoted as Σ_I (input), and Σ_O (output) and static symbols denoted as Σ_S. While the static symbols cannot be changed by the service invocation, the dynamic symbols correspond to input and output data of the service which can be changed by the invocation. Each rule $r \in L$ is a Horn formula [3] and it defines a state transition $r : r^{cond} \rightarrow r^{eff}$ where $cond$ is defined as an expression in logic $\mathcal{L}(\Sigma_I \cup \Sigma_S)$ which must hold in a state before the transition is executed; eff is defined as an expression in logic $\mathcal{L}(\Sigma_I \cup \Sigma_O \cup \Sigma_S)$ describing how the state changes when the transition is executed.

For the SWS Challenge scenario we have chosen the logic $\mathcal{L}$ as being the intersection of Description Logic $\mathcal{SHIQ}(\mathbf{D})$ [4] and Horn Logic [3], extended with data type support, value constraints and integrity constraints, meta-modeling, inequality, (locally) stratified negation and non-recursive function symbols [4].

Grounding

Grounding defines a link between semantic descriptions of services and the underlying technology used for the services invocation (such as how and where the service can be accessed). Although the semantic descriptions are independent on the underlying technology, we use grounding to WSDL for on-the-wire message serialization (WSDL binding), physical Web service access (WSDL service and endpoint) and communication (SOAP).

For purposes of grounding definition for a WSDL description we denote the WSDL schema as S and the WSDL interface as N. Further, we denote $\{x\}_S$ as

---

[3] Please note, that in our approach the choreography defines the observable behavior and the information exchange from a particular participant viewpoint as opposed to the global view adopted by the Web Service Choreography Description Language (WS-CDL) http://www.w3.org/TR/ws-cdl-10/

[4] In fact the logic $\mathcal{L}$ corresponds to the WSML-Flight variant (extended with non-recursive function symbols) of the Web Service Modeling Language (WSML) [8] family of languages.

a set of all element declarations and type definitions of S, and $\{o\}_N$ as a set of all operations of N. Each operation $o \in \{o\}_N$ may have one input message element $m \in \{x\}_S$ and one output message element $n \in \{x\}_S$.

There are two types of grounding used for information and behavioral semantics. The first type of grounding specifies references between input/output symbols of a choreography $X = (\Sigma, L)$ and input/output messages of respective WSDL operations $\{o\}_N$ with schema S. We define this grounding as

$$ref(c, m) \tag{3.3}$$

where $m \in \{x\}_S$, $c \in \Sigma$ and ref is a binary relation between m and c. Further, m is the input message of operations in $\{o\}_N$ if $c \in \Sigma_I$ or m is the output message of operations in $\{o\}_N$ if $c \in \Sigma_O$.

The second type of grounding specifies transformations of data from schema S to ontology $O = (C, R, E, I)$ called lifting and vice-versa called lowering. We define this grounding as

$$lower(c_1) = m \quad \text{and} \quad lift(n) = c_2, \tag{3.4}$$

where $m, n \in \{x\}_S$, $c_1, c_2 \in (C \cup R)$, *lower* is a *lowering transformation function* transforming the semantic description c_1 to the message m, and *lift* is a *lifting transformation function* transforming the message n to the semantic description c_2. Please note that both definitions in Eq. 3.3 and Eq. 3.4 are associated either with WSDL or semantic descriptions. For example, [5] defines the grounding associated with WSMO semantic service model and [14] describes the grounding associated with WSDL descriptions using the Semantic Annotations for WSDL and XML Schema (SAWSDL) specifications [6].

Both types of grounding definitions are used when processing the choreography rules and performing the communication with the service (see Section 10.1.1) while following the underlying definition of WSDL operations and their Message Exchange Patterns (MEPs). Table 3.1 shows basic choreography rules for four basic WSDL 2.0 MEPs[5], (*in-out, in-only, out-only, out-in*) and corresponding WSDL operations. In here, the symbols $c_1, \ldots, c_6$ refer to identifiers of semantic descriptions defined as part of input or output state signature Σ_I or Σ_O of some choreography X (see Eq. 3.2), the symbols msg1, ..., msg6 refer to some XML Schema elements used for input/output messages of operations, $ref(c, m)$ denotes the existence of grounding definition between a semantic description c and a message m (see Eq. 3.3), and w is the prefix for URI http://www.w3.org/ns/wsdl. Please note that a complex rule may exist in the choreography covering more than one invocation and thus combining multiple MEPs in one rule.

The $add(c)$ construct is only a syntactic sugaring and it actually states that a positive fact c is "added" to the reasoning space.

---

[5] http://www.w3.org/TR/wsdl20-adjuncts/#meps

MEP and Rule	WSDL Operation

in-out:
if c_1 then $add(c_2)$
$c_1 \in \Sigma_I,\ ref(c_1, \texttt{msg1})$
$c_2 \in \Sigma_O,\ ref(c_2, \texttt{msg2})$
	```<operation name="oper1" pattern="w:in-out">```
	``` <input messageLabel="In" element="msg1"/>```
	``` <output messageLabel="Out" element="msg2"/>```
	```</operation>```

in-only:
if c_3 then *no action*
$c_3 \in \Sigma_I,\ ref(c_3, \texttt{msg3})$
	```<operation name="oper2" pattern="w:in-only">```
	``` <input messageLabel="In" element="msg3"/>```
	```</operation>```

out-only:
if *true* then $add(c_4)$
$c_4 \in \Sigma_O,\ ref(c_4, \texttt{msg4})$
	```<operation name="oper3" pattern="w:out-only">```
	``` <output messageLabel="Out" element="msg4"/>```
	```</operation>```

out-in:
if *true* then $add(c_5)$
if $c_5 \wedge c_6$ then *no action*
$c_5 \in \Sigma_O,\ ref(c_5, \texttt{msg5})$
$c_6 \in \Sigma_I,\ ref(c_6, \texttt{msg6})$
	```<operation name="oper4" pattern="w:out-in">```
	``` <output messageLabel="Out" element="msg5"/>```
	``` <input messageLabel="In" element="msg6"/>```
	```</operation>```

Table 3.1. MEPs, Rules and WSDL operations

Data Mediation

When the information semantics of the two services is different, i.e. different ontologies are used, the communication cannot take place and the data mediation needs to be performed. The data mediation transforms every incoming message from the terms of the sender's information semantics (the source) into the terms of the receiver's information semantics (the target).

The agent performing data mediation has to automatically perform the transformation of the exchanged messages. Since the interoperability problems can greatly vary in their nature and severity, automatic solution for the detection and solving of data mismatches are not feasible in a business scenario due to the lower-than-100% precision and recall of the existing methods[6]. As a consequence, alignments between heterogenous ontologies have to be created at design-time and used by the data mediation engine at run-time.

An alignment consists of a set of mappings expressing the semantic relationships that exist between the two ontologies. Technically, the mappings are expressed as rules which concretely specify the semantics of mappings present in alignments. In particular, a mapping can specify that classes from two ontologies are equivalent while corresponding rules use logical expressions to unambiguously define how the data encapsulated in an instance of one class can be encapsulated in instances of the second class. Formally, we define an alignment A between two ontologies $O_s = (C_s, R_s, E_s, I_s)$ and $O_t = (C_t, R_t, E_t, I_t)$ as

$$A_{s,t} = (O_s, O_t, \Phi_{s,t}) \tag{3.5}$$

---

[6] The *"Ontology Alignment Evaluation Initiative 2006"* [7] shows that the best five systems' scores vary between 61% and 81% for precision and between 65% and 71% for recall.

where $\Phi_{s,t}$ is the set of mappings m of the form

$$m = <\varepsilon_s, \varepsilon_t, \gamma_{\varepsilon_s}, \gamma_{\varepsilon_t}> \tag{3.6}$$

where ε_s, ε_t represent the mapped entities from the two ontologies while γ_{ε_s}, γ_{ε_t} represent restrictions (i.e. conditions) on these entities such as $\varepsilon_s \in C_s \cup R_s$, $\varepsilon_t \in C_t \cup R_t$ while γ_{ε_s} and γ_{ε_t} are expressions in $\mathcal{L}(C_s \cup R_s \cup E_s)$ and $\mathcal{L}(C_t \cup R_t \cup E_t)$, respectively. Intuitively, the conditions are set on schema elements and as a consequence, they will apply to all the exchange data (i.e. ontology instances) that comply with these schemas.

Please note, that in order to execute the mappings, they need to be grounded to executable rules expressed in a logical language for which a reasoning support is available. Using this grounding, the reasoner becomes the execution engine of these rules. We implement this grounding using the WSML language. Consequently, the set of rules $\rho_{s,t} = \Phi_{s,t}^G$ is obtained by applying the grounding G to the set of mappings Φ. Every mapping rule $mr \in \rho_{s,t}$ has the following form:

$$mr : \bigwedge_{i=1..n}^{\{x\}} mr_i^{head} \leftarrow \bigwedge_{i=1..n}^{\{x\}} mr_i^{body} \tag{3.7}$$

where

$$mr^{head} \in \{x' \text{ instanceOf } \varepsilon \mid \varepsilon \in C_t \text{ and } x' \in \{x\}\} \cup \tag{3.8}$$
$$\{\varepsilon(x', x'') \mid \varepsilon \in R_t \text{ and } \varepsilon(x', x'') \in E_t \text{ and } x', x'' \in \{x\}\}$$

$$mr^{body} \in \{x' \text{ instanceOf } \varepsilon \mid \varepsilon \in C_s \text{ and } x' \in \{x\}\} \cup \tag{3.9}$$
$$\{\varepsilon(x', x'') \mid \varepsilon \in R_s \text{ and } \varepsilon(x', x'') \in E_s \text{ and } x', x'' \in \{x\}\} \cup$$
$$\{\gamma_s \mid \gamma_s \in \mathcal{L}(C_s \cup R_s \cup E_s \cup \{x\})\} \cup$$
$$\{\gamma_t \mid \gamma_t \in \mathcal{L}(C_t \cup R_t \cup E_t \cup \{x\})\}$$

In the above definitions, $\{x\}$ stands for the set of variable used by the mapping rule and x' and x'' are two particular variables.

A mapping rule is formed of a head and a body and it is, as in the case of the transition rules, a Horn formula. The head is a conjunction of logical expressions over the target elements and it constructs the instances of the target ontology which represent the result of the mediation. Please note that by allowing the instantiations of both concepts and relations ($\varepsilon \in C_t$ or $\varepsilon \in R_t$), the mediator can construct all complex relationships that can appear between the concepts in the target ontology. For example, using such mapping rules it is possible to construct instances of the concepts *Person* and *Address* linked by the *hasAddress* relation.

The body is formed of a set of logical expressions over the source entities which represent the data to be mediated, plus (if necessary) a set of logical expressions representing conditions over both the source and the target data.

It is important to mention that the variables are used in such a way to assure that there are no unsafe rules generated (i.e. in the head there are no variables that do not appear in the body). This is achieved by the grounding mechanism, which always (automatically) generates safe rules based on the given set of mappings. In Section 3.3.3 we show examples of mapping rules in WSML.

Process Mediation

Process Mediation handles the interoperability issues which occur in descriptions of choreographies of the two services. In [8], Cimpian defines five process mediation patterns:

a. **Stopping an unexpected message:** when one service sends a message which is not expected by the other service, the mediator stops the message.
b. **Inversing the order of messages:** when one service sends messages in a different order than the the other service expects them to receive, the mediator ensures that messages are supplied in proper order.
c. **Splitting a message:** when a service sends a message which the other service expects to receive in multiple different messages, the mediator splits the message and ensures that all messages are supplied to the service.
d. **Combining messages:** when a service expects to receive a message which is sent by the other service in multiple different messages, the mediator combines those messages and ensures that the combined message is supplied to the service.
e. **Generating a message:** when one service expects to receive a message which is not supplied by the other service, mediator generates the message and supplies the message to the service.

The patterns are implemented using an algorithm by processing both choreographies, i.e. evaluating choreography rules and the information semantics of both services. In sections 10.1.1 and 3.2.3 we show how the algorithm fulfils the patterns (a) – (d). In order to fulfill the pattern (e), the algorithm should be aware of the intention of the messages. For example, if the algorithm is able to distinguish control interactions (e.g. acknowledgements) among all the interactions happening between both services, it could generate an acknowledgment message (assuming the algorithm would be able to assess that a message to be acknowledged was successfully received by the other service). Since we do not give semantics to message interactions, we currently do not address the pattern (e) in our work.

3.2.2 Algorithm

The algorithm for the execution model manages the conversation between two services with applied data and process mediation. Each such a service contains description of information and behavioral semantics, WSDL definition and the grounding according to the definitions in the previous section. These services are usually supplied as a result from the late-binding phase. The Figure 3.1 depicts the main steps

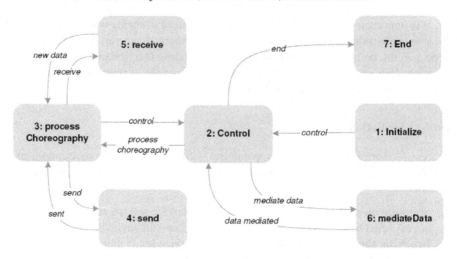

Fig. 3.1. Control State Diagram for the Execution Model

of the execution phase. The algorithm requires inputs and uses internal structures as follows:

Input:

- Service W_1 and service W_2. Each such a service W contains the ontology (information semantics) $W.O$ (Eq. 3.1), the choreography $W.X$ (Eq. 3.2) with set of rules $W.X.L$, WSDL description and grounding (Eq. 3.3, 3.4). In addition, for a rule $r \in W.X.L$, the condition r^{cond} is a logical expression with set of semantic descriptions $\{c\}$, and the effect r^{eff} is a logical expression with set of actions $\{a\}$. For each element a we denote its action name as $a.action$ with values $delete$ or add and a semantic description as $a.c$.
- Mappings Φ between $W_1.O$ and $W_2.O$.

Uses:

- Symbols M_1 and M_2 corresponding to the processing memory of the choreography $W_1.X$ and $W_2.X$ respectively (a memory M is a populated ontology $W.O$ with instance data). The content of each memory M determines at some point in time a state in which a choreography $W.X$ is. In addition, each memory has methods $M.add$ and $M.remove$ allowing to add or remove data to/from M and a flag $M.modified$ indicating whether the memory was modified. The flag $M.modified$ is set to $true$ whenever the method $M.add$ or $M.remove$ is used.
- Symbols D_1 and D_2 corresponding to the set of data to be added to the memory M_1 and M_2 after the choreography is processed. Each D has a method $D.add$ for adding new data to the set.
- A symbol A corresponding to all actions to be executed while processing the choreography. Each element of A has the same definition as the element of the rule effect r^{eff}. A has methods $A.add$ and $A.remove$ for adding and removing actions to/from the set.

- A symbol o corresponding to a WSDL operation of a service and symbols m, n corresponding to some XML data of the message (input or output) of the operation o.

States 1, 2, 7: Initialize, Control, End

```
 1: M₁ ← ∅; M₂ ← ∅
 2: repeat
 3:    M₁.modified ← false; M₂.modified ← false
 4:    D₁ ← processChoreography(W₁, M₁)
 5:    D₂ ← processChoreography(W₂, M₂)
 6:    if D₁ ≠ ∅ then
 7:       Dₘ ← mediateData(D₁, W₁.O, W₂.O, Φ)
 8:       M₁.add(D₁); M₂.add(Dₘ)
 9:    end if
10:    if D₂ ≠ ∅ then
11:       Dₘ ← mediateData(D₂, W₂.O, W₁.O)
12:       M₁.add(Dₘ); M₂.add(D₂)
13:    end if
14: until not M₁.modified and not M₂.modified
```

After the initialization of the processing memory M_1 and M_2 (line 1), the execution gets to the control state when the whole process is managed. It can process choreographies (state 3), mediate the data (state 6) or end the execution (state 7). The execution ends when no modifications of the processing memories M_1 or M_2 has occurred.

State 3: $D = processChoreography(W, M)$

```
 1: A ← ∅; D ← ∅
 2: {Performing rule's conditions and sending data}
 3: for all r in W.X.L : holds(rᶜᵒⁿᵈ, M) do
 4:    A.add(rᵉᶠᶠ)
 5:    for all c in rᶜᵒⁿᵈ : c ∈ W.X.Σ_I do
 6:       send(c, W)
 7:    end for
 8: end for

 9: {Performing delete actions}
10: for all a in A : a.action = delete do
11:    M.remove(a.c)
12:    A.remove(a)
13: end for

14: {Receiving data and performing add actions}
15: while A ≠ ∅ do
16:    c ← receive(W)
17:    if c ≠ null then
18:       for all a in A: (a.action = add and a.c = c) do
```

19:        $D.add(c)$
20:        $A.remove(a)$
21:     **end for**
22:     **end if**
23: **end while**

24: **return** D

The algorithm evaluates the conditions of each rule in the choreography and if its conditions hold the effect is processed, i.e. the algorithm collects all data to be added to the memory or removes existing data from the memory. The whole process is divided into three major steps as follows.

- **Performing rule's conditions and sending data (lines 2-8):** each rule's conditions are evaluated and if they satisfy the content of the memory the rule's effect is added to the set of effects A (line 4). Then, for each input symbol of the rule's condition (line 5), the algorithm sends the data to the service (line 6, see State 4).
- **Performing delete actions (lines 9-13):** all effects with *delete* action are performed, the data of the effect is removed from the memory (line 11) while such effects are removed from A (line 12).
- **Receiving data and performing add actions (lines 14-24):** When there are effects to be processed in A and the new data is received from the service (line 16), it is checked if the new data corresponds to some of the *add* effect from A. In this case, the data is added to the set D (line 19) and the effect is removed from A (line 20).

The result of the algorithm is the set D containing all new data to be added to the memory M. The actual modification of the memory M with the new data is performed in State 2. The algorithm assumes that definition of the choreography rules are consistent with WSDL operations and their MEPs while at the same time no failures occur in services. In lines 14-23 the algorithm waits for every message to be received from the service for every *add* action of the rule's effect. If the definition of the rules was not consistent with WSDL description, the algorithm would either ignore the received message which could in turn affect the correct processing of the choreography (in case of missing *add* action) or wait infinitely (in case of extra *add* action or a failure in a service). For the latter, the simplest solution would be to introduce a timeout in the loop (lines 14-23), however, we do not currently handle these issues in the algorithm. They will be the subject of our future work.

State 4: $send(c, W)$

1: $m \leftarrow lower(c)$
2: **for all** o of which m is the input message **do**
3:     send m to W
4: **end for**

In order to send the data c the algorithm first retrieves a corresponding message definition according to the grounding and transforms c to the message m using the lowering transformation function (line 1). Then, through each operation of which the message m is the input message, the algorithm sends the m to the service W.

State 5: $c = receive(W)$

```
1: if receive m from W then
2:     c ← lift(m)
3:     return c
4: else
5:     return null
6: end if
```

When there is a new data from the service W, the data (message m in XML) is lifted to the semantic representation using lifting transformation function associated with the message (line 2), and the result is returned. In the opposite case, the *null* is returned.

State 6: $c_m = mediateData(c, O_s, O_t, \Phi)$

```
 1: ε ← getTypeOf(c)
 2: εm ← null
 3: for all m =< εs, εt, γεs, γεt >∈ Φ where ε = εs do
 4:     if isMoreGeneral(εt, εm) then
 5:         εm ← εt
 6:     end if
 7:     ρ ← ρ ∪ {mG}
 8: end for
 9: if εm = null then
10:     return null
11: end if
12: cm ← getDataForType(εm, ρ)
13: return cm
```

The first step in the mediation process is to determine the type of the data to be mediated. If this data is a concept instance the algorithm determines its concept. After that, the set of mappings is navigated in order to determine the type of the target, mediated data. Since there could be more mappings from a given source entity to the several other target entities, it is necessary to determine the most general entity to mediate the source data to. Also while traversing the set of mappings, each of them is grounded to WSML and transformed in a set of logical mapping rules. Finally, by using a reasoner engine all the data of the selected target type is retrieved based on the source data and the set of mapping rules.

From the implementation point of view, several optimizations could be applied to this algorithm. First, the mappings rules could be cached in order to avoid their regeneration every time when a new request for data mediation is coming. Second only the mappings and mapping rules that refer to the input source data could be processed in order to reduce the volume of rules that need to be evaluated.

3.2.3 Discussion on Data and Process Mediation

The data mediation ensures that all new data coming from one service is translated to the other's service ontology. Thus, no matter from where the data originates the data is always ready to use for both services. From the process mediation point view, the data mediation also handles the splitting of messages (pattern c) and combining the messages (pattern d). Since the mediated data is always added to both memories (see State 2, lines 8, 12 and the next paragraph for additional discussion) the patterns a) and b) are handled automatically through processing of the choreography rules. In particular, the fact that a message will be stopped (pattern a) means that the message will never be used by the choreography because no rule will use it (the message remains in the memory until the end of the algorithm). In addition, the order of messages will be inverted (pattern b) as defined by the choreography rules and the order of ASM states in which conditions of rules hold. This means that the algorithm automatically handles the process mediation with help of data mediation through rich description of choreographies when no central workflow is necessary for that purpose.

In our algorithm we always add all the data to both choreographies and not only the data which could be of *potential use*, i.e. the data could be used when evaluating a rule's condition. However, since we use the language which allows for the intentional definitions (axioms) which are part of the information semantics and the memory, the data might affect the evaluation of the rule indirectly through such axioms. The evaluation of the potential use of data would thus require a logical reasoning and would influence the scalability and the processing time. On the other hand, we do not expect a significant overhead when storing such additional data, however, we leave the evaluation for the future work.

3.3 Implementation

We have implemented the execution model as part of the established Semantic Web Services framework which includes the Web Service Modeling Ontology (WSMO), the Web Service Modeling Language (WSML) and the Web Service Execution Environment (WSMX). Building upon this framework we then show how the execution model solves the SWS Challenge mediation scenario. In this section we describe the details of the solution architecture together with modeling of necessary services, and ontologies and run through the execution.

3.3.1 WSMO, WSML, and WSMX

WSMO provides a conceptual model and a language for semantic markup describing all relevant aspects of general services which are accessible through a Web service interface. The ultimate goal of such markup is to enable the (total or partial) automation of tasks (e.g. discovery, selection, composition, mediation, execution, monitoring, etc.) involved in both intra- and inter-enterprise integration settings. WSMO defines the underlying model for the WSMX Semantic Web services architecture and execution environment and provides the conceptual model formalised by the Web Service Modeling Language (WSML)[8] family of ontology languages, used to formally describe WSMO elements.

WSMO defines the conceptual model for *ontologies, mediators, services* and *goals*. Please note, that while WSMO defines WSMO Goal for representation of a service requester and WSMO Service for representation of a service provider, both elements have the same structural definition (both include the description of their ontologies and behavioral models). For purposes of service execution operating on ontologies and choreographies, the distinction between the WSMO Goal and the WSMO Service is not important. In addition, the WSMO Goal as well as WSMO service defines a functional description in a form of a capability as conditions which must hold before the execution (called preconditions and assumptions) and conditions which must hold after the execution (called postconditions and effects). In this chapter we do not use them either.

The Web Service Execution Environment (WSMX) is an execution environment that enables discovery, selection, mediation, invocation, and interoperation of Semantic Web services [9, 3]. WSMX is based on the conceptual model provided by WSMO, being at the same time a reference implementation of it. It is the scope of WSMX to provide a test-bed for WSMO and to prove its viability as a mean of achieving dynamic interoperability of Semantic Web services.

For purposes of this chapter we use the WSMO ontology to model the information semantics of the service, and the *choreography interface* definition of WSMO Service/Goal to model the behavioral semantics of services. In addition, we adopt the concept of WSMO mediators for the data and process mediation. For purposes of describing ontologies, choreographies and mediators, we use the WSML language.

3.3.2 Solution Architecture

The SWS Challenge mediation scenario describes a situation where two companies aim to build an automated B2B integration. A trading company, called Moon, uses a Customer Relationship Management system (CRM) and an Order Management system (OMS) to manage its order processing. Moon has signed agreements to exchange Purchase Order (PO) messages with a company called Blue using the RosettaNet standard for PO exchange (PIP3A4). In this scenario, Blue sends a PIP3A4 PO message, including all items to be ordered, and expects to receive a PIP3A4 PO confirmation message. In Moon, various interactions with the CRM and OMS systems must be performed in order to process the order, i.e. get the internal ID for the customer from the CRM system, create the order in the OMS system, add line items into the order, close the order, and send back the PO confirmation. In order for integration to be possible, both Moon and Blue must comply on three interoperability levels - *communication, message* and *process*. We focus on the two latter as in the scenario both companies communicate via SOAP over HTTP. For the message level both partners need to understand the exchanged messages including both the message structure and the semantics of its content. The Blue uses PIP3A4 to define the PO request and confirmation messages, however, the Moon uses a proprietary XML Schema for its OMS and CRM systems. On the process level, the exchange of messages in the right order is an essential requirement for partner integration. The Blue company conforms to the PIP3A4 process while Moon follows its own internal business process.

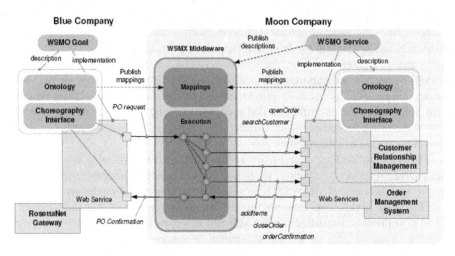

Fig. 3.2. Solution Architecture

Figure 3.2 depicts the solution architecture for the scenario. It includes the existing systems of the Moons back-end applications, i.e. CRM and OMS systems on one side and the Blue's RosettaNet system on the other. The integration of both companies is built in the WSMX middleware which operates on the WSMO semantic descriptions. Thus, both companies must expose their system functionalities to the WSMX middleware using the WSMO ontology for their information models and the WSMO service/goal choreography for their behavioral models together with grounding definitions. In the next section, section 3.3.3, we further show how we model these descriptions.

3.3.3 Modeling of Ontologies and Services

The back-end systems already have their interfaces available in WSDL. The goal of the modeling phase is to represent them semantically and define their grounding.

Ontologies and Grounding

Ontologies describe information models used in semantic service descriptions. In our scenario, we assume that both Blue and Moon use independent ontologies i.e. different ontologies for RosettaNet and CRM/OMS systems[7]. The message level interoperability must be thus reached through mappings between used ontologies which are defined during design-time and executed during runtime.

We assume that all ontologies are not available up-front, thus, we take the existing standards and systems as a basis (i.e. RosettaNet PIP 3A4 and CRM/OMS schemas) and, using the Web Service Modeling Toolkit (WSMT), we create PIP3A4 and CRM/OMS ontologies. WSMT [10] is an Integrated Development Environment (IDE) for Ontology Engineering, Semantic Web Service engineering and Mapping engineering implemented in the Eclipse framework. It aims to support the developer through the full development cycle of Ontologies, Semantic Web Services, and Ontology Mappings through the WSMO paradigm, in order to improve the productivity of the developer and to ensure the quality of the artefacts produced.

During this process we describe the information semantically, i.e. with richer expressivity as opposed to that of the underlying XML schema. When both ontologies are available, we define the mapping between these ontologies, again using WSMT. For example, in listing 8.2, the mapping of *searchString* concept of the *CRM/OMS* ontology to concept *customerId* of the *PIP3A4* ontology is shown. The construct $mediated(X, C)$ represents the identifier of the newly created target instance, where X is the source instance that is transformed, and C is the target concept we map to [8]. Such format of mapping rules is generated from the ontology mapping process by the WSMT ontology mapping tool.

```
axiom aaMappingRule23
    definedBy
        mediated(?X21, SearchCustomerReq)[searchString hasValue ?Y22] memberOf o1#
            SearchCustomerReq
    :- ?X21[businessName hasValue ?Y22] memberOf o2#BusinessDescription.
```

Listing 3.1. Mapping Rules in WSML

In addition, we capture a *logic* of getting from the XML schema level to the semantic level and vice-versa by lifting and lowering transformations.

```
1   /* Lifting rules from XML message to WSML */
2   instance PurchaseOrderUID memberOf por#purchaseOrder
3       por#globalPurchaseOrderTypeCode hasValue "<xsl:value-of select="dict:
            GlobalPurchaseOrderTypeCode"/>"
4       por#isDropShip hasValue IsDropShipPo
5       <xsl:for-each select="po:ProductLineItem">
6           por#productLineItem hasValue ProductLineItem<xsl:value-of select="position()"/>
7       </xsl:for-each>
8       <xsl:for-each select="core:requestedEvent">
9           por#requestedEvent hasValue RequestedEventPo
10      </xsl:for-each>
11      <xsl:for-each select="core:shipTo">
12          por#shipTo hasValue ShipToPo
13      </xsl:for-each>
14      <xsl:for-each select="core:totalAmount">
15          por#totalAmount hasValue TotalAmountPo
16      </xsl:for-each>
```

```
17
18   /* message in WSML after transformation */
19   instance PurchaseOrderUID memberOf por#purchaseOrder
20       por#globalPurchaseOrderTypeCode hasValue "Packaged product"
21       por#isDropShip hasValue IsDropShipPo
22       por#productLineItem hasValue ProductLineItem1
23       por#productLineItem hasValue ProductLineItem2
24       por#requestedEvent hasValue RequestedEventPo
25       por#shipTo hasValue ShipToPo
26       por#totalAmount hasValue TotalAmountPo
```

Listing 3.2. Lifting from XML to WSML

Listing 3.2 shows an example extract of lifting transformation in XSLT (lines 1-16) and the result WSML instance of a RosettaNet message (lines 18-26). Such grounding is identified by an URI which is specified in the lifting/lowering non-functional property of the service (not shown in the example). In a reality, modeling of ontologies, creating the mapping rules and the transformation rules must be performed by a domain expert who poses the knowledge from the B2B domain, related standards as well as relevant skills from ontology engineering.

Choreography and Grounding

In line with Eq. 3.2, the WSMO service choreography contains the definition of the input, output and shared symbols (called state signature or vocabulary) and a set of rules. Using these rules we model the choreography of both RosettaNet and CRM/OMS services separately and for each define the order in which the operations should be correctly invoked. Listing 8.1 shows a fragment of the choreography for the CRM/OMS service. The choreography is part of the semantic descriptions of the service (see WSMO specifications [7] for more details) and it can be developed by a domain expert either manually or semi-automatically, in a tool assisted manner. Even if we are not aware of any existing work concerning automatic generation of choreographies (from WSDL descriptions for example), we envisioned that such an approach might yield good results for simple message exchange patterns but it will always require the support of the human user for more complicated scenarios.

There are two rules defined listing 8.1. The first rule (lines 18-23) defines that the *SearchCustomerReq* will be sent to the service and on result the *SearchCustomerResp* will be expected as the output message. The *SearchCustomerReq* message must be available in the memory (in our case the data for the message will be provided by the Blue RosettaNet after the mediation). The second rule (lines 25-31) defines that the *SearchCustomerResp* must be available in the memory while its *customerId* will be used for the *customerId* of the *CreateNewOrderReq* which will be sent to the service. On result, the *CreateNewOrderResp* will be expected to be received back. The data for the *CreateNewOrderReq* will be again supplied by the Blue RosettaNet after the mediation. All the messages used in the choreography as the input or output symbols refer to the definition of concepts in the ontology imported in line 4 while at the same time the mapping of those symbols to the underlying WSDL messages is defined in lines 6-15.

```
1   choreography MoonWSChoreography
2     stateSignature _"http://example.com/ontologies/MoonWS#statesignature"
3     importsOntology {_"http://example.com/wsml/Moon" }
4     // input symbols
5     in moon#SearchCustomerReq
6        withGrounding { _"http://example.com/MoonCRM#wsdl.interfaceMessageReference(search/in0)"}
7        moon#CreateNewOrderReq
8        withGrounding { _"http://example.com/MoonOMS#wsdl.interfaceMessageReference(openorder/
           in0)"}
9
10    // output symbols
11    out moon#SearchCustomerResp
12       withGrounding { _"http://example.com/MoonCRM#wsdl.interfaceMessageReference(search/out0
           )"}
13       moon#CreateNewOrderResp
14       withGrounding { _"http://example.com/MoonOMS#wsdl.interfaceMessageReference(openorder/
           out0)"}
15       ...
16    transitionRules _"http://example.com/ontologies/MoonWS#transitionRules"
17    // rule 1: search the customer in CRM
18    forall { ?customerReq} with (
19     ?customerReq memberOf moon#SearchCustomerReq
20    ) do
21     add(_# memberOf moon#SearchCustomerResp)
22    endForall
23
24    // rule 2: open the order in OMS
25    forall { ?orderReq, ?customerResp} with (
26     ?customerResp[customerId hasValue ?id] memberOf moon#SearchCustomerResp and
27     ?orderReq[customerId hasValue ?id] memberOf moon#CreateNewOrderReq
28    ) do
29     add(_# memberOf moon#CreateNewOrderResp)
30    endForall
```

Listing 3.3. Moon CRM/OMS Choreography

3.4 Evaluation

Our implementation has been evaluated, by peer-review, according to the criteria defined by the SWS Challenge. The evaluation criteria targets the adaptivity of the solutions – solutions should handle introduced changes by modification of declarative descriptions rather than code-changes. Success level 0 indicates a minimal satisfiability level, where messages between middleware and back-end systems are properly exchanged. Success level 1 is assigned when changes introduced in the scenario require code changes and recompilation. Success level 2 indicates that introduced changes did not entail any code modifications and only declarative parts had to be changed. Finally, success level 3 is assigned when the system is able to automatically adapt to new conditions. In the data mediation scenario we had to make some changes to the code to overcome limitations of the existing data mediation tool (success level 1). For process mediation, we only needed to change the description of the service interfaces (choreographies) according to the changes in back-end systems (success level 2).

3.5 Related Work

The most relevant related work is among other submissions addressing the SWS-Challenge mediation scenario, namely WebML [?] and dynamic process binding for BPEL[13]. They are based on software engineering methods with strong emphasis on graphical modelling of integration process as a central point of integration. However, they do not use logical languages in their data model while they are limitted to expressivity of UML Class Diagrams. On the other hand, WSML comes with powerful rule and F-logic support which caters for reasoning tasks of varying complexity. In addition, Preist et al [14] presented a solution covering all phases of a B2B integration life-cycle, starting from discovering potential partners to performing integrations including mediations. They also address the lifting and lowering of RosettaNet XML messages to ontologies but provide no details for mediation on the ontological level. Their solutions is rather conceptual with missing details about the actual components and algorithms used. Other, more general SWS related work, include IRS-III[15] which is an execution environment also based on WSMO as the underlying conceptual model. Both WSMX and IRS-III have common roots in the UPML framework of [16].

3.6 Conclusion and Future Work

One of the main advantages of our approach is the strong partner de-coupling. This means that when changes occur in back-end systems of one partner, consequent changes in service descriptions does not affect changes in the integration. The integration automatically adapts to the changes in service descriptions as there is no central integration workflow (see the next paragraph for additional comment). On the other hand, changes in back-end system still require manual effort in making changes in semantic descriptions such as ontologies and mapping rules. Although our SWS technology allows for semi-automated approaches in modelling and mapping definitions, it is still a human user who must adjust and approve the results.

It is important to note, however, that this type of integration where no central workflow is necessary is only usable in situations when two public processes (ASM choreographies) are compatible, that is, they may have different order/structure of messages but by adjusting the order/structure the integration is possible. In general, there could be cases where third-party data need to be obtained (e.g. from external databases) for some interactions. Although some of the tihrd-party data can be gathered through the transformation functions of the mapping rules, in some cases, an external workflow could be required to accommodate the integration process. It is our open research work to further investigate such cases in detail.

References

1. Vitvar, T., Mocan, A., Kerrigan, M., Zaremba, M., Zaremba, M., Moran, M., Cimpian, E., Haselwanter, T., Fensel, D.: Semantically-enabled service oriented architecture: Con-

cepts, technology and application. In Service Oriented Computing and Applications, Springer London **1**(2) (2007)

2. Vitvar, T., Kopecky, J., Fensel, D.: WSMO-Lite: Lightweight Semantic Descriptions for Services on the Web. In: ECOWS. (2007)

3. Lloyd, J.W.: Foundations of Logic Programming (2nd edition). Springer-Verlag (1987)

4. Horrocks, I., Sattler, U., Tobies, S.: Practical Reasoning for Expressive Description Logics. In: Proceedings of the 6th International Conference on Logic for Programming and Automated Reasoning (LPAR-1999). Number 1705, Springer-Verlag (1999) 161–180

5. Kopecký, J., Roman, D., Moran, M., Fensel, D.: Semantic Web Services Grounding. In: AICT/ICIW. (2006) 127

6. Kopecky, J., Vitvar, T., Bournez, C., Farrell, J.: Sawsdl: Semantic annotations for wsdl and xml schema. IEEE Internet Computing **11**(6) (2007)

7. Euzenat, J., Mochol, M., Shvaiko, P., Stuckenschmidt, H., Šváb, O., Svátek, V., van Hage, W.R., Yatskevich, M.: Results of the Ontology Alignment Evaluation Initiative 2006. In: Proceeding of International Workshop on Ontology Matching (OM-2006). Volume 225., Athens, Georgia, USA, CEUR Workshop Proceedings (2006) 73–95

8. Cimpian, E., Mocan, A.: Wsmx process mediation based on choreographies. In: Business Process Management Workshops. (2005) 130–143

9. Mocan, A., Moran, M., Cimpian, E., Zaremba, M.: Filling the Gap - Extending Service Oriented Architectures with Semantics. In: ICEBE, IEEE Computer Society (2006) 594–601

10. Kerrigan, M., Mocan, A., Tanler, M., Fensel, D.: The Web Service Modeling Toolkit - An Integrated Development Environment for Semantic Web Services. In: Proceedings of the 4th European Semantic Web Conference (ESWC-2007), System Description Track, Innsbruck, Austria, Springer-Verlag (2007)

11. Mocan, A., Cimpian, E., Kerrigan, M.: Formal model for ontology mapping creation. In: International Semantic Web Conference. (2006) 459–472

12. Roman, D., Scicluna, J.: Ontology-based Choreography of WSMO Services. Wsmo final draft v0.3, DERI (2006) Available at: http://www.wsmo.org/TR/d14/v0.3/.

13. Kuster, U., Konig-Ries, B.: Dynamic binding for bpel processes - a lightweight approach to integrate semantics into web services. In: Second International Workshop on Engineering Service-Oriented Applications: Design and Composition (WESOA06) at 4th International Conference on Service Oriented Computing (ICSOC06), Chicago, Illinois, USA (2006) 00–00

14. Preist, C., Cuadrado, J.E., Battle, S., Williams, S., Grimm, S.: Automated Business-to-Business Integration of a Logistics Supply Chain using Semantic Web Services Technology. In: Proc. of 4th Int. Semantic Web Conference. (2005)

15. Motta, E., Domingue, J., Cabral, L., Gaspari, M.: IRS-II A Framework and Infrastructure for Semantic Web Services. The Semantic Web ISWC 2003. Lecture Notes in Computer Science, Springer-Verlag, Heidelberg **2870** (2003) 306–318

16. Fensel, D., Benjamins, V., Motta, E., Wielinga, B.: UPML: A Framework for knowledge system reuse. In: Proceedings of the International Joint Conference on AI (IJCAI-99), Stockholm, Sweden (1999)

4

A Software Engineering Approach based on WebML and BPMN to the Mediation Scenario of the SWS Challenge

Marco Brambilla[1], Stefano Ceri[1], Emanuele Della Valle[2],
Federico M. Facca[1], Christina Tziviskou[1]

[1] Dipartimento di Elettronica e Informazione, Politecnico di Milano
  P.za Leonardo da Vinci 32, I-20133 Milano, Italy
[2] CEFRIEL
  Via Fucini 2, I-20133 Milano, Italy

Summary. Although Semantic Web Services are expected to produce a revolution in the development of Web-based systems, very few enterprise-wide design experiences are available; one of the main reasons is the lack of sound Software Engineering methods and tools for the deployment of Semantic Web applications. In this chapter, we present an approach to software development for the Semantic Web based on classical Software Engineering methods (i.e., formal business process development, computer-aided and component-based software design, and automatic code generation) and on semantic methods and tools (i.e., ontology engineering, semantic service annotation and discovery).

4.1 Introduction

The Semantic Web promotes the vision of an extended Web of machine- understandable information and automated services that allows knowledge technologies to reach Web-scale. The explicit representation of the semantics of the data and of the services will enable a new Web that provides a qualitatively new level of service. Automated services will improve in their capacity to assist humans in achieving their goals by *understanding* more of the content on the Web, and thus providing accurate filtering, categorization, and searches of information sources. Recent efforts around UDDI, WSDL, and SOAP are concentrating on making the Web more service-centric, allowing for on-the-fly software composition through the use of loosely coupled, reusable software components. However, more work needs to be done before the Web Service infrastructure can support the Semantic Web vision. Semantic Web Services (SWS) address the automation of discovery of services of interest; mediation of data exchanged between the different services; and mediation of processes performing service-enabled tasks.

The emerging field of Semantic Web Services provides paradigms based on program annotation and self-descriptive implementation, to build cross-enterprise applications which favour flexibility, automatic resource discovery, and dynamic evolution.

One of the main problems faced by developers to adopt Semantic Web technologies is the lack of methodological guidelines for the development and the extra cost of semantic annotation of the developed software components. This is mostly because software engineering techniques are seldom used in the context of Semantic Web; hence, no automatic mechanism can be applied for extracting semantic descriptions. Therefore, annotations are still added manually, in a very expensive and subjective manner. In our solution to the Semantic Web Service Challenge, we propose both a method and a toolset for fostering the adoption of Semantic Web Services (i.e., WSMO) in cross-enterprise applications. Two research groups, one from the Web Engineering community from Politecnico and one from the Semantic Web community from CEFRIEL, joined their efforts and expertise in building a structured solution to the design and implementation of Semantic Web applications. The solution exploits Web engineering methods, including visual declarative modeling (i.e., WebML), automatic code generation (locally and globally executable through Semantic Execution Environments such as WSMX), and automatic elicitation of semantic descriptions (i.e., WSMO Ontologies, Goals, Web Services and Mediators) from the design of the application. Global choreography (in W3C sense), front-end, and services implementations are modeled from Business Process models and WebML models, whereas goals, descriptions of Web services (i.e., capability and choreography interface), and descriptions of mediators are automatically generated. The approach also comprises the importing/ exporting of ontologies. The following techniques and notations shall be used for covering the various design aspects:

- High-level design of the global choreography of the interaction between services: we adopt BPMN (Business Process Management Notation) to build process models, involving several actors possibly from different enterprises.
- Design of the underlying data model of the cross-enterprise application: we use extended E-R (Entity Relationship) diagrams or equivalent subset of object oriented class diagrams (whose expressive power is equivalent to WSML Flight) to model the local ontology of the application and to import existing ontologies; we expose the resulting set of ontologies to the underling WSMX;
- Design of web services interfaces, of integration platform, and of application front end: we use visual diagrams representing Web sites and services according to the WebML models [4], including specific hypertext primitives for Web service invocation and publishing [5], and explicit representation of workflows [3].

In this way, instead of coping with textual semantic descriptions of Semantic Web Services, application developers will obtain them from the use of abstractions that are supported by software engineering tools. The use of description generators, sometimes helped by designer's annotations, guarantees the benefits of Semantic Web Services at nearly zero extra-cost, thus positioning the implemented applications within an infrastructure that allows for exible and dynamic reconfiguration.

The SWS challenge aimed at employing semantics-based technologies on a set of problems represented by two scenarios, respectively covering mediation (both for data and processes) and discovery (both static and dynamic). Semantics is clearly needed to address in a flexible way the Discovery scenario, but Software Engineering tools and methods are the right ones to address in a flexible way the Mediation scenario. For this reason we adopt an original mix of Semantic Web and Software Engineering techniques: WSMO [5] as Semantic Web Service approach, Glue [DCC05] as Semantic Web Service discovery engine, WebML [4] as Web engineering model for designing and developing semantically rich Web applications implementing Service Oriented Architecture, and WebRatio [6] as WebML CASE tool[3].

Our experience introduces a significant contribution in the application of Software Engineering techniques to SemanticWeb application design. This chapter reports about the cross-fertilization between the two fields. The chapter is organized as follows: Section 2 presents the background technologies and method used in our approach; Section 3 describes our solution to the mediation scenario of the SWS challenge; Section 4 compares our approach to the related work; and finally, Section 5 summarizes and draws some conclusions on our experience.

4.2 Background technologies

In the following we provide the required background on the languages and tools used for the challenge.

4.2.1 WSMO, WSML and WSMX

The WSMO initiative [5, 6] aims at providing a comprehensive framework for handling Semantic Web Services which includes the WSMO conceptual model, the WSML language [8] and the WSMX execution environment [9].

The Web Service Modeling Ontology (WSMO) is an ontology for describing various aspects related to Semantic Web Services. WSMO defines four modeling elements (ontologies, Web Services, goals and mediators) to describe several aspects of Semantic Web Services, based on the conceptual grounding of the Web Service Modeling Framework (WSMF) [10].

Ontologies provide the formal semantics to the information used by all other components. They serve in defining the formal semantics of the information, and in linking machine and human terminologies.

Web Services represent the functional and behavioral aspects, which must be semantically described in order to allow semi-automated use. Each Web Service represents an atomic piece of functionality that can be reused to build more complex ones. Web Services are described in WSMO from three different points of view: *non-functional properties*, *capabilities* (describing functionalities), and *interfaces*

---

[3] Online demos and further material is available at: http://www.webml.org/ sws-challenge.html.

(describing the behavior). A Web Service can have multiple interfaces, but it has one and only one capability.

Goals specify objectives that a client might have when consulting a Web Service. In WSMO [6], a goal is characterized in a dual way with respect to Web Services: goal's descriptions include the *requested capability* and the *requested interface*.

Finally, *mediators* provide interoperability facilities among the other elements. They aim at overcoming structural or semantic mismatches that appear between the different components that build up a WSMO description. For instance, a ggMediator acts as a mediator between two goals, a wgMediator mediates between a Web Service and a goal, and a wwMediator mediates between two Web Services with mismatching interfaces.

Web Service Modeling Language (WSML) [8] offers a set of language variants for describing WSMO elements that enable modelers to balance between expressiveness and tractability according to different knowledge representation paradigms. The most basic, and least expressive, variant is WSML-Core. WSML Core is separately extended in two different directions by the variants WSML-DL and WSML-Flight, respectively. WSML-Flight is based on a logic programming variant of F-Logic [KLW95]. Web Service Execution Environment (WSMX) is a framework for the automation of discovery, selection, mediation, and invocation of Semantic Web Services. WSMX is based on WSMO and, at the same time, it is a reference implementation of it.

4.2.2 BPMN

Visual workflow models allow to effectively represent business processes, describing enterprise-wide operations, interactions between business partners, and orchestrations of Web services. Several notations have been proposed for workflow design. We adopt Business Process Management Notation (http://bpmn.org), which is associated to the BPML standard, issued by the OMG and the Business Process Management Initiative. The BPMN notation allows one to represent all the basic process concepts defined by the WfMC (http://wfmc.org) model and others, such as data and control flow, activity, actor, conditional/split/join gateways, event and exception management, and others. BPMN activities can be grouped into pools, corresponding to the different participants. BPMN can be used to formalize the orchestration of the services performed by the mediator in a WSMO semantic Web context. Figure 4.7 shows a BPMN model of the interaction between the parties of the mediation scenario. This model is a high level representation of the behaviour of the mediator.

4.2.3 WebML and WebRatio

WebML [4] is a high-level notation for data- and process- centric Web applications. It allows specifying the conceptual modeling of Web applications built on top of a data schema used to describe the application data, and composed of one or more hypertexts used to publish the underlying data.

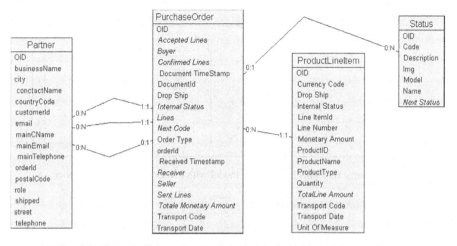

Fig. 4.1. The E-R diagram for the data model used of the initial Mediator.

The WebML data model is the standard Entity-Relationship (E-R) model extended with an Object Query Language [13]. Figure 4.1, described in details in Section 4.3.2, is an E-R representation of the data needed for the Challenge scenario. The expressive power of the WebML E-R model can be compared to the WSML-Flight language (the detailed comparison can be found in [14]).

Upon the same data model, it is possible to define different hypertexts (e.g., for different types of users or for different publishing devices), called *site views*. A site view is a graph of *pages*, allowing users from the corresponding group to perform their specific activities. Pages consist of connected *units*, representing at a conceptual level atomic pieces of homogeneous information to be published: a unit displays instances of an entity, possibly restricted by a *selector*. Units within a Web site are related to each other through *links*, representing navigational paths and carrying data from a unit to another, to allow the computation of the hypertext. WebML allows specifying also update *operations* on the underlying data (e.g., the creation, modification and deletion of instances of entities or relationships) or operations performing other actions (e.g. sending an e-mail). In [3] the language has been extended with operations supporting process specifications.

To describe Web Services interactions, WebML includes some Web Service primitives [5]. Web Services operation symbols correspond to the WSDL classes of Web Service operations: Request-response, Response, Solicit, and One-way units can be used in WebML for describing Web Service interactions.

Request-response and One-way operations are triggered when the user navigates one of their input links; from the context transferred by these links, a message is composed, and then sent to a remote service as a request. Solicit-response and Notification are instead triggered on the service-side by the reception of a message. Indeed, these units represent the publishing of a Web Service, which is exposed and can be invoked by third party applications. In the case of One-way, the

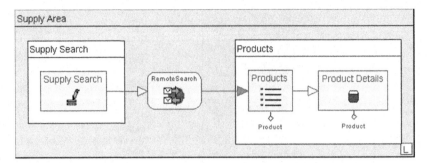

Fig. 4.2. Example of WebML hypertext model with invocation of remote service - a

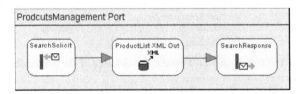

Fig. 4.3. Example of WebML hypertext model with invocation of remote service - b

WebML specification may dictate the way in which the response is built and sent to the invoker. Moreover, Web Services publishing units cannot have output links leading to pages, because there is no user interaction involved in the response to the caller. Another operation typically involved in Web Service interactions is the `Adapter` unit, which is able to apply any kind of XSLT transformation to a XML document. This unit is often used in conjunction with the `XML-In` unit or the `XML-Out` unit: the first is used to import canonic XML data (formatted according a particular XSD) into the database, the latter to extract database instances and convert them to the a canonic XML format.

Figures 4.2 and 4.3 shows a hypertext example that includes the model of a Web Service call and of the called service. *Supply Area* of Figure 4.2 is an area of a Web site for supply management. The employee can browse the *SupplySearch* page, in which the *SearchProducts* entry unit permits the input of search criteria. navigating the link outgoing the entry unit, a request message is composed and sent to the *RemoteSearch* operation of a Web Service. The user then waits for the response message, containing a list of products satisfying the search criteria. From these options, a set of instances of *Product* are created, and displayed to the user by means of the *Products* index unit in the *Products* page; the user may continue browsing, e.g., by choosing one of the displayed products and looking at its details. Figure 4.3 represents the model of the *RemoteSearch* service invoked by the previously described hypertext. The interaction starts with the *SearchSolicit* unit, which denotes the reception of the message. Upon the arrival of the message, an XML-out operation extracts from the local data source the list of products and formats the resulting XML document. The *SearchResponse* unit produces the response message for the invoking Web Service.

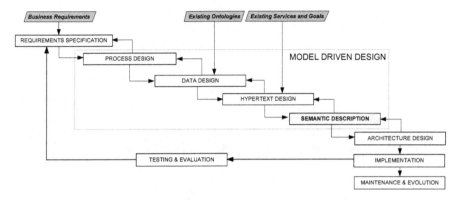

Fig. 4.4. Phases in the development process of semantic Web applications.

The WebML language is *extensible*, allowing for the definition of customized operations and units. It has been implemented in the CASE tool WebRatio [6], a development environment for the visual specification of Web applications and the automatic generation of code for the J2EE platform. The design environment is equipped with a code generator that deploys the specified application and Web Services, by automatically generating all the necessary pieces of code, including data extraction queries, Web Service calls, data mapping logics, page templates, and WSDL service descriptors.

4.3 Our solution to the mediation scenario of the SWS challenge

In this section we describe the general approach to the SWS challenge scenarios. We adopt a software engineering approach to the issue, by defining and following a clearly specified development process, as shown in Figure 4.4. In line with the classic Boehm's Spiral model and with modern methods for Web and software engineering, the development phases must be applied in an iterative and incremental manner, in which the various tasks are repeated and refined until results meet the business requirements.

Requirements specification collects and formalizes the essential information about the application domain and expected functions. *Process design* focuses on the high-level schematization of the (possibly distributed) processes underlying the application. *Data design* organizes the main information objects identified during requirements specification into a comprehensive and coherent domain model, that may comprise importing of existing ontologies. *Hypertext design* is the activity that transforms the functional requirements into one or more Web services and Web site views embodying the needed retrieval and manipulation methods. Hypertext design may comprise importing or referencing existing services and goals. It exploits high level models, which let the architect specify how content elements are published within pages, how services provide information to requesters, and how hypertext elements

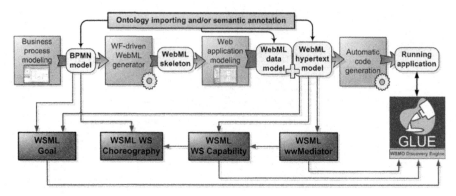

Fig. 4.5. Overall design methodology for Semantic Web Service-based applications.

are connected by links to form a navigable structure. *Semantic description* of the application provides the bases for ontological annotation and reasoning ; it consists in a set of tasks, partially automated, that aim at providing a set of semantic specifications of the application to be implemented. The other phases of Figure 4.4 are outside of the scope of the Challenge.

4.3.1 Integration of Web engineering and Semantic Web tools

For each step of the development process shown in Figure 4.5, a set of techniques and tools are used. Figure 4.5 provides more details on the core development phases. The blue blocks highlight the basic steps for the development process of Semantic Web applications. The various steps produce some artifacts (BPMN models, WebML skeletons, data models, hypertext models), possibly enriched by imported ontological descriptions (on top of Figure 4.5). These "conventional" software engineering artifacts are exploited for deriving the set of WSMO specifications (at the bottom of Figure 4.5):

- the description of the mediator can be extracted from the hypertext describing the mediator;
- the Web Services capability description is derived from the hypertext model;
- the choreography information is derived from the Business Process (BP) model;
- and the user goals are derived from both the BP model and the hypertext model.

This approach seamlessly fits into traditional Software Engineering methods and techniques based on system modeling (i.e. Model Driven Design and Model Driven Architectures); therefore, existing CASE tool for Model Driven Design (MDD) can be easily extended for supporting the process. We choose to adopt an approach mainly based on the Software Engineering methods and techniques for the mediation scenario and an approach mainly based on the Semantic Web technologies for the discovery scenario, that will be discussed in another chapter.

In line with the classic Boehm's Spiral model and with modern methods for Web and Software Engineering, the development phases can be applied in an iterative and

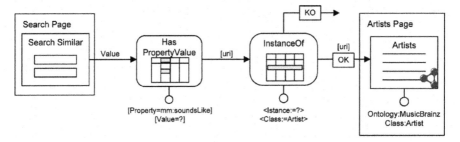

Fig. 4.6. Example of WebML model exploiting the Semantic Web units.

incremental manner, in which the various steps are repeated and refined until results meet the business requirements [14]. Further details on the approach and relative examples can be found in [15].

In order to support the query over ontologies, new WebML units have been devised [16]. In particular we extended the WebML basic primitives provided by the hypertext model (e.g., Index and Data units) to support ontological data sources (e.g., RDF/OWL ontologies) and we provided a new set of primitives specifically designed to exploit ontologies characteristics and reasoning over them. These new units are aggregated primitives that, depending on the type of parameters, execute differently. The units (SubClassOf, InstanceOf, HasProperty, HasPropertyValue, PropertyValue, SubPropertyOf) aim at providing explicit support to advanced ontological queries. They allow to extract classes, instances, properties, values; to check existence of specific concepts; and to verify whether a relationship holds between two objects.

Figure 4.6 depicts a fragment a WebML application that allows to retrieve artists or albums whose names sound in a similar way to the name specified by the user. The ontology adopted in the example is the MusicBrainz ontology [17]. The value submitted in the form is passed to the HasPropertyValue unit that extracts a set of URIs of instances (albums or artists) that have value as value of the mm:soundsLike property. The set of URIs is then passed to the InstanceOf unit that checks if they are instances of the class Artist. In this case, the URIs are passed over through the OK link to an Index unit showing list of Artists, otherwise the URIs are passed on the KO link to publish a list of Albums (not shown in the figure).

In general, each WebML semantic unit can automatically extract a RDF description of its contents. The designer has to specify how he wants to use the RDF fragments; for instance, it is possible to aggregate the fragments of all the units in the page and publish the aggregate at the bottom of the page, as a global semantic annotation of the page itself; another option could be to maintain them separated and publish the RDF annotation for each unit in the page. For instance, annotations can be generated as RDF expressions [18].

Besides the units for ontological data query, we introduce also three new units working at a upper level: the Set Composition operation unit is able to per-

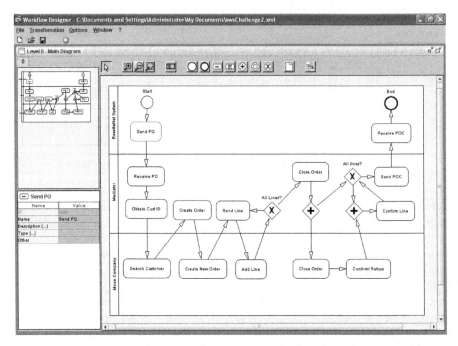

Fig. 4.7. The BPMN model of the Mediator from Blue-to-Moon.

form classic set operations (i.e., union, intersection, difference) over two input sets of URIs, considering the hierarchy of the URIs involved; the `Import Ontological Source` unit adds a remote or local data source that must be consistent with ontological model of the web application (it's validated against it before being added to the ontology); and finally, the `Describe` unit returns the RDF description of an URI, thus enabling data exporting and semantic annotation of pages.

We present our approach by following the evolution of the SWS Challenge requirements of the mediation scenario: every phase we address corresponds to one of the SWS Challenge workshops. In the first place we provide an overview of the initial solution. Then we give some insight about how we coped with the changing requirements and about the effort required to adapt our solution to the subsequent new scenario specifications.

4.3.2 First phase of the challenge

The modeling of the mediator started from the design of the data model. The RosettaNet message was analyzed and a corresponding WebML E-R diagram was obtained from it. We identified four main entities: PurchaseOrder, Partner, Status, and ProductLineItem as shown in Figure 4.1.

As showed by relationships in Figure 4.1, each PurchaseOrder instance has: one of more ProductLineItem instances, three Partner instances representing respectively the Buyer, the Seller and the Receiver. The entity Status tracks the status of each PurchaseOrder.

Once the WebML data model was completed, we started modeling the Web Service providing the mediation feature. An high level Business Process Modeling Notation (BPMN) model is created representing the mediator (see Figure 4.7), which formalizes the orchestration of the Moon Web Services, and defines states pertaining to the mediation process according to the scenario specification. Then, the BPMN model is used to automatically generate a WebML skeleton that is manually refined to complete the design of the mediator. The final model for the Blue to Moon mediator is reported in Figure 4.8. Each row of the model depicted in the Figure corresponds to a specific step that the mediator must perform. Each of these steps comprises a set of specific operations on the received messages or on the local data. We exemplify in details the first two steps of the mediator, namely (i) the reception of the RosettaNet message and its forwarding to the legacy system; and (ii) the selection of the Buyer Partner. First, we modeled the operation receiving the RosettaNet message and forwarding the order to the legacy system:

1. As soon as the order is received (`Pip3A4PurchaseOrderRequest` Solicit Unit), the Pip3APurchaseOrder is converted (`Lifting` Adapter Unit) and stored in the database (`StorePip3A4PurchaseOrder` Unit), the status of the current Pip3APurchaseOrder is set to "To Be Processed" (`SetProcessStatus` Connect Unit, that creates new relationship instances between objects) and the Acknowledge message is returned to the service invoker (`SendReceiptAcknowledgement` Response Unit).
2. Next, the Buyer Partner is selected (`SelectBuyer` Selector Unit, that retrieves data instances according to a specified selector condition) and a message to query the Customer Relationship Management service (CRM) is created (`Lowering` Adapter Unit) and sent to the legacy system (`ObtainMoonCustomerID` Request-Response Unit). Once a reply has been received, the CustomerId is extracted from the reply message (`Lifting` Adapter Unit) and stored in the data model (`StoreCustomerID` Modify Unit). The status of the order is set to "CustomerId received" (`SetProcessStatus` Connect Unit).

Analogous operations are performed for the remaining steps (lines 3 to 5 in Figure 4.8).

Figure 4.9 shows the corresponding process required at the legacy system for receiving order lines:

1. For each line confirmation (`OrderLineItemConfirmation` Solicit Unit), the status is extracted (`Lifting` Adapter Unit), the relative order and line stored in mediator database are selected (`SelectOrder` and `SelectLineItem` Selector Units), and the status of the stored line is modified according to the received confirmation (`SetLineStatus` Modify Unit). Eventually the Acknowledge message is returned to the service invoker (`OrderLineItemReceiptAck` Response Unit).

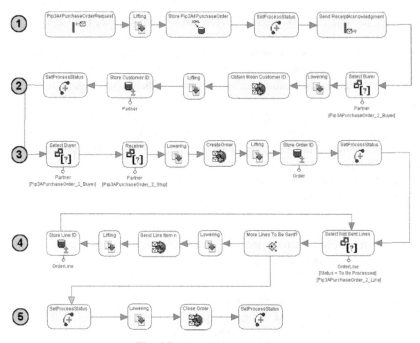

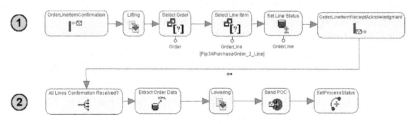

Fig. 4.8. Blue-to-Moon mediator

Fig. 4.9. Moon-to-Blue mediator.

2. When all the lines have been received (`AllLinesConfirmationRecei-
   ved?` Switch Unit), the XML serialization of the data for the current Pip3A-
   PurchaseOrder is extracted (`ExtractOrderData` XML-Out Unit) and a RosettaNet Purchase Order Confirmation (POC) message is created (`Lowering`
   Adapter Unit) and sent to the RosettaNet client (`SendPOC` Request Unit) and
   the status of the order is set to "Rosetta PO Confirmation sent" (`SetProcess-
   Status` Connect Unit).

The SOAP messages transformation to and from the WebML data model are performed by proper WebML units (`Adapter` units) that apply XSLT transformations;
XSLT stylesheets can be designed with an XML-to-XML visual mapping tool. A
prototype tool is included in our toolsuite, but any other tool can be used (e.g., IBM
Clio [19]).

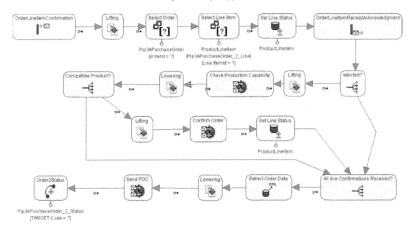

Fig. 4.10. The WebML model of the modified portion of the Mediator (cfr. Figure 4.9).

4.3.3 Second phase of the challenge

To test the flexibility of the solutions proposed by participants to the challenge, the SWS challenge organizers introduced some changes in the scenarios. The approaches we initially used to solve the two scenarios permitted us to address the new changes in a easy way. This also proved that our initial choice of adopting a Software Engineering approach for the mediation scenario and a Semantic Web approach for the discovery scenario was good. In the Phase II of the challenge, the new requirements of the mediation scenario imposed a change in the format of the exchanged messages and a change in the mediation process. The change in the format required an adjustment of the data model: we introduced a new relationship between the entity ProductLineItem and the entity Partner. Then we modified the mediator process: when the Stock Management system is unable to fulfill a request from the customer and replies that the particular line item cannot be accepted, the new Mediator contacts the legacy Production Management system in order to search an alternative product. To fulfill this new requirement, we changed the mediator by introducing a chain of operations needed to query the new Production Management Web Service (Figure 4.10).

4.3.4 Third phase of the challenge

Phase III of the challenge did not introduce any substantial new requirement, therefore we concentrated on improving and refining our previous solution solving some of the open issues in our approach. In the previous challenge edition we did not completely address some of the changes to the Mediation scenario. Among them we did not consider the process changes required in order to deal with the introduction of the optional shipment address for each line item. According to the modified scenario, line items must be grouped according to their shipment address and for each group an independent new order has to be sent to the Moon legacy system. We improved

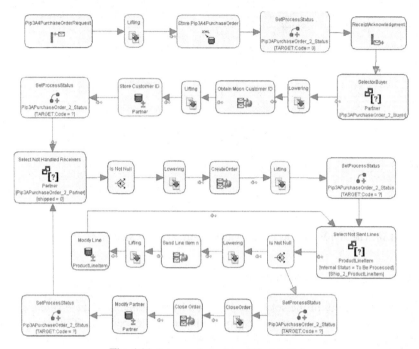

Fig. 4.11. Improved version of the Mediator

our mediator handling this requirement (see Figure 4.11): i.e., we introduced a loop over every shipment address associated to the incoming RosettaNet purchase order; inside the loop, a new shipment order for every different address is created, and each line item with that address is added to the new order; finally the order is closed, and the next address, if available, is processed.

4.3.5 Fourth phase of the challenge

The scenarios for the fourth phase of the challenge involved a totally new discovery scenario, where a buyer of computer wants to choose among competing services offering computers and related accessories[4], depending on information that can be provided by the services themselves. This challenges current technologies of the participants requiring dynamic services discovery and composition. In some sense, this also extends the concept of mediation, explicitly introducing the idea of selection and negotiation. Therefore, we applied to the new discovery solution some techniques borrowed from the mediation design.

At conceptual level we model both goal and Web Services making explicit differences among:

---

[4] http://sws-challenge.org/wiki/index.php/Scenario:_Discovery_
II_and_Composition

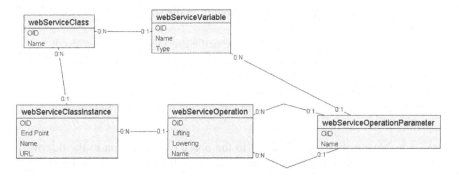

Fig. 4.12. The ER metamodel for the dynamic service invocation in Phase IV.

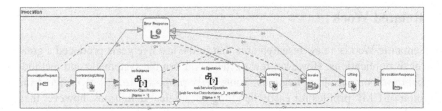

Fig. 4.13. The WebML model of the dynamic service invocation in Phase IV.

- *"discovery" capabilities*, which are static description of the service in terms of functional properties,
- *"selection" capabilities*, which are static or dynamic non functional descriptions;
- *"negotiation" capabilities*, which are description of the service that need to be evaluated by invoking one or more operation of the service (for describing the choreography we relay on WebML).

These aspects are explained in details in the chapter dealing with our discovery solution. At this stage, we only highlight that some changes to the mediation and invocation modeling have been applied too. In particular, dynamic service invocation is needed.

To address this aspect, we specify a more detailed metamodel describing the services, and we exploit this metamodel to dynamically invoke services. The metamodel is shown in Figure 4.12 and comprises the concepts of Web Service Classes (with related variables) and respective Web Service Instances (with related operations and parameters).

The WebML model of the dynamic invocation of services is shown in Figure 4.13: a general purpose *Invocation* service is defined, that incapsulates the dynamic invocation behaviour, consisting of the following steps:

- the incoming invocation request (containing the name of the service to be invoked) is lifted to the internal model;

- the webServiceClassInstance corresponding to the specified service name is retrieved;
- the wsOperation corresponding to the specified service name is retrieved;
- the incoming invocation request data is lowered to the specific Web service format;
- the actual Web service is invoked;
- the Web service response is lifted to the internal data format and returned to the caller.

Similar techniques have been applied to the phase of negotiation in the discovery scenario too. With this approach we introduce an additional level of service call, but we keep the invocation in the general model very clean.

4.4 Related Work

The Semantic Web is a new research area that in the last five years produced a great number of publications. However, few of them concern the systematic and methodological development of applications. Some early proposals (e.g., [20]) offered the definition of UML profiles for easily handling ontological definitions; however they haven't been adopted because of the lack of an overall methodology. A number of researches concentrated on the development of tools to support the generation of semantic descriptions for existing Web Services [21, 22, 23]. [24] presents an engineered approach to extraction of semantic annotations from XML schemas and documents to be published in dynamic Web applications. Most of these tools still require the learning of the annotation language used (e.g., OWL-S or WSMO) and hence do not rise the level of abstraction required from developers. Furthermore, they do not exploit the advantages of conceptual models of the Web Services to semi-automatically derive any part of the semantic descriptions.

Our research effort is more similar to the recent efforts of the Object Management Group (OMG)[5]. The OMG proposed the Ontology Definition Metamodel (ODM) [25] to define a suitable language for modeling Semantic Web ontology languages and hence Semantic Web applications in the context of the Model Driven Architecture (MDA) [26]. In [27] MIDAS, a framework based on MDA to model and develop Semantic Web applications, is introduced. The proposed framework focuses on the creation of Semantic Web Services and associated WSML descriptions using a UML model according to the MDA approach. This proposal inherits the limits of the MDA approach: the use of a UML model is not always fitting the Semantic Web needs, and often the model is too far from the implementation details to provide an effective automatic code generation. Furthermore, MIDAS does not provide a clear overall roadmap to the design of Semantic Web applications. The work of the W3C has created a Software Engineering Task Force dedicated to the Semantic Web[6] but its work is still under development. These proposals can be regarded as first contributions to

---

[5] http://www.omg.org/
[6] http://www.w3.org/2001/sw/BestPractices/SE/

the field, but they still do not provide a clear roadmap to the design of Semantic Web applications.

Other research efforts are converging on the proposal of combining Semantic Web Services (SWS) and Business Process Management (BPM) to create one consolidated technology, which we call Semantic Business Process Management (SBPM) [28]. This is based on the fact that mechanization of BPM can be addressed through machine-accessible semantics, that can be naturally provided by SWS frameworks (e.g., WSMO).

In the last years some efforts from the Web Engineering field have been redirected towards methodologies for developing Semantic Web Information Systems. Traditional Web design methodologies (like OOHDM [29]) and new approaches (like Hera [30]) are now focusing on designing Semantic Web applications. However, these methodologies are not supported by an effective CASE tool and they concentrate only on Semantic Web Portals instead of the development of Semantic Web Services.

Other works related to the mediation problem have been developed within the SWS Challenge. In particular, [31] proposed a solution based on a SOA engineered framework called jABC/Jeti, that for some aspects is similar to our solution. [KKR06] solved the process mediation using a BPEL engine, embedding it in the DIANE framework that provides for the data mediation; a similar solution was provided by the Meteor-S team [33]. The solution proposed by DERI [34], based on the WSMO/WSMX framework [5] is perhaps the most interesting solution and the most different with respect to ours. The DERI solution to the mediation scenario is purely semantic. The entire architecture has been developed for the semantic web from its origin, and this provides native support to internal reasoning, ontology storage, and so on. The schema describing RosettaNet PIP 3A4, Customer Relationship Management (CRM), Order Management (OM) are ontologized and Semantic Web Services for the CRM and the OM are generated together with the Goal templates for the service requester.

However, only limited research efforts are concerned with the environments, methods, and tools for the systematic development of semantic Web applications. A wide set of tools for supporting the generation of semantic descriptions for existing Web resources (e.g., services) have been developed [21] [35]. In the context of DERI, tool support to the development is provided by WSMT [23]. However, these tools they are intended for ontology experts and consider the annotation process as completely separated from the actual service development. This requires mastering of the annotation languages (e.g., OWL-S or WSMO) and hence do not help to widen the adoption of semantic Web and semantic Web services in the software engineering community.

4.5 Conclusions

This chapter summarized our experience of applying Semantic Web Service and Web engineering techniques in the mediation scenario of SWS Challenge 2006. We addressed the mediation problems of the challenge with the design and implementation of the wwMediator through the usage of the conceptual languages BPMN and WebML, supported by the CASE tool WebRatio and its companion BPMN workflow editor.

Our approach extends the design flow supported for conventional Web applications [4] which leads the designer from the process modeling to the running Web application, by producing some intermediate artifacts (BPMN models, WebML skeletons, data models, hypertext models). Such models are enriched by imported ontological descriptions and are exploited for semi-automatically generating WSMO-compliant semantic. The merits of our solution are: the rooting in the tradition of Software Engineering, the use of sophisticated, up-to-date Web Enginnering technology, and the extension of the methods to the Semantic Web. We have given the maximum attention to the methodology specification and to the practical applicability of the approach, thanks to CASE tools and code generators that ease the work of designers and developers, who can benefit of automatically generated semantic annotations and WSMO-compliant components. We believe that development methods and tools for the Semantic Web should not be different from the classic paradigms which are now dominating software design and deploymen. Therefore, Semantic Web developers should adapt classic (UML-based) methods and tools hosted by classic tool frameworks (such as Eclipse). We fully agree with Charles Petrie's words: *"If semantic technology has a future — and I'm sure that it does — it's in Software Engineering"* [3]. Our participation to the challenge is a first attempt in this direction. Indeed, the ability of our solution to adapt to changes is mostly the merit of our use of enhanced Software Engineering methods and platforms. Our future work aims at implementing a complete extension of the WebML methodology towards the design of Semantic Web Services applications, supported by a design environment based upon WebRatio [6].

References

1. Ceri, S., Fraternali, P., Bongio, A., Brambilla, M., Comai, S., Matera, M.: Designing Data-Intensive Web Applications. Morgan Kauffmann, San Francisco, CA, USA (2002)
2. Manolescu, I., Brambilla, M., Ceri, S., Comai, S., Fraternali, P.: Model-driven design and deployment of service-enabled web applications. ACM Trans. Internet Techn. **5**(3) (2005) 439–479
3. Brambilla, M., Ceri, S., Fraternali, P., Manolescu, I.: Process modeling in web applications. ACM Trans. Softw. Eng. Methodol. **15**(4) (2006) 360–409
4. Fensel, D., Lausen, H., Polleres, A., de Bruijn, J., Stollberg, M., Roman, D., Domingue, J.: Enabling Semantic Web Services: The Web Service Modeling Ontology. Springer-Verlag New York, Inc., Secaucus, NJ, USA (2006)
5. Valle, E.D., Cerizza, D.: The mediators centric approach to automatic web service discovery of glue. In Hepp, M., Polleres, A., van Harmelen, F., Genesereth, M.R., eds.: MEDIATE2005. Volume 168 of CEUR Workshop Proceedings., Amsterdam, The Netherlands, CEUR-WS.org (December 2005) 35–50 online http://CEUR-WS.org/Vol-168/MEDIATE2005-paper3.pdf.

6. WebModels s.r.l.: Webratio site development suite (2007)
   http://www.webratio.com.
7. Roman, D., Keller, U., Lausen, H., de Bruijn, J., Lara, R., Stollberg, M., Polleres, A., Feier, C., Bussler, C., Fensel, D.: Web Service Modeling Ontology. Applied Ontologies **1**(1) (2005) 77 – 106
8. de Bruijn, J., Lausen, H., Polleres, A., Fensel, D.: The web service modeling language wsml: An overview. In: Proceedings of the 3rd European Semantic Web Conference (ESWC 2006). Volume 4011 of Lecture Notes in Computer Science, LNCS., Springer (6 2006)
9. Haller, A., Cimpian, E., Mocan, A., Oren, E., Bussler, C.: WSMX - A Semantic Service-Oriented Architecture. In: Proceedings of the 2005 IEEE International Conference on Web Services (ICWS'05), Washington, DC, USA, IEEE Computer Society (2005) 321–328
10. Fensel, D., Bussler, C.: The web service modeling framework wsmf. Electronic Commerce Research and Applications **1**(2) (2002) 113–137
11. de Bruijn, J., Lausen, H., Polleres, A., Fensel, D.: The web service modeling language: An overview. In: Proc. of the European Semantic Web Conference. (2006)
12. Kifer, M., Lausen, G., Wu, J.: Logical foundations of object-oriented and frame-based languages. J. ACM **42**(4) (1995) 741–843
13. Berler, M., Eastman, J., Jordan, D., Russell, C., Schadow, O., Stanienda, T., Velez, F.: The object data standard: ODMG 3.0. Morgan Kaufmann Publishers Inc., San Francisco, CA, USA (2000)
14. Brambilla, M., Ceri, S., Facca, F.M., Celino, I., Cerizza, D., Valle, E.D.: Model-driven design and development of semantic web service applications. ACM Trans. Internet Techn. **8**(1) (2007)
15. Brambilla, M., Celino, I., Ceri, S., Cerizza, D., Della Valle, E., Facca, F.M.: A Software Engineering Approach to Design and Development of Semantic Web Service Applications. In: Proceedings of the 5th International Semantic Web Conference (ISWC 2006). (Nov 2006)
16. Facca, F.M., Brambilla, M.: Extending webml towards semantic web. In: WWW - World Wide Web Conference. (2007) 1235–1236
17. MusicBrainz: Musicbrainz project (2007) http://musicbrainz.org.
18. W3C: Rdfa primer 1.0: Embedding rdf in xhtml (2007) http://www.w3.org/TR/xhtml-rdfa-primer/.
19. Hernández, M.A., Miller, R.J., Haas, L.M.: Clio: a semi-automatic tool for schema mapping. SIGMOD Rec. **30**(2) (2001) 607
20. Djuric, D., Gasevic, D., Devedzic, V., Damjanovic, V.: Uml profile for owl. In Koch, N., Fraternali, P., Wirsing, M., eds.: ICWE. Volume 3140 of Lecture Notes in Computer Science., Springer (2004) 607–608
21. Elenius, D., Denker, G., Martin, D., Gilham, F., Khouri, J., Sadaati, S., Senanayake, R.: The owl-s editor - a development tool for semantic web services. In Gómez-Pérez, A., Euzenat, J., eds.: ESWC. Volume 3532 of Lecture Notes in Computer Science., Springer (2005) 78–92
22. Jaeger, M.C., Engel, L., Geihs, K.: A methodology for developing owl-s descriptions. In Panetto, H., ed.: Proceedings of the INTEROP-ESA'05 Workshops, Geneva, Switzerland, Hermes Science Publishing (2005) 153–166
23. Kerrigan, M.: D9.1v0.2 web service modeling toolkit (wsmt). Technical report, DERI (2005) http://www.wsmo.org/TR/d9/d9.1.

24. Reif, G., Gall, H., Jazayeri, M.: Weesa: Web engineering for semantic web applications. In: Proceedings of the 14th International Conference on World Wide Web, New York, NY, USA, ACM Press (2005) 722–729

25. OMG: Ontology definition metamodel (2007) http://www.omg.org/cgi-bin/doc?ad/06-05-01.pdf.

26. OMG: Model driven architecture (2007) http://www.omg.org/cgi-bin/doc?omg/03-06-01.

27. Acuña, C.J., Marcos, E.: Modeling semantic web services: a case study. In: ICWE '06: Proceedings of the 6th international conference on Web engineering, New York, NY, USA, ACM Press (2006) 32–39

28. Hepp, M., Leymann, F., Domingue, J., Wahler, A., Fensel, D.: Semantic business process management: A vision towards using semantic web services for business process management. In: ICEBE '05: Proceedings of the IEEE International Conference on e-Business Engineering, Washington, DC, USA, IEEE Computer Society (2005) 535–540

29. Lima, F., Schwabe, D.: Application Modeling for the Semantic Web. In: 1st Latin American Web Congress (LA-WEB 2003), Empowering Our Web, 10-12 November 2003, Sanitago, Chile, IEEE Computer Society (2003) 93–102

30. Vdovjak, R., Frasincar, F., Houben, G.J., Barna, P.: Engineering Semantic Web Information Systems in Hera. J. Web Eng. 2(1-2) (2003) 3–26

31. Kubczak, C., Steffen, B., Margaria, T.: The jabc approach to mediation and choreography. 2nd Semantic Web Service Challenge Workshop (June 2006)

32. Küster, U., König-Ries, B.: Discovery and mediation using diane service descriptions. In: Third Workshop of the Semantic Web Service Challenge 2006 - Challenge on Automating Web Services Mediation, Choreography and Discovery, Athens, GA, USA (November 2006)

33. Wu, Z., Harney, J.F., Verma, K., Miller, J.A., Sheth, A.P.: Composing semantic web services with interaction protocols. Technical report, LSDIS Lab, University of Georgia, Athens, Georgia (2006)

34. Zaremba, M., Vitvar, T., Moran, M., Hasselwanter, T.: WSMX discovery for sws challenge. In: Third Workshop of the Semantic Web Service Challenge 2006 - Challenge on Automating Web Services Mediation, Choreography and Discovery, Athens, GA, USA (November 2006)

35. Patil, A.A., Oundhakar, S.A., Sheth, A.P., Verma, K.: Meteor-s web service annotation framework. In: Proceedings of the 13th international conference on World Wide Web (WWW 2004), New York, NY, USA, ACM Press (2004) 553–562

36. Petrie, C.J.: It's the programming, stupid. IEEE Internet Computing 10(3) (2006) 95–96

Service-oriented Mediation with jABC/jETI

Christian Kubczak[1], Tiziana Margaria[2], Bernhard Steffen[3], and Ralf Nagel[3]

[1] TU Dortmund, Chair of Software Engineering
   `christian.kubczak@tu-dortmund.de`
[2] Universität Potsdam, Chair of Service and Software Engineering
   `margaria@cs.uni-potsdam.de`
[3] TU Dortmund, Chair of Programming Systems
   `steffen@cs.tu-dortmund.de, ralf.nagel@tu-dortmund.de`

Summary. This chapter shows how we solved the Mediation task in a model driven, service oriented fashion using the jABC framework for model driven development and its jETI extension for seamless integration of remote (Web) services. In particular we illustrate how atomic services and orchestrations are modelled in the jABC, how legacy services and their proxies are represented within our framework, and how they are imported into our framework, how the mediator arises as orchestrations of the testbed's remote services and of local services, how vital properties of the Mediator are verified via model checking in the jABC, and how jABC/jETI orchestrated services are exported as Web services. Besides providing a solution to the mediation problem, this also illustrates the agility of jABC-based solutions, which is due to what we call eXtreme Model Driven Design, a new paradigm that puts the user process in the center of the development and the application expert in control of the process evolution.

5.1 Introduction

We solve the Mediation task in a model driven, service oriented fashion using the jABC framework [8, 10, 19] for model driven development and its jETI extension for seamless integration of remote (Web) services. After a brief sketch of jABC's origin (Sect. 5.2) and philosophy (Sect. 5.3), this chapter shows how we model atomic services and orchestrations in the jABC (Sect. 5.4 and 5.5), how we represent legacy services and their proxies within our framework (Sect. 5.6), how we import them into the framework, how we compose the mediator's model as an orchestration of the testbed's remote services and of local services (Sect. 5.7), how we verify properties of the Mediator via model checking in the jABC (Sect. 5.8), and how to systematically export jABC/jETI orchestrated services as Web services (Sect. 5.9).

The jABC is a flexible framework for service development based on Lightweight Process Coordination [21] and eXtreme Model Driven Design [18]. Users easily develop services and applications by composing reusable building-blocks into (flow-) graph structures that can be animated, analyzed, simulated, verified, executed, and compiled. We will sketch here how to handle the mediator design and the remote integration of Web services.

An extension to this basic approach by a technique that automatically generates the workflow from declarative specifications is described in Chapter 7.

Before addressing our solution to the Mediator problem from Sect. 5.7 onwards, we briefly summarize the origin of the jABC as service Development Environment for Intelligent Network services in Sect. 5.2, and the underlying formal model for Services and orchestrations in Sect. 5.3 and 5.4.

5.2 Service Oriented development for Telecommunications

Service-Oriented Design has driven the development of telecommunication infrastructure and applications, in particular the so-called Intelligent Network (IN) Services, since the early 90s. Intelligent Networks have changed the world of telecommunication: practically everybody has already made use of IN services, e.g., for Televoting (0137 Service) on TV or radio, toll-free calls (0180 resp. 800 Service) for teleshopping, prepaid or credit card calls, or the familiar Virtual Private Networks. To satisfy the growing expectation on IN services, a flexible Service Definition Environment is a must.

In 1994-96 we were involved in the development of an innovative Service Definition environment for Intelligent Networks, as part of a telecommunication project that involved large firms like Siemens and Siemens Nixdorf, but also software houses, consulting firms, and academia (the University of Passau), and that resulted in the development of the first predecessor of the jABC [28, 20].

The realization of new IN services was complex, error prone, and extremely costly until a service-oriented, feature-based architecture, a corresponding standardization of basic services and applications in real standards, and adequate programming environments came up: they set the market, enabled flexibilization of services, and dramatically reduced the time to market.

Thinking about this experience, we noticed that a central role in its success was ascribed to the introduction of *incremental formal methods*, realized in particular through *constraint-based* formal verification techniques. The impact of those techniques was sensible in all phases of the project: it contributed to the project in technical, scientific, managerial, and marketing areas [3]. In [20], we reviewed our 10 years of experience in service engineering for telecommunication systems from the point of view of Service-Oriented Design then and now. In particular, we were establishing a link to the notions used by the service-oriented programming (SO) community.

The novelty of our approach consisted of introducing a declarative specification layer, which was used for the construction of the desired services according to *global constraints* guaranteeing executability and other consistency conditions. These constraints were the basis for an on-line verification via model checking during the interactive service design process. Important for the success of the method was the high performance and the availability of diagnostic information in the case of failure: Several hundred constraints had to be checked in real-time, and the diagnostic information had to reflect the responsible constraint violations as concisely as possible, while preserving as much of the structure of the developed service as possible.

5.3 Basic Concepts of the jABC Modeling Framework

The jABC is a flexible framework for model-driven service development based on Lightweight Process Coordination (LPC) [21].

The LPC approach is *coarse-grained* in the sense that it renounces a detailed model of the system functionality (which would be infeasible in the considered industrial settings). Thus it naturally fits to the application to Web services, which are coarse-grained remote functionalities whose implementation is not disclosed.

The coordination is *lightweight* in the sense that it allows a programming-free definition of system-level behaviors based on the coarse models of the functionalities. In the Challenge, some of those functionalities are Web services, and the coordination expresses orchestrations of local or remote (Web) service entities.

The LPC approach puts *behaviours* in the center of the modelling and design approach. Instead of the architectural aspect, as in SOA approaches, or of information objects, as in approaches rooted in database and information systems, we have runs and processes as the central entity of attention. The conceptual background to this point of view is that of formally sound process-based communicating systems, as e.g. in process algebras like CCS, CSP, LOTOS, and in standardized industrial languages like SDL. We support both modelling the system behaviours in term of coarse grain processes, and, thanks to the mathematically sound formal models underlying those models, also a mathematically sound analysis of the models' behaviours. In the jABC, we can prove the conformance of the models to behavioural properties expressed in modal logics specifically developed to describe system runs: temporal logics, like LTL, CTL, μ-calculus. The adopted proof paradigm is called *model checking*. It has meanwhile reached maturity in high-assurance branches of industry like hardware design, and its scientific and economical relevance are witnessed by the 2008 ACM Turing Award to its inventors Ed M. Clarke, Allen Emerson and Joseph Sifakis.

The verification of the models is for the jABC an essential requirement: we target on certifiable orchestrations of coarse grained service compositions, where the certification concerns the coordination level (i.e. the process) rather than the complete implementation.

The first implementation of LPC was based on a general purpose environment for the management of complex processes, METAFrame Technologies' *Agent Building Center* ABC [25]. The ABC offered built-in features for the programming-free coordination and the management of libraries of functional components, which was based on so-called *Service Logic Graphs*, which managed the inter-component or inter-tool flow of control. The current jABC is an evolution of the ABC, and in particular it has maintained complete compliance to the LPC approach.

The power and adequacy of this approach have been successfully used in industrial scenarios that combined heterogeneous architectures with black/grey-box implementation. This is the regular case when using Web services. The challenge is precisely how to handle this partial knowledge in an independent, understandable, and manageable way: an ideal approach should be

- *expressive* enough to capture the coordination tasks, like steering tools, obtaining and evaluating responses, and taking decisions that direct the control flow within a system-level behaviour,
- *non-intrusive*, i.e. we cannot afford having to change the code of the subsystems, and this both for economical reasons and lack of feasibility: most applications, and all Web services are behaviourally complete black boxes,
- *intuitive and controllable* without requiring programming skills. This implies that we need a lightweight, possibly graphical approach to coordination definition, and that easy and timely validation of coordination models should be available.

The Service Logic Graphs provide an adequate abstraction mechanism to be used in conceptual modelling because they direct developers to the identification and promotion of interactions as first-class citizens, a pre-condition for taming the complexity of system construction and evolution. In our solution, we have adopted a coarse-grain approach to modelling system behavior, that accounts for the required simplicity and allows direct animation of the models as well as validation via model checking at the application level.

Adequacy Considerations

In order to steer services composed of several independent subservices that intercommunicate, one must be able to coordinate a heterogeneous set of services in a context of heterogeneous platforms. This task exceeds the capabilities of today's service composition tools, which typically cover only the needs of specific (homogeneous) technologies and of their immediate periphery. We thus need an approach capable of developing a formal coordination layer on top of existing blackbox implementations which rapidly evolve.

Due to the blackbox availability of the services, the coordination is necessarily *coarse grained*. Due to the rapid evolution of the services (with volatile, ad hoc services, that have lifecycles of one week to three months, as observed e.g. in the Web 2.0 domain) the coordination must be extremely *lightweight*: there is no hope of having the resources for "reprogramming" new orchestrations in a traditional way once a service varies. Adaptions and changes have to be easy and programming-free. Taken together, this defines a 'meta-level' on which

- service providers and aggregators are used to think,
- test cases and test suites can be easily composed and maintained,
- usage scenarios can be configured and initialized,
- critical consistency requirements (including version compatibility and frame conditions for executability) are easily *formulated*, and
- error diagnosis and repair must occur.

5.4 jABC as Service Assembly Framework

In the jABC, developing an application consists of the behaviour-oriented combination of building blocks, called SIBs (Service Independent Building blocks), on a

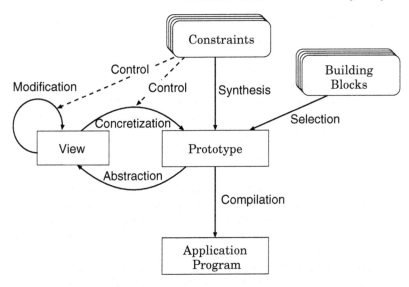

Fig. 5.1. The Service Creation Process

coarse-granular level. Service orchestrations, like the Mediator, are therefore simply compositions of SIBs, which themselves comprise functionality, ranging from elementary statements to relatively large procedures steering e.g. complex application machinery, to Web Services. In the Challenge scenarios we have a mix of local SIBs (like the Receive POR SIB in Fig. 5.2 and all those with the same icon, and jETI SIBs like the Moon SIBs in the same figure, that serve as proxies within the jABC for the remote Web Services that run on the Challenge's testbed in Innsbruck. The corresponding service creation process is shown in Fig. 5.1.

Behaviour-Oriented Development:

Behaviour-oriented development means combination of Service Independent Building Blocks (SIBs) on a *coarse* granular level, typically understandable by the application expert/user. SIBs are software components with a particularly simple interface, which enables one to view them semantically just as input/output transformations. Additional (interaction) structure can also be captured, but is not (yet) subject to the formal synthesis and verification methods offered by the jABC environment.

SIBs are identified at the application level. They are understandable by application experts and not tied to specific infrastructure of programming units. Usually they encompass a number of 'classical' programming units (be they procedures, classes, modules, services, or functions), and are organized in application-specific collections. In contrast to (other) component-based approaches, e.g., for object-oriented program development, the jABC focusses on *dynamic* behavior: (complex) functionalities are graphically stuck together to yield flow graph-like structures called Service Logic Graphs (SLGs) embodying the application behavior in terms of their control flow.

SLGs are independent of the paradigm of the underlying programming language, which may, e.g., be an object-oriented language: here the coarse granular building blocks are themselves implemented using all the object oriented features, and only their combination is organized operationally. In particular, we view this flow-graph structure as a control-oriented coordination layer on top of data-oriented communication mechanisms enforced e.g. via RMI, CORBA or (D)COM. Accordingly, the purely graphical combination of the SIBs behaviors happens at a more abstract level, and can be implemented in any of these technologies.

Incremental Formalization:

The successive enrichment of the application-specific development environment is two-dimensional. Besides the library of application specific SIBs, which dynamically grows whenever new functionalities are made available, jABC supports the dynamic growth of a hierarchically organized library of *constraints*, controlling and governing the adequate use of these SIBs within application programs. This library is intended to grow with the experience gained while using the environment, e.g., detected errors, strengthened policies, and new SIBs may directly impose the addition of constraints. It is the possible *looseness* of these constraints which makes the constraints highly reusable and intuitively understandable. Here we consciously privilege understandability and practicality of the specification mechanisms over their completeness.

Library-Based Consistency Checking:

Throughout the behaviour-oriented development process, jABC offers access to mechanisms for the verification of libraries of constraints by means of model checking (Sect. 5.5). The model checker individually checks hundreds of typically very small and application- and purpose-specific constraints over the flow graph structure. This allows concise and comprehensible diagnostic information in the case of a constraint violation (see later Fig. 5.6), since the feedback is provided on the Service Logic Graph, i.e. at the application level rather than on the code.

These characteristics are the key towards distributing labor according to the various areas of expertise. Typically, we distinguish:

Programming Experts, the software engineers responsible for the software infrastructure, the runtime-environment for the compiled services, as well as the programming of the SIBs.

Domain Modelling Experts: They build, use, modify, and curate the underlying domain models, typically in some knowledge basis that can be expressed via ontologies, These experts classify the SIBs, typically according to technical criteria like their version or specific hardware or software requirements, their origin (where they were developed) and, here, most importantly, according to their intent for a given application area. The resulting classification scheme is the basis for the constraint definition in terms of modal formulas and for the automatic generation of the SLGs with the LTL guided synthesis technique explained in Chap. 7.

Application Experts: They develop concrete applications just by defining their Service Logic structure. This happens without programming: they graphically combine building blocks into coarse-granular flow graphs and graphically configure the data path. These flow graphs can be immediately executed by means of an interpreter, in order to validate the intended behavior (rapid prototyping). Model checking guarantees the consistency of the constructed graph with respect to a constraint library.

Additionally, **End Users** may customize a given (global) service according to their needs by parametrization and specialization. This was desired for example in the original IN project [3].

The resulting overall lifecycle for application development using jABC is two-dimensional: both the application and the environment can be enriched during the development process.

5.4.1 The Service Model

The jABC has a very simple **service model** for atomic services. A SIB always consists of the following:

- a *UID*: a globally unique name used to internally identify a special class of a SIB. Every instance of the service shares this identifier.
- a *Name*: A locally unique name of the SIB, used to identify it within a flow graph.
- a *Label*: A string displayed for this SIB inside a flow graph. This is useful for (end-user) presentation purposes, and can be changed by the users as desired. It does not have to be unique, unlike the *Name* and the *UID*. Different Services may share one label.
- a *Class*: The underlying Java class implementation of a Service.
- a *Taxonomy information*: a structured set of labels that characterize the SIBs tool, subsystem, or purpose and properties of the service. This is freely defined by the domain expert, it forms the knowledge basis on which to perform model checking and reasoning. Here foots the semantic approach of the Mediation solution. As an example, Fig. 5.5 a) shows the domain expert point of view: taxonomy information classifies here the imported SIBs for the Mediation as Blue and Moon SIBs.
  In case no semantic information is available, the package and class name of the Java implementation are taken as a default value. One can specify customized classifications by using the taxonomy editor or changing the value manually. At the moment we support only tree structures. Fig. 5.2 shows the programmer's view: Taxonomy information is expressed syntactically like "virtual" Java package names.
- a set of *formal parameters* that enable a more general usage of the block (e.g. Customer ID). In the Challenge, this is the set of input and output parameters of a service. Technically, there is no difference between inputs and outputs, therefore a distinction requires an appropriate naming of the parameters. Parameters are pairs $\langle names(keys), value \rangle$, whereby the values can also refer to variables inside jABC's execution context.

- a list of outgoing *branches* which direct the flow of execution in dependence of the results of the SIB's execution. This list can be declared as fixed (immutable) or flexible (mutable) inside the SIB's implementation (see "Class"). Only mutable branch lists can be modified during modelling.
- *execution code*: for the Challenge services it is a Java adapter that realizes via jETI the remote service invocation. In case of local components it is the actual code that realizes the functionality.
- *Icon*: A PNG (pixel) or SVG (vector) image used to graphically represent the SIB inside the taxonomy (see Fig. 5.5 a)) and the flow graph on the jABC GUI (see Figs. 5.6, 5.7 and 5.8).

Additionally, SIBs are decorated by optional plugin annotations. These are realized through Java interfaces inside a service's implementation (see "Class"). When a plugin interface is implemented for a SIB, the corresponding jABC plugin can access the SIB and perform its task. Examples of such interfaces are the tracer interface (for service execution inside the jABC), the Genesys interface (for the Genesys code generator, that compiles the SLG into code for a target external execution platform), or the model checker interface, that decorates the service with labels, here the semantic annotations used to define the semantic service properties.

The freedom for the plugins and interfaces is ample: each plugin used by the jABC framework could specify any number of interfaces which can take nearly every kind of additional data to be used by the SIB. Note that there are no restrictions on the code level: we allow here the full expressive power of Java.

SIBs are semantically classified in our design environment in terms of a taxonomy, which reflects the essentials of their abstract profile. A taxonomy is a directed acyclic graph, where sinks represent SIBs, which are atomic entities in the taxonomy, and where intermediate nodes represent groups, that is sets of modules satisfying some basic property (expressed as predicates). The use of taxonomy information is discussed in detail in Chap. 7, that shows how we use it as a basis for the automatic synthesis of the workflow.

It is easy to see that the *name, taxonomy, class, formal parameters*, and *branches* of this service model provide a very abstract characterization of the services, which will be used later to check the consistency of the orchestrations. The computational portion is encapsulated in the execution code, which is independent of the orchestration level, thus it is written (or, as in this application, generated) once and then reused across the different scenarios.

5.4.2 Service Logic Graphs as Service Composition Models

Service Orchestrations, called in the jABC Service Logic Graphs (SLGs), are internally modelled as Kripke Transition Systems (KTS) [23] whose nodes represent elementary SIBs and whose edges represent branching conditions (see Fig. 5.6):

Definition 1.
A Service Logic Graph *is defined as a triple* $(S, Act, Trans)$ *where*

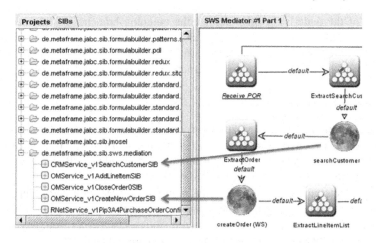

Fig. 5.2. The SWS Mediator SIBs and the abstract process model

- *S represents the (named) occurrences of SIBs*
- *Act is the set of possible branching condition*
- $Trans = \{(s, a, s')\}$ *is a set of transitions where* $s, s' \in S$ *and* $a \in Act$.

Through this non-standard abstraction in our model we obtain a **separation of concerns** between the control-oriented orchestration layer, where the user is not troubled with implementation details while designing or evaluating the applications, and the underlying data-oriented communication mechanisms enforced between the participating subsystems, which are hidden in the SIB implementation. Our tools support the automatic generation of SIBs according to several communication mechanisms for Web services and for other widespread platforms (CORBA, RMI, and other more application-specific ones), as done e.g. in the jETI application [26, 17].

Fig. 5.2 shows one perspective on the taxonomic classification of the SIBs: projectwise, here the SWS.Mediation project. Abstract SIBs, as imported from the WSDL, are shown in the SIB palette on the left, and are instantiated in an SLG by drag and drop to the right canvas. SIBs that refer to Moon's Web services have a moon icon, the other SIBs in this SLG are implemented in Java in the jABC, and they have the typical jABC icon.

5.4.3 Hierarchy

The jABC supports a truly hierarchical design, where SLGs are allowed to make full use of other already existing SLGs. Figure 5.7 shows how this works in practice (cf. [27] for a detailed discussion): Within an abstraction step a (part of a) service is stored as a SIB Graph, which directly becomes itself available as a new SIB. Beside the identifier and the name of the macro the formal parameters and the outgoing branches have to be specified. The parameters of the macro can be mapped to (selected) parameters of the underlying SIBs. Similarly, the set of (un-set) outgoing branches of the underlying SIBs defines the outgoing branches of the macro. As usual, the resulting hierarchy is a design and management aid without any influence on the execution time: during the execution SIB Graphs are automatically unfolded (concretized) and the underlying graph structure is executed by the Tracer.

5.4.4 Tracer Execution

From the execution point of view, an SLG is interpreted as a graph, where the actually executed sequence (a path in the graph) is determined at runtime by results of the execution of the actual SIBs. The execution of the individual SIBs is delegated by the tracer to the corresponding execution environment.

This reflects our policy of separation between orchestration and computation: it embodies the superposition of the orchestration on the components' code and it enables a *uniform view* on the service functionalities, abstracting from any specific technical details like concrete data formats or invocation modalities.

Inter-component communication is realized via parameter passing and tool functionality invocation by function calls which, via their arguments, pass abstract data to the adapters encapsulating the underlying functionalities. The functionalities can be accessed via jETI, using SOAP, or CORBA, or Java RMI. In the concrete setting of the Challenge, the input data for the services are XML messages.

5.5 Model Checking-Based High-Level Compliance Validation

Correctness and consistency of the application design is fully automatically enforced in the jABC via *model checking*. The impact of this approach on the efficiency of design and documentation is dramatic in industrial application scenarios.

We developed a game based model checker dedicated to this application scenario [6]: it is optimized for dealing with detailed diagnosis information, in order to allow verification in real time and extensive investigations in case of unverified properties. Concretely, the algorithm verifies whether a given (behavioral) model satisfies (temporal) properties expressed in a user friendly, natural language-like macro language. In particular:

- the *properties* express correctness or consistency constraints the entire service (e.g., the Mediator) is required to respect.
- the *models* are directly the Service Logic graphs, whereby SIB names correspond to atomic propositions, and branching conditions correspond to action names.

Classes of constraints are formed according to the application domain, to the subsystems, and to the purposes they serve. This way it depends on the global goals of an application, which constraints are bound to its coordination model.

5.5.1 The Logic

The overall on-line verification during the design of a new application case captures both local and global constraints.

Local Constraints.

Local constraints specify requirements on single SIBs, as well as their admissible later parameterization.

Whereas the specification of single SIBs is done simply by means of a predicate logic over the predicates expressed in the taxonomy, parametrization conditions are formulated in terms of a library of corresponding predicates. The verification of local constraints is invoked during the verification of the global constraints.

Global Constraints: The Temporal Aspect.

Global constraints allow users to specify causality, eventuality and other vital relationships between SIBs, which are necessary in order to guarantee test case well-formedness, executability and other frame conditions.

A test case property is global if it does not only involve the immediate neighbourhood of a SIB in the SLG[4], but also relations between SIBs which may be arbitrarily distant and separated by arbitrarily heterogeneous submodels. The treatment of global properties is required in order to capture the essence of the expertise of designers about do's and don'ts of design in this application domain, e.g. which SIBs are incompatible, or which can or cannot occur before/after some other SIBs. Such properties are rarely straightforward, sometimes they are documented as exceptions in thick user manuals, but more often they are not documented at all, and have been discovered at a hard price as bugs of previously developed product versions. This kind of domain-specific knowledge accumulated by experts over the years is particularly worthwhile to include in the design environment for automatic reuse. Governance, business rules, and compliance constraints are other examples of properties often expressible at this level.

Global constraints are expressed internally in the *modal μ-calculus* [11, 12]. The following negation-free syntax defines μ-calculus formulas in positive normal form. They are as expressive as the full modal μ-calculus but allow a simpler technical development.

$$\Phi ::= A \mid X \mid \Phi \wedge \Phi \mid \Phi \vee \Phi \mid [a]\Phi \mid \langle a \rangle \Phi \mid \nu X. \Phi \mid \mu X. \Phi$$

In the above, $a \in Act$, and $X \in Var$, where A is given by the SIB taxonomy, *Act* by the library of branching conditions, and *Var* is a set of variables. The fixpoint operators νX and μX bind the occurrences of X in the formula behind the dot in the usual sense. Properties are specified by *closed* formulas, that is formulas that do not contain any free variable.

The formulas are interpreted with respect to a fixed labeled transition system $\langle S, Act, \rightarrow \rangle$, and an environment $e : Var \rightarrow 2^S$. Formally, the semantics of the μ-calculus is given by:

---

[4] I.e., the set of all the predecessors/successors of a SIB along all paths in the model.

$$[\![X]\!]e = e(X)$$
$$[\![\Phi_1 \vee \Phi_2]\!]e = [\![\Phi_1]\!]e \cup [\![\Phi_2]\!]e$$
$$[\![\Phi_1 \wedge \Phi_2]\!]e = [\![\Phi_1]\!]e \cap [\![\Phi_2]\!]e$$
$$[\![[a]\Phi]\!]e = \{\, s \mid \forall s'.\ s \xrightarrow{a} s' \implies s' \in [\![\Phi]\!]e \,\}$$
$$[\![\langle a \rangle \Phi]\!]e = \{\, s \mid \exists s'.\ s \xrightarrow{a} s' \wedge s' \in [\![\Phi]\!]e \,\}$$
$$[\![\nu X.\Phi]\!]e = \bigcup \{S' \subseteq \mathcal{S} \mid S' \subseteq [\![\Phi]\!]e[X \mapsto S']\}$$
$$[\![\mu X.\Phi]\!]e = \bigcap \{S' \subseteq \mathcal{S} \mid S' \supseteq [\![\Phi]\!]e[X \mapsto S']\}$$

Intuitively, the semantic function maps a formula to the set of states of the KTS of an SLG for which the formula is "true". Accordingly, a state s satisfies $A \in \mathcal{A}$ if s is in the valuation of A, while s satisfies X if s is an element of the set bound to X in e. The propositional constructs are interpreted in the usual fashion: s satisfies $\Phi_1 \vee \Phi_2$ if it satisfies one of the Φ_i and $\Phi_1 \wedge \Phi_2$ if it satisfies both of them. The constructs $\langle a \rangle$ and $[a]$ are *modal operators*; s satisfies $\langle a \rangle \Phi$ if it has an a-derivative satisfying Φ, while s satisfies $[a]\Phi$ if each of its a-derivatives satisfies Φ. Note that the semantics of $\nu X.\ \Phi$ (and dually of $\mu X.\Phi$) is based on Tarski's fixpoint theorem [30]: its meaning is defined as the greatest (dually, least) fixpoint of a continuous function over the powerset of the set of states.

For application experts, it is important to provide a natural language-like feeling for the temporal operators. As indicated by the examples below, the standard logical connectors turned out to be unproblematic. We omit the formal definition of **next**, **generally**, **eventually**, and **until** here, as they are standard.

5.6 Using jETI for Remote Service Inclusion and Execution

jETI (Java Electronic Tool Integration framework [16, 29, 1]) is a framework for including remotely provided third party functionalities as remote services (both REST and Web) as SIBs within the jABC, and to communicate with them seamlessly from within the jABC. As for all jABC extensions, jETI is available as a plugin.

As shown in Fig. 5.4, it can generate basic service types (SIBs) from the WSDL file of a third party service, and export the orchestrated/choreographed services inside the jABC (the SLGs), as Web services.

Fig. 5.3 shows the distributed architecture of this infrastructure. SIBs represent the atomic functionality of an involved service. Within the jABC, domain-specific SIB palettes are shareable among projects, and organised in a project-specific structure using project-specific terminology. This is a simple way for adopting or adapting to different ontologies within the same application domain. Domain-specific SIB palettes are complemented by a library of SIBs that offer basic functionality (e.g.

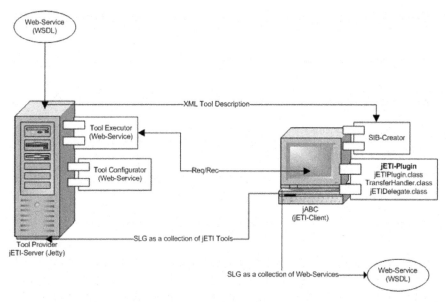

Fig. 5.3. The jETI architecture.

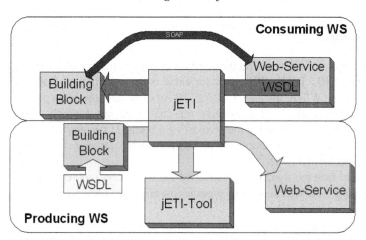

Fig. 5.4. Consuming and producing web services with jABC/jETI.

SIBs for I/O or memory handling), control structures (for loops, and threads) or handling of data structures like matrices (e.g. extensively used in our bioinformatics
applications [15]). Fig. 5.5 a) shows the palette of SIBs imported from the Blue and
Moon service descriptions, as they are displayed in the taxonomy view of jABC's
inspector.

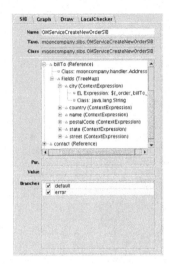

Fig. 5.5. a) Taxonomy view for the Mediator SIB Palette: (jETI-) SIBs imported from the WSDLs and **b)** Hierarchical input parameters of the generated SIB OMServiceCreateNewOrder

Including Web services

To use Web service components inside the jABC it is only necessary to provide a valid WSDL file or URL. jETI's SIB generator extracts the information about the functions defined in the WSDL file and creates a SIB for each function. Input parameters are handled as hierarchical SIB parameters: this enables the user to freely define input values for the Web service, using the preexisting graphical user interface of the jABC. In Fig. 5.5 b) we see for example the hierarchical rich parameter structure of the OMServiceCreateNewOrder SIB.

This is useful to face the dynamic scenarios of the Mediation problem without need of programming: if a Web service changes its interface, we only need to reimport the WSDL into a (new) SIB.
By generating Web service SIBs, the *execution* of the service remains on the server. The SIBs simply serve as proxies for the Web services, which, in this example, are called using the Apache Axis framework [2].

From XML to Java Objects

Using the mechanism described in the previous paragraph, services may take *Java* objects bound to the XML schema of the message as an input. This way we can now deal with "real" objects representing orders within the mediation model. The message is received by a *Java* component and automatically parsed and bound.

To specify the message object as an input of our service model we use *Model-Parameters*: while *SIB-Parameters* are input parameters defined for a single building

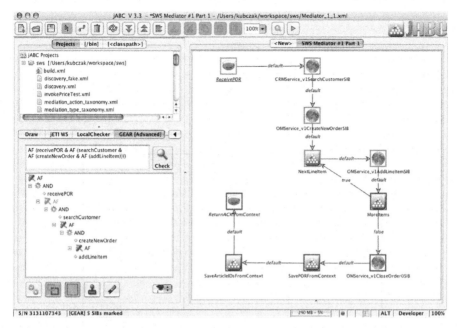

Fig. 5.6. Receiving a POR - Modelchecked SLG, Mediator #1 Part 1

block, *Model-Parameters* are parameters defined for the whole SLG. Therefore once the received message is transformed into an object, this is also defined as a parameter of the service model.

Response messages from the mediator are handled analogously: as described above, they become output parameters written to the execution context of an *SLG*.

5.7 Solving the SWS Mediation with jETI/jABC

When we entered the SWS Challenge back in 2006, we first solved the mediation scenario described in Chap. 2 without any specific additional enhancements to the jABC. This meant that we had to program (in Java)

- WSDL import functionality,
- transformations from the WSDLs to SIBs, and
- the communication with the individual Web services.

These solutions, presented at the Budva (June 2006) and Athens, GA (Nov. 2006) Workshops, were purely oriented to a professional use of model driven design, as supported in the jABC, for the creation of bespoke applications. We used SIBs and SLGs for the functionalities and workflows respectively, and we provided the mediator as a Java application. Seen from today's point of view, this solution used the

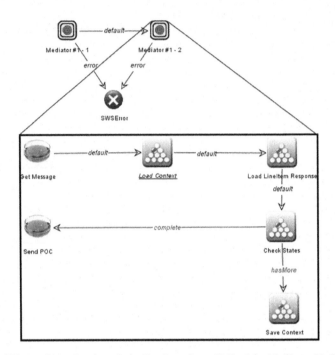

Fig. 5.7. Sending a PurchaseOrderConfirmation - SLG of the Mediator #1, Part 2

jABC framework only to ease the work of a programmer.

One year later, at Innsbruck (June 2007) and Stanford (November 2007) we had proceeded to providing an *infrastructure* that systematically aids the integration of external (Web) services, the communication with them at runtime, and the provision of the mediator services as Web services themselves, enhancing the entire jABC/jETI framework.

In this section we illustrate the agility of our current framework-based solution by considering two mediation scenarios described in Chap. 2: the basic mediation scenario between the *Blue* customer and the *Moon* company, that we call here Mediation scenario #1, and an elaboration of this scenario that extends Moon's capabilities (called here Mediation scenario #2) - each Mediator consisting of two services. This shows the impact of our

- automatic WSDL import functionality, our
- automatic generation of SIBs from the WSDLs, and the
- jETI communication framework (Sect. 5.6), which makes the communication with (remote) SIBs transparent to the user of the Framework.

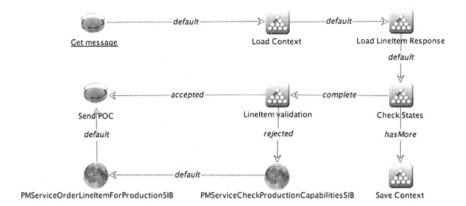

Fig. 5.8. Sending a PurchaseOrderConfirmation with LineItems - SLG of the Mediator #2, Part 2

In particular, the automatic generation of SIBs from the WSDLs describing the communication with *Moon*'s and *Blue*'s backend services made a huge difference. Due to the automatic WSDL import, this feature is very easy to use: one only needs to provide the URL for the WSDL descriptor of the Web service, and the corresponding SIB shows up in the SIB palette, ready to be used for orchestrations. Together with the jETI framework, this totally frees the user from worrying about remote integration and communication, both at design time and at runtime.

Both mediation scenarios are similar in structure. As illustrated in Fig. 5.9 and 5.10 on the original Challenge's schemata, they both consist of two services, each modeled in their own SLG:

- Receiving a PurchaseOrderRequest: this service takes a RosettaNet *PIP3A4PurchaseOrderRequest* from Blue and forwards it to the Moon system, handling the whole order submission procedure (due to the different granularity of the Moon and Blue services). This service is shared by both scenarios. The corresponding final SLG is reported in Fig. 5.6.
- Sending a PurchaseOrderConfirmation: this service waits for all ordered items to be confirmed by Moon's backend system and sends a RosettaNet *PIP3A4PurchaseOrderConfirmation* back to the Blue client. Depending on the scenario, this service refers only to Moon's Order Management System or also to its Production Management System. Its SLGs are reported in Fig. 5.7 and 5.8, respectively.

The following two subsections describe the modelling of the original mediation scenario and of its elaboration.

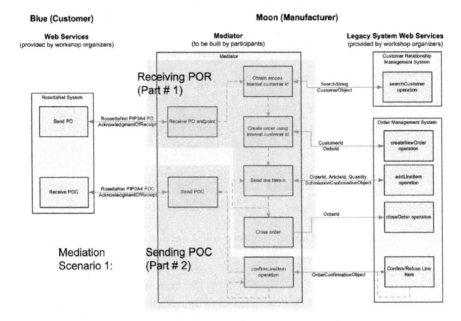

Fig. 5.9. Decomposition of Mediation Scenario #1: the Receiving POR and the Sending POC services

5.7.1 The Original Mediation Scenario - #1

The *mediation* scenario concerns making a legacy order management system interoperable with external systems that use a simplified version of the RosettaNet PIP3A4 specifications[5]. It concerns therefore finding an adequate *orchestration* that adapts two conversation partners that mismatch both in the interaction protocol and in the granularity and format of data. Its three main components are

- the **Company Blue**, a customer (service requester) ordering products. The SIBs in our solution that communicate with Blue's endpoint are indicated visually in the SLGs by an icon with blue liquid
- the **Mediator**, the sought-for piece of technology providing automatic or semi-automatic mediation for the Moon company, and
- the **Legacy System** of the Moon Company. To manage its order processing, Moon uses two back-end systems: a Customer Relationship Management system (CRM) and an Order Management System (OMS), both accessible on the SWSC testbed through public Web services described using WSDL. The SIBs in our solution that communicate with Moon's endpoints are indicated visually in the SLGs by an icon with a picture of the moon's surface.

---

[5] http://www.rosettanet.org/PIP3A4

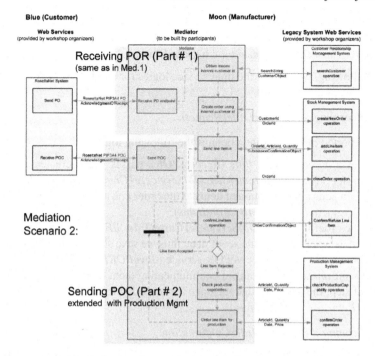

Fig. 5.10. Decomposition of Mediation Scenario #2: the same Receiving POR and extended Sending POC services

While the external interfaces must follow the RosettaNet specification, internally Moon uses a propriety legacy system whose data model and message exchange patterns differ from those of RosettaNet. Participants shall basically enable Moon to "talk RosettaNet" and implement the *Purchase Order receiving role* part of the interaction described in the RosettaNet PIP 3A4.

Both the Moon legacy systems and the customer Web services (Blue) are provided by the challenge organizers as technical infrastructure accessible online, and cannot be altered by the participants.

Outline of the Solutions

The generic structure of the solution, shared by all our successive improvements, is as follows:

- extract the *relevant* information from the *PurchaseOrderRequest*
- call Moon's Customer Relation Management (CRM) to find the customer data inside the database, if the customer already has an account.
- Use the *CustomerID* to create an order using Moon's Order Management System (OMS).
- add *LineItems* as needed and then

- close the order.
- Finally the middle layer receives an *OrderConfirmationObject* and
- sends a *PurchaseOrderConfirmation* back to Blue.

In the following, we present the final service logics for the three services that are required to solve both scenarios.

Service 1: Receiving a PurchaseOrderRequest.

Its SLG is reported in Fig. 5.6 and contains the following logic:

- it receives a message from *Blue* (*ReceivePOR*), parses it and creates an order (*CRMService_v1SearchCustomerSIB, OMService_v1CreateNewOrderSIB*).
- A loop then adds all the contained items to the order one at a time (*NextLineItem, OMService_v1AddLineItemSIB, MoreItems*).
- Finally the order is closed (*OMService_v1CloseOrderSIB*).
- Both models work on the same set of data, thus we save all the information in the execution context of the ReceivePOR service (*SavePORFromContext, SaveArticleIDsFromContext*) as a means of communicating them to the next service.
- In a final step, the acknowledge message for receiving the POR is sent to *Blue's* service (*ReturnACKFromContext*).

Service 2: Sending a PurchaseOrderConfirmation.

This service (see Fig. 5.7) waits for a message sent by *Moon* confirming the availability of all the items.

- When the message is received (*Get message*)
- the context information stored by the previous service is retrieved in the new execution context (*Load Context*).
- The response is then parsed (*Load LineItem Response*)
- and checked for more items to come (*Check States*).
- Since there is a single message for each line item we save the context once again if we have to wait for another response (*Save Context*),
- we finally send a *PurchaseOrderConfirmation* once all items have been processed (*Send POC*).
- As in any jABC service, the *SWS Error* SIB provides also here the default jABC error handling.

5.7.2 Adding the Production Management System: Mediation Scenario #2

Mediation scenario #2 is identical in its first phase (service 1) to the previous scenario, but addresses some additional requirements concerning the second phase for purchase order confirmation: it offers on-demand production of items not available in stock. This extension of the functionality led to the following changes in our solution:

Once the OMS's responses of all items are received, instead of sending directly a PurchaseOrderConfirmation there is a conditional treatment based on an additional evaluation (*LineItem validation*):

- The item is accepted if it is in stock and the process ends by sending the confirmation as described in scenario #1.
- Otherwise, we check with Moon's Production Management service whether the missing items can be produced on demand. To this aim we invoke two new backend services at *Moon*'s legacy system. The corresponding SIBs are of course again generated from the corresponding WSDLs. The SIBs (*PMServiceCheckProductionCapabilitiesSIB* and *PMServiceOrderLineItemForProductionSIB*) check Moon's capability to produce the missing items and order its production. If this is successful, the process ends by sending the corresponding confirmation, thus reducing an order's rejection only to the case where it is neither on stock nor it can be produced on demand.

Fig. 5.8 shows the resulting SLG, which turns out to require only minor modifications wrt. its predecessor shown in Fig. 5.7. For better layout of the logic we hide here the error handling aspect in this picture. In reality, there is for each SIB a mandatory error branch, that enables possibly specific treatment of errors.

5.8 Verifiying the Mediator

A central feature of jABC is its rich family of plugin extensions. They include *GEAR*, our Model Checker for the full μ-calculus [12]. GEAR [10] enables us to semantically verify our approach by expressing behavioral properties of the Mediator as temporal logic formulas in μ-calculus or in one of its derived logics, like the branching time logic CTL [4]. A frequent pattern of behavioral properties easily expressible in these logics concerns *precedence* requirements. As an example, we request that a *receivePOR* must precede a *searchCustomer* which in turn must precede a *createNewOrder* and this must occur before an *addLineItem*. This is expressed in the internal CTL syntax for GEAR as

AF (receivePOR & AF (searchCustomer & AF (createNewOrder
    & AF (addLineItem))))

whereby AF p means *on every path starting in this state, property* p *will eventually occur (at least once)*.

Fig. 5.6 shows the modelchecked Mediator service Part 1, where a POR is received. GEAR highlights in green the path (the set of nodes) for which this property holds. Additionally, on the left it shows both the property and its subformulas: clicking on a node, the satisfied (resp. unsatisfied) subformulas turn green (resp. red), and clicking on a subformula all the satisfying nodes turn green. Our previous experience has shown that this direct feedback is greatly appreciated in particular by less experienced users since it simplifies debugging complex processes directly on the model.

We can also model the entire Mediator in a hierarchical fashion: the model of each Mediator part is exported as a SIB, as in Fig. 5.7. The Service of the Part 2 is connected by a virtual edge, that is taken upon successful termination of the Part 1

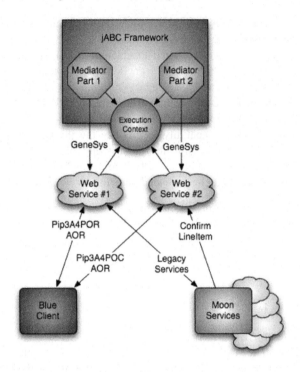

Fig. 5.11. Architecture of the jABC/jETI SWS Mediator

graph. This way we have a single graph, even if the execution of Part 2 starts asyn-
chronously, and thus we can also express and check properties of the entire Mediator.

5.9 Automatic Web Service Generation in Practice

Our initial solution worked, but it required execution inside the jABC Tracer. We
wanted however to provide the Mediator *automatically* as intermediate Web service
between the *Blue* customer and *Moon*'s legacy system, participating to this three-
party choreography (or four, if we consider that the mediator requires two services).

The missing components to achieve this concerned a robust and possibly automatic technology for providing the orchestrated services as autonomous Web services. This is solved by a new generic component of the *jETI* framework [26, 14, 29],
which is provided as a plugin within *jABC*. As we discussed in [13], initially we
thought it would be quite easy. However, the solution turned out to be heavily dependent on rather peculiar features and capabilities of a number of 'standard' tools and
software layers, which required specific care far beyond what one would expect for
a 'mature technology'.

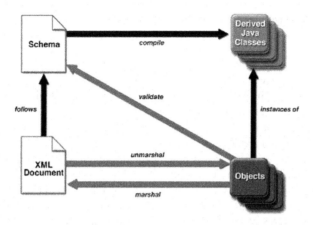

Fig. 5.12. Data Binding in Java 6

In the following we briefly sketch the different approaches we tried out, followed by our current solution, which extends the jABC with a specific functionality realized itself as a jABC process (Fig. 5.14).

5.9.1 Basic Technology

There are two dual approaches for implementing Web services in general: *code first* and *contract first*:

- In a *code first* approach, some implemented functionality is available that should be published as a Web service. The related WSDL file is ideally generated by the used Web services framework at deployment.
- In a *contract first* approach, one starts by writing a WSDL by hand (or tool-supported) and then generates the Web service's stubs and skeletons with a generation tool usually provided by the used Web services framework.

We investigated both approaches, as described in detail in [13]. Fig. 5.11 gives an overview of our current solution (architecture and flow). Once the mediator's services had been modelled as described in the previous section, we could automatically generate a fully functional Web service serving as a communication component between *Blue* and *Moon*. As before, we first had to export the model to plain and stand-alone Java using *GeneSys*, followed by the *Contract first* approach to Web service generation: Java 6 has a fully integrated Web service support, providing an integrated web server and an easy to use services framework. So we can just deploy and execute the resulting application, and the service is up and running. We describe in the following in detail the systematic process.

5.9.2 Web Service Generation: the final process

Whether the SLG Mediator is manually composed, as just described, or automatically generated, as described in Chap. 7, it has at the end to be able to communicate with the Web services on the Challenge testbed. The most natural way of achieving this is by providing the Mediator itself as a Web service, and deploying it somewhere with free communication to the Testbed.

To this aim, we extended the jABC with the capability of creating a Web service from an arbitrary traceable jABC model. This section describes the organization of this Web Service generator, that is now bundled in the jETI plugin for jABC.

The chosen approach is to create executable Java code from the given jABC model using the Genesys code generation framework [7] and add some wrapper classes which publish this generated class as a Web service. As Web service framework we choose JAX-WS [9], which is part of the Java 6 distribution. For the creation of the Web Service we need some additional information that cannot be fully inferred from the model alone, such as imported XSD definitions and input/output types of the Web service, as well as a way to append this meta information to the model. This is realized by a dedicated annotation editor, the *AppendWSInfo* SIB, with a special grammar that represents exactly the required data. Figure 5.13 shows the WS Metadata for the Mediator process, that has been added by the *AppendWSInfo* SIB.

The Web service generation process results in a complete Web service, with all its sources and dependencies being generated into a temporary directory and then packaged to a ZIP file.

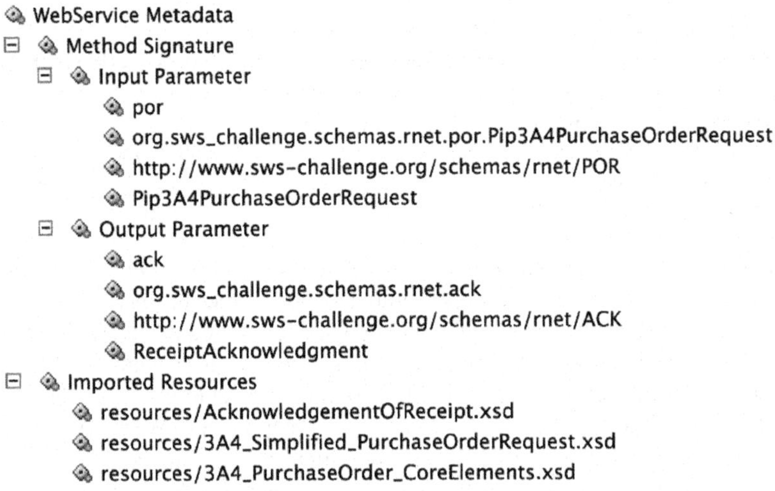

    ✦ WebService Metadata
    ☐ ✦ Method Signature
        ☐ ✦ Input Parameter
            ✦ por
            ✦ org.sws_challenge.schemas.rnet.por.Pip3A4PurchaseOrderRequest
            ✦ http://www.sws-challenge.org/schemas/rnet/POR
            ✦ Pip3A4PurchaseOrderRequest
        ☐ ✦ Output Parameter
            ✦ ack
            ✦ org.sws_challenge.schemas.rnet.ack
            ✦ http://www.sws-challenge.org/schemas/rnet/ACK
            ✦ ReceiptAcknowledgment
    ☐ ✦ Imported Resources
        ✦ resources/AcknowledgementOfReceipt.xsd
        ✦ resources/3A4_Simplified_PurchaseOrderRequest.xsd
        ✦ resources/3A4_PurchaseOrder_CoreElements.xsd

Fig. 5.13. Metadata for Web service generation

The Web Service generation process has been modelled itself as a jABC process graph, shown in Fig. 5.14, that orchestrates a number of (new) SIBs which implement the required functionalities. This model has then been extruded[6] using Genesys to enable its seamless integration into the jABC/jETI GUI.

We now explain the Web service generation process stepwise, along the structure of its SLG.

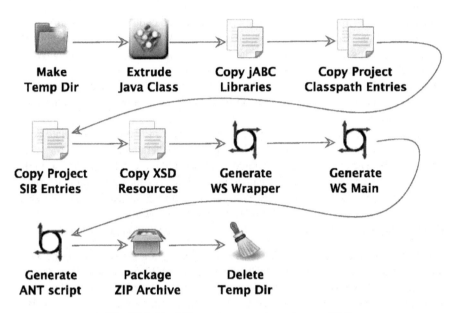

Fig. 5.14. The Web service generator process as SLG

Make Temp Dir creates a dedicated temporary directory for the work of the subsequent SIBs.

Extrude Java Class takes the target SLG to be provided as a Web service and generates the corresponding Java code using the Genesys *JavaClassExtruder*. The result is a Java class that performs the same tracing of the model as it would be done by the jABC Tracer.

Copy jABC Libraries The generated Java class depends on some core jABC libraries. Here, we search the Classpath for those libraries and add them to the temporary directory.

Copy Project Classpath Entries Additional libraries required by the project can be specified as project classpath entries within jABC. They are also necessary to run the final Web service, thus this SIB copies those project specific JARs to the temporary directory.

---

[6] For Java targets, Genesys can produce either pure code, which is native Java, or *extruded* code, that runs outside of the jABC within a lightweight version of the Tracer, that is itself part of the delivered code.

Copy Project SIB Entries copies all the SIB classes of this project to the temporary directory. These are required for the extruded trace.

Copy XSD Resources If the Web service's interface definition contains more than simple XSD types, one can provide XSD type definition files that are shipped with the Web Service. This information is taken from the Web Service Metadata annotation, as explained above.

Generate WS Wrapper generates the endpoint source code using a Velocity template and the *Message Signature* subtree of the WS Metadata definition. This class contains the annotations required by the JAX-WS framework (@Web-Service, @WebParam, @WebResult).

Generate WS Main then generates the main class of the Web service from a velocity template. In this main class the previously created endpoint class is instantiated and started.

Generate ANT Script creates an ANT build script from a velocity template containing predefined targets to compile and run the generated classes.

Package ZIP Archive Here all generated and copied files are packaged into a single ZIP file for easier delivery. The path to the ZIP file is exported as a model parameter. This means that it is provided as as 'procedure parameter' in the extruded model, giving the caller the ability to specify the output file.

Delete Temp Dir Finally, the temporary directory is cleaned up and deleted.

Most of the elements of this Web service generator are not specific to the Web service technology. We expect that its realization as a jABC model based on components packaged as SIBs, followed by code generation of the entire SLG will provide a template to be reused for other exporters to specific technologies, like e.g. CORBA or other domain-specific specialized formats.

5.10 Related Work

A detailed comparison with the WebML/Webratio approach is provided in Chap. 9.

Concerning the other Mediation solutions, we are certainly very close to the ASM format used by WSMO-LX: Our SLGs have a formal semantics as Kripke Transition Systems, which is also a state machine based formalism. SLGs were initially exported as list of transitions, thus close even in the notation to ASMs. However, the WSMO Solution does not make any use of the formal model underlying the ASMs, while we take advantage of ours both for verification purposes of the SLGs, as shown here in Sect. 5.8, and for the semantic enhancement of the SIBs with formal properties (atomic propositions in the SLTL logic). We use in fact these properties also to create taxonomies then used for the automatic generation of the SLGs from declarative descriptions of the desired workflows, as shown in Chap. 7. That solution is the closest to the planning-based one described in Chap. 6. The Diane mediation solution was realized as a normal, manually produced Java program, without any generation from a modelling layer. It represents therefore the state-of-the-art starting point of programming in an IDE, without any kind of high-level modelling.

Relative to the state of the art in Workflow systems for Web services, the popular tools used in other communities, like e.g. Taverna [24] in bioinformatics, would likely encounter great difficulty of application for the SWS Challenge. The point is that they are dataflow-oriented modelling tools born on top of fine granular grid computing projects: activities there concern basic data management operations on a grid such as Put, Get, Connect, ProxyCommand - quite a different granularity from the user-level addressed in jABC/jETI and in the Challenge. Moreover, their provenance is not from a software engineering/programming environment background, nor from a process model semantics and formal verification culture. Thus they address the process design and management with a focus on explicit model of data connections. This is already emerging as a limit in their original area of application, where Web services communicate via a few, simple datatypes. Handling complex structures like the Challenge's business objects (as shown in Fig. 5.5 b)) would exceed their capabilities and original purpose.

Regarding Web services standards, jABC supports meanwhile also BPEL as a graphical entry notation [5] alternative to the SLG format, and it supports code generation for the Active BPEL and Oracle BPEL engines. We could have therefore also formulated the flows as BPEL processes, and executed them on one of those platforms. However, since BPEL has no clean formal semantics, we would have lost the formal methods support offered by jABC, which is in our opinion a central asset of the environment.

Regarding the standards of Semantic Web, our SLGs are very close to the processes expressible in OWL-S [22]. We may decide to export our SLGs in that format too in the near future.

5.11 Conclusions and Ongoing Work

We have discussed our model driven, service oriented solution to the Mediation task with the intent to also illustrate the agility of jABC-based solutions: users easily develop services and applications by composing reusable building-blocks into (flow-) graph structures that can be animated, analyzed, simulated, verified, executed, and compiled. In particular, we have proceeded to providing an *infrastructure* that systematically aids the integration of external (Web) services, the communication with them at runtime, and the provision of the mediator services as Web services themselves, enhancing the entire jABC/jETI framework.

This approach is adequate whenever one wants to put the user process at the center of the development and the application expert in control of the process evolution - in our opinion the key to agility.

Currently, we are investigating this new paradigm of user-centric process/system design, which we call eXtreme Model Driven Design, in various dimensions: we address how it can be technically further supported, how it complements classical software/service development, and which are the natural limitations of this approach. The SWS challenge provides an interesting scenario for this investigation, in particular as it allows one to compare the own solutions with solutions proposed by others for the same problem scenarios.

References

1. A. Arenas, J. Bicarregui, and T. Margaria. The FMICS view on the verified software repository, proc. integrated design and process technology. In *IDPT 2006*. Society for Design and Process Science, June 2006.
2. *Apache Axis Web Service Framework*, 2007. http://ws.apache.org/axis/.
3. V. Braun, T. Margaria, B. Steffen, H. Yoo, and T. Rychly. Safe service customization. In *Proc. IN'97, IEEE Communication Soc. Workshop on Intelligent Network*. IEEE Comm. Soc. Press., May 1997.
4. E.A. Emerson. Temporal and modal logic. In *J. van Leeuwen, editor*, Handbook of Theoretical Computer Science, volume B, pages 995–1072. MIT Press/Elsevier, 1990.
5. J. Gaeb. Entwicklung eines BPEL-Plugins für das jABC-Framework. Master's thesis, Universität Dortmund, 2007.
6. *GEAR Model Checker*, 2007. http://jabc.cs.uni-dortmund.de/opencms/opencms/jabc/plugins/gear.html.
7. *GeneSys Code Generation*, 2007. http://jabc.cs.uni-dortmund.de/opencms/opencms/jabc/plugins/genesys/index.html.
8. *jABC Website*, 2007. http://www.jabc.de.
9. *JAX-WS Developers' Website:*, 2007. https://jax-ws.dev.java.net/.
10. Sven Jörges, Christian Kubczak, Ralf Nagel, Tiziana Margaria, and Bernhard Steffen. Model-driven development with the jABC. In *HVC - IBM Haifa Verification Conference*, LNCS 4383, Haifa, Israel, October 23-26 2006. IBM, Springer Verlag.
11. D. Kozen. Results on the propositional mu-calculus. In *Proc. ALP'82, 9th Colloquium on Automata, Languages and Programming, LNCS 140*, pages 348–359, Aarhus, DK, July 1982. Springer Verlag.
12. D. Kozen. Results on the propositional mu-calculus. *TCS N.27*, pages 333–354, 1983.
13. C. Kubczak, T. Margaria, B. Steffen, and S. Naujokat. Service-oriented mediation with jETI/jABC: Verification and export. In *Worksh. on Service Composition & SWS Challenge, part of WI-IAT'07, the IEEE/ WIC/ ACM Int. Conf. on Web Intelligence, November 2007, Stanford (CA)*, volume ISBN-10: 0-7695-3028-1. IEEE CS, 2007.
14. T. Margaria. Web services-based tool-integration in the ETI platform. *SoSyM, Int. Journal on Software and System Modelling*, 4(2):141–156, May 2005.
15. T. Margaria, C. Kubczak, M. Njoku, and B. Steffen. Model-based design of distributed collaborative bioinformatics processes in the jABC. In *Proc. ICECCS 2006, 11th IEEE International Conference on Engineering of Complex Computer Systems, Stanford (CA)*, pages 169–176. IEEE CS, August 2006.
16. T. Margaria, C. Kubzcak, and B. Steffen. Bio-jETI: a service integration, design, and provisioning platform for orchestrated bioinformatics processes. *BioMed Central (BMC) Bioinformatics 2008; Supplement dedicated to Network Tools and Applications in Biology 2007 Workshop (NETTAB 2007) ISSN 1471-2105. Published online 2008 April 25. doi: 10.1186/1471-2105-9-S4-S12.*, 9 (Suppl 4): S12, 2008.
17. T. Margaria, H. Raffelt, B. Steffen, and M. Leucker. The LearnLib in FMICS-jETI. In *Proc. ICECCS 2007, 12th IEEE Int. Conf. on Engineering of Complex Computer Systems*, pages 340–349. IEEE CSoc. Press., July 2007.

18. T. Margaria and B. Steffen. From the how to the what. In *VSTTE: Verified Software—Theories, Tools, and Experiments, Proc. IFIP Working Conference, Zurich, Oct 2005*, volume LNCS 4171. Springer, 2005.
19. T. Margaria and B. Steffen. Service engineering: Linking business and it. *IEEE Computer, issue 60th anniv. of the Computer Society*, pages 53–63, October 2006.
20. T. Margaria, B. Steffen, and M. Reitenspieß. Service-oriented design: The roots. In *ICSOC 2005: 3rd ACMSIGSOFT/SIGWEB Int. Conf. on Service-Oriented Computing*, LNCS N.3826, pages 450–464, Amsterdam, December 2005. Springer Verlag.
21. Tiziana Margaria and Bernhard Steffen. Lightweight coarse-grained coordination: a scalable system-level approach. *STTT*, 5(2-3):107–123, 2004.
22. D. Martin, M. Burstein, D. McDermott, S. McIlraith, M. Paolucci, and K. Sycara et al. Bringing semantics to web services with OWL-S. In *World Wide Web*, volume 10, page 243277. Springer, 2007.
23. M. Müller-Olm, D. Schmidt, and B. Steffen. Model-checking: A tutorial introduction. In *Proc. SAS'99*, pages 330–354. LNCS 1503, Springer Verlag, September 1999.
24. T. Oinn, M. Addis, J. Ferris, D. Marvin, and M. Senger et al. Taverna: a tool for the composition and enactment of bioinformatics workflows. *Bioinformatics*, 20(17):3045–3054, 2004.
25. B. Steffen and T. Margaria. Metaframe in practice: Intelligent network service design. In *Correct System Design - Issues, Methods and Per-spectives, E.-R. Olderog and B. Steffen (eds.), LNCS 1710*, pages 390–415. Springer Verlag, 1999.
26. B. Steffen, T. Margaria, and V. Braun. The electronic tool integration platform: Concepts and design. *Int. Journal on Software Tools for Technology Transfer (STTT)*, 1(2):9–30, 1997.
27. B. Steffen, T. Margaria, V. Braun, and N. Kalt. Hierarchical service definition. In *Annual Review of Communication*, pages 847–856. Int. Engineering Consortium Chicago (USA), IEC, 1997.
28. B. Steffen, T. Margaria, A. Claßen, V. Braun, and M. Reitenspieß. An environment for the creation of intelligent network services. In *(invited contribution) Annual Review of Communication*, pages 919–935. Int. Engineering Consortium Chicago (USA), IEC, November 1996.
29. Bernhard Steffen, Tiziana Margaria, and Ralf Nagel. Remote Integration and Coordination of Verification Tools in jETI. In *Proc. ECBS 2005, 12th IEEE Int. Conf. on the Engineering of Computer Based Systems*, pages 431–436, Greenbelt (USA), April 2005. IEEE Computer Soc. Press.
30. A. Tarski. A lattice-theoretical fixpoint theorem and its applications. *Pacific Journal of Mathematics*, 5, 1955.

6

A Declarative Approach using SAWSDL and Semantic Templates Towards Process Mediation

Karthik Gomadam[1], Ajith Ranabahu[1], Zixin Wu[2], Amit P. Sheth[1] and John Miller[3]

[1] kno.e.sis center, Wright State University, Dayton, OH
   kgomadam@gmail.com,{ranabahu.2,amit.sheth}@wright.edu
[2] Nextag Corporation, San Mateo, CA
   wuzixin@gmail.com
[3] LSDIS Lab, Department of Computer Science, University of GA, Athens, GA
   jam@cs.uga.edu

Summary. In this paper we address the challenges that arise due to heterogeneities across independently created and autonomously managed Web service requesters and Web service providers. Previous work in this area either involved significant human effort or in cases of the efforts seeking to provide largely automated approaches, overlooked the problem of data heterogeneities, resulting in partial solutions that would not support executable workflow for real-world problems. In this paper, we present a planning-based approach to solve both the process heterogeneity and data heterogeneity problems. We adopt a declarative approach to capture the partner specifications external to the process and demonstrate the usefulness of this approach in adding more dynamism to Web processes. Our system successfully outputs a BPEL file which correctly solves a non-trivial real-world problem in the SWS Challenge.

Semantic Templates, Process Mediation, Semantic Web Services, SAWSDL, SWS Challenge

6.1 Introduction

Web services are software systems designed to support interoperable machine-to-machine interactions over a network. They are the preferred standards-based way to realize Service Oriented Architecture (SOA) computing. A problem that has seen much interest from the research community is that of automated composition (i.e., without human involvement) of Web services. The ultimate goal is to realize Web service compositions or Web processes by leveraging the functionality of autonomously created services. While SOAs loosely coupling approach is appealing, it inevitably brings the challenge of heterogeneities across these independently developed services. Two key types of heterogeneities are those related to data and process. It is necessary and critical to overcome both types of these heterogeneities in order to organize autonomously created Web services into a process to aggregate their power.

Previous efforts related to Web service composition considered various approaches, and have included use of HTN [1], Golog [2], classic AI planning [3], rule-based planning [4]

model checking [5], theorem proving [6] etc. Some solutions involve too much human effort; some overlook the problem of data heterogeneities. Overcoming both process and data heterogeneities is the key to automatic generation of executable process.

One of the metrics for evaluating the solution is to measure the flexibility of a solution. The objective is to minimize the human effort required when the execution scenario is modified. We adopt a declarative approach towards achieving a greater degree of flexibility. Our solution externalizes the partner and the process requirements from the process control flow. Various variable parameters including QoS requirements, data and functional requirements are specified using semantic templates in a declarative manner. In the event of a change in the environment, one can reconfigure the process by changing the external specification.

In our solution, we extend GraphPlan[7], an AI planning algorithm, to automatically generate the control flow of a Web process. Our extension is that besides the preconditions and effects of operations, we also take into consideration in the planning algorithm the structure and semantics of the input and output messages. This extension reduces the search space and eliminates plans containing operations with incompatible messages. Our approach for the problem of data heterogeneity is a data mediator which may be embedded in the middleware or an externalized Web service. By separating the data mediation from the process mediation, we allow the process mediation system concentrate on generating the control flow. This separation of concerns also makes it easier to analyze the control flow.

The key benefits of our solution are

1. The ability to automatically generate executable workflow that addresses both control flow and data flow considerations (in our current implementation it is a BPEL process specification).
2. A pattern-based approach for loop generation in planning.
3. A loosely coupled data mediation approach and a context-based ranking algorithm for data mediation.
4. Declarative approach towards specifying requirements that makes it easier to manage change.

We demonstrate the above capabilities using a case/scenario in the 2006 SWS Challenge.

The remainder of this paper is organized as follows. We first give some background information of the problem of Web service composition in section 6.2, and then introduce a motivating scenario in section 6.3. The next two sections form the technical core of this paper—section 6.4 presents a formal definition of semantic Web services and Semantic Templates, and section 6.6 discusses the automatic Web service composition capability.

Finally, we give conclusions and future work in section 6.7.

6.2 Background and Related Work

6.2.1 Background

There are two categories of partners that are described within the Web services domain, namely the service provider and service requester. A service provider presents its Web service functionality by providing a set of operation specifications (or operations for short). These operations allow service requesters to use the services by simply invoking them. These operations might be inter-dependent. The dependences can be captured using precondition, effect, input, and output specifications of the operation. Using these available operations, a service requester performs one or more inter-related steps to achieve the desired goal. These steps can be best viewed as activities in a process and can be divided into smaller and more concrete sub-steps, and eventually invocations of concrete operations. Specifications by service requesters and providers are often times autonomously created. This causes heterogeneities to exist between the requester and provider when Web services need to interoperate as part of a composition of Web services. Two key types of heterogeneities may exist – the data related and the communication/process related. We say that process heterogeneity exists when the goal of the service requester cannot be achieved by atomically invoking exactly one operation once. On the other hand, data heterogeneity exists when the output message of an operation has different structure or semantics from the input message of the consecutive operation.

It is also important that we use a framework that has the flexibility to support both functional and non-functional requirements for service discovery. Such a framework must allow service providers to publish their non-functional capabilities. In such a framework the criteria for selection must not be too restrictive, since it may be very difficult to find services that exactly match the requirements. The requester must be able to specify the expected level of match for the different aspects of the request. For example, a requester can specify that an exact match is needed with respect to the operation while a *sufficiently similar* match would suffice for the input and output parameters.

SAWSDL

We describe Web services and Semantic Templates (discussed next) in SAWSDL. SAWSDL [8] is a W3C standard to add semantics to Web services descriptions. SAWSDL does not specify a language for representing the semantic models, e.g., ontologies. Instead, it provides mechanisms by which concepts from the semantic models that are defined either within or outside the WSDL document can be referenced from within WSDL components as annotations. Semantic annotations facilitate process composition by eliminating ambiguities. We annotate a Web service by specifying Model References for its operations as well as Model References and Schema Mappings for the input and output message of its operations. We also extend SAWSDL by adding preconditions and effects as in our W3C submission on WSDL-S [9] for an operation, which will be discussed in later sections.

Rao et al. [3] discuss the use of the GraphPlan algorithm to successfully generate a process. While it is good to consider the interaction with the users, their approach suffers from the extent of automation. Also this work, unlike ours does not consider the input/output message schema when generating the plan, though their system does give alert of missing message to the users. This is important because an operation's precondition may be satisfied even when there is no suitable data for its input message. Another limitation of their work is that the only workflow pattern their system can generate is sequence, although the composite process may contain other patterns. As the reader may observe from the motivation scenario, other patterns such as loops are also frequently used.

Duan et al. [10] discuss using the pre and post-conditions of actions to do automatic synthesis of Web services. This is initiated by finding a backbone path. One weakness of their work is the assumption that task predicates are associated with ranks (positive integers). Their algorithm gives priority to the tasks with higher rank. However, this is clearly invalid if the Web services are developed by independent organizations, which is the common case and the main reason leading to heterogeneities.

Pistore et al. [11] propose an approach to planning using model checking. They encode OWL-S process models as state transition systems and claim their approach can handle non-determinism, partial observability, and complex goals. However, their approach relies on the specification of OWL-S process models, i.e., the users need to specify the interaction between the operations. This may not be a realistic requirement in a real world scenario where multiple processes are implemented by different vendors.

6.3 Motivating Scenario

The 2006 SWS Challenge mediation scenario version 1 is a typical real-world problem where distributed organizations are trying to communicate with each others . A customer (depicted on the left side of the figure) desires to purchase goods from a provider (depicted on the right side of the figure). The anticipated process, i.e., the answer of this problem, is depicted on the middle of the figure which should be generated by a mediation system automatically. Both process and data heterogeneities exist in this scenario. For instance, from the point of view of the service requester called Blue, placing an order is a one-step job (send PO), while the service provider called Moon, involves four operations (searchCustomer, createNewOrder, addLineItem, and closeOrder). The message schemas they use are not exactly the same. For example, Blue uses fromRole to specify the partner who wants to place an order, while Moon uses billTo to mean the same thing. The structures of the message schemas are also different. To make matters worse, an input message may involves information from two or more output message, for example, the operation addLineItem requires information from the order request message by Blue and the newly created order ID from the output message of operation createNewOrder. In order to solve this problem successfully and automatically, the composition system at least should be able to do the following: generate the control flow of the mediator that involves at least two workflow patterns (Sequence and Loop) based on the specification of the task and the candidate Web service(s), and convert (and combine if needed) an input message to an acceptable format annotated with appropriate semantics.

6.4 Declarative Approach towards Solution

One of the evaluation measures to determine the efficiency of the composition approach is the ability to manage change with minimal programming efforts. Systems developed using conventional approaches where the requirements and the services are not externalized from the actual system itself, may often prove to be inflexible. To overcome this limitation, we adopt an declarative approach to capture the requirements of the process and the service description of partner services. Our system generates a plan based on the requirement and discovers partner services based on their descriptions. A Web process is then generated that can be deployed and executed. When there is a change in the requirement, a new process can be generated using the changed requirements. The requirements are captured as semantic template and partner services are described using SAWSDL. The non-functional properties of both the requirement and the service can be captured using WS-Policy. We define a new class of assertions called business assertions that can be added to WS-Policy to describe business level non-functional properties such as shipment destinations and shipment weight. It is our belief that the availability of visual XML editors and WSDL editors would make it easier to change these specifications. Further, this externalization eliminates re-compilation of the system for each change.

6.4.1 Semantic Templates

A semantic template captures the functional and non-functional requirements of a service requestor. It allows service requesters to semantically describe their requirements. Similar to SAWSDL the semantics are captured using the model reference attribute.The elements in a semantic template are the template term, operation, input, output, and term policy. The model reference attribute in a template term captures the domain requirement which is a concept in a classification hierarchy such as the NAICS industry classification hierarchy. In addition to the domain attribute, a template term also consists of one or more operations. The model reference attribute in the operation element carries a reference to a concept in a semantic meta-model that provides a richer description of the operation including its behavioral aspects. Each operation element has input and output elements. The model reference attribute of the input and the output elements is a concept in the semantic meta-model that describes their schema. The non-functional requirements are captured using the term policy element. Each term policy element is a collection of assertions. The term policy element can be attached to a operation, template term or to the entire semantic template. [12] and [13] discuss the Semantic Template in great detail. However for the sake of clarity and completion we describe the semantic template briefly.

Formally semantic templates are defined by:

Definition 1. *A semantic template ψ is a collection of template terms* $= \{\theta | \theta$ *is a template term*$\}$. *A template term* $\theta = \{\omega, M_r^\omega, I_\omega, O_\omega, \pi_\omega, p_\omega, e_\omega\}$ *is a 7-tuple with:*

- ω: *the operation*
- M_r^ω: *set of operation model references*
- I_ω: *operation inputs and their model references*
- O_ω: *operation outputs and their model references*
- π_ω: *operation level term policy and the non-functional semantics*
- p_ω: *operation precondition*
- e_ω: *operation effect*

The template term $\theta_s = \{\epsilon, \epsilon, \epsilon, \epsilon, \pi_s, \epsilon, \epsilon\}$ *defining just the term policy defines semantic template wide term policies.*

Figure 6.1 illustrates the conceptual model of a semantic template.

6.4.2 Business assertions in WS-Policy

The motivating scenario illustrates the importance to model the non-functional properties towards enhancing the discovery of partner services. In this section we present our approach to declaratively specify the non-functional properties of both a request as well as a service. The WS-Policy specification provides a flexible grammar for describing the non-functional properties. The WS-Policy specification defines a policy as a collection of alternatives; each policy alternative is a collection of assertions [14]. Leveraging this flexibility, we define a new class of assertions called business assertions to capture business level non-functional metrics. Examples of these metrics in the Muller service include maximum weight of shipment and shipping destinations. When used by service providers, they are attached to the SAWSDL service descriptions in the same manner as WS-Policy, using WS-PolicyAttachment.The elements of a business assertion are described in Table 6.1. These assertions are illustrated in the business policy example in Figure 6.2

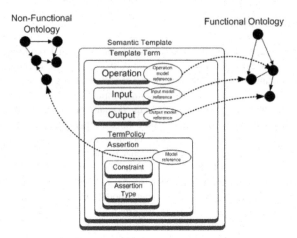

Fig. 6.1. Conceptual Model of Semantic templates

6.4.3 Formal model of abstract Web services:

WSDL is a widely accepted industry standard (a W3C recommendation) for describing Web services. SAWSDL is expressive for functional and data semantics, and sufficient to solve the problem of semantic discovery and data mediation. We extend SAWSDL by adding pre-conditions and effects in the operations for process mediation. Preconditions and effects are necessary because not all the states of a Web service are represented by the input/output message. For example, both a book buying service and book renting service may take as the input the user ID and the ISBN, and give as the output the status *succeed* or *fail*. Importance of pre-condition and effects have been recognized by major semantic Web services initiatives including OWL-S, WSMO and WSDL-S, here we do that by extending the emerging standard of SAWSDL.

For the purpose of service composition, our model only focuses on the abstract representation of Web services, i.e., operations and messages, but does not consider the binding detail. Before giving our formal model, we need to introduce some definitions of the basic building blocks. Most classic AI planning problems are defined by the STRIPS representational language (or its variants like ADL), which divides its representational scheme into three components, namely, states, goals, and actions. For the domain of Web service composition, we extend the STRIPS language as the representational language of our method.

- **Extended state:** We extend a state by adding a set of semantic data types in order to ensure that the data for the input message of an operation is available before the operation is invoked. An extended state s has two components: s = <SSF, SDT >, where:
  - SSF is a set of status flags, each of which is an atomic statement with a URI in a controlled vocabulary. SSF defines the properties of the world in the specific state. We use ternary logic for status flags, thus the possible truth values are True, False, and Unknown. We use the open-world assumption, i.e., any status flag not mentioned in the state has the value unknown.
  - SDT is a set of semantic data types representing the availability of data. A semantic data type is a membership statement in Description Logic of a class (or a union of

Business As-sertion Element	Definition	Example
Assertion Ex-presssion	captures a unit assertion. Assertion expressions can either be quantitative or logical.The *ignorable* tag from the WS-Policy specification can be added to an assertion expression to indicate that the assertion encapsulated in this expression can be ignored during policy matching.	
Assertion Concept	The *ontology concept* that describes the entity of the assertion	
Assertion Operator	The fulfillment condition that this assertion will satisfy in case of a guarantee or the condition that needs to be satisfied in case of a requirement	In the cost constraint illustrated in the above example, the lessthan operator is the assertion operator.
Assertion Constraint	Captures the value of the assertion expression. Each assertion constraint has a constraint value and a unit that denotes the unit in which the constraint is expressed in.	In the cost constraint illustrated in the above example, 50 is the constraint value and Amer-icanDollar is the unit. The unit is usually a ontology concept. This mapping allows us to represent unit conversion rules in the ontology.
Assertion Options	When the assertion expression can have multiple values, one or more either is guaranteed or required, they are represented as options. Options contains assertion constraints	In the business assertion example, the provider agrees to a 2 day shipping if express shipping option is chosen and a 5 day delivery if priority shipping is chosen.

Table 6.1. Elements in a Business Assertion

classes) in an ontology. An example state could be: $<\{$ orderComplete=True, order-Closed=False $\}, \{$ ontology1#OrderID$(Msg_1)\} >$

The reason why we use predicate logic for status flags is because it is simple for the user to specify the values of status flags in predicate logic, and computationally efficient. On the other hand, we use description logic for semantic data types since it makes it easier to express relationships such as sub-class relationships.

- **Abstract semantic Web service** [13]: Our definition of an abstract semantic Web service is built upon SAWSDL [8] An abstract semantic Web service SWS can be represented as a vector: $SWS = (sop_1, sop_2, , sop_n)$ Each sop is a semantic operation, which is defined as a 6-tuple: sop = $<op, in, out, pre, eff, fault>$where,
  - *op* is the semantic description of the operation. It is a membership statement of a class or property in an ontology.
  - *in* is the semantic description of the input message. It is a set of semantic data types, stating what data are required in order to execute the operation.

```
<wspba:businessAssertion>
  <wspba:assertionExpression type="OWLPolicy#QuantitativeAssertionType">
    <wspba:assertionConcept>QoSOWL#ProductCost</wspba:constraintConcept>
    <wspba:assertionOperator>QoSOWL#LessthanOperator</wspba:constraintConcept>
    <wspba:assertionConstraint>
      <wspba:constraintValue>1200</wspba:constraintValue>
      <wspba:constraintUnit>OWLUnits#AmericanDollar</wspba:constraintUnit>
    </wspba:assertionConstraint>
    <wspba:assertionStatus>OWLPolicy#PolicyGuarantee</wspba:constraintType>
  </wspba: businessAssertion>
<wspba:businessAssertion>
  <wspba:assertionExpression type="OWLPolicy#LogicalAssertionType">
    <wspba:assertionConcept>QoSOWL#CreditRating</wspba:assertionConcept>
    <wspba:assertionOperator>QoSOWL#AtLeastEquals</wspba:assertionOperator>
    <wspba:assertionConstraint>
      <wspba:constraintValue>AAA+</wspba:constraintValue>
      <wspba:constraintUnit>OWLUnits#DUNS-Rating</wspba:constraintUnit>
    </wspba:assertionConstraint>
    <wspba:assertionExpression>
    <wspba:assertionStatus>OWLPolicy#PolicyRequirement</wspba:assertionStatus>
  </wspba: businessAssertion>
  <wspba: businessAssertion>
    <wspba:assertionOptions>
      <wspba:assertionGroup>
        <wspba:assertionExpression type="OWLPolicy#LogicalAssertionType">
          <wspba:assertionConcept>OWL-QoS#ShipmentType</wspba:constraintConcept>
          <wspba:assertionOperator>QoSOWL#EqualOperator</wspba:constraintConcept>
          <wspba:assertionConstraint>
            <wspba:constraintValue>QoSOWL#Priority</wspba:constraintValue>
          </wspba:assertionConstraint>
        </wspba:assertionExpression>
        <wspba:assertionExpression type="OWLPolicy#QuantitativeAssertionType">
          <wspba:assertionConcept>OWL-QoS#ShipmentTime</wspba:constraintConcept>
          <wspba:assertionOperator>QoSOWL#EqualOperator</wspba:constraintConcept>
          <wspba:assertionConstraint>
            <wspba:constraintValue>5</wspba:constraintValue>
            <wspba:constraintUnit>OWLUnits#BusinessDays</wspba:constraintUnit>
          </wspba:assertionConstraint>
        </wspba:assertionExpression>
      </wsbpa:assertionGroup>
      <wspba:assertionGroup>
        <wspba:assertionExpression type="OWLPolicy#LogicalAssertionType">
          <wspba:assertionConcept>OWL-QoS#ShipmentType</wspba:constraintConcept>
          <wspba:assertionOperator>QoSOWL#EqualOperator</wspba:constraintConcept>
          <wspba:assertionConstraint>
            <wspba:constraintValue>QoSOWL#Express</wspba:constraintValue>
          </wspba:assertionConstraint>
        </wspba:assertionExpression>
        <wspba:assertionExpression type="OWLPolicy#QuantitativeAssertionType">
          <wspba:assertionConcept>OWL-QoS#ShipmentTime</wspba:constraintConcept>
          <wspba:assertionOperator>QoSOWL#EqualOperator</wspba:constraintConcept>
          <wspba:assertionConstraint>
            <wspba:constraintValue>2</wspba:constraintValue>
            <wspba:constraintUnit>OWLUnits#BusinessDays</wspba:constraintUnit>
          </wspba:assertionConstraint>
        </wspba:assertionExpression>
      </wspba:assertionGroup>
      <wspba:assertionStatus>QoSOWL#PolicyGuarantee</wspba:assertionStatus>
  </wspba:businessAssertion>
```

Fig. 6.2. Example Business Policy

- *out* is the semantic description of the output message. It is a set of semantic data types, stating what data are produced after the operation is executed.
- *pre* is the semantic description of the precondition. It is a formula in predicate logic of status flags representing the required values of the status flags in the current state before an operation can be executed.
- *eff* is the semantic description of the effect. It can be divided into two groups: positive effects and negative effects, each of which is a set of status flags describing how the status flags in a state change when the action is executed.
- *fault* is the semantic description of the exceptions of the operation represented using classes in an ontology.

Table 6.2 illustrates an example of the representation of part of the Order Management System Web service described in our running scenario.

sop	sop_1	sop_2	sop_3
op	CreateNewOrder	AddLineItem	CloseOrder
in	CustomerID	LineItemEntry,Order	OrderID
out	OrderID	AddItemResult	ConfirmedOrder
pre		orderComplete $\wedge$ orderClosed	orderComplete $\wedge$ orderClosed
eff	negative:{orderComplete, orderClosed}	positive:{orderComplete}	positive: { orderClosed }
fault	sop_1 fault	sop_2 fault	sop_3 fault

Table 6.2. Representation of Order Management System Web service

6.5 Discovering Services

In this section we discuss the hierarchy-based matching algorithm. for discovering services The algorithm exploits the hierarchical structure of service definitions and the semantic template to compute the level of similarity between them. We define a mapping between the elements in the service structure hierarchy and the elements in the structure hierarchy of the semantic template. This mapping is illustrated in Figure 6.3. The elements in the service structure hierarchy are then compared with their mapped counterparts in the structural hierarchy of the semantic template.

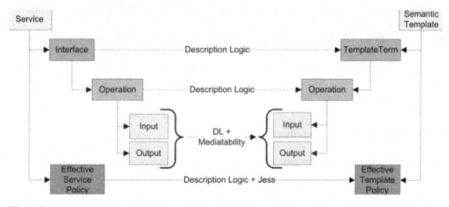

Fig. 6.3. Mapping Between Elements in Service Structure Hierarchy and Semantic Template Hierarchy

6.5.1 Overview of the Hierarchy-based Matching Algorithm

Adopting an approach that exploits the hierarchy found in service descriptions allows us to customize the comparison technique for each of the service elements. While techniques based on description logic can help in determining the semantic similarity and can be used in matching the interface and operation elements. They would not be sufficient for matching the data objects , however, because when comparing data objects one must also consider the structural similarity between them in addition to the semantic similarity.

We define a weighted scheme to compute the match score. The weights are determined by the *matchlevel* attribute of each element defined in the semantic template. This weighted scheme is used in ranking the discovered services. The rest of this section discusses the matching approach for different elements and the ranking of discovered services.

6.5.2 Description Logic Based Matching

We employ a description logic-based matching for identifying the semantic similarity between the ontological concepts captured in the modelreference attributes of the elements in the service structure and semantic template hierarchies. The similarity measure can be one of *subsumption-similar*, *equivalence*, or *generalized-similar* defined as:

- **Equivalence**: The interface element is equivalent to the templateterm element, if the ontological concepts represented by their respective modelreferences are either the same or equivalent. The equivalence measure is similarly defined for operations, input and output elements.
- **Generalized-Similar**: The interface element is *generalized-similar* to the templateterm element , if the ontology concept represented by modelreference attribute of the interface element *subsumes* the ontology concept represented by the modelreference attribute of the templateterm element. For example, a service whose domain is electronics would be *generalized-similar* to a semantic template for personal computers since electronics subsumes personal computers in the NAICS ontology illustrated in The *generalized-similar* measure is similarly defined for operations, input and output elements..
- **Subsumption-Similar**: The interface element is *subsumption-similar* to the templateterm element , if the ontology concept represented by modelreference attribute of the interface element *is subsumed by* the ontology concept represented by the modelreference attribute of the templateterm element. The *subsumption-similar* measure is similarly defined for operations, input, and output elements.

6.5.3 Non-functional Matching

In this section we describe the approach to matching non-functional requirements during service discovery. Non functional requirements consist of certain quality of service (QoS) guarantees the service provider advertices and possibly the service requestor would expect other than the functional capabilities such as security and reliability. These non-functional aspects are usually expressed using policies. To match non-functional requirements, we match the policies of the provider and the requestor. We first create the normalized effective policy for the operations in the service and in the semantic template. The procedure for creating the normalized policy is described in [14]. The effective policy of a service operation is the disjunction of the service policy, the interface policy and the operation policy. The normalized effective policy of a service operation is the normalized form of the effective policy of the operation. We define this policy as the effective provider policy. The effective policy of a semantic template operation is the disjunction of the template policy, templateterm policy and the operation policy. The normalized effective policy of a semantic template operation is the normalized form of the effective policy of the operation. We define this as the effective requestor policy. [14] describes two modes for policy matching: (1) The *Lax* mode in which assertions marked

Requestor Assertion Operator	Provider Assertion Operator	Jess Rule	Example
$<, >, \leq$	$<, >, \leq, \geq$ $=$	(Requestor Assertion Operator, Provider Assertion Value, Requestor Assertion Value)	Requestor assertion expression: Memory >512 MB; Provider assertion expression: Memory $<2GB$;Jess rule: $(>, 2048, 512)$.
$=$	$<, \leq, >, \geq,$ $=$	(Inverse of provider operator, Provider Assertion Value, Requestor Assertion Value)	Requestor assertion expression: Memory $= 512$ MB; Provider assertion expression: Memory $<2GB$;Jess rule: $(>, 2048, 512)$.

Table 6.3. Generating Jess Rules From Assertion Expressions

as *ignorable* can be ignored. It is not necessary for such assertions to match for the policies to match and (2) The *Strict* mode in which all the assertions must match for the two policies to match. In our policy matching approach we adopt the lax mode.

Given two policies, the first step is to identify the equivalent business assertions. This is done by comparing the assertion concept elements of the business assertions in the two policies. Two business assertions are equivalent if the ontology concepts described in their assertion concept elements are equivalent. The two policies are said to match, if all pairs of equivalent assertions that are not ignorable match. To match a pair of equivalent business assertions, we first identify the type of the assertion expression. If the assertion expression is quantitative, then they are compared using the Jess framework. Assertion expressions that are logical are compared using description logics.

In case of quantitative assertion expressions, we first ensure that both expressions are expressed in the same assertion unit. If not, we convert the provider assertion expression into the same unit as the requestor assertion expression. We assume that the rules for unit conversion are modeled in the ontology.Once the units are normalized, a Jess is rule is created from the assertion expressions. This rule is evaluated and if it evaluates to True, then we say the assertions match. The approach to creating the rule is determined by the assertion operator of the assertion expression obtained from the effective requestor policy. This is described in Table 6.3. The assertions expressions are said to match if the rule can be asserted.

Logical expressions are evaluated using description logics. If the provider assertion value subsumes or is equivalent to the requestor assertion, then we deem the expressions are a complete match. If the requestor assertion value subsumes that of the provider, then we deem it a partial match. If the subsumption or equivalence relationship cannot be determined between the provider and requestor assertion units, we check if there is a property in the schema that relates the assertion concept elements. If such a property P exists, we check if P holds between the provider and requestor assertion values. We deem a match, if P holds. The following example illustrates this better. The provider assertion expression is : Shipment destination is Europe. The client assertion expression is: Shipment destination is Germany. The provider assertion unit is a continent and the requestor assertion unit is a country. From the ontology

(ISOCountries.rdf available at the web resource[4]), we identify that *belongs_to* property exists between country and continent. We check in the ontology, if Germany *belongs_to* Europe. Since it does, we deem it a match.

6.6 Automatic Web service composition

6.6.1 Formal definition of Web service composition

A semantic Web service composition problem involves composing a set of semantic Web services (SWSs) to fulfill the given requirements, or in our case a Semantic Template. Figure 6.4 illustrates our approach.

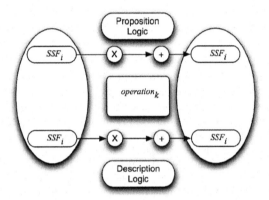

Fig. 6.4. Business Process Levels

A semantic operation ($Operation_k$ in figure 6.4) has to be checked by the *satisfy* operator (X in figure 6.4)against the current extended state before it can be added in the process specification. After it is added, a successor extended state is created by applying the *apply* (+ in figure 6.4) operator. We will give the formal definition of *satisfy* and *apply* operators below. For convenience, we use the following notations.

Satisfy operator is a function mapping an extended state s_i and a semantic operation sop_k to T or F. Formally $textitsatisfy$ is defined as:

Definition 2. *satisfy:* $(s_i, sop_k) \rightarrow \{T, F\}$
This function maps to T (in such case, s_i satisfies sop_k and is written as: $s_i \times sop_k$) if and only if:

- $\epsilon(Pre(sop_k), SSF(s_i)) = True$, *where $\epsilon(f, v)$ is an evaluation of formula f based on the truth values in v.*
- $(Onto \cup SDT(s_i)) \models in(sop_k)$, *where Onto is the ontology schema for semantic data types.*

---

[4] http://knoesis1.wright.edu/swsc/

Notation	Explanation
SSF(s)	The set of status flags of extended state s
Value(s)	The truth value of a status flag sf in extended state s
SDT(s)	The set of semantic data types of extended state s
in(sop)	The input messages of semantic operation sop
pre(sop)	The output messages of semantic operation sop
eff(sop)	The effect of semantic operation sop
positive(eff)	The positive effects of eff
negative(eff)	The negative effects of eff

Table 6.4. Representation of Order Management System Web service

That is, the precondition of sop_k holds based on the truth values of the status flags in state s_i, and the semantic data types of s_i together with the ontology schema entails the input of sop_k. For example, the following state satisfy the operation sop_3 in table 6.2:

¡ $\{orderComplete = True, orderClosed = False\}, \{ontology1\#OrderID(Msg_x)\}$¿

Here the semantic data type *OrderID* comes from an output message of any previous operation, or the initial message of the Semantic Template, so we put Msg_x in the above example.

Apply operator is a function mapping an extended state si and a semantic operation sop_k to a new extended state s_j. Formally this is defined as

Definition 3. *apply:* $(s_i, sop_k) \rightarrow s_j$
Alternatively, we write $s_i + sop_k \rightarrow s_j$ *This operator does the transition both on status flags and semantic data types.*

- *For status flags:*

$$\forall sf \in positive(eff(sop_k)), value(sf, s_j) = True$$
$$\forall sf \in negative(eff(sop_k)), value(sf, s_j) = False$$
$$\forall sf \in (eff(sop_k)), sf(s_j) = sf(s_i)$$

That is, a status flag in the positive effects is true in s_j, a status flag in the negative effects is false in s_j, while any status flag in s_i but not in the effect is assumed to be unchanged in s_j.
- *For semantic data types:* $SDT(s_j) = SDT(s_i) \cup out(sop_k)$ *That is, the semantic data types (membership statements) in s_j are the union of the semantic data types in s_i and the output of sop_k.*

As an example, if we apply the operation sop_3 in 6.2 to the state

$$< \{orderComplete = True, orderClosed = False\}, \{ontology1\#OrderID(Msgx)\} >$$

we will get a new state:

$$< \{orderComplete = True, orderClosed = True\}, \{$$
$$ontology1\#OrderID(Msgx),$$
$$ontology1\#ConfirmedOrder(sop_3OutMsg)\} >$$

6.6.2 Composition of semantic Web services

We consider a SWS composition problem as an AI planning problem such that the semantic operation template defines the initial state and the goal state of the problem specification: **Initial state** is the extended state at the beginning of the process. It is defined by the precondition and initial message of the semantic operation template ψ.

$$s_0 = < ssf_0(sopt), in(sopt) >$$

Goal state is a requirement of the extended state at the end of the process. It is defined by the goal and output of sopt.

$$goalstate = < gl(sopt), out(sopt) >$$

Composition of semantic Web services is a function

$$swsc : (sopt, SWS_s) \rightarrow plan$$

Where,

- sopt is a semantic operation template.
- SWSs is the set of the semantic operations in the semantic Web services.
- *plan* is a DAG (Directed Acyclic Graph) of operations. Every topological sort of the DAG (say one of them is $sop_1, sop_2, , sop_n$) must conform to the following restrictions:
  - $s_0 \times_i pre(sop_1), in(sop_1) \; \xi$
  - $s_0 + sop_1 \rightarrow s_1$
  - $s_{i-1} \times_i pre(sop_i), in(s_i) \; \xi$
  - $s_{i-1} + sop_1 \rightarrow s_i$
  - $s_n \times goalstate$

That is, every topological sort of the plan must transform the initial state into the goal state by conforming to the *satisfy* and *apply* operators. Loops are generated in a post-process step that is explained in section 6.6.6.

6.6.3 Planning For Process Mediation

AI planning is a way to generate a process automatically based on the specification of a problem. Planners typically use techniques such as progression (or forward state-space search), regression (or backward state-space search), and partial-ordering. These techniques attempt to use exploration methods such as searching, backtracking, and/or branching techniques in order to extract such a solution. There are two basic operations in every state-space-based planning approach. First, the precondition of an action needs to be checked to make sure it is satisfied by the current state before the operation can be a part of the plan. Second, once the operation is put into the plan, its effect should be applied to the current state and thus produce a consecutive state. We address the significant differences between classic AI planning and semantic Web service composition as follows:

1. Actions in AI planning can be described completely by its name, precondition, and effect, while Web services also include input and/or output message schema.

2. For AI planning, it is assumed that there is an agreement within an application on the terms in the precondition and effect. Terms with same name (string) mean the same thing, while terms with different name (string) mean different things. For example, in the famous block world scenario, if both block and box exist in the precondition/effect, they are treated as different things. This obviously does not carry over to the resources on the Web, thus it is necessary to introduce semantics in Web service composition.

3. More workflow patterns such as loops are desired in Web service composition. We address this problem by a pattern-based approach.

As discussed in the previous sections, both Web services and the specification of the task, i.e., Semantic Template are described in extended SAWSDL standard, so the terms in the precondition, effect, and input/output messages reach an agreement which is captured by the ontologies. For the first two types of differences we mentioned above, to apply AI planning techniques to semantic Web service composition, any state-space-based planning algorithm needs to be revised according to the following criteria.

1. State space should include status flags, as in the existing AI planning approaches, and semantic data types to represent the availability of data.

2. For each candidate action, besides checking its precondition against the status flags in the current state, it is also necessary to check its input message schema against the semantic data types in the current state. This reduces the search space and eliminates plans containing operations whose input message is unavailable in the state.

3. Since the states and the actions/operations are semantically annotated by referring to ontologies, the checking in the previous step involves reasoning based on the ontologies, not just comparing the name of the terms.

4. Once an action/operation is added into the plan, not only the status flags are updated by applying the effect, the semantic data types should also be updated by put a new semantic data type based on the output message schema.

6.6.4 Discovering Services

6.6.5 Extended GraphPlan Algorithm

Although most AI planning algorithms are suitable for the task here, we use GraphPlan algorithm [7]. It is sound and complete thus we can always construct correct plans if there exist any, and its compact representation of the states makes it space efficient while doing a breadth-first style search. It also uses mutex links to avoid exploring some irrelevant search space. Like other classical AI planning algorithms, GraphPlan only considers the precondition and effect of actions, thus does not take into account the input/output message of actions. Our approach requires an extension of the algorithm to accommodate the semantic data types defined above. An operation may only be added in the next action level when its preconditions hold based on the current state level of the planning graph and the data types of the input message of the operation can be entailed by the union of ontology and the current state level. When an operation is placed in the next action level, its effects as well as output data types are applied to the current state level, and thus produce the next state level. Afterwards, mutex links between actions must be evaluated and placed so that they may be used when backtracking through the graph for the solution. Note that the creation of the mutex links should also consider the semantic data types accordingly.

6.6.6 Pattern-Based Approach For Loop Generation

GraphPlan algorithm may generate plans only with sequence and AND-split workflow patterns [15]. However, loops are also a frequently used pattern. Loop generation (or iterative planning) itself is a difficult and open problem in AI. Much work on iterative planning is based on theorem-proving [16]. It is believed by Stephan and Biundo [17] and other researchers that iterative planning cannot be carried out in a fully automatic way. [18] proposes a new way that is not tied to proving a theorem, but it is only correct for a given bound or a certain class of simple planning problems. Here we proposed a pattern-based approach for loop generation. It is based on the observation of frequently used patterns of iterations. For example, in the motivation scenario, the order request includes multiple line items (an array of line items) while the addLineItem operation takes as input only one line item. It is obvious that the process needs to iterate all the line items in the order request. We may extract the pattern as follows. If an operation has an input message including an element with semantic annotation SDT_i and attribute maxOccurs in XML Schema whose value is 1, while the matched (see satisfy operator) semantic data type in the current state is from an output message where the corresponding element in that message has maxOccurs with value unbounded or greater than 1, then a loop is needed for this operation to iterate the array. Our approach avoids the computationally hard problem by restricting possible patterns of loops. The limitation is that the patterns need to be identified and put in the code beforehand.

Lifting and Lowering Mechanism of Data Mediation

The data mediation approach is primarily based on the lifting and lowering mechanism presented in [8]. This section looks in detail of how this lifting and lowering mapping schema functions. The base technique is to convert the message into an intermediate semantic data model and re-convert the semantic data model back into the required specific format. Converting from the message to the intermediate model is known as *lifting* and the reverse conversion is known as lowering. It is important to note that the data heterogeneities cannot be overcome merely by attaching an ontology reference. These conversions require specific references to templates or other conversion resources in order to carry out the lifting and lowering. Due to the use of XML as the primary message format, the most commonly used intermediate model is also XML and hence the conversion references are often references to XSLT documents.

To understand the importance of this approach rather than the direct use of XSLT to transform between each and every message format consider the following example. Given that there are five heterogeneous (but convertible) messages that requires conversion from message A. If direct conversion is used this requires ten conversion specifications. If the intermediate semantic model is used this conversion would require a total of twelve conversion specifications. The advantage of the intermediate model can be seen when there is another message added along with A. This will double the number of conversion specifications if direct conversion is used. However if the intemediate model is used it results only in the addition of two new conversion specifications. It can be clearly seen that the intermediate model approach is the scalable mediation strategy.

in Figure 6.5 we describe the different heterogeneities that can exist between two XML schemas and how such heterogeneities can effect the mediations as discussed in [19]

Heterogeneities / Conflicts	Examples - conflicted elements shown in color		Mediatability
Attribute level Incompatibilities – *differences that arise because of using different descriptions for semantically similar attributes*			
Naming conflicts Two attributes that are semantically alike might have different names (synonyms) Two attributes that are semantically unrelated might have the same names (homonyms)	*Web service 1* Student(Id#, Name) *Web service 1* Student(Id#, Name)	*Web service 2* Student(SSN, Name) *Web service 2* Book (Id#, Name)	
Data representation conflicts Two attributes that are semantically similar have different data types or representations	*Web service 1* Student(Id#, Name) Id# defined as a 4 digit number	*Web service 2* Student(Id#, Name) Id# defined as a 9 digit number	* Mapping WS2 Id# to WS1 Id# is easy with some additional context information while mapping in the reverse direction is most likely not possible.
Data scaling conflicts Two attributes that are semantically similar might be represented using different precisions	*Web service 1* Marks 1-100	*Web service 2* Grades A-F	* Mapping WS1 Marks to WS1 Grades is easy with some additional context information while mapping in the reverse direction is most likely not possible.
Entity level Incompatibilities – *differences that arise because of using different descriptions for semantically similar entities*			
Naming conflicts Semantically alike entities might have different names (synonyms) Semantically unrelated entities might have the same names (homonyms)	*Web service 1* EMPLOYEE (Id#, Name) *Web service 1* TICKET (TicketNo, MovieName)	*Web service 2* WORKER (Id#, Name) *Web service 2* TICKET (FlightNo, Arr. Airport, Dep. Airport)	A semantic annotation on the entities and attributes (provided by *SAWSDL.modelReference*) will indicate their semantic similarities.
Schema Isomorphism conflicts Semantically similar entities may have different number of attributes	*Source* PERSON (Name, Address, HomePhone, WorkPhone)	*Target* PERSON (Name, Address, HomePhone)	The additional information from the source that is not in the target can be disregarded. Hence mediatability is 1.
Abstraction Level Incompatibility – *Entity and attribute level differences that arise because two semantically similar entities or attributes are represented at different levels of abstraction*			
Generalization conflicts Semantically similar entities are represented at different levels of generalization in two Web services	*Web service 1* GRAD-STUDENT (ID, Name, Major)	*Web service 2* STUDENT(ID, Name, Major, Type)	* WS2 defines the student entity at a much general level. A mapping from WS1 to WS2 requires adding a Type element with a default 'Graduate' value, while mapping in the other direction is a partial function.
Aggregation conflicts Two semantically similar entities, one represented as an aggregate of another	*Web service 1* PROFESSOR (ID, Name, Dept)	*Web service 2* FACULTY (ID, ProfID, Dept)	* A set-of Professor entities is a Faculty entity. When the output of WS1 is a Professor entity, it is possible to identify the Faculty group it belongs to, but generating a mapping in the other direction is not possible.
Attribute Entity conflicts Semantically similar entity modeled as an attribute in one service and as an entity in the other	*Web service 1* COURSE (ID, Name, Semester)	*Web service 2* DEPT(Course, Sem, ...)	* Course modeled as an entity by WS1 is modeled as an attribute by WS2. With definition contexts, mappings can be specified in both directions.

* Interoperation between services needs transformation rules (mapping) in addition to annotation of the entities and/or attributes indicating their semantic similarity (matching).

Fig. 6.5. Different Heterogeneities

6.7 Conclusions and Future Work

This paper presents an automatic approach for Web service composition, while addressing the problem of process heterogeneities and data heterogeneities by using a planner and a data mediator. Specifically, an extended GraphPlan algorithm is employed to generate a BPEL process (the currently supported workflow patterns are sequence, AND-split and loop) based on the task specification (Semantic Template) and candidate Web services described in SAWSDL. Data mediation can be handled by assignment activities in the BPEL, or by a data mediator which may be embedded in a middleware or an externalized Web service. While the BPEL process is running, it calls the data mediator to convert (and combine if necessary) the available messages into the format of the input message of an operation which is going to be invoked. A context-based ranking algorithm is employed in the data mediator to select the best element from the source messages if more than one element has acceptable semantics for the target element.

Our experiment shows that our systems solved the problem in SWS challenge 2006 mediation scenario successfully, which is a non-trivial challenging problem that involves process and data heterogeneities. We consider our approach to be highly flexible, since the only thing a user need to change for a new scenario is the task specification (Semantic Template).

Our future work includes supporting more workflow patterns especially OR-Split, the propogation/scopes of semantic data types in messages, and non-functional semantics.

References

1. Sirin, E., Parsia, B., Wu, D., Hendler, J., Nau, D.: Htn planning for web service composition using shop2. Journal of Web Semantics **1**(4) (2004) 377–396
2. Narayanan, S., Mcilraith, S.A.: Simulation, verification and automated composition of web services. In: WWW '02: Proceedings of the 11th international conference on World Wide Web, New York, NY, USA, ACM Press (2002) 77–88
3. Rao, J., Dimitrov, D., Hofmann, P., Sadeh, N.: A mixed initiative approach to semantic web service discovery and composition: Sap's guided procedures framework. In: ICWS. (2006) 401–410
4. Ponnekanti, S.R., Fox, A.: Sword: A developer toolkit for web service composition. (2001)
5. Traverso, P., Pistore, M.: Automated composition of semantic web services into executable processes (2004)
6. Rao, J., Küngas, P., Matskin, M.: Logic-based web services composition: From service description to process model. In: ICWS. (2004) 446–453
7. Russell, S.J., Norvig, P.: Artificial Intelligence: A Modern Approach. Pearson Education (2003)
8. for WSDL, S.A., working group, X.S.: Semantic annotations for wsdl and xml schema. Technical report, W3 Consortium (2007)
9. Akkiraju, R., Farrell, J., Miller, J., Nagarajan, M., Schmidt, M., Sheth, A.P., Verma, K.: Web service semantics – wsdl-s. Technical report, LSDIS Lab and IBM Corporation (2004)
10. Duan, Z., Bernstein, A.J., Lewis, P.M., Lu, S.: A model for abstract process specification, verification and composition. In: ICSOC. (2004) 232–241
11. Pistore, M., Traverso, P., Bertoli, P., Marconi, A.: Automated synthesis of composite bpel4ws web services. In: ICWS. (2005) 293–301
12. Gomadam, K., Ranabahu, A., Ramaswamy, L., Sheth, A.P., Verma, K.: A Semantic Framework for Identifying Events in a Service Oriented Architecture. In: ICWS. (2007) 545–552
13. Verma, K.: Configuration And Adaptation of Semantic Web Processes. PhD thesis, University of Georgia (2006)
14. working group, W.S.P.: Web services policy 1.2 - framework (ws-policy)
15. van der Aalst, W., Hofstede, A.: Yawl: Yet another workflow language (2002)
16. Biundo, S.: Present-day deductive planning. In Bäckström, C., Sandewell, E., eds.: Current Trends in AI Planning: Proceedings of the 2nd European Workshop on Planning (EWSP-93), Vadstena, Sweeden, IOS Press (Amsterdam) (1994) 1–5
17. Stephan, W., Biundo, S.: Deduction-based refinement planning. Technical Report RR-95-13 (1995)
18. Levesque, H.J.: Planning with loops. In: IJCAI. (2005) 509–515
19. Nagarajan, M., Verma, K., Sheth, A.P., Miller, J.A., Lathem, J.: Semantic interoperability of web services - challenges and experiences. In: ICWS. (2006) 373–382

7

Automatic Generation of the SWS- Challenge Mediator with jABC/ABC

Tiziana Margaria[1], Marco Bakera[2], Christian Kubczak[2], Stefan Naujokat[2], and Bernhard Steffen[2]

[1] Chair of Service and Software Engineering, Universität Potsdam (Germany),
margaria@cs.uni-potsdam.de
[2] Chair of Programming Systems, TU Dortmund (Germany),
{marco.bakera, christian.kubczak, stefan.naujokat, steffen}@cs.
uni-dortmund.de

Summary. We show how to apply a tableau-based software composition technique to automatically generate the mediator's service logic, as a declarative alternative to the mediator solution presented in Chap. 5. Here we use an LTL planning (or configuration) algorithm originally embedded in the ABC and in the ETI platforms. The algorithm works on the basis of the existing jABC library of available services (SIB library) already introduced in Chap. 5, and it uses an enhanced description of their semantics that is given in terms of a taxonomic classification of their behaviour (modules) and abstract interfaces/messages (types). The resulting approach is a forward synthesis algorithm that users can configure to provide the set of shortest, or cycle-free, or all orchestrations, that satisfy the given LTL specification.

7.1 The SWS Challenge Mediator

The ongoing Sematic Web Service Challenge [22] proposes a number of increasingly complex scenarios for workflow-based service mediation and service discovery. We use here the technology presented in [11] to automatically generate (or synthesize) a process that realizes the communication layer for the Challenge's initial mediation scenario.

In this scenario, a customer (technically, a client) initiates a Purchase Order Request specified by a special message format (RosettaNet PIP3A4) and waits for a corresponding Purchase Order Confirmation according to the same RosettaNet standard. The seller however does not support this standard. Its backend system or server awaits an order in a proprietary message format and provides appropriate Web Services to serve the request in the proprietary format. As client and server here speak different languages, there is a need for a mediation layer that adapts both the data formats and also the granularity.

Of course we can easily define the concrete process within our jABC modelling framework, as we have shown in Chap. 5 and in the past [12, 6, 7].

To provide a more flexible solution framework, especially to accommodate later *declarative specification changes* on the backend side or on the data flow, we show here how to synthesize the whole mediator using the synthesis technology introduced in [11] and explained

module name	input type	output type	description
Mediator			Maps RosettaNet messages to the backend
startService	{*true*}	*PurOrderReq*	Receives a purchase order request message
obtCustomerID	*PurOrderReq*	*SearchString*	Obtains a customer search string from the req. message
createOrderUCID	*CustomerObject*	*CustomerID*	Gets the customer id out of the customer object
buildTuple	*OrderID*	*Tuple*	Builds a tuple from the orderID and the POR
sendLineItem	*Tuple*	*LineItem*	Gets a LineItem incl. orderID, articleID and quantity
closeOrderMed	*SubmConfObj*	*OrderID*	Closes an order on the mediator side
confirmLIOperation	*OrderConfObj*	*PurOrderCon*	Receives a conf. or ref. of a LineItem and sends a conf.
Moon			The backend system
searchCustomer	*SearchString*	*CustomerObject*	Gets a customer object from the backend database
createOrder	*CustomerID*	*OrderID*	Creates an order
addLineItem	*LineItem*	*SubmConfObj*	Submits a line item to the backend database
closeOrderMoon	*OrderID*	*TimeoutOut*	Closes an order on the backend side
confRefLineItem	*Timeout*	*orderConfObj*	Sends a conf. or ref. of a prev. subm. LineItem

Table 7.1. The SWS mediation Modules

in [9]. We proceed here exactly along the lines already presented in that paper.

In the following, we show in Sect. 7.2 how to use the SLTL synthesis methodology to generate the mediator workflow based on a knowledge base that expresses the semantics of the concrete types from the SWS mediator scenario, then in Sect. 7.3 we add a more business-level-like abstraction to the knowledge base, and in Sect. 7.4 we show how this leads to a looser solution, and how this solution can be step-wisely refined towards the first solution by adding business-level knowledge to the problem definition, in a declarative way. Subsequently, Sect. 7.5 describes how to work with the synthesis tool, Sect. 7.6 illustrates the plan generation, and Sect. 7.7 sketches the service-oriented realization of the synthesis process. Finally, Sect. 7.8 discusses related work and Sect. 7.9 draws some conclusions and sketches ongoing work.

7.2 The Concrete Mediator Workflow

7.2.1 Abstract Semantics: Taxonomies for Modules and Types

Table 7.1 shows the modules identified within the system. They represent at the semantic level the collection of basic services available for the mediator. In order to produce a running solution as demonstrated in Stanford in November they are then bound (grounded) to the concrete SIBs that in the jABC constitute the running services. How this happens is sketched in [19].

This information about the single modules is complemented by simple ontologies that express in terms of *is-a* and *has-a* relations properties over the types and the modules of the scenario. We call these relations Taxonomies. The taxonomies regarding the mediation scenario are shown in Fig. 7.1 (Type Taxonomy) and Fig. 7.2 (Module Taxonomy).

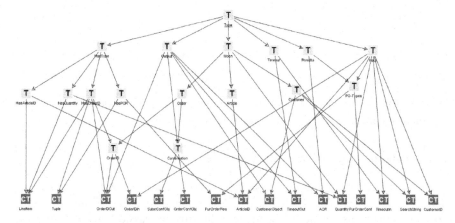

Fig. 7.1. The SWS Challenge Mediator Type Taxonomy

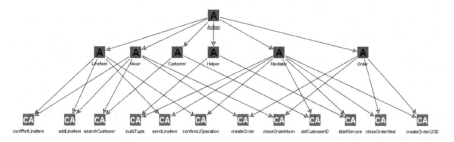

Fig. 7.2. The SWS Challenge Mediator Module Taxonomy

This information is expressed in a Prolog-like fashion in a concrete knowledge base which is used by the synthesys algorithm.

7.2.2 The Concrete Knowledge Base

The synthesis tool takes as input a textfile with the definitions of the taxonomies (module and type taxonomy), the module descriptions, and some documentation. The first line of the file declares a name for the knowledge base:

```
$program(sws_challenge).
```

The file contains statements (one per line) of facts in the following three forms:

- `tax(type, output, customerObject).`
- `tax(module, mediator, sendLineItem).`
- `module(searchCustomer, searchString, customerObject).`

The two first statements show how to specify the type and module taxonomy:

- The first line declares `customerObject` as a subtype of the `output` type.

- The second line declares module `sendLineItem` to be a `mediator` module.

The third statement form is used to specify the relation between input and output types for particular modules. It describes the module definition as already presented in Table 7.1: the `searchCustomer` module takes a `searchString` as input type and produces a `customerObject` output type.

This way it is possible to concisely represent the taxonomies of Fig. 7.1 and 7.2 as well as the module description of Table 7.1 in one single file.

7.2.3 Semantic Linear-time Temporal Logic

The loose specification language supported by the synthesis is the *Semantic Linear-time Temporal Logic* (SLTL)[16], a temporal (modal) logic comprising the taxonomic specifications of types and activities. This lifts the classical treatment of types and activities in terms of actions and propositions to a semantical level in a way typical today in the context of the semantic Web.

Definition 1 (SLTL).

The syntax of Semantic Linear-time Temporal Logic (SLTL) is given in BNF format by:

$$\Phi ::= \, \mathsf{type}(t_c) \mid \neg\Phi \mid (\Phi \wedge \Phi) \mid <a_c> \Phi \mid \mathbf{G}(\Phi) \mid (\Phi \mathbf{U} \Phi)$$

where t_c and a_c represent type and activity constraints, respectively, formulated as taxonomy expressions.

SLTL formulas are interpreted over the set of all *legal coordination sequences*, i.e. alternating type correct sequences of types and activities[3], which start and end with types. The semantics of SLTL formulas is now intuitively defined as follows[4]:

- $\mathsf{type}(t_c)$ is satisfied by every coordination sequence whose first element (a type) satisfies the type constraint t_c.

- Negation $\neg$ and conjunction $\wedge$ are interpreted in the usual fashion.

- Next-time operator $<>$:
  $<a_c> \Phi$ is satisfied by coordination sequences whose second element (the first activity) satisfies a_c and whose *continuation*[5] satisfies Φ. In particular, $<tt> \Phi$ is satisfied by every coordination sequence whose continuation satisfies Φ.

- Generally operator **G**:
  $\mathbf{G}(\Phi)$ requires that Φ is satisfied for every suffix[6] satisfies Φ.

---

[3] During the description of the semantics, types and activites will be called *elements* of the orchestration sequence.

[4] A formal definition of the semantics can be found online.

[5] This continuation is simply the coordination sequence starting from the third element.

[6] According to the difference between activity and type components, a suffix of a coordination sequence is any subsequence which arises from deleting the first 2n elements (n any natural number).

- Until operator **U**:
  (ΦUΨ) expresses that the property Φ holds at all type elements of the sequence, until a position is reached where the corresponding continuation satisfies the property Ψ. Note that ΦUΨ guarantees that the property Ψ holds eventually (strong until).

The definitions of continuation and suffix may seem complicated at first. However, thinking in terms of path representations clarifies the situation: a subpath always starts with a node (type) again. Users should not worry about these details: they may simply think in terms of pure activity compositions and should not care about the types, unless they explicitly want to specify type constraints.

The online introduction of *derived operators* supports a modular and intuitive formulation of complex properties.

7.2.4 Declarative LTL Specification for the Concrete Mediator

For the mediator, we look for a workflow (a service coordination) that satisfies the following requirement:

The mediator service should produce a Purchase Order Confirmation.

The corresponding formal specification formulated in SLTL is simple: we need to start the service (module **startService**) and reach the result `PurOrderCon` (a type). We may simply write: (`startService < PurOrderCon`) where the symbol < denotes a derived operator meaning *before* or *precedes* and is defined as

$$\mathtt{f1} < \mathtt{f2} =_{df} \mathbf{F}(\mathtt{f1} \wedge \mathbf{F}(\mathtt{f2}))$$

The jABC process model shown in Fig. 7.3(a) resembles very closely the expected required solution.

If we adopt the very fine granular model of the types shown in Table 7.1, a natural choice given the SWS Challenge problem description, this is in fact the only solution.

In this setting, we use abstract type names in the taxonomy to model de facto almost the concrete operational semantics: we distinguish for instance an `OrderID` from an `OrderConfObject`, modelling the described application domain at the concrete level of datatypes and objects - a direct rendering of what happens at the XML level, or for programs in the memory and on the heap. This is however already a technical view, and it corresponds to lifting the concrete, programming-level granularity of data to the semantic level: the resulting ontology is as concrete as the underlying program.

This is however not the intention of Service Orientation, nor of the semantic web: the idea there is to decouple the business-level view (captured at the semantic level) from the technical view of a specific implementation, in order to allow a coarser description of business-level workflows and processes that then must be concretized and grounded to a running implementation. In the following we show how this can be done, also including automatic synthesis.

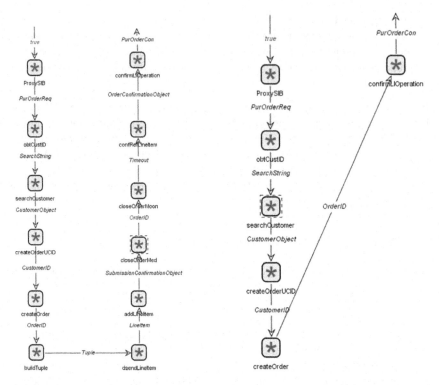

Fig. 7.3. (a) The synthesised SWS mediator (standard) and **(b)** Using loose types: the new solution

7.3 Abstract Semantics: Using Abstraction and Constraints

For a specifier and definer of the business domain it is much more realistic to say that the modules concerned with orders work on an `Order` type, which is a business-level abstraction for order-related objects and records, and to leave further distinctions to a problem-specific refinement of the desired solutions via constraints added separately at need.

For the abstract semantics we work on the taxonomies. The taxonomy design and module specification decides here the balance between concreteness and flexibility (looseness). In this specific case, we change the definition of the modules that deal with orders as shown in Table 7.2: they now operate on the abstract `Order` type. We can be as concrete, or as abstract and generic as we wish, and choose the suitable description level driven by the semantics or application domain modelling. This abstraction determines how much flexibility we build in into our solutions. At the one extreme we can have very specific types, as fine granular as a description in terms of structural operational semantics [13]. In this case, solutions are type-determined, and basically render the concrete labelled transition system underlying the manually programmed solution as in Fig. 7.3(a). At the other extreme one could also use one

module name	input type	output type	description
Mediator			Maps RosettaNet messages to the backend
buildTuple	*Order*	*Tuple*	Builds a tuple from the orderID and the POR
closeOrderMed	*SubmConfObj*	*Order*	Closes an order on the mediator side
confirmLIOperation	*Order*	*PurOrderCon*	Receives a conf. or ref. of a LineItem and sends a conf.
Moon			The backend system
createOrder	*CustomerID*	*Order*	Creates an order
closeOrderMoon	*Order*	*TimeoutOut*	Closes an order on the backend side
confRefLineItem	*Timeout*	*Order*	Sends a conf. or ref. of a prev. subm. LineItem

Table 7.2. The SWS Mediation Modules with abstract `Order`

generic type and model the process structure solely by means of temporal constraints. However, most flexible is a hybrid approach which combines loose taxonomies, types and module descriptions with temporal constraints in order to arrive at an adequate specification formalism.

No matter the choice, the algorithm covers the whole spectrum, leaving it free to the application domain designer to determine where to be precise and where to be loose, leaving space for exploring alternatives and tradeoffs.

7.4 A Loose Solution, and its Declarative Refinement

7.4.1 The base case

If we now solve the planning problem with the modified module description and the original goal, we obtain a much shorter solution, shown in Fig. 7.3(b). This is due to the fact that the module specifications now refer to the abstract type *Order*. As a consequence, closeOrderMoon is a suitable direct successor of createOrder. This solution corresponds to a degenerate workflow where an empty order is sent.

7.4.2 Refinement1: Nonempty Orders

Since in the normal case orders contain items, the business expert needs to be more precise in the specification of the solution, adding knowledge by means of SLTL constraints. If one just knows that the items are referred to via the LineItem type, one may simply refine the goal as follows:
      (startService < LineItem < PurOrderCon)
  This way, we have added as additional intermediate goal the use of a LineItem type. Accordingly, at least one of the modules {addLineItem, sendlineItem} must appear in the required minimal workflow. We see the result in Fig. 7.4(a): this solution coincides with the previous one till the createOrder module, then the type mediator buildTuple is added, after which sendLineItem satisfies the intermediate goal. The remaining constraint at that point is simply the reaching of the final type

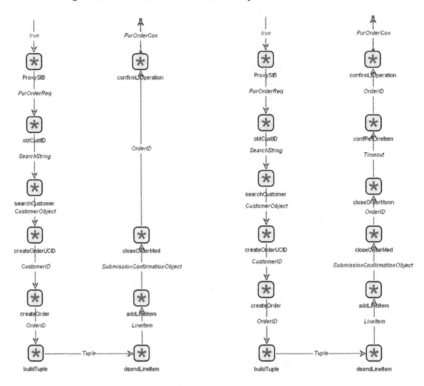

Fig. 7.4. (a) Adding a LineItem: the new solution and **(b)** Adding a Confirmation: the complete loose solution

PurOrderCon, which is done by generating the sequence CloseOrderMediator followed by CloseOrder.

This solution however corresponds only to the first part of the Web service realizing the mediator. There is in fact a subsequent second service that realizes the confirmation part of the mediator.

7.4.3 Refinement2: Confirmed Nonempty Orders

To cover the second part as well, we have to additionally specify that we need to see a confirmation, e.g. as confRefLineItem module:

```
(startService < LineItem <
        confRefLineItem < PurOrderCon)
```

This generates the solution of Fig. 7.4(b), which includes also the rest of the sequence shown in Fig. 7.3(a).

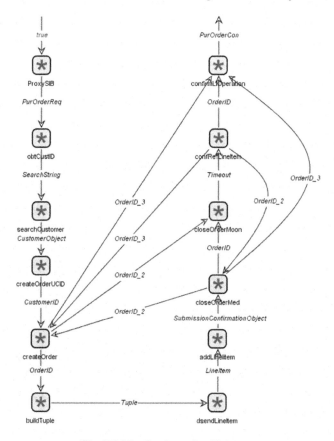

Fig. 7.5. The Configuration Universe

7.5 How to work with the Synthesis Tool

The synthesis tool takes as input the text file containing the knowledge base: the module and type taxonomy, the module descriptions, and some documentation for the integrated hypertext system. It is steered from the ABC GUI. There, users can input the SLTL formulas that describe the goal and can ask for different kinds of solutions. The tool produces a graphical visualization of the satisfying plans (module compositions), which can be executed, if the corresponding module implementations are already available, or they can be exported for later use.

The knowledge basis implicitly describes the set of all legal executions. We call it *configuration universe*, and it contains all the compatible module compositions with respect to the given taxonomies and to the given collection of modules. Fig. 7.5. shows the configuration universe that emerges when simply considering the atomic, concrete input/output types.

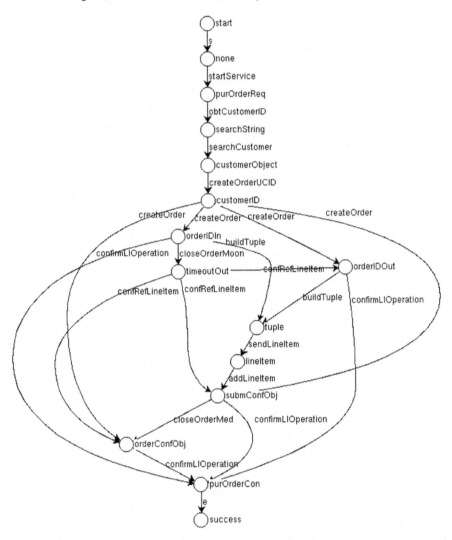

Fig. 7.6. The Minimal (i.e. cycle free) Solutions

7.5.1 Specifying Solution Types

Users never see the configuration universe. They have a number of simple options to state which kind of solutions they would like to have displayed.

- **minimal** solutions denotes plans that achieve the goal without repetition of configurations. In particular, this excludes cycles.
- **shortest** solutions returns the set of all minimal plans that are also shortest, measured in number of occurring steps.
- **one shortest** solution returns the first shortest plan satisfying the specification.

- **all** solutions returns all the satisfying solutions, which includes also cyclic ones.

Minimal plans generated for our working example are shown in Fig. 7.6. Since these plan descriptions are directed acyclic graphs, it is rather simple to select and execute one plan.

If we require all plans, in this simple case we are returned the configuration universe. As we see in the lower part of Fig. 7.5, it contains a loop that successively handles the line items.

The typical user interaction foresees a successive refinement of the declarative specification by starting with an initial, intuitive specification, and asking typically for shortest or minimal solutions, and using the graphical output for inspection and refinement.

This is exactly what we did in Sect. 7.3, where we used abstract types to enlarge the solution space and then tightened successively the LTL specification by adding salient characteristics that yield a good declarative characterization of the desired solutions.

7.6 Plan Generation in Detail

In the following $\langle a \rangle true$, meaning *next follows an* a *step*, will be abbreviated by $\langle a \rangle$, and $\mathcal{T}$ the whole set of types of the taxonomy. Based on these conventions, we are now going to describe the tableau-based synthesis for the following simple example specification

$$\phi = \langle startService \rangle < PurOrderCon$$

and the configuration universe in Fig. 7.5.

7.6.1 The Synthesis Algorithm

The algorithm produces internally the proof tree shown in Figures 7.7 and 7.8 and it is built following the presentation outlined in [20].

Intuitively, the proof proceeds forward, from an initial configuration where we have no type prescriptions (None) and the complete formula still to satisfy.

The guiding formula is successively *split* in a subformula that restricts the current state and the next step, and a rest concerning a deeper future. The constraints at the current state concern *admissible* types, which preselect (as preconditions) the set of modules from which to choose at this stage. Admissible modules that satisfy the next step constraint give rise to a *reduction* step: these modules are added to the tree and the algorithm continues from the configurations (output-type, rest-formula). Emptyness of the set of admissible modules means failure of the corresponding attempt to find a solution. The formulas arising as intermediate steps and their evaluations in the concrete example are presented in Fig. 7.10. They help to understand how the algorithm successively develops the proof tree, which is now illustrated in more detail.

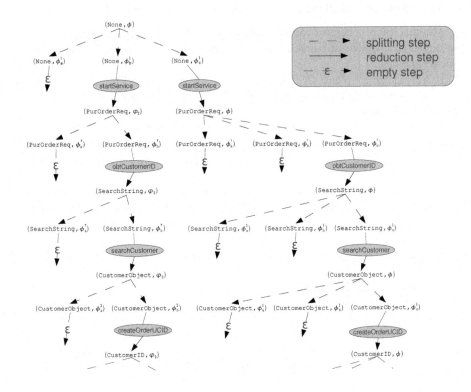

Fig. 7.7. Proof tree (upper part)

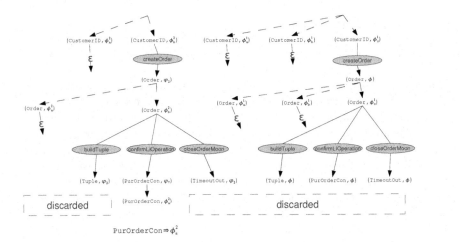

Fig. 7.8. Proof tree (lower part)

7.6.2 Example: Applying the Algorithm

As the technique [20] relies on the declarative specifications of the plan provided by the LTL formula ϕ, this is broken down in the first step into the following equivalent formula in basic LTL, where U is the *strong until* operator[7]:

$$
\begin{aligned}
\phi &= \langle startService \rangle < PurOrderCon \\
&= F(\langle startService \rangle \wedge F(PurOrderCon)) \\
&= true \ U \ (\langle startService \rangle \wedge \overbrace{(true \ U \ PurOrderCon)}^{\varphi_2}) \\
&\underbrace{\hspace{5cm}}_{\varphi_1}
\end{aligned}
$$

The first step of the algorithm searches for input types that are admissible for the given specification. For our example we do not have any precondition here, so all the input types qualify, symbolized by input type None.

We thus start with the configuration (None, ϕ).

These configurations are called *continuation constraint*: they express the sub-problem still to be solved at any stage of the proof derivation, in the context of a partial solution. The algorithm reduces the initial configuration stepwise by unrolling the specification on one hand and applying admissible modules on the other hand. The occurring configurations are reported in Fig. 7.10.

The split and reduction steps in the proof tree are carried out with respect to the outcome of the *adm* function to determine the set of (locally) admissible modules. Outcomes relevant for the proof tree are depicted in Fig. 7.10, which refers to Table 7.1. Please note that we are here in a relaxed setting, where the types *Order ID* and *OrderConfObj* are identified.

The root of the tableau in Fig. 7.7 describes the situation when no module has been applied and the overall formula has to be satisfied. Starting from this initial configuration a *split*-function splits up the property into several new continuation constraints that need to be validated. Mainly this splitting technique relies on the inherent splitting character of LTL's until-operator. This step produces (in our case three) new subproblems.

Each new subproblem can be reduced by applying an admissible module via the reduction operator *red*. This results into a new continuation constraint that takes into account the execution of that module.

If the split step produces a local specification that cannot be satisfied, the corresponding reduction step is denoted by ϵ if it yields the empty set, by a contradiction symbol if the local specification is inconsistent (this does not occur in this example), and in both cases it closes this branch of the tableau without a solution.

This exposition is only for illustration of the principle. Users do not see the proof tree. They directly obtain the set of legal solutions as shown in Sect. 7.5.

---

[7] The formula $\phi = \phi_1 \ U \ \psi$ is decomposed into the two formulas ψ and $\phi_1 \wedge \langle adm(\phi) \rangle \phi$, expressing that either ψ holds directly in this state, or ϕ_1 holds here locally and in all its reachable successors until a successor is reached where ψ holds.

$$split(\phi) = split(\varphi_1) \cup \{true \wedge \langle adm(true)\rangle \phi\}$$

$$split(\varphi_1) = \{\phi_a \wedge \phi_b | \phi_a \in split(\langle startService\rangle) \text{ and } \phi_b \in split(\varphi_2)\}$$

using

$$split(\langle startService\rangle) = \{\langle startService\rangle\}$$

$$split(\varphi_2) = \{split(PurOrderCon) \cup \{true \wedge \langle adm(true)\rangle \varphi_2\}$$

$$= \{\{\underbrace{PurOrderCon}_{\phi_a^2}\} \cup \underbrace{\{true \wedge \langle adm(true)\rangle \varphi_2\}}_{\phi_b^2}$$

it follows that

$$split(\varphi^1) = \{\underbrace{\langle startService\rangle \wedge PurOrderCon}_{\phi_a^1},$$

$$\underbrace{\langle startService\rangle \wedge true \wedge \langle adm(true)\rangle \varphi_2}_{\phi_b^1},$$

$$\underbrace{true \wedge \langle adm(true)\rangle \phi}_{\phi_c^1}\}$$

$$red(\phi_b^1) = red(< startService >) \wedge red(< adm(true) > \varphi_2)$$

$$= true \wedge \varphi_2$$

$$red(\phi_c^1) = \phi$$

$$red(\phi_b^2) = \varphi_2$$

Fig. 7.9. (a) Configurations occurring in the proof tableau

$$adm(\phi_a^1) = adm(< startService >) \cap adm(PurOrderCon)$$

$$= \{startService\} \cap \emptyset$$

$$= \emptyset$$

$$adm(\phi_b^1) = adm(< startService >) \cap adm(< adm(true) >$$

$$(true \ U \ PurOrderCon))$$

$$= \{startService\} \cap adm(true)$$

$$b = \{startService\}$$

$$adm(\phi_c^1) = \mathcal{T}$$

$$adm(\phi_a^2) = \emptyset$$

$$adm(\phi_b^2) = adm(< adm(true) > \varphi_2)$$

$$= \mathcal{T}$$

$$adm(true) = \{startService\}$$

$$adm(PurOrderReq) = \{obtCustomerID\}$$

$$adm(SearchString) = \{searchCustomer\}$$

$$adm(CustomerObject) = \{createOrderUCID\}$$

$$adm(CustomerID) = \{createOrder\}$$

$$adm(Order) = \{buildTuple, closeOrderMoon, confirmLIOperation\}$$

Fig. 7.10. (b) Terms occurring in the proof tableau

7.7 Implementing the Synthesis Process as a jABC Orchestration

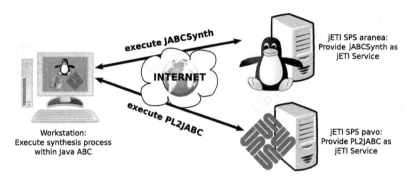

Fig. 7.11. jETI remote execution architecture for synthesis

To enable easy integration of our legacy systems, such as the synthesis algorithm and the converter from old ABC's graph file format to jABC's graph file format, we modelled the complete synthesis process within the jABC. The process is now realized itself as a Service Logic Graph containing remote execution calls via jETI to those legacy services. The user of these services does not need to care about maintaining over ten year old software, but rather can simply use it for the intended purpose. Figure 7.11 illustrates the distributed architecture of the synthesis process, which includes remote calls to our legacy services.

Fig. 7.12 shows the Service Logic Graph that is executed to perform the synthesis. The individual steps of the process are described in the following. Table 7.3 gives an overview of the data exchange between the process' elements.

- **CollectModules** We require that the modules themselves provide the synthesis process with their type and behaviour information. Technically, this is achieved by a Java interface `EtiSynthesis`. Implementing this interface, the module provides the type information via a certain method. The CollectModules SIB searches all the modules of the current jABC project that implement this interface. This set of modules is then written to the jABC execution context and can be used by the following SIBs.
- **LoadSymbolicTypes** This SIB reads the symbolic type mapping from a given text file. At the current state of development, this text file maps *symbolic names* to a set of *unique type identifiers* that are provided by the previously introduced EtiSynthesis interface. It is planned for the future to replace this simple mapping by a more general taxonomy concept. This will allow the modules to be further grouped, so that the requirement to the synthesis can be specified more loosely.
- **GenerateQuery** Here the SLTL formula for the synthesis is created from the previously collected modules using the symbolic type mapping. The SIB iterates over all symbolic type names and adds corresponding compatibility constraints

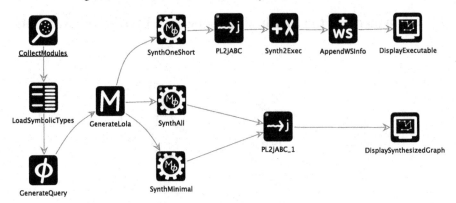

Fig. 7.12. The Synthesis process, itself a jETI/jABC SLG

to the SLTL formula. Furthermore, the SIB contains parameters to set start and goal types, as well as the option to specify additional constraints.

- **GenerateLola** This SIB translates the information about the modules and types into Lola format. LOLA was in the early '90s a logic language for deductive databases. We used it since 1994 as a text format for the file that defines the configuration universe in terms of modules, types, module taxonomy and type taxonomy, and it is part of the legacy synthesis system. Different from our original approach, the type information is now equivalently encoded into the query file. This Lola file plus the SLTL formula are input to the vintage ABC synthesis algorithm of [4].

- **SynthOneShort** This is where the actual synthesis algorithm is invoked. As already mentioned, it is embedded in the old version of the ABC, which was written in C. Thus for execution this SIB accesses remotely a jETI service provider in Dortmund, where a server with a very old version of C and of the ABC is running, and where the ABC synthesis is installed.

- **PL2jABC** Of course, the synthesis' output is a graph file for the old ABC, in PLGraph format. To enable further processing or displaying of the synthesized model, the file needs to be converted to jABC file format. This is also done by an externally provided service, via a jETI call to the corresponding service provider.

- **Synth2Exec** This SIB transforms the graph into its dual view (SIBs → edges, edges → SIBs), as the legacy synthesis associates edges with actions (since it has an internal Labelled Transition System representation) whereas the jABC considers SIBs to perform the actions. After this step, the graph contains the real SIBs that constitute the mediator.

- **AppendWSInfo** The jETI Web Service Generator requires some meta information about the processed graph model. AppendWSInfo appends this information according to the models parameters. The meta information includes imported XSD type definitions as well as the service's interface definition. This meta information is described in detail in Chap. 5, where we explain how we generate Web services from jABC's SLGs.

SIB	Input	Output
CollectModules	*none*	ModuleSet
LoadSymbolicTypes	*none*	SymbolicTypeMap
GenerateQuery	ModuleSet, SympolicTypeMap	Query
GenerateLola	ModuleSet, SymbolicTypeMap	Lola
SynthOneShort	Query, Lola	PLGraph
PL2jABC	PLGraph	jABCGraph
Synth2Exec	jABCGraph	ExecutableJABCGraph
AppendWSInfo	ExecutableJABCGraph	ExecutableJABCGraph
DisplayExecutable	ExecutableJABCGraph	*none*

Table 7.3. Type behaviour of the SIBs for the synthesis process

- **DisplayExecutable** Finally, the resulting SLG of the mediator is displayed within the jABC for manual inspection and modification (cf. Fig. 7.13).

After completion of the synthesis process, one can now use the jETI Web Service Generator to export the graph as a Web Service, or use the Genesys library to produce a binary executable for the workflow.

7.8 Related Approaches

Our approach was introduced 1993 ins [17, 4] and applied in [18, 10] and [21] to synthesize Statecharts, CAD design processes, and heterogeneous verification algorithm for concurrent systems, respectively. The idea of LTL guided process composition has later been taken up by others: Bacchus and Kabanza [1] extensively discuss their technique that implements a first order extension of LTL, Mandell and McIlraith use LTL in the context of BPEL compositions [8], and Falcarin et al. [23] use LTL as a starting point for their compositions, transforming single LTL formulas to finite state automata, then composing them to a global specification, and finally finding the correct shortest solutions as the acyclic accepting paths in that automaton.

Concerning the relation with planning, the state variables in an LTL formula are directly fluents: their value changes from state to state along the process, and the formulas describe mutual dependencies naturally and compactly. In this sense, there is a close kinship between the temporal logic mentality and event calculus [14] or logics for timing diagrams [3]: all three describe what is true at what time, associating the evolution of time with a succession of states, and offering a well chosen set of operators to express dependencies between temporal variables along possible paths within models.

The fundamental advantages of LTL guided synthesis over planning are the following:

- the supported guidance is process driven and not state driven. Therefore the control it offers can in general depend on the entire history of predecessors, and not only on the current state. This is extremely efficient in focussing the search, resulting in small memory usage and quick execution.

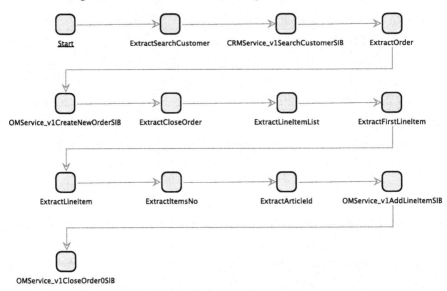

Fig. 7.13. The Mediator's SLG resulting from the synthesis process

- it is decoupled from the (internal) state of a solver/planner: the search control information relates exclusively to properties of the domain knowledge, not on any information on the internal state of an algorithm, which is often the case for planning techniques in order to capture and encode the relevant history aspects (what is enabled, what is true, etc.) that govern the correct chaining of transitions, i.e. the temporal/causal/precedence aspects. In contrast, a user of our technique does not need to know anything about the algorithm underlying the solver/planner.

Among the mediation approaches described in this book, the planning technique by Sheth et al. of Chap. 6 is the closest to ours. It is very similar in its perspective, but in a sense dual in its technical realization. We both adopt

- separation of control and data
- declarative requirement specifications, and
- a loose coupling mechanism, very important for obtaining a manageable process synthesis, and
- we both propose a pattern-based approach to dealing with loops.

However, in contrast to their data and state-centric approach, our synthesis framework is behaviour oriented, giving the technical realization a quite different look. E.g., where Chap. 6 exploits the multitude of data elements to detect a loop structure, our approach is based on a repetitive occurrence of events, where they match tuples, we introduce symbolic data mediation functionality based on ontological descriptions (see e.g. [15]), and were they define the planning problem via initial and goal states, we use temporal formulas as a loose goal specification.

7.9 Conclusions

We have applied the automatic tool composition feature of the ABC/ETI platform as a synthesis tool for the mediator. Our LTL-based synthesis approach is not restricted to compute one solution, but it may compute all (shortest/minimal) solutions, with the intent to provide maximum insight into the potential design space.

In future we plan to investigate various forms of synthesis approaches in order to compare their application profiles. In particular, we are interested in comparing game-based methods which work via synthesis of winning strategies with the described tableau-based methods, that construct a linear model as a result of proof construction. We also plan to enhance the user-friendliness in terms of graphical support for the declarative specifications, for example by means of the Formula Builder [5] and by the use of patterns [2].

References

1. F. Bacchus and F. Kabanza. Using temporal logics to express search control knowledge for planning. *Artificial Intelligence*, 116(1-2):123 – 191, 2000.
2. M. Dwyer and J.Corbett G. Avrunin. *Specification Patterns Website.* http://patterns.projects.cis.ksu.edu/.
3. Kathi Fisler. Toward diagrammability and efficiency in event-sequence languages. *STTT, Int. J. on Software Tools for Technology Transfer*, 8(4-5):431–447, 2006.
4. B. Freitag, B. Steffen, T. Margaria, and U. Zukowski. An approach to intelligent software library management. In *Proc. 4th Int. Conf. on Database Systems for Advanced Applications (DASFAA '95), National University of Singapore, Singapore*, 1995.
5. S. Jörges, T. Margaria, and B. Steffen. Formulabuilder: A tool for graph-based modelling and generation of formulae. In *Proc. ICSE'06*, May 2006.
6. C. Kubczak, T. Margaria, B. Steffen, and S. Naujokat. Service-oriented mediation with jETI/jABC: Verification and export. In *Worksh. on Service Composition & SWS Challenge, part of WI-IAT'07, the IEEE/ WIC/ ACM Int. Conf. on Web Intelligence, November 2007, Stanford (CA)*, volume ISBN-10: 0-7695-3028-1. IEEE CS, 2007.
7. C. Kubczak, T. Margaria, C. Winkler, and B. Steffen. An approach to discovery with miAamics and jABC. In *Worksh. on Service Composition & SWS Challenge, part of WI-IAT'07, the IEEE/ WIC/ ACM Int. Conf. on Web Intelligence, November 2007, Stanford (CA)*, volume ISBN-10: 0-7695-3028-1. IEEE CS, 2007.
8. Daniel J. Mandell and Sheila A. McIlraith. Adapting BPEL4WS for the semantic web: The bottom-up approach to web service interoperation. In *Proc. ISWC2003, Sundial Resort, Sanibel Island, FL (USA), LNCS N.2870, 2003, pp. 227 - 241, Springer Verlag*, 2003.
9. T. Margaria, M. Bakera, H. Raffelt, and B. Steffen. Synthesizing the mediator with jABC/ABC. In *EON-SWSC 2008, Proc. 6th Int. Worksh. on Evaluation of Ontology-based Tools and the Semantic Web Service Challenge, Tenerife, Spain, June 2008*. CEUR-WS, http://ftp.informatik.rwth-aachen.de/Publications/CEUR-WS/Vol-359/Paper-4.pdf, 2008.
10. T. Margaria and B. Steffen. Backtracking-free design planning by automatic synthesis in METAFrame. In *Proc. FASE'98, Lisbon(P), LNCS, Springer Verlag*, 1998.

11. T. Margaria and B. Steffen. LTL guided planning: Revisiting automatic tool composition in ETI. In *SEW: 31st Annual Software Engineering Workshop*. IEEE Computer Society Press, March 2007.
12. T. Margaria, C. Winkler, C. Kubczak, B.Steffen, M. Brambilla, D. Cerizza S. Ceri, E. Della Valle, F. Facca, and C. Tziviskou. The SWS mediator with WebML/WebRatio and jABC/jETI: A comparison. In *Proc. ICEIS'07, 9th Int. Conf. on Enterprise Information Systems*, Funchal (P), June 2007.
13. G.D. Plotkin. a structural approach to operational semantics. *Journal of Logic and Algebraic Programming*, 60-61:17–140, 2004.
14. M. Shanahan. The event calculus explained. In *LNAI (1600):409-430*. Springer Verlag, 1999.
15. B. Steffen, T. Margaria, and V. Braun. The electronic tool integration platform: Concepts and design. *Int. Journal on Software Tools for Technology Transfer (STTT)*, 1(2):9–30, 1997.
16. B. Steffen, T. Margaria, and A. Claßen. Heterogeneous analysis and verification for distributed systems. *SOFTWARE: Concepts and Tools*, 17(1):13–25, 1996.
17. B. Steffen, T. Margaria, and B. Freitag. Module configuration by minimal model construction. In *Tech. rep. MIP 9313, Universität Passau, Passau (D)*, 1993.
18. B. Steffen, T. Margaria, and M. von der Beeck. Automatic synthesis of linear process models from temporal constraints: An incremental approach. In *Proc. AAS'97, ACM/SIGPLAN Int. Workshop on Automated Analysis of Software, Paris (F),(affiliated to POPL'97), pp. 127-141.*, 1997.
19. B. Steffen and P. Narayan. Full lifecycle support for end-to-end processes. *IEEE Computer*, 40(11):64–73, Nov., 2007.
20. Bernhard Steffen, Tiziana Margaria, and Burkhard Freitag. Module configuration by minimal model construction. Technical Report MIP-9313, University of Passau, Germany, December 1993.
21. Bernhard Steffen, Tiziana Margaria, and Ralf Nagel. Remote Integration and Coordination of Verification Tools in jETI. In *Proc. ECBS 2005, 12th IEEE Int. Conf. on the Engineering of Computer Based Systems*, pages 431–436, Greenbelt (USA), April 2005. IEEE Computer Soc. Press.
22. *SWS Challenge Workshops: Website.*   http://sws-challenge.org/wiki/index.php/Workshops.
23. J. Yu, J. Han, Y. Jin, and P. Falcarin. Synthesis of service compositions process models from temporal business rules.

Part II

Mediation Solutions Comparisons

Comparison: Mediation Solutions of WSMOLX and WebML/WebRatio

Maciej Zaremba[1], Raluca Zaharia[1], Andrea Turati[2], Marco Brambilla[3], Tomas Vitvar[4], and Stefano Ceri[3]

[1] Digital Enterprise Research Institute, National University of Ireland, Galway, Ireland, `firstname.lastname@deri.org`
[2] CEFRIEL, Milan, Italy, `andrea.turati@cefriel.it`
[3] Department of Electronics and Information Technologies, Technical University of Milan, Italy, {`mbrambil,ceri`}`@elet.polimi.it`
[4] The Semantics Technology Institute Innsbruck, University of Innsbruck, Austria, `tomas.vitvar@sti2.at`

Summary. In this chapter we compare the WSMO/WSML/WSMX andWebML/WebRatio approaches to the SWS-Challenge workshop mediation scenario in terms of the utilized underlying technologies and delivered solutions. In the mediation scenario one partner uses RosettaNet to define its B2B protocol while the other one operates on a proprietary solution. Both teams shown how these partners could be semantically integrated.

In this chapter we compare the WSMO/WSML/WSMX and WebML/WebRatio approaches to the SWS-Challenge workshop mediation scenario in terms of the utilized underlying technologies and delivered solutions. In the mediation scenario one partner uses RosettaNet to define its B2B protocol while the other one operates on a proprietary solution. Both teams shown how these partners could be semantically integrated.

8.1 Introduction

This chapter compares two different approaches to semantic integration of a RosettaNet-enabled client with legacy systems in the context of the Semantic Web Services Challenge. Here we compare the submissions to the mediation problem based on WSMO[6], WSML [8], WSMX[3] of the Digital Enterprise Research Institute[5] and WebML/WebRatio [4] approach provided by the joint team of Technical University of Milan, DEI[6] and Cefriel[7].

---

[5] http://www.deri.org
[6] http://www.dei.polimi.it
[7] http://www.cefriel.it

The solutions of both groups differ quite substantially in terms of the underlying technologies. The DERI team based its solution on the WSMO conceptual framework for Semantic Web services which comes from the relatively young Semantic Web research area, while DEI-Cefriel followed the path of well-established Software Engineering methods. We compare the similarities and differences of the provided solutions mainly with respect to the data and process modeling, execution environments, tool support, but also from the perspective of dealing with changes in the integration requirements.

8.2 Comparison

Both submissions have successfully addressed the SWS-Challenge Moon mediation scenarios. In this section we elaborate on the similarities and differences on the approaches taken by DERI and DEI-Cefriel to the mediation tasks.

Underlying Technologies

WebML is a high-level notation language for data- and process- centric Web applications. It allows specifying the conceptual modeling of Web applications built on top of a data schema used to describe the application data, and composed of one or more hypertexts used to publish the underlying data. The WebML data model is the standard Entity-Relationship (E-R) model extended with Object Query Language (OQL) constraints. The hypertext model is specified through pages and units. Each WebML unit has its own well defined semantic and its execution complies with its semantic. The composition of different units lead to the description of the semantic of hypertext or Web services. The language is extensible, allowing for the definition of customized operations and units. To describe Web service interactions, WebML has been extended with Web service units [5]. In particular the `Request-Response` and `One-way` operations are used to consume external Web services, while the `Solicit` and `Response` units are used to publish Web services. In [3] the language has been extended with operations supporting process specifications, and a further modeling level was added to the framework, allowing to start workflows/orchestrations using a BPMN model that is later automatically translated to a WebML skeleton to be refined by designers.

The WebML methodology has been implemented in a prototype that extends the CASE tool WebRatio[8], a development environment for the visual specification of Web applications and the automatic generation of code for the J2EE platform. The design environment is equipped with a code generator that deploys the specified application and Web services in the J2EE platform, by automatically generating all the necessary pieces of code, including data extraction queries, Web service calls, data mapping logics, page templates, and WSDL service descriptors. The overall framework is shown in Figure 8.1: the modeling and design aspect rely on high-level

---

[8] http://www.webratio.com

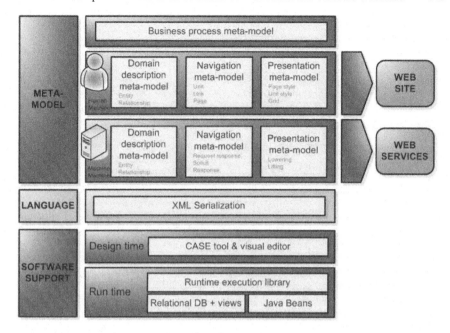

Fig. 8.1. The WebML/WebRatio Framework

BPMN model, which is instantiated for user- and machine- oriented applications, with appropriate primitives for domain description, hypertext navigation specification, and presentation design. The outcome of human-oriented application design is a website, whilst the machine oriented case results in a service-oriented application. Technically speaking, the project models are stored as XML serializations, that in turn are translated by code, and documentation generation, that produce running applications.

The DERI approach follows the Web Services Modeling Ontology (WSMO) framework reflecting four top elements by explicitly modeling Goals, Web services, Ontologies and Mediators. The solution provided by DERI is technically realized using WSMX - a Semantic Web service middleware facilitating tasks like service discovery, composition, mediation and execution. WSMX is a component-based middleware following the Service Oriented Architecture (SOA) principles of loose-coupling. Major WSMX components include: **Data Mediation** (handles the mismatches at instance level between heterogeneous ontologies), **Process Mediation** (deals with solving the interaction mismatches between the Goal and the Web service), **Discovery** (determines matching services for the given Goal), **Choreography Engine** (drives the conversation between service requester and providers following their public processes - WSMO Choreographies defined using ontologized Abstract State Machines(ASM)[7]). Ontology-to-ontology mediation (OO-Mediation between heterogenous ontologies) is reflected in the Data Mediation WSMX component while goal-to-Web service mediation (WG-Mediation facilitating communi-

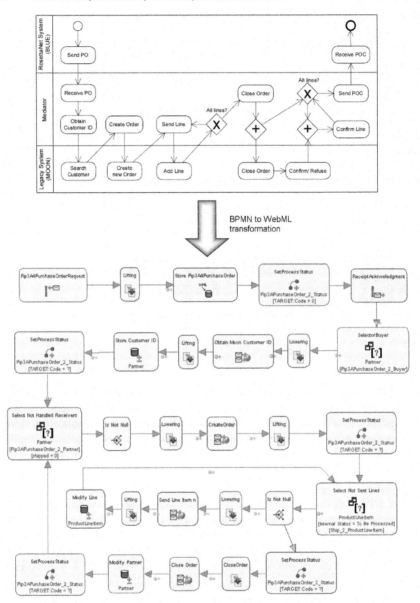

Fig. 8.2. The BPMN and WebML Models of Blue to Moon Mediator

cation between Goal and Web service) is handled by the Process Mediation WSMX
component.

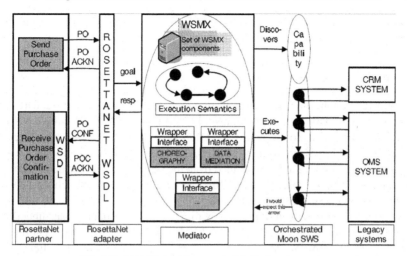

Fig. 8.3. WSMX Architecture in Mediation Scenario

Modeling of WSMO elements can be performed using WSMT[9] or WSMO Studio[10]. WSMT is a collection of tools for management of Semantic Web Services (e.g. WSMO service and ontology editor and visualizer, WSMX monitoring, etc.).

On the other hand, WebML focuses more on the modeling of the WSMO WW-Mediators (Web service-to-Web service mediation) and of the internal logics of the services (if they need to be developed), that are defined through visual diagrams representing the execution chains, while little emphasis is given to the design of the Goals and of the other semantic aspects. Indeed, the approach provides a semi-automatic extraction of WSMO Goal and Web service behaviour from the designed models, that need to be refined later by the designer.

In the WSMOLX approach, the following artefacts have to be created and applied to the WSMX middleware to get full system integration: ontologies for both involved parties (i.e. service requestors and providers), bidirectional XML–WSML adapters and lifting/lowering rules, WSMO Goals and Services, data mediation mapping rules between heterogenous otologies. Each artefact must be registered with WSMX in order to be utilized during the runtime phase. Once these artefacts are provided, the WSMX framework will handle all aspects of the communication: discovery of a WSMO Web service that will fulfill the requester's Goal, mediation between the involved parties, WSDL service invocations including lowering from/lifting back to WSML and Web service execution.

The WSMX runtime architecture is shown in Figure 8.3. Instance data is sent from the RosettaNet enabled Blue company in its native XML data format to the dedicated adapter where it is lifted to the semantic level and from there it is sent to WSMX as a WSMO Goal. The PIP3A4-WSMX and CRM/OMS-WSMX adapters

---

[9] http://wsmt.sourceforge.net
[10] http://www.wsmostudio.org

were developed for handling the lifting and lowering between XML schema and ontologies in the mediation scenario.

Data Model

The WSMOLX solution starts with creating ontologies, with existing standards and systems as their basis, namely RosettaNet PIP 3A4 and CRM/OMS schemas. Next, Semantic Web services for the CRM and OMS systems of the Blue legacy system as well as Goal templates, conforming to PIP3A4, for the service requestor are created. In addition, a grounding must be defined from the semantic (WSMO) descriptions to the syntactic (WSDL) descriptions. Lifting and lowering has to be defined between utilized ontologies and XML data models.

The DEI-CERFIEL solution starts with designing the data model underlying the RosettaNet messages with an extended E-R model. Three main entities are identified: the Pip3A4PurchaseOrder, the Partner and the ProductLineItem. Each Pip3APurchaseOrder instance is related with one or more ProductLineItem instances, one Partner representing the Buyer, one Partner representing the Seller and one Partner representing the Receiver. Every ProductLineItem instance may have one Partner representing a Receiver for the single line. Only the essential data for the scenario was modeled under this approach.

Both teams provided expressive data models reflecting domain specific knowledge and exchanged messages on the data schema and instance level. WebML allows to specify a data model describing the domain data structure as an Entity-Relationship (E-R) or, equivalently, a UML class diagram. WebML E-R diagram provides rich notation for specifying structure and relationships between concepts occurring in the given domain and it allows to impose simple constraints over the modeled domain by using WebML-OQL. Logic rules are not explicitly supported, however the authors showed that the expressive power of the model is very close to WSML-Flight. DERI used the WSML-Rule variant, a fully-fledged ontology language with rule support. SWS-Challenge mediation scenario data model did not require to utilize complex rules while modeling the ontology. Thus, despite of using more expressive language by DERI, both underlying data models were quite similar in terms of their expressiveness. Both teams modeled existing concepts, their attributes and relationships between these concepts without imposing additional constraints over the data models taking advantage of the expressiveness provided on the level of UML class diagrams. In both cases, mature tools exist to edit underlying data models: for WSMO, WSMT and WSMO Studio are available, while for WebML one can use the WebRatio CASE tool.

Process Model

Provided solutions differ quite significantly with respect to the process modeling. The joint team DEI-Cefriel followed a Software Engineering approach to model

Moon orchestration, while DERI specified orchestration using the ontologized Abstract State Machines[7] formalism which falls into process execution based on underlying rich knowledge base formalism. In the utilized Abstract State Machines (ASM), an ontology constitutes the underlying knowledge representation and transition rules are specified in terms of logic formulas. ASM provide a precise and executable model for specifying processes allowing simulation (e.g. deadlock, livelock freedom detection) and elaborate reasoning over the model. DERI focused on the executable aspect of the ASM, not utilizing process simulation since there is currently no tool for WSML supporting ASM simulation. Execution of the ontologized ASM has been carried out by ASM Engine used both in WSMX Choreography and Orchestration. ASM-based modeling allows to model processes in a more flexible way, supporting *strong decoupling* between service requester and service provider where delivery of exchanged messages do not have to be explicitly modeled. Instead the internal ontology of the ASM Engine will be populated with allowed messages and it is up to the state of the execution and the transition rules to determine and evaluate the usability of the available information.

In the WebML approach, RosettaNet, the Moon CRM and ORM related messages are modeled as a part of the same process, *tightly coupling* the Moon mediation process with the RosettaNet client. This coupling is embedded within the design of the WW-Mediatior, specified as a WebML operation chain triggered by a Web service call. The DERI approach is more flexible by being more client independent, where the orchestrated service is not aware of any incoming or outgoing RosettaNet messages. It simply specifies messages in its native ontology and it is up to the Data Mediator to resolve and mediate data heterogeneities between service requester and service provider.

Listing 8.1 shows a fragment of the WSMO Choreography for the CRM/OMS service. The Choreography is described from the service point of view thus the rule says that in order to send a *SearchCustomerResponse* message, the *SearchCustomerRequest* message must be available. By executing the action of the rule (*add(SearchCustomerResponse)*), the underlying operation is invoked according to the grounding definition of the corresponding message which in turn results in receiving instance data from the Web service.

```
choreography MoonChoreography
    stateSignature
        in moon#SearchCustomerRequest withGrounding { ... }
        out moon#SearchCustomerResponse withGrounding { ... }

transitionRules MoonChoreographyRules
    forall {?request} with (
        ?request memberOf moon#SearchCustomerRequest
    ) do
        add(_# memberOf moon#SearchCustomerResponse)
    endForall
```

Listing 8.1. CRM/OMS Choreography

In WebML/WebRatio after modeling the data structures, a high level BPMN model is created representing the mediator (see Figure 8.2 for the mediation from

Blue to Moon); this model formalizes the orchestration of the Moon Web services and defines states pertaining to the mediation process as defined in the SWS-Challenge specification. Then, the BPMN model is used to automatically generate a WebML skeleton that is manually refined to complete the design of the mediator. The final model for the Blue to Moon mediator is reported also in Figure 8.2:

1. In the first line, as soon as the order is received (Solicit unit), the Pip3A4Pur-chaseOrder is converted to the Canonic XML (Adapter unit) and stored in the database (XML-In unit), the status of the current Pip3APurchaseOrder is set to "To Be Processed" (Connect unit) and the Acknowledge message is returned to the service invoker (Response unit).
2. Next, the Buyer Partner is selected (Selector Unit) and a message to query the CRM service is created (Adapter unit) and sent to the Moon Legacy System (Request-Response unit). Once a reply has been received, the CustomerId is extracted from the reply message (Adapter unit) and stored in the data model (Modify unit). The status of the order is set to "CustomerId received" (Connect unit).
3. For each Receiver Partner in the order (Selector unit) a message for the createNewOrder operation is created (Adapter unit) and sent to the Moon Legacy System (Request-Response unit). Once a reply has been received, the OrderId is extracted from the reply message (Adapter unit) and stored in the data model (Modify unit). The status of the order is set to "OrderId received"(Connect unit).
4. Next, the ProductLineItem instances related to current Pip3APurchaseOrder and Receiver Partner are processed by a cycle: at every interaction a message for a single line is created and sent to the Moon Legacy System (Request-Response unit), and the received LineId is stored (Modify unit).
5. Finally when all the lines have been processed the message for the closeOrder operation is created (Adapter unit) and sent to the Moon Legacy System (Request-Response unit) and the status of the order is set to "Order closed" (Connect unit). If there are still Receiver Partner to be processed, the loop starts again.

Data Mediation

As mentioned before, WSMX puts a strong emphasis on mediation, allowing the interacting participants to be completely decoupled so that they do not need to directly comply with the requirements of the other party.

The WSMOLX solution requires the user to create mappings between the domain ontologies (OO-Mediator) with the help of the WSMT Data Mediation plugin. At runtime, the Data Mediator component performs mediation at the level of the exchanged messages following the mappings (OO-Mediator) defined during the design time. Listing 8.2 shows an example mapping of $searchString$ concept of the CRM/OMS ontology to concepts $cusomterId$ of the $PIP3A4$ ontology following the model defined in [8]. The construct $mediated(X, C)$ represents the identifier of the newly created target instance, where X is the source instance that is transformed, and C is the target concept we map to.

```
axiom mapping001 definedBy
  mediated(X, o2#searchString) memberOf o2#searchString :–
  X memberOf o1#customerId.
```

Listing 8.2. Mapping Rules in WSML

In WebML, the SOAP messages transformation to and from the WebML data model are performed by proper WebML units (`Adapter` units) that apply XSLT transformations; XSLT stylesheets are designed with the visual mapping tool (a fragment is reported in Listing 8.3).

```
<xsl:template match="//po:Pip3A4PurchaseOrderRequest">
  <xsl:variable name="fromId" select="./core:fromRole//core:businessName/core:FreeFormText"/>
  <xsl:variable name="toId" select="./core:toRole//core:businessName/core:FreeFormText"/>
```

Listing 8.3. Fragment of the XSLT for Mapping RosettaNet Messages to the WebML Data Model

In the WebML approach, the notion of data mediation and data mapping from one RosettaNet to the Moon specific data model is encoded in XSLT transformations that can be reused, but they do not exploit ontological information. XSTL transformations provide a one-to-one mapping between XML documents. New transformations need to be devised for new message models. In short-term it is a faster solution; however, if the number of clients using different data formats grows, then scalability becomes an issue for the WebML approach. For each customer it is required to change and redefine the orchestrated business process. For instance, when considering customers using other data formats and following different message exchange patterns, new OO-Mediators and WW-Mediators need to be designed. This can be partially avoided when there is no need to process the content of the messages, simply by not checking the format of the incoming message and lifting it to the internal model dynamically according to the incoming message format.

Tool Support

It is also worth overviewing the maturity of both solutions and respective tools in the design as well as the execution phase. Currently, there is a better tool support for WebML modeling, especially on the process modeling level. A good support is already provided for editing WSMO elements (e.g., ontologies, Goals), but only a basic support currently exists for editing processes in the form of ontologized ASMs and no support for simulation and model testing. However, the tools utilized throughout the development lifecycle of the WSMOLX submission are being actively developed (WSMO editor, Data Mediation, WSMX, others). Some of them are not yet as mature as the WebRatio CASE tool especially in terms of ontologized ASM-based process modeling. However, other modeling aspects involved in the semantic integration, like for instance WSMO ontology editing using WSMT, are already supported by quite advanced and user-friendly functionality.

8.2.1 Comparison Table

The comparison of the two solution is summarized in the Table 8.1.

8.2.2 Coping with the scenario changes

Both solutions were able to comply with the changes required by the second version of the mediation scenario. In particular, as regards the WebML solution, the scenario changes required to update the data model by introducing the fact that there may be a receiver for each single item lines. With regard to the process mediation, the BPMN model was updated to consider the new loop required to handle a different receiver and to invoke the production Web service. Accordingly, data mappings have also been updated. The cost of copying with the changes was relatively low and it required less than one day of work.

For the WSMOLX based solution, minor changes were required in the ontology similar to the case of the WebML data model. Also the Choreography of the Moon service had to be updated to model the loop required in the changes introduced in the second version of the scenario. Lack of process simulation and graphical support for ontologized ASM modeling requires good understanding of this technology and the DERI team was able to incorporate the required changes also within less than one day. Nevertheless, it is acknowledged that it would take longer for a person unfamiliar with this formalism to make the necessary changes, while the WebML solution is more likely to be grasped and modified reasonably quick even by a non-expert.

8.3 Conclusion

In this chapter we have compared two different approaches to the SWS-Challenge mediation scenario. The mediation requirements are very similar to a real world situation, where two partners having different B2B protocols want to interact with each other, but also complex enough to stress both compared solutions and to evidence their advantages and disadvantages. While the WebML based solution exploits well-established Software Engineering methods that allow some de-coupling and reuse, the WSMO based solution goes beyond the standard way of system integration allowing for a better de-coupling and reusability of the modeled elements.

The WebML based solution offers a mature and easy to use design environment totally based on a visual paradigm, with a set of automatic facilities for partial generation of semantic descriptions and definitions. From the WSMOLX user perspective the most difficult part is modeling ontologized ASM-based processes what should be accommodated in a more user-friendly way. However an easy visual paradigm is available, facilitating modeling of other WSMO elements (e.g., ontologies, Goals, etc.) involved in the semantic integration.

Future activities will focus on the refinement of the two approaches, also for coping with the new challenge scenarios that will be proposed. Both teams were

Feature	WebML/WebRatio	WSMO/WSMX
Data Model Design	ER-model manually created from analyzing the RosettaNet messages and adding status information. Used to keep the data persistent.	Independent ontologies created both from analyzing the Blue RosettaNet messages and internal data requirements by Moon's legacy services.
Process Mediation Design	WebML model structure with standard units generated from BPMN model. Units are then configured and other units are added from the library manually (no need for any implementation, no code generation, just component configuration).	The process mediation is modeled explicitly using an ontologized ASM that represents the orchestration of the mediation service or the choreography of the invoked services. The orchestration and the choreographies are hence decoupled.
Data Mediation Design	XSLT mapping designed within a visual environment to lift SOAP messages to the WebML data model and lower the data selected from the WebML data model to a SOAP message.	WSMT data mediation plugin for creating OO-Mediators. Additionally, dedicated bidirectional XML–WSML adapters generated semi-automatically are used for handling ontology lifting and lowering.
Web service publishing	Generic standard units for receiving SOAP messages.	Generated WSs are internally published on Axis2 or as JAX-WS services.
Web service invocation	Generic standard units for calls to Web services that are configured (at design time or at runtime) to invoke the Web services.	WSMX Invoker component handles all communication with services using grounding information provided in SWS descriptions.
Process Mediation Execution	The designed mediator represents the process that will be executed. The configuration of the execution environment is automatically obtained from the model.	WSMO Choreography and Orchestrations modeled during the design time are directly executable.
Data Mediation Execution	Incoming and outgoing messages, according to the modeled mediator are lowered to the internal data model calling the preconfigured XSLT mapping.	Handled automatically by the Data Mediator component by applying the OO-mediators (expressed as data mapping rules) on exchanged messages level.
Execution Monitoring	The WebRatio runtime offers default logging facilities that store all the execution threads. Standard WebML units can be used to develop a dedicated monitoring hypertext.	WSMX execution is presented as components' events flow on the Java SWING-based panel.

Table 8.1. Comparison of the Presented Solutions

able to handle the scenarios separately up to now and hence we are confident that both technologies employed will be able to propose an effective solution for the new scenario. The WebML based solution will further exploit the integration with the Glue discovery engine by exploiting it for the discovery phase and modeling within WebML a solution to dynamically compose and invoke the services according to the discovery results. The WSMO based solution will incorporate service discovery via *AchieveGoal* construct into its Orchestration allowing late-binding and runtime service composition.

References

1. Roman, D., Keller, U., Lausen, H., de Bruijn, J., Lara, R., Stollberg, M., Polleres, A., Feier, C., Bussler, C., Fensel, D.: Web Service Modeling Ontology. Applied Ontologies **1**(1) (2005) 77 – 106
2. de Bruijn, J., Lausen, H., Polleres, A., Fensel, D.: The Web Service Modeling Language: An Overview. In: Proc. of the European Semantic Web Conference. (2006)
3. Vitvar, T., Mocan, A., Kerrigan, M., Zaremba, M., Zaremba, M., Moran, M., Cimpian, E., Haselwanter, T., Fensel, D.: Semantically-enabled service oriented architecture: Concepts, technology and application. In Service Oriented Computing and Applications, Springer London **1**(2) (2007)
4. Ceri, S., Fraternali, P., Bongio, A., Brambilla, M., Comai, S., Matera, M.: Designing Data-Intensive Web Applications. Morgan Kauffmann (2002)
5. Manolescu, I., Brambilla, M., Ceri, S., Comai, S., Fraternali, P.: Model-driven design and deployment of service-enabled web applications. ACM Trans. Internet Techn. **5**(3) (2005) 439–479
6. Brambilla, M., Ceri, S., Fraternali, P., Manolescu, I.: Process modeling in Web applications. ACM Trans. Softw. Eng. Methodol. **15**(4) (2006) 360–409
7. Roman, D., Scicluna, J.: Ontology-based Choreography of WSMO Services. Wsmo final draft v0.3, DERI (2006) Available at: http://www.wsmo.org/TR/d14/v0.3/.
8. Mocan, A., Cimpian, E., Kerrigan, M.: Formal model for ontology mapping creation. In: International Semantic Web Conference. (2006) 459–472

9

Comparison: Mediation on WebML/WebRatio and jABC/jETI

Marco Brambilla[1], Stefano Ceri[1], Emanuele Della Valle[2], Federico M. Facca[1], Christian Kubczak[3], Tiziana Margaria[4], Bernhard Steffen[5], and Christian Winkler[4]

[1] Dipartimento di Elettronica e Informazione, Politecnico di Milano, Italy,
   {mbrambil,ceri,facca}@elet.polimi.it
[2] CEFRIEL, Milano, Italy, dellava@cefriel.it
[3] Chair of Software Engineering, Technical University of Dortmund, Germany,
   christian.kubczak@cs.uni-dortmund.de
[4] Chair of Service and Software Engineering, University of Potsdam, Germany,
   {margaria,winkler}@cs.uni-potsdam.de
[5] Chair of Programming Systems, Technical University of Dortmund, Germany,
   steffen@cs.uni-dortmund.de

Summary. In this chapter we compare two solutions to the mediation scenario of the SWS challenge that are based on the use of WebML [1] and of the jABC [2, 3] as modeling and execution platforms. In particular, first we give a general overview of the differences among the to approaches, and then we compare in the details the two solutions for the SWS challenge.

We use selected parts from the mediation scenarios to keep the comparison simple but expressive. Looking on the advanced scenarios would be more complex but would obviously lead to the same results.

9.1 Introduction

Both presented solutions adopt a model based approach, supported by model driven design tools and environments. This allows modeling the mediator in a graphical high level modeling language and supports the derivation of an executable mediator from these models. The solutions are thus similar in their spirit, and we provide here a description and comparison of the similarities and differences, at the modeling, language, tool, and change management levels.

The complete discussion on the two solutions can be found in Chap. 4 and 5. Hence we do not go into the solutions' details here but give a brief description of both submissions in Sect. 9.2 and 9.3. In Sect. 9.4 we compare the applied techniques of both approaches in details and in Sect. 9.5 we present a reduction of the two solutions to their mere common essence before we conclude in Sect. 9.6.

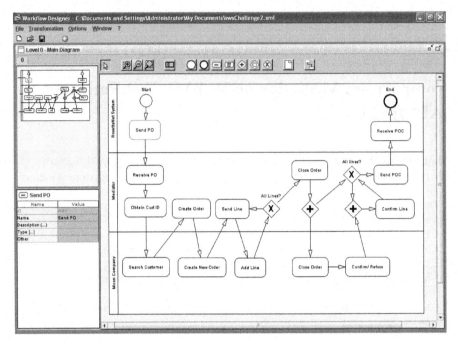

Fig. 9.1. The BPMN editor integrated in the WebML editing environment.

9.2 Designing the Mediator with WebML

The solution for the mediation problem starts by designing the data model under-lying the RosettaNet messages with an extended E-R model. We identified three main entities: the Pip3A4PurchaseOrder, the Partner and the ProductLineItem. Each Pip3A4PurchaseOrder instance is related with one or more ProductLineItem in-stances, one Partner representing the Buyer, one Partner representing the Seller and one Partner representing the Receiver. Every ProductLineItem instance may have one Partner representing a Receiver for the single line.

Then the WebML solution models the high-level scenario of the challenge using BPMN (see Fig. 9.1). This model includes all parts of the scenario on the whole – Blue's side as well as the mediator and Moon's side – and describes the scenario workflow.

This model is used as a guidance in the production of two WebML models that implement the workflow's functionality. The BPMN workflow is split by a corre-sponding annotation of the BPMN model into two separate WebML models that represent two independent parts of the process: sending a purchase order and receiv-ing acknowledgments for the ordered items. The generation of WebML diagrams is based on an algorithm that populates the WebML diagram with the standard general purpose units mentioned before, e.g. for receiving Web service calls and calling Web services and sending Web service responses, according to the BPMN model. The design of the mediator is refined manually by configuring existing units and adding

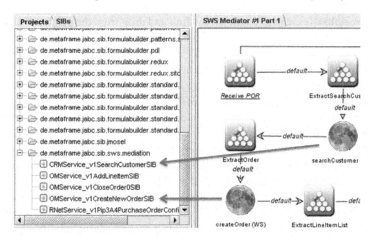

Fig. 9.2. The SWS Mediator SIBs and the abstract process model

new ones from the WebML unit library (no new unit had to be developed to cope with the mediation scenario). It could be possible also to model the mediator without storing data but working only in memory. The data storage was preferred to allow a better monitoring of the mediation process. The conversion from RosettaNet messages is handled by `Adapter` units that are configured by a proper XSLT stylesheet that transforms messages in an XML format compatible with WebML's internal data format. In the same way conversion to and from Moon legacy messages are handled by proper XSLT stylesheets that act as templates for SOAP messages and that are then populated by runtime queries during the workflow execution.

9.3 Designing the Mediator with jABC

The modeling process with the jABC framework is strongly control flow driven. The mediation task is analyzed under this aspect and then mapped into a jABC model consisting of *Service Independent Building Blocks* (SIBs) that are derived from WSDL[6] descriptions of the provided services and a palette of standard SIBs for data extraction and control flow management called *common services* that are delivered with the jABC. In the Mediator scenario we have a rather flat domain structure for the SWS specific services (see Fig. 9.2 left): we only distinguish SWS services from common services, and we import the entities in the domain of discourse (part of an underlying ontology) through the WSDL import.

We compare here the user-designed solution described in Chap. 5. Since it is closer to the WebML/WebRatio approach than the synthesized solution of Chap. 7 it enables a more interesting comparison.

---

[6] Web Services Description Language (`http://www.w3.org/TR/wsdl`)

The workflow is created manually, by drag and drop from the palette of automatically produced SIBs[7]. It is executed using the Tracer plugin, the jABC interpreter for jABC service models, which uses the jETI[8] facility to communicate with the remote services provided by the SWS Challenge hosts.

We publish and provide the resulting jABC Mediator service itself as a Web service with the technology provided by jETI as described in Chap. 5. Obviously this implies that (Java) code has to be generated from the created model using jABC's code-generator plugin *'Genesys'*.

When moving from one scenario level to the next, the data adaptation requires only the reimport of the changed WSDL descriptions into SIBs, which is automatic. The process adaptation requires a manual modification of the workflow (called Service Logic Graph or SLG), which happens graphically in the jABC. For comparison, in our declarative approach based on LTL guided synthesis described in Chapter 7 the modification of the workflow might be achieved by just adding/modifying the LTL formulas that describe the new desired workflow and running the synthesis again.

9.4 Comparison

Table 9.1 summarizes the profiles of the two solutions, which we describe in more detail below.

Table 9.1: Comparison of the presented technologies

Function	WebML	jABC
BPMN model	Manually modelled from the SWSC task description. Manually annotated to steer the WebML generation to meet the challenge's needs.	Not a distinct model, just an abstract jABC graph.
Mediator control flow	WebML model structure with standard units generated from BP model. Units are then configured and other units are added from the library manually (no need for any implementation, no code generation, just component configuration).	Manually created SLG along the SWSC task description (by refining the abstract model equivalent to the BPMN model), using automatically generated- and standard SIBs.
	continued on next page	

---

[7] Automatic generation of the workflow from declarative specifications is also possible as described in Chap. 7.

[8] Java Electronic Tool Integration; an extension of the jABC framework to seamlessly integrate remote (Web) services.

continued from previous page

Function	WebML	jABC
Data Management	ER-model manually created from analyzing the RosettaNet messages and adding status information. Used to keep data persistent.	Not necessary here due to WSDL import. The data for the mediator are kept in the session memory. ER-model possible, manually created from analyzing the RosettaNet messages.
Web Service invocation	Generic standard units for calls to WSs	Automatically generated SIBs representing WS functions and containing the WS call.
Web Service publishing	Generic standard units for receiving, processing and storing SOAP messages. This allow the design and publishing of complex workflows behind published services.	WSs automatically generated from jABC SLGs and published.
Passing data to a Web Service	Data must be included in the SOAP messages. SOAP (XML) message templates have to be created in advance.	Data is passed to the WSs via the generated SIB parameters provided as Java objects (general jABC mechanism).
Receiving data from a Web Service	Data are extracted from the raw SOAP messages.	Data is received from the WSs via the generated SIB parameters (s. above) that are correct by construction.
Handling XML messages	Standard units for handling XML messages exist, performing XSL transformations on XML messages.	No need to handle raw XML messages.
Monitoring User Interface	Standard units to generate web pages, displaying database data.	Monitoring of flow graphs and state information within the SLG Tracer (interpreter).
Execution outside the modeling environment	Autom. generation of standard J2EE application deployable into any J2EE application server.	Autom. generation of standalone executable application.
Checking mechanisms	Checking mechanism based on the semantic of the single units.	LocalChecker to verify local constraints concerning a single SIB. ModelChecker to verify temporal logic constraints on models.
Service heterogeneity	Extensible support for any Web service platform.	Extensible support for local and remote services (WS, CORBA, jETI, etc.)

9.4.1 Workflow

WebML covers the high level specification of the business flow by means of BPMN models. A coarse WebML skeleton is automatically generated from the BPMN model. This model contains standard units for the Web service calls. Other functions that are necessary to complete these calls have to be configured to meet the actual requirements.

The jABC abstract model is essentially equivalent to the BPMN model. It can be refined manually into the mediator graph. As done here, the main domain specific (peculiar to the SWS Challenge) components (SIBs) used in this model are automatically generated from the Web service's WSDL descriptions. The SLG also contains standard control SIBs (provided with the jABC as a library) to realize the specific control flow for the SWSC scenario descriptions.

9.4.2 Data Model

The WebML model comprises a data description model consisting of an Entity-Relationship model (E-R) that is derived from analyzing the data structures in the RosettaNet messages. This E-R model is used to store the BP's data as well as status information regarding the state of the process execution. It is also possible to use in memory data storage as configuration option.

The jABC mediator does not use persistent data storage since it keeps the information in the session memory. The same E-R model could however also be realized persistently via the *DB-Schema* plugin, if necessary. In this case the corresponding E-R model would be created in the jABC and using this model, a corresponding schema could automatically be created on a JDBC[9] compliant database system. Databases can be accessed using a common SIB palette provided by the DB-Schema plugin.

9.4.3 Dealing with WS

The WebML solution offers four generic WS-related functional units to use or realize a Web service's functionality: two units to issue calls to a WS, one for sending a request and one for also waiting for a response, and two units to provide a WS functionality, one to wait for a request and one for also sending a reply. See Chap. 4 for more details.

These units are parameterized (configured) with the WSDL description and with SOAP message templates that realize the particular WS functionality and return the results of the WS call as SOAP message. These units can also be configured dynamically at runtime passing as parameter the dynamic end point, as shown in the discovery scenario. Such feature is particular useful if combined with dynamic `Adapter` units since it allows to interact with arbitrary Web services and to store the results in the internal data model regardless of the invoked Web services. The feature is adopted in the discovery scenario, to support dynamic binding of services according to user goals and QoS (see Chap. 11).

While WebML choses generic templates for the communication with Web services, the jABC solution realizes a dedicated access to external Web services: for each WS functionality, a separate SIB is automatically generated from the corresponding WSDL description. These SIBs are already fully instantiated: they provide access to the data exchanged with the WS through automatically generated SIB parameters, that can be accessed in each jABC model. The data translation to/from the parameters from/into the SOAP message that in the end is exchanged with the service, is also generated into the SIBs and happens implicitly at execution time. The jABC is specifically designed to make these communication details transparent to the user. Besides a simplified user experience, this also supports agility: the virtualization of (distributed) middlewares and platforms allows one to flexibly exchange service implementations without touching the process model at all.

---

[9] Java DataBase Connectivity (http://java.sun.com/javase/technologies/database/)

Similarly, a stand-alone WS (including the corresponding WSDL) can be generated from each jABC SLG and automatically provided on a web server.

9.4.4 Service heterogeneity

A model driven approach like the one offered by WebML is platform independent in principle. The code corresponding to the modeling primitives can be extended in order to ground to different Web service standards or customized services. This allow a great flexibility and requires, due to the generality of the models, few changes to the modeling primitives.

jABC is designed to be a uniform hub between different external technologies: services and components realized in heterogeneous technologies are handled within the jABC at the SIB and at the SLG level in a uniform way. The SIB model is independent of the technology in which the SIBs are implemented. In this mediator we use Web services, in other applications CORBA components, Java or C, C++, C# code, or just local or remote functionalities made available over an API. Similarly, the SLGs are uniform orchestration models, independent of the technology, platform, or language in which they are going to be exported. Here we export the mediator as Web service implemented in Java, but we could as well export it as BPEL orchestration, or any other target programming language and deployment technique the Genesys plugin and the deployment units support.

The advantage is that users who compose models from functionalities, as is the case for this mediator, are offered a simple, uniform level at which they use and access the SIBs and at which they compose the SLGs, independently of the heterogeneity of technologies.

9.4.5 Dealing with XML messages

To deal with Web services WebML has to prepare the corresponding SOAP (XML) messages, that are passed to the units that execute the call to a WS. If a WS returns a result, this value has to be extracted from the returned SOAP message as well. To do so, WebML offers standard units that perform (lifting and lowering) XSL transformations on XML messages. Eventually this operations can be performed directly in units that perform the actual Web service calls. The use of lifting and lowering adapters grants a more generic approach since they can be configured dynamically.

As in the jABC there is no need to deal with raw XML messages, no such special functions are required. The messages are created within the SIBs according to the structure prescribed by the original WSDL, which is reflected later in the structured parameters of the SIBs and thus known to them.

9.4.6 Execution outside the modeling environment

The use of a Model Driven Design principle enable the total decoupling between the WebML models and the final application code. The WebML code generator allow to transform WebML models into running Web applications, including Web portals, Web services, and Web based workflows. In particular current version enable the generation of J2EE Web applications that can be deployed to any J2EE compliant application server (e.g., Tomcat). In principle, since WebML models are not bound to any specific implementation, it is also possible to generate Web applications for platform different from J2EE, such as .NET. This will require to define a new set of transformation scripts for new target platforms and the relative set of code libraries.

jABC's code generation facility allows the automatic generation of applications from SLGs that are completely independent from the jABC framework and can be executed stand-alone, as if they had been programmed manually. In the given scenarios this capability was used to provide the modeled mediator SLG as a Web service implemented in pure Java. The generation for independent execution is a central difference from other systems that support execution only inside the own interpreter/tracer, or to extruders, i.e. code generators that support the external execution outside the design platform by including with the exported code an own mini-runtime environment.

Since jABC's code generator plugin is retargetable, by selecting a different target language/platform with a few clicks we can as well provide the mediator as a "simple" Java application or applet, or choose another programming language for code generation.

9.4.7 Checking mechanisms

WebML provides checking mechanisms both at the level of BPMN diagrams and WebML models, ensuring that the designed models are consistent with the semantics of the adopted primitives and hence that the code generation process can be completed without errors. For example, if a needed parameter is missing in input to a unit, the verification tool, provides the user with this information and assists the user into the completion of the model.

jABC provides two checking mechanisms to support the modeling process. To verify constraints concerning single SIBs, the LocalChecker plugin can be used. Preconditions as e.g. provision of correct values for all necessary SIB parameters can be ensured this way. The second verification tool is the ModelChecker plugin (named GEAR[10]) that allows to specify constraints in temporal logics that are applied to jABC's models. For example in the SWSC scenario, the ModelChecker could be used to ensure that the closeOrder service is not invoked unless the addLineItem service was called at least once.

Both checking tools can be invoked manually or can be configured to support the modeling process by continuously checking the models and giving spontaneous feedback if the user models any errors. jABC's checking facilities were not used in the early SWSC scenarios but were applied in the advanced solutions.

9.4.8 State Monitoring

The WebML language offers standard abilities to display information from a relational database on a web page. This functionality can be efficiently used to monitor the state of the modelled workflow, as this information is stored in a relational database as well. The runtime offers also the chance to log each single component interaction, including WS interactions.

The jABC offers white box monitoring via its SLG interpreter, the Tracer plugin, which allows monitoring variables and communication activity of the whole hierarchical SLG. At wish this can be done separately for each hierarchy level and each thread, in case of a distributed execution. Additionally, the LearnLib [4] and TestLib plugins support validation and monitoring of black box systems. Not only can the behaviour of black boxes be observed at run time. It may also be systematically learned, resulting in a user-level behavioural model. This feature has not yet been used in the SWS Challenge.

---

[10] Game-based, Easy And Reverse model-checking (`http://jabc.cs.uni-dortmund.de/gear/`)

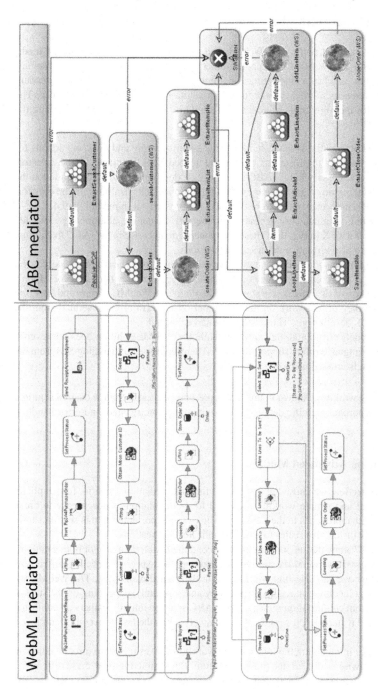

Fig. 9.3. The compared Mediators: Functional correspondence of the WebML (left) and jABC (right) solutions

9.5 Boiling Down to the Essence

Fig. 9.3 compares the first part of the WebML and the jABC workflows for the first mediation scenario, with a layout that respects the functionalities within the mediator solutions.
Each horizontal bar matches a single functional entity in the scenario. Taking into account
the discussed differences, it is easy to reduce both solutions to their common essence. The
result demonstrates the high grade of conceptual similarity of both solutions concerning the
modeling style.

- As mentioned before, the WebML model needs a pair of *lifting* and *lowering* actions for
  each Web service call to create and decode the needed XML messages. These transformations are not necessary in the jABC solution, as it does not treat communication at the
  level of exchanging raw XML messages. So all the service units dealing with the transformation of XML messages in the WebML model are crossed out in red in Fig. 9.4.
- All units dealing with database access in the WebML model are additionally identified
  and crossed out with **X** in Fig. 9.4. These components do not arise in the jABC modelling,
  which allows to also virtualize these access functions.
- In the jABC solution some SIBs are used that extract values from the incoming RosettaNet
  message's type and create new types from these values that are then used for Moon's
  services. The task of these SIBs is in some way analogous to WebML's *lifting* and *lowering*
  units, though they do not work on raw XML but on the Java types generated from the
  services WSDL descriptions. Those SIBs are marked with **#**.
- The jABC models error handling explicitly while the WebML solution does not (even if
  the modeling language offers support for that). Therefore the error handling SIB from the
  jABC solution is crossed using **X**.

The remaining workflow, shown in Fig. 9.5, represents the essence of the desired solution,
abstracted from approach-specific details of the communication, storage, and error handling
choices.

9.5.1 Comparing Advanced Models

For the previous section, we chose the first part of the first mediation scenario, for simplicity
reasons. The small and simple workflows created for both solutions made it easy to break
down the presented approaches to their essence. The example presented in this section shows
that the found conclusion also scales to more complicated applications.

Fig. 9.6 and 9.7 show the second part of the second mediation scenario for both solutions.
Once again it is possible to find the aforementioned approach-specific modeling differences
but apart from this, we can also find a difference in the logical realization. The WebML solution handles each incoming message immediately and separately, depending on the state of
the received line item confirmation message. The jABC solution initially gathers all confirmation messages, and it starts to process them successively when the last item confirmation was
received.

This difference in modeling the logics of the workflow makes it hard to directly compare
the solutions pointwise as done in the previous section. But abstracting from these differences
and from the approach-specific modeling properties again leads to quite similar pictures. The
different details of the presented solutions reflect the different focuses of the used tools. Despite that, even the granularity level of both tools proved to be quite similar as the size of the
resulting models does not differ significantly.

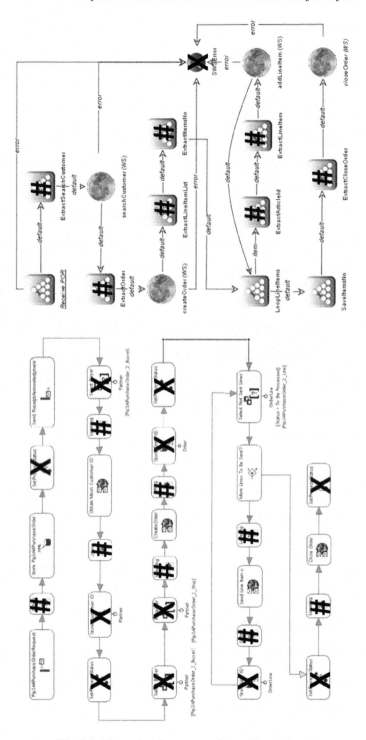

Fig. 9.4. Abstracting from approach-specific entities.

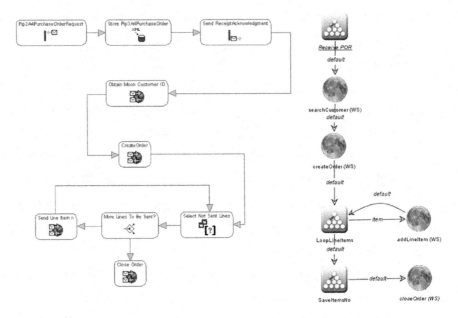

Fig. 9.5. The Reduced WebML and jABC solutions

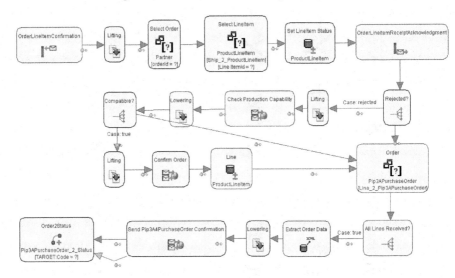

Fig. 9.6. WebML mediator part 2 (scenario 2).

9.6 Conclusion

In this chapter we presented two solutions to the mediation in the Semantic Web service scenario. The two approaches, WebML and jABC, offer two different views on the mediation problem, both in terms of the design-time modeling of the solution and of the runtime execution platform. The applied tools focus on different aspects and so both approaches present advantages and drawbacks.

jABC offers a more abstract and synthetic view of the solution, e.g., disregarding some grounding details of the communication. Modeling with the jABC framework is control driven and it aims at the transparent integration of services in heterogeneous environments. For the user (modeler) it makes no difference what kind of services (e.g. local or remote) are used or how they are implemented. All services appear in a uniform way, as SIBs. The idea of service oriented architecture is strongly maintained in the jABC. Thus it can be seen as a system-integration platform allowing the user to select from heterogeneous services and to compose them (orchestrate them) in a workflow.

On the other hand, WebML offers a wider coverage of the technical details and of the efficient runtime execution. The WebML approach is based on software engineering and web engineering practices, while jABC takes more advantage of the SOA and Web service design fields. Both the methods are not natively meant to face Semantic Web applications, but both proved to adapt rather well to this new class of problems.

References

1. Ceri, S., Fraternali, P., Bongio, A., Brambilla, M., Comai, S., Matera, M.: Designing Data-Intensive Web Applications. Morgan Kauffmann (2002)
2. Steffen, B., Margaria, T., Nagel, R., Jörges, S., Kubczak, C.: Model-Driven Development with the jABC. In: HVC - IBM Haifa Verification Conference. LNCS N.4383, Springer Verlag (2006)
3. Universität Dortmund: jABC Website. (2007) http://www.jabc.de.
4. Raffelt, H., Steffen, B., Berg, T.: LearnLib: A library for automata learning and experimentation. In: ACM SIGSOFT FMICS'05, Lisbon, P, ACM Press (2005) 62–71

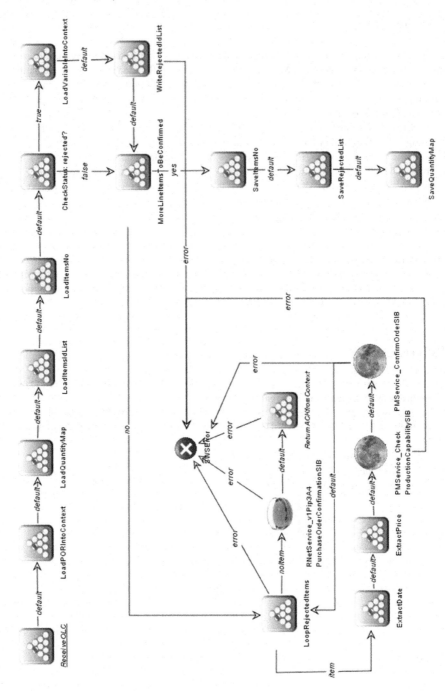

Fig. 9.7. jABC mediator part 2 (scenario 2)

Part III

Discovery Individual Solutions

10

Instance-based Service Discovery with WSMO/WSML and WSMX

Maciej Zaremba[1], Matthew Moran[1], and Tomas Vitvar[2]

[1] Digital Enterprise Research Institute,
National University of Ireland, Galway, Ireland,
`firstname.lastname@deri.org`
[2] The Semantics Technology Institute Innsbruck,
University of Innsbruck, Austria,
`tomas.vitvar@sti2.at`

Summary. In this chapter we present the solution based on WSMO[6], WSML [8]) and WSMX[3] to solving SWS Challenge discovery tasks. Web Service Modeling Ontology (WSMO) provides a model for Semantic Web services used for defining *ontologies*, *services*, *goals* and *mediators*. Web Service Modelling Language (WSML) provides a family of ontology languages used to formally describe WSMO elements used for service modelling, while Web Service Execution Environment (WSMX) is a middleware platform used for discovery, composition, execution and mediation of Semantic Web services. WSMO, WSML and WSMX form a coherent framework covering all aspects of the Semantic Web services that we use to address SWS Challenge discovery scenario.

10.1 Discovery with Data Fetching

Semantic descriptions enhance various descriptive parts of services. The parts regarding service invocation (such as how and where the service can be accessed) are reused, thus so called grounding from semantic level to the underlying technology for service invocation must be defined. In our approach we use grounding to WSDL which is used for on-the-wire message serialization (WSDL binding), physical Web service access (WSDL service and endpoint) and communication (SOAP). Semantic input messages are transformed to the XML representing the input message (lowering) and passed to the underlying operation which responds with an output message in XML. The output messages are transformed to the corresponding semantic output data (lifting).

We define two phases for the discovery process, namely (1) *Web Service Discovery* and (2) *Service Discovery*. Web Service Discovery operates on the capability descriptions of the Goal $\mathcal{G}_F$ and Web service $\mathcal{W}_F$ without any data being taken into account. The matching is defined by the following set-theoretic relationships [13]: (1) exact match, (2) subsumption match, (3) plug-in match, (4) intersection match and (5) disjointness. Exact match denotes perfect match between $\mathcal{G}_F$ and $\mathcal{W}_F$. Subsumption match indicates that $\mathcal{W}_F$ is more specific than request in $\mathcal{G}_F$, e.g., Goal specifies a request of finding a connection from Galway to Dublin, while service offers bus transportation between these two locations. Plug-in match indicates the case where $\mathcal{W}_F$ is more general then what is requested in $\mathcal{G}_F$, e.g, Goal specifies search for Apple laptops while service offers assorted laptops. Intersection match indicates some common parts between $\mathcal{W}_F$ and $\mathcal{G}_F$, e.g., $\mathcal{W}_F$ specifies packaged flight and hotel deals in Europe while $\mathcal{G}_F$ requests flight only. If the Goal and the Web service match, based on relationships 1-4, then service discovery is performed where it is checked if the service can satisfy the specifics of the service request, by consulting the data of the Goal and the service. If all data is not available, it needs to be obtained from the service by performing so called *data fetching*. In this section we further elaborate on the service discovery phase and define the algorithm.

The service requester is de-coupled from the service provider through separate Goal and Web service descriptions. For the purposes of our work we use definitions from WSMO-Lite for semantic description of both parties using the following types of semantics: *information*, *functional*, and *behavioral* [14]. Details of these semantics are also presented in "Mediation using WSMO, WSML and WSMX" Chapter.

For the service discovery we define the matching function

$$s \leftarrow matching(\mathcal{G}, \mathcal{W}, \mathcal{B}_{gw}), \qquad (10.1)$$

where $\mathcal{G}$ and $\mathcal{W}$ is a Goal and a service description respectively and $\mathcal{B}_{gw}$ is a common knowledge base for the Goal and the service. The knowledge base contains data which must be *directly* (through descriptions $\mathcal{G}_O$ and $\mathcal{W}_O$) or *indirectly* (through data fetching) available so that the matching function can be evaluated. The result s of this function can be: (1) $match$ when the match was found (in this case all required data in $\mathcal{B}_{gw}$ is available), (2) $nomatch$ when the match was not found (in this case all required data in $\mathcal{B}_{gw}$ is available), or (3) $nodata$ when some required data in $\mathcal{B}_{gw}$ is not available and thus the matching function cannot be evaluated.

We denote the description of the Web service and the Goal as $\mathcal{W}$ and $\mathcal{G}$ respectively. For each such description, $\mathcal{D}$, we denote the information semantics as $\mathcal{D}_O$, the capability as $\mathcal{D}_F$, and choreography as $\mathcal{D}_X$.

We further assume that all required data for the Goal is directly available in the description $\mathcal{G}_O$. The data fetching step is then performed for the service when the matching function cannot be evaluated (the result of this function is $nodata$). We then define the knowledge base as:

$$\mathcal{B}_{gw} = \mathcal{G}_O \cup \mathcal{W}_O \cup \{y_1, y_2, ..., y_m\}, \qquad (10.2)$$

where $\{y_i\}$ is all additional data that needs to be fetched from the service in order to evaluate the matching function.

Further, we denote $\mathcal{W}_X$ as the data-fetch interface of the service $\mathcal{W}$ with output symbols Σ_O and input symbols Σ_I. The matching function can be then evaluated if data $\{y_i\}$ can be fetched from the service through the data fetch interface if input data Σ_I is either initially available in the knowledge base $\mathcal{B}_{gw}$ (data directly available from the Goal or Web service ontologies) or the input data becomes available during the processing of the interface.

In addition, as illustrated in Figure 10.1, we only fetch the data from the interface if this data can be used for evaluation of the matching function (in general the data-fetch interface can provide data not required for the matching – see the rule $r3$ in Figure 10.1). In $\mathcal{B}_{gw}$ full circles denote available information while dotted circles denote unavailable information which can be obtained through the data-fetch interface. However, since the fetching operation can be costly in terms of the generated communication, only the parts of $\mathcal{B}_{gw}$ which are referenced from the Goal effect ϕ^{eff} should be fetched.

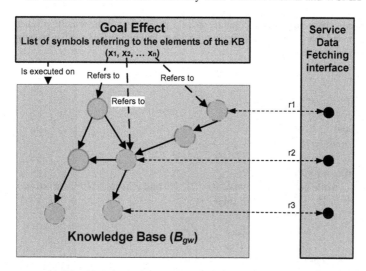

Fig. 10.1. Minimization of the Provider Interactions

Let ϕ^{eff} be the effect of the Goal capability $\mathcal{G}_F$, L be the set of rules of the data-fetch interface $\mathcal{W}_X$, and let Σ_O be the set of output symbols of that interface. Then, we only use the rule $r \in L$ iff exists $x \in r^{eff}$, $x \in \Sigma_O$ such that $x \in \phi^{eff}$. Please note that this rule can be in addition executed if the input data is available during processing (i.e. r^{cond} holds in the $\mathcal{B}_{gw}$) (see the algorithm in Section 10.1.1).

10.1.1 Algorithm

In algorithm 1, the matching function is integrated with the data fetching which provides instance data for the concepts referred from the Goal effect ϕ^{eff}. The algorithm operates on inputs, produces outputs and uses internal structures as follows:

Input:
- Web service W for which we denote W_O as the Web service ontology with initial instance data and $\mathcal{W}_X$ as data-fetch interface of the Web service with rule base L. In addition, for each rule $r \in L$ we specify the data of the rule effect r^{eff} as $r.data$ and the action $r.action$ with values add, $update$, $delete$ meaning that if the rule is executed the action performs the effect of the rule, i.e. changing the state by adding, updating or deleting data in the memory (knowledge base).
- Goal description G for which we denote G_O as the Goal ontology with initial instance data and G^{eff} as the Goal capability effect. For W and G it must hold that they match at abstract level (Web service discovery).

Output:
- Boolean variable s indicating the result of the matching function between W and G, i.e. $match$ or $nomatch$.

Uses:
- Processing memory M containing data fetched during execution of rules of the data fetching interface.

- Knowledge base B_{gw} which contains data for processing of the matching function.
- Boolean variable $modified$ indicating whether the knowledge base has been modified or not during the processing.

1: $B_{gw} \leftarrow G_O \cup W_O$
2: $M \leftarrow B_{gw}$
3: **repeat**
4:    $modified \leftarrow false$
5:    $s \leftarrow matching(G, W, B_{gw})$
6:    **if** $s = nodata$ **then**
7:       **while** get r from L: $holds(r^{cond}, M)$ **and** $r.data \in G^{\textit{eff}}$ **and not** $modified$ **do**
8:          **if** $r.action = add$ **then**
9:            $add(r.data, M)$
10:           $add(r.data, B_{gw})$
11:           $modified \leftarrow true$
12:          **end if**
13:          **if** $r.action = remove$ **then**
14:           $remove(r.data, M)$
15:          **end if**
16:          **if** $r.action = update$ **then**
17:           $update(r.data, M)$
18:           $update(r.data, B_{gw})$
19:           $modified \leftarrow true$
20:          **end if**
21:       **end while**
22:    **end if**
23: **until** $s \neq nodata$ **or not** $modified$

Algorithm 1: Minimized Data Fetching for Discovery

The algorithm tries to fetch data from the service by processing the service's data-fetch interface. For each rule present, which can be executed, it checks whether its result will provide any information referenced by $G^{\textit{eff}}$. For example $G^{\textit{eff}}$ may refer to the concept *price* of a given product which is unavailable in the B_{gw}, however a rule exists which can result in an instance of the *price* concept being obtained. Once the data fetching operations are executed and new facts are added, updated or removed, a $modified$ flag is set to true and B_{gw} can be matched again. This cycle ends when no data can be fetched from the interface or the matching function can be evaluated (the result is $match$ or $nomatch$).

The algorithm assumes that the rules of the data-fetch interface can be executed independently. In particular this means that if there is a symbol referencing a concept in the knowledge base and there is a rule which can fetch the data for that concept, there is no other rule which needs to be executed prior in order to execute the rule fetching the data. Although our assumption that more realistic scenarios of data fetching should have independent rules (see Section 10.3.1), we acknowledge that this is an open issue of our approach which we plan to investigate in our future work.

The algorithm uses independent memory (memory M) from the knowledge base (B_{gw}) for processing the data-fetch interface. This allows that already-obtained data cannot be removed from the knowledge base while, at the same time, correct processing of the interface is ensured. The memory M is used not only for data but also for control of interface processing (in general, the content of the memory does not need to always reflect the content of the knowledge base). According to the particular interface definition, the data can be fetched step-wise allowing minimization of the interactions with the service during discovery. This also aligns with the strong decoupling principle when services are described semantically and independently from users' requests. For example, during the service-creation phase a service provider (creator) does not know which particular data will be required for a particular data-fetch (in general, matching with a Goal could require some or all defined data which depends on the definition of the request). The interface defined using rules allows to get only the data which is needed for the matching (for example in some cases only price is needed, in other cases a price and location of the selling company could be needed, if offered by the service depending on what is referred in the user request).

10.2 Solution to SWS-Challenge Discovery

In this section we describe the case scenario from the SWS Challenge used to demonstrate our approach to discovery. The scenario is depicted in figure 10.2, a user wants to buy certain products and ship them to a certain location. A user accesses the e-marketplace called Moon where a number of companies such as Muller and Racer have registered their services (we further refer to Muller and Racer as *service providers*). Moon runs a (1) web portal through which it provides services to users and (2) the WSMX middleware system through which it facilitates integration between users and service providers.

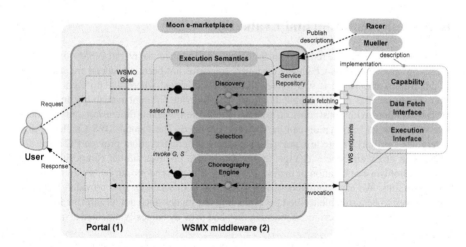

Fig. 10.2. Architecture for the Scenario

We make the following assumptions which hold for both, the service interface model definition and implementation of the scenario.

- Service providers and Moon both use WSMO for Web service description. Service providers make their WSMO service descriptions available to Moon. The payload of messages exchanged is represented in WSML. We assume that both service requesters and providers maintain adapters to their back-end systems which provide lifting and lowering operations between their existing technology (e.g. WSDL, XML Schema) and WSML.

- All service providers utilize a common ontology maintained by the Moon e-marketplace. This assumption reflects the fact that we assume no data interoperability issues between service providers and the Moon e-marketplace.

- Each service requester provides purchase and shipment requests in one message. As we focus on discovery, we do not deal with service composition in this example. However, in general, purchase and shipment could be two separated services provided by two independent service providers.

- A user defines requests through a Web portal's user interface. The Web portal generates a WSMO Goal corresponding to the request, sends it to WSMX, receives the response, and presents the result back to the user.

- The execution process is run in WSMX after the receipt of the Goal, including discovery with fetch of the required data from services, selection of the best service, and its invocation. Although we present the complete process, the contribution in this chapter is only in the model for the dynamic data-fetch interface integrated with discovery. Other parts of the process, i.e. semantic matching for discovery and selection are not subject of our contribution in this work.

- During the execution process, the message exchange pattern between the user and the Moon is simplified to request-response only (e.g. the user could approve a selected service or select a service himself before the invocation). This assumption reflects the fact that meta-interactions between users and the middleware system are not of our interest at this point.

10.3 Implementation and Evaluation

In this section we detail the required modeling steps and explain the overall WSMX-based discovery process. Two SWS Challenge discovery scenarios has been introduced and addressed by our framework. The first was related to package shipment where five different shippers offer various purchasing and shipment options. They provide different availability and pricing for their services with constraints on package destination, weight, dimension and shipment date where not all information can be statically provided. The second SWS-Challenge discovery use-case tackles product provisioning where different vendors provide PC hardware where their stock and prices change very often. It also involves simple composition since sometimes only a combination of the devices from different vendors can satisfy user requests and constraints. We have comprehensively addressed both scenarios and provided Web services proven to be a suitable testbed for evaluating our model since not all information could be provided in service descriptions meaning they had to be dynamically obtained at discovery-time.

Both the descriptions of WSMO Goals and Web services include elements for describing *capabilities*. We use the following parts of WSMO Capabilities in our service discovery:

- **Preconditions** describe conditions which must hold in a state required before the service can be executed. WSMO Preconditions map to ϕ^{pre} of the capability descriptions.

- **Postconditions** describe conditions in a state which must hold after the service is executed. WSMO Postconditions map to ϕ^{eff} of the capability descriptions.

From the perspective of a Goal description, the capability describes the functionality that the owner of the Goal wishes to achieve from a Web service. Correspondingly, the capability of a Web service describes the functionality offered by that service. To a large extent, the responsibility of a discovery mechanism, in the context of WSMO, is to find services whose capability matches that of the provided Goal.

In addition, the Web service interface defines *choreography* and *orchestration* allowing the modeling of external and internal behavior of the service respectively. We define the interface for data-fetch using a specific choreography *namespace*[3] allowing to distinguish a specific meaning for its usage from the meaning of the interface defining execution choreography used for consuming the service functionality within the same WSMO service.

10.3.1 WSDL to Choreography Mapping

The modeling of Semantic Web service behavioral descriptions is, to a significant extent, based on existing Web service standards. We map existing WSDL service descriptions to the WSMO Semantic Web services where additional descriptions can be provided. Mapping from existing, syntactic service descriptions to the semantic layer is the first step of the modeling process after which resulting descriptions can be aligned by the domain expert.

XML Schema defined in the WSDL can be mapped to the given domain ontology using Semantic Annotations of Web Service Description Language and XML Schema (SAWSDL [15]) which provides a generic and agnostic mechanism for semantically annotating Web services. As described in [14], the SAWSDL allows to annotate WSDL schema elements with elements from the information semantics and WSDL interfaces with behavioral semantics of the service. In addition, the extension of WSDL 2.0 comes with the notion of so called *safe methods*, relevant from the dynamic discovery point of view. When the *safe* attribute of an operation is set to *true*, the operation indicates that it has an informative character and will not cause any real world effect when invoked (e.g. like agreeing to buy something). For the purpose of our work, safe operations may be mapped to the data-fetch interface allowing a user to find out more about the functionality of the service. Figure 10.3 presents this mapping. WSDL operations without the *safe* attribute are mapped to the service execution interface.

10.3.2 Modeling Ontologies, Goals and Services

We base examples on a simple composition service for computer hardware, where PC hardware stock and price information is not available in the service description and needs to be fetched during the service discovery. We also emphasize how this communication is minimized by looking at the concepts referred to in the Goal capability. In section 10.3.3 we further describe the evaluation of our implementation in the broader context of the SWS Challenge requirements. In order to implement the scenario, we first need to create semantic models for ontologies, Goals and services. We describe these models in the following sub-sections. We present examples of ontologies, services and Goals definition in WSML using the following prefixes to denote their respective namespaces: *do* – domain ontology, *df* – data fetch interface, *gl* – Goal ontology.

Ontologies

Ontologies provide rich data models used for the definition of Goals and services. In our scenario we use a common domain ontology with additional ontologies to define specific axioms or concepts used by the descriptions of services and/or Goals.

---

[3] we specify the URI for the namespace as *"http://wsmx.org/datafetch#"*

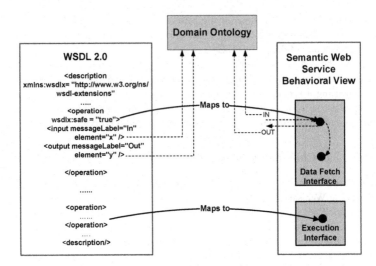

Fig. 10.3. WSDL 2.0 to Semantic Web service Mapping

The common ontology defines shared concepts used in the description of the Goal and services, such as *Location, Notebook, DockingStation*, etc. In addition, we use the common ontology to specify named relations for services and Goals. Specific ontologies for Goals and services declare axioms that define the relations to represent their conditions. An analogy for this approach are interfaces in programming languages like Java. The interface declares some functionality but does not say how this should be implemented. Using this approach, we define a set of relations in the common ontology which represent the axioms that a service may need to define. Listing 10.1 shows the simple definition for the *isCompatible* relation from the common ontology and its implementation in the service ontology.

```
1   /* isCompatible relation in the domain ontology */
2
3   relation do#isCompatible (ofType do#Notebook, ofType
4   do#DockingStation)
5
6   /* implementation of the isCompatible relation in the service
7   ontology */
8
9   axiom isCompatibleDef definedBy
10      ?notebook[do#GTIN hasValue ?gtinX]
11      memberOf do#Notebook and
12      ?dockingstation[do#supportsGTIN hasValue ?gtinY]
13      memberOf do#DockingStation
14      and ?gtinX = ?gtinY) implies
15      do#isCompatible(?notebook, ?dockingstation).
```

Listing 10.1. *isCompatible* relation

The relation *isCompatible* is true if the notebook sold by the service provider can be used with one of the available docking stations. This axiom can be used in the Goal query to check compatibility of the two components.

Services

We focus on the description of the data-fetch interface of one of the vendors service showing how and which data can be fetched during discovery. In listing 10.2, the first rule (line 14) describes how to get the list of notebook prices depending on the user location. A user-location (*location* variable) is taken from the notebook quote request. For the listing of notebooks the location matters and first the location of the client has to be checked. Computer hardware vendors can send their hardware only to some of the countries and availability of shipment to the given location is checked by evaluating $mo\#isAvailable(?clientLocation)$ rule.

```
1
2    stateSignature WSVendorStatesignature
3
4        in do#NotebookListReq withGrounding { _"http://sws−challenge.org/vendor.wsdl#(VendorPort/
             listNotebooks/in0)"}
5        in do#WebCamListReq withGrounding { _"http://sws−challenge.org//vendor.wsdl#(VendorPort/
             listWebCams/in0)"}
6        out do#NotebookList
7        out do#WebCamList
8
9    interface df#WSVendorDataFetchInterface
10       choreography WSVendorDataFetchChoreography
11           ...
12           transitionRules WSVendorDataFetchTransitionRules
13           /* Rule 1: Request for the list of notebooks */
14               forall {?notebookListReq} with (
15                   ?notebookListReq[mo#location hasValue ?clientlocation]
16                   memberOf do#NotebookListReq and
17                   ?clientLocation memberOf mo#Location and
18                   mo#isAvailable(?clientLocation)
19               ) do
20                   add(_# memberOf do#NotebookList)
21               endForall
22
23           /* Rule 2: Request for the list of Web cameras*/
24               forall {?webcamsListReq} with (
25                   ?WebCamsListReq memberOf do#WebCamListReq
26               ) do
27                   add(_# memberOf do#WebCamList)
28               endForall
```

Listing 10.2. Vendor data fetching interface

If notebooks are not shipped to the client location, no data will be fetched, since the client will not be able to buy from this vendor due to the address constraints. For example, notebooks may be sold only in US for tax and shipment reasons while other, lightweight items (e.g. Web cameras) may be shipped all over the world. In the definition of the second rule there are no constraints over the client's location and available Web cameras may be sold to any location in the world. Concepts *NotebookListReq*, *WebCamsListReq* and *NotebookList*, *WebCamList* are defined as input and output vocabularies respectively. The relation *isAvailable* is described in the common ontology and its axiom is provided in the Web service ontology.

Goals

The example Goal for the scenario describes the user's aim to buy a laptop and docking station and to ship them to a specific location. In addition, the Goal specifies a preference that price be used for selection of the best service where multiple matching services are discovered. The Goal as in listing 10.3 is defined for our scenario with respect to the implementation of the matching function following the algorithm 1 (we discuss this implementation in section 10.3.3). The Goal expression contains references to two concepts, namely mo#Notebook and mo#DockingStation.

```
1    Goal GoalPurchaseHardware
2        nfp
3            _"preference" hasValue "?price"
4            ...
5        endnfp
6        ...
7        capability GoalPurchaseHardwareCapability
8        postcondition
9            definedBy
10           ( ?x[do#price hasValue ?priceX, do#hddGB hasValue ?hddGBX, do#memoryMB hasValue ?
                 memMBX]
11              memberOf do#MacNotebook and ?memMBX >= 512 and ?hddGBX > 40 and
12           ?y[do#price hasValue ?priceY] memberOf do#DockingStation
13              and isCompatible(?x,?y)
14              and ?price = (?priceX + ?priceY)
15              and ?price < 2000).
16       ...
```

Listing 10.3. User Goal in WSMO

Instances of these two concepts are not available in the static Web service description and have to be fetched during the discovery phase as specified in algorithm 1. The Goal defines the capability postcondition specifying how to get a quote for the product while at the same time the product must be available to be shipped to the location specified by the notebook request. Hard constraints are expressed over the parameters of the laptop. It must have at least 512 MB RAM and over 40 GB hard drive capacity. Additionally, a compatible docking station should be ordered. The previously-defined axiom *isCompatible* is used for this purpose. The overall price of both components should not exceed 2000 Euro.

10.3.3 Implementation

The scenario is implemented as follows: when the Goal is generated out of the request specified by the user, it is sent to the WSMX system. WSMX starts a new operational thread (execution semantics) which first invokes the discovery component which in turn returns a list of services matching the Goal. This list is passed to the selection component to select the service that best fits the user request. Control passes to the choreography engine which uses the choreography descriptions of the Goal and service respectively, to drive the message exchange with the discovered service. This section describes the implementation of the algorithm 1 within the discovery component of WSMX. The details about other parts of the execution process can be found in our previous work in [16].

After the discovery phase, the execution semantics starts the conversation by processing the execution choreographies of the Goal and selected service resulting in invoking and consuming of the service capability by the user.

Section 10.1 describes two steps for discovery. A prototype for the *Web service discovery* is under development in the WSMO working group. The implementation, described here, focuses on the steps of *Service discovery* matching and *data-fetching*. A match between the Goal and Web services is determined on the knowledge base created out of their descriptions, including instance data (both available from the descriptions and fetched). The Goal capability defines a query (listing 10.3) which is used to query the knowledge base.

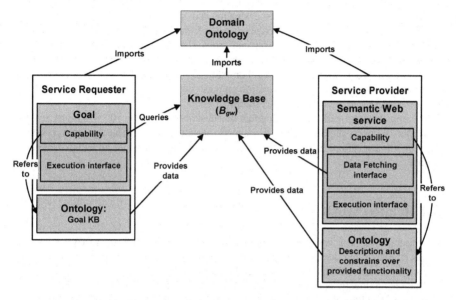

Fig. 10.4. Knowledge Base B_{gw}

According to the algorithm 1 in section 10.1, the knowledge base B_{gw} is created for every Goal and Web service from the repository as shown in figure 10.4. Initially, the knowledge base imports all concepts from the domain ontology and data from both Goal and Web service descriptions. If the data-fetch interface is available then parts of it may be able to obtain the instance data of some of the concepts referred to in the Goal query. In our case, data fetching will be executed for $Notebook$ and $DockingStation$ provisioning. Once the knowledge base is populated with up-to-date information on available notebooks and docking stations, a query such as the one defined in listing 10.3, can be performed on the KB. It is worth noting that, thanks to this approach, only the necessary parts of the data-fetch interface will be utilized and no unnecessary communication will be generated. If the result of the evaluation is $true$, we add the Web service to the list E of Web services to the position determined by the preference. If the result of the evaluation is $false$, match of the next service from the list is attempted. Otherwise, the cycle ends and the next service from the repository is processed. We briefly discuss this implementation in the next section 10.3.4.

10.3.4 Evaluation

Our implementation was evaluated to successfully address the scenario with dynamic PC hardware product data fetching, where various constraints over the hardware parameters (like HDD capacity, type and speed of the processor, etc.), customer location and overall price had to be considered, scoring success level 2 (i.e., introduced changes did not entail any code modifications but only declarative parts had to be modified). The implementation proved to be generic

as only modifications of the WSMO Goals were necessary in order to correctly handle introduced changes. No changes in WSMX code or in the descriptions of the services were required
– only the Goal requests had to be changed.

In the initial version of our work it was not possible to distinguish between dynamically
fetched data required for the user request evaluation and data which is irrelevant resulting from
fetching from all *safe* endpoints exposed via data-fetch interface. The introduction of our optimization allowed to fetch only the relevant data which significantly decreased communication
with the service especially since multiple service endpoints were provided for fetching information on different kinds of products. For example for the Goal of buying a laptop with
compatible docking station only information on these two products were fetched leaving out
all other unreferenced, though available, information.

The implementation of the matching function described in section 10.3.3 was able to handle targeted discovery requirements of the scenario at success level 2. The algorithm presented
here allows to use various implementations of matching functions which adhere to its defined
interface.

10.4 Related Work

Other discovery approaches described in this book like DIANE, miAamics, SWE-ET are in
obvious relation to our discovery. In this section we give a broader overview of other existing
discovery approaches related to our Instance-based Discovery.

There is no directly comparable work in the SOA standards area which would allow for
the fetching of additional data to aid discovery at run-time. UDDI and ebXML registries allow
for search of the services only on the static, category level providing insufficient support for
automated discovery when using fine-grained search requests. Determining suitability and
details of the functionality offered by services advertised in service registries for the request
at hand remains a manual task. However, WSDL 2.0 safe methods could be seen as a step in
direction (see WSDL2.0 primer[4]) of introducing dynamism in the discovery process. Also, in
Dziembowski's W3C position paper [17] there is a need for the instance-based Web service
discovery highlighted but with a very limited proposal on how this should be achieved.

The problem of insufficient static descriptions for fine-grained discovery requests within
dynamic domains has been addressed using CORBA's *Trading Service* in the eMarketplace
domain [18] where dynamic properties of a offered functionality exposed as a CORBA object
can be calculated within a business's private space and where results can be integrated into
the *Trading Service* discovery process. *Trading Service* consists of name-value property pairs
which can be either static or dynamic. In the case of a dynamic property, the external *Dynamic Property Evaluator* entity residing within the business provider private space is called.
Dynamic Property Evaluator returns different results depending on the current state of the
business provider (e.g., its current stock, prices or date and time of the day) and client's request. It is worth noting that due to the code-based representation of CORBA actual evaluation
of the *Trading Service* is carried out in the client's code while our semantic-based approach
allows to shift the overall discovery process to the middleware requiring the client only to
provide a fine-grained request. A similar approach to dynamic service functionality aspects is
currently missing in SOA and our work attempts to fill this gap.

Research into goal-based discovery for WSMO and WSMX takes a step-wise approach
with both theoretical and implementation concerns addressed at each stage. Three strategies

---

[4] http://www.w3.org/TR/wsdl20-primer/

have been investigated in this manner. The first is keyword-based discovery [13], which uses an algorithm that matches keywords, identified from the Goal description, with words occurring in various parts of the Web service description, namely in, non-functional properties, concept names and predicate names. The second strategy is for a lightweight Semantic Web services discovery component for the WSMX platform and is described in [19]. This approach models a service in terms of the objects it can deliver. The term object, in this sense, means something of value the service delivers in its domain of interest. A third strategy is based around the use of quality-of-service attributes as described in [20] and implemented by the authors as a WSMX component. Upper level ontologies describing various domains for quality-of-service attributes are provided and non-functional properties are introduced to the service descriptions whose meanings are defined in these QoS ontologies. Our approach to service discovery is compatible with each of the matching strategies as it extends the matching power by requesting data from the service that is not directly available in its description. In [21], contracting is identified as an activity that may take place between the requester and provider once the initial discovery has identified candidate services.

The discovery mechanisms in OWL-S relies on subsumption reasoning to match a service profile of a service request with candidate service profiles published by service providers as described in [9]. As with the WSMO efforts, they acknowledge that a *negotiation* phase may be necessary after discovery to allow requesters and providers agree on quality of service issues. However, they do not address the problem of fetching additional data from the service at discovery-time to enable a more informed match to be made. Our approach can be considered as pre-contracting as we concentrate on the retrieval of additional data from the service provider to make a more exact match during discovery.

10.5 Summary

In this chapter we have presented an approach for semantic discovery supporting realistic late-binding performed at run-time and with emphasis on minimizing any additional communication. The fine granularity of both client request and service functionality descriptions, expressed semantically, allows a greater degree of accuracy when matching requester Goals to candidate Web services. We are aware that this approach, due to the logical reasoning, computational complexity and generated communication overhead, is scalable only for a limited number of services, therefore data fetching and detailed evaluation takes place in the final phase of the discovery process, and is preceded by category-based matchmaking and static description semantic discovery. Applying optimization to dynamic data-fetching decreases the generated communication, especially for more complex services that offer a broad range of functionality (e.g. a warehouse offering multitude of products with different constraints on shipment and different pricing options). Combining the dynamic data-fetch mechanism with existing WSMO discovery approaches brings the target of runtime service late-binding close, facilitating the volatile and frequently-changing nature of services in SOA.

Our future work is planned to extend our discovery framework in two directions: (1) support for service contracting, (2) evaluation of the technique with large number of services. Service functionality details disclosed during the discovery phase should be propagated downwards to the service execution phase once the client (or middleware acting on the behalf of client) decide to consume the dynamically proposed functionality. It is worth noticing that data fetched during the discovery can be used for constructing a client-service contract with a certain time period of validity. However, an additional protocol would be required for finalizing such a contract, which may also require negotiation with the service. Our discovery framework has been successfully applied to the SWS-Challenge discovery problems where several Web services have been semantically described and their safe operations been exposed via data-fetch interfaces. We plan to evaluate the applicability of our approach to a greater number of services from different domains, to examine the scalability of the advantages obtained through using semantic descriptions with the data-fetch mechanism, over purely informal and static service descriptions.

References

1. Roman, D., Keller, U., Lausen, H., de Bruijn, J., Lara, R., Stollberg, M., Polleres, A., Feier, C., Bussler, C., Fensel, D.: Web Service Modeling Ontology. Applied Ontologies 1(1) (2005) 77 – 106
2. de Bruijn, J., Lausen, H., Polleres, A., Fensel, D.: The Web Service Modeling Language: An Overview. In: Proc. of the European Semantic Web Conference. (2006)
3. Vitvar, T., Mocan, A., Kerrigan, M., Zaremba, M., Zaremba, M., Moran, M., Cimpian, E., Haselwanter, T., Fensel, D.: Semantically-enabled service oriented architecture: Concepts, technology and application. In Service Oriented Computing and Applications, Springer London 1(2) (2007)
4. Preist, C.: A conceptual architecture for semantic web services. In McIlraith, S., Plexousakis, D., Harmelen, F.v., eds.: Third International Semantic Web Services Conference (ISWC). Volume LNCS 3298., Hiroshima, Japan, Springer (2004) 395–409
5. Baida, Z., Gordijn, J., Omelayenko, B.: A shared service terminology for online service provisioning. In: Proceedings of the 6th international conference on Electronic commerce. ACM Press, Delft, The Netherlands (2004) 1–10
6. Fensel, D., Keller, U., Lausen, H., Polleres, A., Toma, I.: What is wrong with web services discovery. In: W3C Workshop on Frameworks for Semantics in Web Services - Position Paper., Innsbruck, Austria, (2005)
7. Keller, U., Lara, R., Lausen, H., Polleres, A., Fensel, D.: Automatic Location of Services. In: 2nd European Semantic Web Symposium (ESWS2005), 29th May - June 1st. (2005)
8. Martin, D., Burstein, M., Hobbs, J., Lassila, O., McDermott, D., McIlraith, S., Narayanan, S., Paolucci, M., Parsia, B., Payne, T., Sirin, E., Srinivasan, N., Sycara, K.: Owl-s: Semantic markup for web services, w3c member submission. Technical report, W3C (2004)
9. Paolucci, M., Kawamura, T., Payne, T., Sycara, K.: Semantic matching of web services capabilities. In: 1st International Semantic Web Conference (ISWC). (2002) 333–347
10. Dogac, A., Tambag, Y., Pembecioglu, P., Pektas, S., Laleci, G., Kurt, G., Toprak, S., Kabak, Y.: An ebXML infrastructure implementation through UDDI registries and RosettaNet PIPs. In: Proc. of the 2002 ACM SIGMOD International Conference on Management of Data. (2002) 512–523
11. Voskob, M.: UDDI Spec TC V4 Requirement - Taxonomy support for semantics. OASIS, 2004. http://www.oasis-open.org. (Technical report)
12. Vitvar, T., Mocan, A., Kerrigan, M., Zaremba, M., Zaremba, M., Moran, M., Cimpian, E., Haselwanter, T., Fensel, D.: Semantically-enabled service oriented architecture : concepts, technology and application. Service Oriented Computing and Applications 2(2) (2007) 129–154
13. Keller, U., Lara, R., Lausen, H., Polleres, A., Predoiu, L., Toma, I.: WSMO D10.2 Sematic Web Service Discovery available at http://www.wsmo.org/TR/d10/v0.2/d10.pdf. Technical report (2005)

14. Vitvar, T., Kopecky, J., Fensel, D.: WSMO-Lite: Lightweight Semantic Descriptions for Services on the Web. In: ECOWS. (2007)
15. Farrell, J., Lausen, H.: Semantic Annotations for WSDL and XML Schema available at http://www.w3.org/TR/sawsdl/. Technical report (2007)
16. Haselwanter, T., Kotinurmi, P., Moran, M., Vitvar, T., Zaremba, M.: WSMX: A Semantic Service Oriented Middleware for B2B Integration. In: ICSOC. (2006) 477–483
17. Dziembowski, K.:   Dynamic service discovery.   In: A position paper for the W3C Workshop on Web Services for Enterprise Computing, available at http://www.w3.org/2007/01/wos-papers/gestalt. (2007)
18. Schade, A., Facciorusso, C., Field, S., Hoffner, Y.: Advanced Dynamic Property Evaluation for CORBA-Based Electronic Markets. In: Second International Workshop on Advanced issues of E-Commerce and Web-Based Information Systems. (2000) 109–116
19. Friesen, A., Grimm, S.: DIP WP4 Service Usage, D4.8 Discovery Specification, available at http://dip.semanticweb.org/documents/D4.8Final.pdf. Technical report (2005)
20. Hauswirth, M., Porto, F., Vu, L.H.: P2P and QoS-enabled Service Discovery Specification, available at http:/dip.semanticweb.org/documents/D4.17-Revised.pdf. Technical report (2006)
21. Lara, R., Olmedilla, D.: Discovery and Contracting of Semantic Web Services. Technical report (2005)

11

Using Glue to Solve the Discovery Scenarios of the SWS-Challenge

Andrea Turati[1], Emanuele Della Valle[1], Dario Cerizza[1], and Federico M. Facca[2]

[1] CEFRIEL,
Via Fucini 2, I-20133 Milano, Italy,
firstname.lastname@deri.org
[2] Dipartimento di Elettronica e Informazione, Politecnico di Milano
P.za Leonardo da Vinci 32, I-20133 Milano, Italy
firstname.lastname@elet.polimi.it

Summary. In this chapter we present SWE-ET, which is the solution that we proposed for the SWS-Challenge. SWE-ET is a conjunction of two components: one is the WebRatio framework, which is mainly used to solve the Mediation scenarios, and the other is Glue, which is used to solve the Discovery scenarios. This chapter focuses on the Discovery scenarios, therefore we describe all the features of Glue in details while we partially describe WebRatio by discussing only those features that have been exploited to solve the Discovery scenarios of the Challenge.

11.1 Introduction

The number of Web Services is constantly increasing and users spend more and more time to locate the one that best fits their needs. An automated method for locating services [1] is necessary to limit the user intervention.

Several success stories about the most common Web Service approach to discovery (e.g., UDDI [2], ebXML registry [3], etc.) tell us that they can be effectively used within an organization in order to collect services that run within its own borders. However, in spite of the benefits, the current solutions fail to escape organizational borders and finding external useful services can be a very consuming process. We believe that is necessary to enable inter-operability between different organizations, and not only intra-operability within a single organization.

Outside the organizational border quite often, decision taking involve a complex negotiation that has to take into account the existence of different view points. We prefer to refer to such different view points with the notion of "polarization". In communications and psychology, "polarization" is the process whereby a social or political group is divided into two opposing sub-groups with fewer and fewer members of the group remaining neutral or holding an intermediate position. We believe such a process occurs quite often in reality and results in a fragmented market, each sub market having its own standards. In case of "polarization" is very difficult to agree on using a common terminology. UDDI and ebXML, being syntactic, are very difficult to deploy in presence of polarization.

Our research on Web Service discovery lead us to believe that *semantics* is a key ingredient in handling polarization. *Ontologies* can be used to capture the different point of view and *rules* can be use to encode domain-specific notion of matching. Extending Web Service discovery with ontologies and rules results not only in a better trade-off between precision and recall, but also in handling polarization by avoiding to require service requesters and service provider to commit to a common set of ontologies. We conceived as well as implemented such idea in a Semantic Web Service discovery engine named Glue [DCC05], which we used to solve the SWS-Challenge.

Actually, CEFRIEL and Politecnico di Milano jointly proposed a solution to the SWS-Challenge named SWE-ET (Semantic Web Engineering – Environments and Tools), by combining CEFRIEL's Glue discovery engine with the WebRatio framework from Politecnico di Milano. In particular, WebRatio mainly addresses the Mediation scenario of the Challenge while Glue deals with the Discovery scenario.

In this chapter we focus on our solution to the Discovery scenario of the SWS-Challenge. In Section 11.2 we describe the conceptual model of WSMO, that Glue extends. In Section 11.3 we describe the extension we made to the conceptual model of WSMO, the execution semantics of Glue and some implementation details. Then, we depict the discovery scenarios addressed by Glue (Section 11.4) and finally we present our solution in Section 11.5. At the end, we point out some conclusion and future works.

11.2 WSMO as starting point

One of the recent works that aim at addressing the discovery of Web Services by exploiting semantics is the Web Service Modeling Ontology (WSMO) [5, 6]. WSMO is a conceptual model that aims at facilitating the discovery of Semantic Web Services. In particular, it is an ontology defining four modeling elements (Ontologies, Web Services, Goals and Mediators).

Ontologies form the data model upon which the other four elements are built.

Web Services include the functional and behavioral aspects, which must be semantically described in order to allow semi-automated use. Web Services are described in WSMO from three different points of view: *non-functional properties*, *capabilities* (describing functionalities), and *interfaces* (describing the behavior).

A *Goal* describes the end user perspective in terms of the function that the user desires and the way in which he/she wishes to invoke the service. It is characterized in a dual way with respect to Web Services: goal's descriptions include the *requested capability* and the *requested interface*.

Finally, *Mediators* provide methods to overcome structural or semantic mismatches that appear between the other top elements of WSMO. There are four types of Mediator. An ontology-to-ontology mediator (*ooMediator*) can be used to resolve mismatches between two different ontologies. A Web Service-to-Goal mediator (*wgMediator*) allows users to state that a given Goal can be fulfilled by the specified Web Service, while a Goal-to-Goal mediator (*ggMediator*) can be used to state the relationship between two Goals. Finally, a Web Service-to-Web Service mediator (*wwMediator*) can be used to state that a given Web Service has some relationship with another Web Service.

The WSMO conceptual model can be formalized in terms of the Web Service Modeling Language (WSML) [8], which provides a set of language variants for describing WSMO elements with different levels of expressivity and reasoning complexity.

11.3 Glue

The Glue conceptual model of discovery is an extension of the WSMO model. Unlike WSMO, we explicitly distinguish classes and instances of both Web Services and Goals. Actually, such distinction is mentioned in the WSMO documentation, which admits the existence of both "abstract" and "concrete" services/goals, but is completely neglected by WSMO implementations. However, classes and instances allow users to write their service/goal descriptions more easily fostering the reuse of already defined elements.

We define a *Goal class* as a kind of template representing an abstract request for a generic type of service. This way, a requester has only to fill in such template with concrete values, by creating a corresponding *Goal instance*.

The same approach is used to define a *Web Service class*, which is a description of a generic type of service. Web Service classes represent abstract services, while concrete services can be described creating appropriate *Web Service instances*. In a following section, we show an example of such classes and instances.

Another distinctive feature of Glue is the explicit central role assigned to the wgMediators in the discovery process. In Glue, a wgMediator includes rules that evaluate whether a Web Service instance provides the service required by a Goal instance (i.e. a Web Service matches the Goal instance) or not.

Glue considers the whole discovery process divided in three subsequent phases:

- *set-up time*, when ontologies, Web Service classes, Goal classes and mediators are created and loaded into the system;
- *publishing time*, when the providers create Web Service instances and publish them into the system;
- *discovery time*, when a user creates a Goal instance and submits it to the system to start the matchmaking process and consequently gets the list of Web Service instances that match the Goal instance.

11.3.1 Execution Semantics

In Glue, the matchmaking process is a composite procedure, which is graphically represented in Figure 11.1 by means of a UML activity diagram.

As said before, this procedure is fired when a user submits a Goal instance to Glue. At the beginning (steps 1, 2 and 3), Glue checks the existence of a Goal class corresponding to the given Goal instance. Then it tries to use ggMediators to translate the user Goal instance in an equivalent instance expressed using a different terminology (cf. steps 4, 5, 6 and 7). Indeed, if a ggMediator exists, Glue uses the rules within the ggMediator to translate the goal in an equivalent one expressed in another terminology. This is a loop that can be re-iterated, for example to gradually reduce the polarization and make the user's point of view closer to the providers' one consequently. If more then one ggMediator exists, this loop can result in a goal expansion similar to the query expansion mechanism largely adopted in Information Retrieval.

For each identified Goal class, Glue looks for the wgMediator that is able to handle such Goal class (steps 8, 9 and 10), that is the wgMediator having that Goal class as *target*. By inspecting the *sources* of the identified wgMediator, it gets the Web Service classes (step 9) that potentially satisfy the request because they offer a service that is of the same type of the one requested in the corresponding Goal class. At that point, Glue extracts the Web Service instances that are related to the previously identified Web Service classes (step 10). Finally, Glue executes the matchmaking process evaluating all the obtained Web Service instances

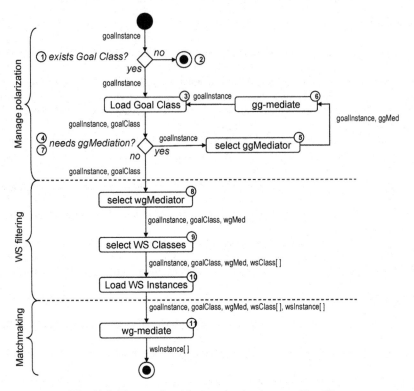

Fig. 11.1. The matchmaking process implemented by Glue.

against the Goal instance, by running the rules included into the wgMediator within a reasoner (step 11). The entry rule of the wgMediator takes the Goal instance description along with a set of Web Service instance descriptions as input and returns a subset of the Web Service instances, which are the only ones that satisfy all the rules (i.e. provides the service requested in the Goal instance). Actually, the result is a ranked list of Web Service instances.

11.3.2 Implementation

Glue an open-source[3] discovery engine implemented in Java. It is built on an open-source F-logic inference engine named Flora-2 [8] that runs over XSB[4], an open source implementation of tabled-prolog and deductive database system. Flora-2 provides only the reasoning support, while Glue wraps the inference engine and builds a WSMO infrastructure around it. For this reason, Web Service and Goal descriptions are represented in F-logic, as well as ontologies and mediators.

The basis of Glue infrastructure is a set of facilities for insertion and retrieval of WSMO elements. In addition, Glue provides a Web Service endpoint that allows developers to integrate Glue into their infrastructure as a service. The Web Service interface of Glue exposes

---

[3] http://sourceforge.net/projects/sws-glue
[4] http://xsb.sourceforge.net/

two methods. The first one is used to put the element descriptions into the internal repository, while the second one activates the actual discovery process.

In addition, for the SWS-Challenge we exploit the WebRatio framework to provide an end-user interface, which is Web-based and user-friendly. Through such graphical interface, a user can fill in an HTML form which represents a Goal class and submit the input to the system. WebRatio takes the user inputs and creates a corresponding Goal instance, then submits it to Glue and starts a discovery process for that Goal instance. When Glue returns the list of the matching Web Service instances, WebRatio shows them to the end user, who may choose among them the one to be invoked. To do this, internally we used a WebML model which shares the model of the goal with Glue.

11.4 The discovery scenarios

During the first year of the SWS-Challenge, the organizers proposed two different Discovery scenarios, with increasing difficulty.

The first discovery scenario of the SWS-Challenge requires to automatically provide the best shipping option among different shipment services for the purchased goods (see Figure 11.2). The set of shipment Web Services offers different destinations, delivery times, prices, and pick-up policies. Hence according to the shipment details, not all the services are suitable. The organizers provided implementations of several shipping services, each of them with a WSDL and a more concise natural language description.

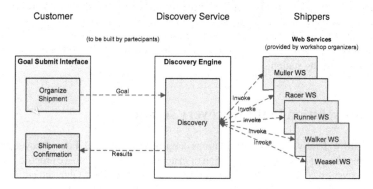

Fig. 11.2. SWS challenge - Discovery scenario overview.

What makes the scenario interesting is (i) the realistically heterogeneous nature of the services descriptions, which focus on different characteristics, (ii) the presence of polarization, and (iii) the domain specific notion of "matching".

As we introduced in Section 11.1, the scenario presents the *polarization* problems between requesters and providers enumerated in Table 11.1.

Moreover, the scenario requires several *domain specific notions of matching*:

- *Products*: a provider completely matches a request if all the requested categories of products are available and it partially matches in case a subset is available.

Aspect	Requester	Provider
Products	concrete list of products	set of products
Shipment Location	concrete location	set of locations
Shipment Price	preferences / restrictions (like less than 100)	concrete value, resp. functional dependency on selected products
Payment Method	concrete list of accepted payment methods	concrete list of accepted payment methods
Units	specific of the requester's country	specific of the provider's country

Table 11.1. Differences between providers' and requesters' point of views.

- *Shipment Location*: A service advertises the locations where it ships to; if the requester wish to send goods in Bristol and the supplier ships to Europe, then an exact matching exists.
- *Payment Method*: both the requester and supplier advertise a list of acceptable payment methods. A complete match exists if at least one payment method is in common between requester and supplier.

In order to test the solutions, the organizers provided a set of heterogeneous shipment goals expressed in natural language. An example of such goal is: send one package (length 10, width 2, height 3 inches; weight 20 lbs) from California to Bristol (UK) for less than 120$.

The organizers of the SWS-Challenge proposed another scenario that is different from the one previously described and is focused on the purchase of products. The interesting issues arose by this scenario are: (i) the dynamic invocation of the providers to get the list of the products that they sell, (ii) the need to manage user preferences such as "at least 512 MB of RAM" and (iii) the request of composite goals such as "a laptop with 40 GB of hard disk and a compatible docking station".

11.5 Our solution to the discovery scenarios

The standard Web Service discovery solutions described in Section 11.1 do not cover polarization and encoding of domain specific notion of matching. In this section, we propose a solution to the Discovery scenario described in the previous section exploiting Glue and putting accent on the use of rules.

The first phase of the development of the solution concerns the creation of all the elements involved in the discovery process (i.e. the *set-up time* and *published time* described in Section 11.3). This implies the creation of the ontologies as first step.

11.5.1 Ontologies

Each ontology defines a set of concepts within a domain and the relationships between them. In particular, we modeled four ontologies including date-time, location, products and shipments. Listing 11.1 shows an excerpt of such ontologies. It includes the definitions of some concepts (both geographical concepts, like `italy`, and temporal concepts like `dateTime`, that is an `instant` enriched with a `date` and a `time`) and axioms (like `calculateWeightForPricing`, which encodes the rules to compute the weight used to determine the price of a package).

The development of these ontologies was kept to the minimum necessary. This implies that, for example, our date-time ontology is not expressive enough to model the generic notion of "business day".

```
1   // temporal aspects
2   dateTime::instant[ date=>date, time=>time ].
3   before(X,Y) :– before(X.date,Y.date)); ((equal(X.date,Y.date), before(X.time,Y.time)).
4
5   // geographical aspects (i.e., taxonomy of continents, countries, nations and cities)
6   worldwide.
7   europe::worldwide.
8   italy::europe.
9   checkContainmentOfPickupLocation(Request, Provider) :–
10    Request[pickupLocation−>X], Provider[pickupLocations−>>Y], (X=Y;X::Y).
11
12  // price aspects (e.g., dimensional weight)
13  calculateWeightForPricing(ActualGoodWeight,GoodDimension,CalculatedWeightForPricing) :–
14    DimensionalWeight is (GoodDimension.l*GoodDimension.w*GoodDimension.h)/166,
15    (
16      (ActualGoodWeight > X , CalculatedWeightForPricing is ActualGoodWeight);
17      (ActualGoodWeight = X , CalculatedWeightForPricing is ActualGoodWeight);
18      (ActualGoodWeight < X , CalculatedWeightForPricing is DimensionalWeight)
19    )
20  .
```

Listing 11.1. Ontologies modeled for the discovery scenario.

11.5.2 Goals

Secondly, we focused on the user side, that is the design of the Goal classes. We defined two classes of goals, one for the shipment and one for the purchase. Listing 11.2 shows the Goal class description (named `goalClass_Shipment`) that models a generic shipment request (lines 1 to 19). In addition, it also shows the description of a possible Goal instance (named `goalInstance`) that a user could create: it asks for a service that is able to ship a specific good (given its weight, its dimensions and other data) at a given time from Stanford to Sacramento.

```
1   /* The Shipment Goal Class */
2   goalClass_Shipment::goalClass[
3     capability=>capabilityGoal_Shipment::capabilityGoal[
4       postcondition=>requestsShipmentService
5     ]
6   ].
7
8   requestsShipmentService[
9     requestedPickupLocation=>location,
10    requestedDeliveryLocation=>location,
11    currentDateTime=>dateTime,
12    requestedPickupDateTimeInterval=>dateTimeInterval,
13    requestedDeliveryDateTime=>dateTime,
14    requestedDeliveryModality=>deliveryModality,
15    requestedGuarantee=>guarantee,
16    goodWeight=>float,
17    goodDimension=>dimension,
18    requestedShipmentPriceInterval=>priceInterval
19  ].
20
```

```
21   /* A Shipment Goal Class Instance */
22   goalInstance:goalClass_Shipment[
23     capability->_#:capabilityGoal_Shipment[
24       postcondition->_#:requestsShipmentService[
25         requestedPickupLocation->stanford,
26         requestedDeliveryLocation->sacramento,
27         currentDateTime->_#:dateTime[
28           date->_#:date[dayOfMonth->28,monthOfYear->4,year->2006],
29           time->_#:time[hourOfDay->23,minuteOfHour->0,secondOfMinute->0]
30         ],
31         requestedPickupDateTimeInterval->_#:dateTimeInterval[
32           start->_#:dateTime[...],
33           end->_#:dateTime[...],
34         ],
35         requestedDeliveryDateTime->_#:dateTime[...],
36         requestedDeliveryModality->letter,
37         requestedGuarantee->guaranteeYes,
38         goodWeight->10,
39         goodDimension->_#:dimension[l->100,w->100,h->100],
40         requestedShipmentPriceInterval->_#:priceInterval[start->0,end->1000]
41       ]
42     ]
43   ].
```

Listing 11.2. The shipment Goal class and an example of a possible Goal intance.

11.5.3 Web Services

Concerning the provider side, we created a Web Service class modeling a generic shipment service and a Web Service class representing a generic purchasing service. In both cases, we modeled all the restrictions that must hold in order to invoke the service as assumptions, and the results provided by the service as postconditions. Listing 11.3 shows the description of the Web Service class for the shipment services (named `wsdClass_Shipment`) and an instance of it. The instance, named `wsdInstance_Shipment13`) describes the service provided by Muller: it can deliver goods in north and south America, Africa, Asia and Europe.

```
1    /* The Shipment Service Class */
2    wsdClass_Shipment::wsdClass[
3      capability=>capabilityWSD_Shipment::capabilityWSD[
4        assumption=>restrictionsOnShipmentService,
5        postcondition=>providesShipmentService
6      ]
7    ].
8
9    restrictionsOnShipmentService[
10     minNumOfHoursBetweenOrderAndPickup=>integer,
11     maxNumOfDaysBetweenOrderAndPickup=>integer,
12     maxNumOfDaysBetweenOrderAndPickup=>integer,
13     maxNumOfDaysBetweenOrderAndDelivery=>integer,
14     minPickupDTInterval=>integer,
15     maxPickupDTInterval=>integer,
16     maxGoodWeight=>float,
17     weightToDimensionalWeightThreshold=>float
18   ].
19
20   providesShipmentService[
21     pickupLocations=>>location,
22     deliveryLocations=>>location,
23     pickupTimeInterval=>timeInterval,
24     price=>>shipmentPricing
25   ].
```

```
26
27
28    /* An instance of the Shipment Service Class */
29    wsdInstance_Shipment13:wsdClass_Shipment[
30      nonFunctionalProperties->_#[ dc_publisher->'Muller'],
31      capability->_#:capabilityWSD_Shipment[
32        assumption->_#:restrictionsOnShipmentService[
33          minNumOfHoursBetweenOrderAndPickup=>0,
34          maxNumOfDaysBetweenOrderAndPickup=>2,
35          maxNumOfDaysBetweenOrderAndPickup=>5,
36          minPickupDTInterval=>7200,
37          maxPickupDTInterval=>259200,
38          maxGoodWeight=>50,
39        ],
40        postcondition->_#:providesShipmentService[
41          pickupLocations->>{northAmerica,africa,asia,europe},
42          deliveryLocations->>{northAmerica,africa,asia,europe},
43          pickupTimeInterval->_#:timeInterval[...],
44          price->>{ _#:shipmentPricing[
45            location->worldwide,
46            deliveryModality->deliveryModality,
47            guarantee->guaranteeNo,
48            basePrice->10,
49            pricePerWeight->5],
50        }
51      ]
52    ]
53  ].
```

Listing 11.3. The shipment service class and an instance of it.

11.5.4 Mediators

Finally, we created the wgMediators that connect Web Service classes to Goal classes and include the rules that handle both polarization and domain specific notion of matching. During the discovery process execution, by evaluating those rules by means of a reasoner Glue checks whether a specific Web Service instance satisfies a given Goal instance.

In our case, we wrote the rules by using the F-logic syntax and we created two wgMediators. A wgMediator links the Web Service class representing a generic shipment service to the Goal class representing a generic request of a shipment and includes the rules that evaluate the degree of matching between a Goal instance and a Web Service instance. Another wgMediator is responsible for checking which real purchasing services satisfy a given purchasing request.

As mentioned before, wgMediators are the core of the matchmaking process in Glue. Since the objective of a wgMediator is to implement the rules that allow the system to check if a Web service satisfies a goal, such rules have to deal with the different representations of Goals and Web Services (i.e. polarization).

The content of a wgMediator can be structured at developer's pleasure: the number of rules as well as their extent depend on the developer's preferences. Anyway, usually there is one special rule that we call *entry rule* because is the one that returns the references to all Web service instances that match the Goal instance. Internally, the entry rule calls many other rules in turn, which are responsible for checking if a single aspect of the Goal instance is satisfied by the Web Service instance considered at the moment in which the rules are executed.

In Listing 11.4, the first rule (lines 1-3) addresses the first polarization problem described in Section 11.4 by allowing a supplier to state that it sells "computers" and matching the service with a goal in which a requester states that he wants a "notebook" (which is a subclass of computer). Indeed, this rule states that when a service provides a product X, then this service provides all products that are sub-classes of X as well. The second rule (lines 5-7) encodes a domain specific notion of exact match between a goal and a service by stating that an exact match occurs when all the required products listed into the goal are also present in the list of the provided products. Similarly, the third rule (lines 9-11) states that when a product is present both in the goal description and in the service description then there is a partial match.

```
1   SubsumeAllProducts[providesSubsumedProducts->>{Y}] :-
2     SubsumeAllProducts[providesProducts->>X],
3     (Y=X;Y::X).
4
5   exactMatch_Products(RequestsPurchaseService,ProvidesPurchaseService) :-
6     L=collectset{X|RequestsPurchaseService[requestedProducts->>X]},
7     ProvidesPurchaseService[providesSubsumedProducts+>>L].
8
9   partialMatch_Products(RequestsPurchaseService,ProvidesPurchaseService) :-
10    RequestsPurchaseService[requestedProducts->>X],
11    ProvidesPurchaseService[providesSubsumedProducts->>X].
```

Listing 11.4. Three rules that manage sets of products.

In a similar manner, the following rule addresses the second polarization problems of Section 11.4, because it enables a match between a goal and a Web service in the case that a required location is in the list of the location covered by the service as well as in the case that a location covered by the service contains the required location (e.g., the service is able to pickup/delivery goods in Europe while the goal asks for pickup/delivery a good in Italy).

```
1   checkContainmentOfPickupAndDeliveryLocation(RequestsShipmentService,ProvidesShipmentService
       ) :-
2     RequestsShipmentService[requestedPickupLocation->X],
3     ProvidesShipmentService[pickupLocations->>Y],
4     (X=Y;X::Y),
5     RequestsShipmentService[requestedDeliveryLocation->H],
6     ProvidesShipmentService[deliveryLocations->>K],
7     (H=K;H::K).
```

Listing 11.5. A rule that checks the locations of pick-up and delivery.

Besides the rules directly included into a wgMediator, during the matchmaking process other external rules can be evaluated. Indeed, some ontologies can also include rules that apply to the concepts defined in them. An example is the rule – contained in the shipment service ontology – described in Listing 11.6, which calculates the price that a service requires for the shipment. First of all, it filters the services on the basis of the location and the modality of delivery that a user required into the goal description: i.e. if the set of the locations stated for the service does not contain the location required by the user that wrote the goal description, then the service is discarded. Then, for each service, it calculates the price of the shipment taking into consideration the base price and the price per weight that the service entails for the required location and required delivery modality, as well as the weight of the good to be shipped.

```
1   calculateShipmentPrice(ShipmentPricing,Location,DeliveryModality,Guarantee,GoodWeight,
       PriceCalculated) :-
2     (Location::ShipmentPricing.location;Location=ShipmentPricing.location),
3     (DeliveryModality::ShipmentPricing.deliveryModality;DeliveryModality=ShipmentPricing.
       deliveryModality),
4     (Guarantee=ShipmentPricing.guarantee;Guarantee=guaranteeNo),
5     PriceCalculated is (ShipmentPricing.basePrice + (GoodWeight-1)*ShipmentPricing.pricePerWeight
       ).
```

Listing 11.6. A rule that calculates the price of a shipment.

11.5.5 Ranking

Into a wgMediator it is possible to define several entry rules - each of them is related to a different level of matching between the Goal and the Web Services. The level of matching related to an entry rule R depends on the rules invoked by R. For example, the top level is assigned to the entry rule that invokes all the rules (checking the satisfiability of all the aspects of the Goal), while lower levels are assigned to the entry rules that invoke subsets of the rules (checking the satisfiability of only some features required in the Goal). In particular, during the creation of the entry rules of the wgMediator, it is possible to choose which are the rules that have to be satisfied for every specific matching level. This way we obtain discrete levels of ranking like "exact", "subsume", or "partial". For example, for the shipment scenario we defined four levels of ranking of the discovery results, allowing for choosing an alternative shipment solution when no exact match is found (see Table 11.2).

Rank	Checked Constraints
1	All restriction checked.
2	Shipment price is not checked.
3	No check for pickup interval.
4	Only weight and location are checked.

Table 11.2. The ranking criteria for the shipment service discovery.

11.5.6 Dynamic parameters

Initially, Glue assumed that every Web Service description was statically available because it assumed no dynamic dependencies between Web Service instances and the Goal instance. However, in many real scenarios a service exposes one or more operations for negotiating the service itself. Such operations are intended to be invoked for retrieving dynamic information that may be used to perform a more precise matchmaking. This is the case of the shipping scenario of the SWS-Challenge, in which a service provides an operation that returns the price for the delivery of a product, which is dynamically calculated on the basis of the goods to be shipped.

The operations that return information without producing any other effect are named *safe methods* in WSDL 2.0 and we call *data-fetching* the invocation of such operations. Glue has been extended to invoke such operations during the matchmaking process, by delegating the invocation to the application in which Glue is integrated – in the case of the SWS-Challenge, an external invocation component implemented within the WebRatio framework. The invocation occurs whenever Glue needs more information to evaluate a rule of the wgMediator, during the matchmaking process. The need for more information arises when the description of a Web Service instance does not include the value of a feature, which is required to the rule that checks if that value satisfies the one requested in the Goal instance. This can happen because that feature provided by the service vary in time or depends on the request.

In the case that a service includes special parameters that need to be fetched (e.g. shipping price), its description has to be annotated with special tags, which point out what parameters are "dynamic".

For example, Listing 11.7 shows how the *price* of the Muller service has been modeled in order to enable data-fetching. In particular, a tag stating that it is necessary to invoke the *invokePrice* operation of the Muller service in order to retrieve the actual values of the price has been added. In addition, the request message (*invokePriceRequest*) that has to be sent to start the data-fetching has been added to Muller's description.

```
1   wsdInstance_Shipment11:wsdClass_Shipment[
2     nonFunctionalProperties->_#[
3       dc_title->'Muller Shipment Service'
4       ... ],
5     capability->_#:capabilityWSD_Shipment[
6       assumption->_#:
7       restrictionsOnShipmentService[
8         maximalGoodWeight->50,
9         ... ],
10      postcondition->_#:
11           providesShipmentService[
12           pickupLocations->>{africa, ...},
13           price->>{
14           _#:shipmentPricing[
15           basePrice->0, //negotiate_operation://Muller/invokePrice(out Price)
16           pricePerWeight->0,
17           additionalPricePerCollect->(−1)
18           ] ...
19    ].
20    invokePriceRequest[
21      country=>location,
22      packageInformation[
23        weight=>integer,
24        lenth=>integer,
25        height=>integer,
26        width=>integer
27      ]
28    ].
```

Listing 11.7. The description of the Muller service including the dynamic data-fetching parameter.

In order to take into consideration the data-fetching, the execution semantics of Glue was divided into two subsequent steps. The first step of the discovery runs the rules of the wg-Mediator on the static descriptions of the Web Service instances, ignoring the parameters that have been tagged as "dynamic". The second step takes the result set of the services returned by the previous step and runs again the rules of the wgMediator only on those services whose description contains some dynamic parameters and only after the invocation of the service and the retrieval of the actual values of the dynamic parameters.

Splitting the matchmaking process into two subsequent phases speeds up the discovery task because the invocation of the safe methods of the services – which can be slow due to the bandwidth of the communication channel, the execution speed of the machine in which resides the service and so on – is executed only for the services that survive to the first step, in which the other "static" parameters are checked.

11.6 Conclusion and Future Work

In this chapter we described our solution to the SWS-Challenge focusing on the Discovery scenarios. For this reason, we deeply described our discovery engine named Glue and we showed how we were able to successfully address the SWS Challenge Discovery scenario. Such results mainly relies on our refinement of WSMO discovery conceptual model which consist in:

- introducing the notion of class of Goals and class of Web Services;
- using rules encoded in wgMediators to handle domain specific notion of matching; and
- redefining the discovery process as a composite procedure where the discovery of the appropriate mediators and the discovery of the appropriate services is combined.

The descriptions of all the elements are coded in an F-logic syntax. However, we aim at a better formalization of the Glue model by means of a new language that is independent from the underlying reasoner. For this reason, we are going to design and implement a completely new version of the Glue architecture which takes advantages from the conceptual model of Glue and, at the same time, allows users to customize and monitor the execution semantics.

Acknowledgements

This work has been partially supported by the Italian FIRB project NeP4B and the IST FP6 European project SEEMP.

References

1. Keller, U., Lara, R., Lausen, H., Polleres, A., Fensel, D.: Automatic location of services. In: ESWC. (2005) 1–16
2. OASIS UDDI Technical Committee: The uddi technical white paper. Technical report, OASIS (2004)
3. OASIS/ebXMLM Registry Technical Committee: Oasis/ebxml registry services specification v3.0. Technical report, OASIS (2005)
4. Della Valle, E., Cerizza, D.: The mediators centric approach to automatic web service discovery of glue. In: MEDIATE2005. Volume 168 of CEUR Workshop Proceedings., CEUR-WS.org (2005) 35–50
5. Fensel, D., Lausen, H., Polleres, A., de Bruijn, J., Stollberg, M., Roman, D., Domingue, J.: Enabling Semantic Web Services – The Web Service Modeling Ontology. Springer (2006)
6. Roman, D., Keller, U., Lausen, H., de Bruijn, J., Lara, R., Stollberg, M., Polleres, A., Feier, C., Bussler, C., Fensel, D.: Web Service Modeling Ontology. Applied Ontologies 1(1) (2005) 77 – 106
7. de Bruijn, J., Lausen, H., Polleres, A., Fensel, D.: The web service modeling language: An overview. In: Proceedings of the 3rd European Semantic Web Conference (ESWC2006), Budva, Montenegro, Springer-Verlag (2006)
8. Yang, G. Kifer, M., Zhao, C., Chowdhary, V.: Flora-2 user's manual (2004)

Semantic Service Discovery with DIANE Service Descriptions

Ulrich Küster and Birgitta König-Ries

Institute of Computer Science
Friedrich-Schiller-University Jena
07743 Jena, Germany
ukuester|koenig@informatik.uni-jena.de

Summary. In this chapter, we introduce the DIANE Service Description (DSD) and show how it has been used to solve the discovery problems stated in the scenarios of the SWS-Challenge. We explain our solution as of the fifth SWS-Challenge workshop in Stanford, CA, USA (November 2007) and provide a discussion about its strengths but also shortcomings.

12.1 What is DSD?

The goal of service-oriented computing is the ability to dynamically discover and invoke services at run-time, thus forming networks of loosely-coupled participants. The most important prerequisite is an appropriate semantic service description language – and with *DIANE Service Description* (DSD) [KKRM05, KKRKS07a] we provide such a language together with an efficient matchmaking algorithm.

One main difference between DSD and other semantic service description languages is its own lightweight ontology language that is specialized for the characteristics of services and can be processed efficiently at the same time. The basis for this ontology language is standard object orientation which is extended by four additional elements:

- Services perform world-altering operations (e.g., after invoking a shipment service, a package will be transported and a bill will be issued) which is captured by *operational elements*. We view this is the most central property of a service, thus, in DSD, services are primarily described by their effects – all other aspects (as flow of information, choreography etc.) are seen as secondary, derived properties. An effect is comprehended as the achievement of a new *state*, which in DSD is an instance from a state ontology.
- Service providers offer more than one effect, e.g. a shipment provider offers shipment to a multitude of possible locations and for various types and sizes of packages. On the other hand requesters typically accept different services with different properties, e.g. a fast and expensive shipping or an inexpensive but slower one. Both is captured in DSD by *aggregational elements*. Thus, the effect of a service (request or offer) is typically a *set of states*. For offers, these are the states the service can potentially create, for requests these are the states the requester is interested in. In DSD, sets are declaratively defined which leads to descriptions as trees (see examples in the next section).

- Services allow to choose among the offered effects (e.g. as a matter of course all shipment providers allow to input the package being transported and to select where to pick it up and where to ship it) which is captured by *selecting elements*. In DSD, selecting elements are represented as variables that can be integrated into set definitions, thus leading to configurable sets. Therefore, a service offer in DSD is represented by its effects as configurable sets of states.
- The appropriateness of different service offers and their effects is varying for a given requester (e.g., in the first scenario, a more expensive shipment provider will still be accepted, but a less expensive one will be preferred) which is captured by *valuing elements*. In DSD, these elements are represented by using *fuzzy sets* instead of crisp ones in request descriptions. Set based descriptions allow expressing that quite different services are acceptable for a requester. Using fuzzy instead of crisp sets in these descriptions additionally allows to include all preferences of the requester in a request description – the larger the fuzzy membership value of a service in the described service set, the higher the preference of the requester for that particular service.

For processing a semantic service description language, an efficient *matchmaking algorithm* is needed. For a given DSD offer description o and a given DSD request r, a matchmaker has to solve the following problem: What configuration of o's crisp effect sets is necessary to get the best fitting subset of r's fuzzy effect sets. Or – in other words – how well is o's offer contained in what r requests and how should o be configured to maximize this value? Our implementation answers this by stepping through the graphs of o and r synchronously in order to calculate the matching value in $[0, 1]$ as well as the optimal configuration of the variables. As the preferences are completely included in r, in contrast to existing approaches, our matcher does not need to apply any heuristics and thus is able to operate deterministically.

In order to interact with a service, DSD assumes a simple choreography. During matchmaking several web safe *estimation operations* may be performed where operations of the service are called, which provide information (like the price of a package given its weight) but do not imply a contract between the provider and the client (in this case the matchmaking agent). After the best match is found that service can be invoked by executing a single *execution operation* which is supposed to produce the offered effects.

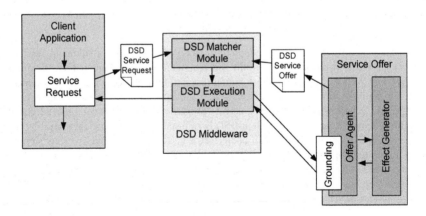

Fig. 12.1. DIANE Middleware architecture

The proposed concepts are implemented in the DIANE middleware. The overall architecture of the system is depicted in Figure 12.1. On the left hand side, the client is shown. It runs an application that at some point in time requests an external service to provide some functionality. The service request is formulated using DSD (e.g. by filling a predefined semantic request template) and sent to the middleware. There, the matcher module compares it to the available service offers. When a matching result is found, it is configured appropriately and passed on to the execution module. This module then invokes the service using its grounding and finally returns the execution results to the client application. More detailed information how to integrate semantic service requests into existing processes using the DIANE Middleware can be found in [KKR06b].

12.2 Solving the SWS-Challenge discovery problems with DSD and the DIANE framework

The SWS Challenge poses two set of discovery problems, one related to finding a shipping provider for a given shipping request, the other one related to purchasing of IT hardware. At the previous SWS-Challenge workshops we have presented the most complete solution to those problems [KKRK06, KKR06a, KKR07b, KKR07a]. The complete solution including all offer and request descriptions, all additional files, an executable version of the DIANE Middleware and a technical description how to get the solution running can be found on the SWS-Challenge wiki[1].

In this section, we provide an in-depth description of our solution. We describe how offers and requests for the first and the second scenario have been described using DSD and particularly elaborate on the difficulties we encountered and how we solved them. At the end of the section we explain how services are invoked automatically by the DIANE middleware, either to gather additional information during the matchmaking or to invoke the best matching service found. We conclude this chapter with a discussion of the strengths and shortcomings of our approach.

12.2.1 Offer descriptions for the first scenario

Figure 12.2 shows the offer description of the Muller shipment service as an example for all shipping services used in the first discovery scenario. We use *GDSD*, an informal UML like graphical notation of DSD for our illustrations because it is more compact and easier to understand than the more formal *FDSD* notation. By the example of the Muller service we detail in the following how the various aspects of the shipper's textual description from the scenario have been captured in our DSD descriptions of the services.

Figure 12.2 shows a service instance presenting a profile (the grounding has been ommitted) that offers a single effect set (diagonal lines in the upper left corner of a concept denote a DSD set). The set of Shipped states that can be created by the service are characterized by the *property conditions* of that set: The service collects a cargo at a certain pickup time and ships it from fromAddress to toAddress for a certain price within the stated shippingTime.

---

[1] http://sws-challenge.org/wiki/index.php/Solution_Jena

OFFER:

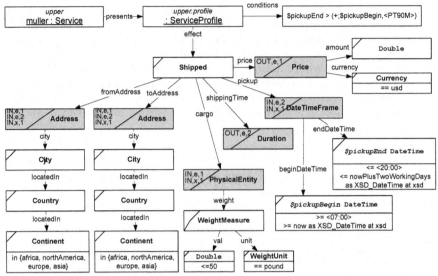

Fig. 12.2. Excerpt from the DSD description for the Muller shipment service.

Offer input and outputs

Inputs (the configurability of an offer) and outputs of a service are described as variables and directly integrated into the description. In GDSD variables are denoted by grayed rectangles. Different types of variables are denoted by markers on the left side of a variable. The same concept may serve as variable for different purposes, thus multiple markers are allowed. The marker IN, e, 1 on the fromAddress set in Muller's description for instance denotes that the value of this set needs to be given as input for the first estimation operation. More precisely IN declares the variable as input, while OUT would have specified an output, e is used to distinguish between web-safe estimation operations (e) and the final execution of the service (x) and the following number (1) is used to distinguish between different operations (more on this below).

Restrictions on package size and weight

Muller requires packages to weigh less than fifty pounds. This condition has to be captured by the cargo set in Muller's description using an appropriate *property condition*. As you can see in Figure 12.2 the cargo set's weight property points to a set of WeightMeasures whose value property in turn points to a set of Double values. By the *direct condition* "<= 50" this set of Double values is restricted to contain only values that are equal or smaller than fifty. Restrictions on the maximum length or width of a package could be added in a similar fashion by adding additional property conditions to the cargo set.

Restrictions on the operation range of the service

Muller operates only in Africa, Asia, Europe and North America. Thus the `fromAddress` and `toAddress` sets have been restricted in a similar way as the `cargo` set. Countries and continents are loaded from a location ontology and the direct condition "in {africa, northAmerica, europe, asia}" on the `Continent` set refers to the names of those ontological continent instances.

Shipping price

Muller does not publish shipping prices but provides an endpoint where prices can be inquired dynamically providing certain input data (like shipping addresses and the weight of the cargo). Such dynamicity is supported by the DIANE framework using *estimation operation* as introduced in Section 12.1. The marker `OUT,e,1` on the `price` set in Muller's description denotes that the value for this set can be inquired by executing the associated first estimation operation. Accordingly both addresses and the cargo need to be given as input to inquire about the price (markers `IN,e,1`). Details on how the estimation operation is actually executed and how the handling of estimation operation is integrated into the matchmaking process will be given in Section 12.2.5. The other services (Runner, Racer, Weasel and Walker) did not offer an endpoint to inquire dynamically about the price and instead specified rules how to compute the price depending on the specifications of the shipping operations. Unfortunately DSD lacks direct support for such rule based computations. Therefore auxiliary endpoints to compute the shipping price have been created for those services similar to the one that was offered by Muller already. During matchmaking the computation of the shipping price is delegated to those endpoints in the same way that Muller's endpoint is used.

Pickup and shipping times

All services made similar restrictions to available pickup times for collection. In the case of Muller collection is possible between 7am and 8pm. This is encoded in Figure 12.2 using according direct conditions ">= <07:00>" and "<= <20:00>" on the properties of the `pickup` set similarly as described above. Additionally, collection is only possible in the future (but in the case of Muller no advance notice was required) and at most two working days in advance. To deal with these temporal aspects we exploited the fact that DSD instances are internally represented as Java classes and created special `Date`, `Time` and `DateTime` instances now, `today` or `todayPlusTwoWorkingDays`. These instances contain code that accesses the system time to capture the intuitive semantic. In the case of `todayPlusTwoWorkingDays` Sundays are not considered working days (which is why we could not use an expression like "now + <P2D>"). Finally the services made restrictions on the length of the pickup interval (in the case of Muller at least 90 minutes). This requires to pose a condition on an arithmetic combination of attributes (the end of the pickup interval minus the begin of the pickup interval has to be greater than a certain duration). Such so-called *multi attribute conditions* can be added to the conditions property of a `ServiceProfile`. In Figure 12.2 the condition "$pickupEnd > (+;$pickupBegin,<PT90M>)" references the sets labelled $pickupEnd and $pickupBegin and states that values for the former must be greater than values for the latter plus a duration of ninety minutes. Originally, this was not supported by DSD. If the required pickup interval is given in the request it is easy to check whether this interval adheres to the restrictions of an offer. If, however, a request does not give a precise interval but, for instance, only specifies that collection is impossible after or before certain times, the matchmaker has to determine an interval that suits both the requirements of the offer as well as the needs of the requester. Note that this interval has to be determined automatically in order to be able to configure the offer automatically to facilitate automated invocation of estimation as well as execution operations. However, in the presence of multi attribute conditions an optimal configuration of an offer cannot be determined locally for the attributes anymore. Currently, our matchmaker does not support globally optimized configuration under such conditions. The current implementation guarantees that any determined configuration is correct, but the algorithm is not complete. Under certain circumstances the matchmaker will fail to determine an optimal or even any valid configuration at all although such a configuration exists. It is planned to address this issue in our future work.

Finally, the offers declare the expected shipping times depending on the pickup time and whether the shipping is national or international. Muller for instance ships in 2/3 (domestic/international) business days if collected by 5pm. Like in the case of the shipping prices DSD does not support such rule based evaluations directly. To overcome this limitation we created auxiliary services to compute the shipping time within an estimation operation (exactly like the shipping prices). Therefore the shippingTime set is declared as an out value of the second estimation operation (marker OUT, e, 2) and the addresses and the pickup interval are declared as input of that estimation operation (markers IN, e, 2).

12.2.2 Request descriptions for the first scenario

Overall DSD request descriptions are built similarly to DSD offer descriptions. Figure 12.3 shows the request corresponding to Goal C3 of the first discovery scenario. The structure of the request resembles the one of the Muller offer. Addresses, and the cargo to be shipped are provided. While the price is specified as a set (denoted by the diagonal line in the upper left corner of the concept), addresses and the cargo to be shipped are provided as concrete instances because no variation is allowed by the requester. Note that the city instances ("bristol" and "moonCity") in the addresses refer to ontological instances, because the city property – unlike street, email or zipCode which are of the primitive String type – refers to a complex entity type with publicly known instances stored in the ontology. Thus state and country where the two cities are located in will be read from the ontology and do not have to be encoded in the request.

No pickup or shipping time is specified since Goal C3 poses no requirements on these properties. It does however specify a price limit of $20. This could have been modelled by a direct condition "<= 20" on the amount property of the Price set. Instead we chose to additionally model preference for lower prices by using a fuzzy Double set for the amount property. The fuzzy direct condition "~==[0,20] 0" requests the set to be fuzzily equal to 0 where the given interval [0,20] denotes the boundaries of the fuzzy equal. Thus the double value 0 will match perfectly (membership value 1), all values greater than 20 will not match at all (membership value 0) and values in between 0 and 20 will match with linearly decreasing membership value.

Goal D1 differs from the other discovery goals in that this goal asks for shipment of two packages and thus enforces two invocations of the corresponding shipping provider service. In our first solution this goal could not be expressed with DSD. However, DSD's effect sets provide a natural mechanism to deal with such requests. The standard semantic of a DSD request effect set is that one (the best) effect out of the specified effect set should be provided. *Iteration directives* on any set in a DSD description may be used to change this semantic. In Figure 12.4 the iteration directive "<Best 2 1>" within the PhysicalEntity set describing the cargo to

REQUEST:

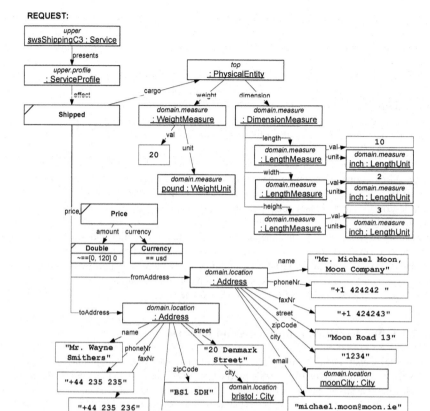

Fig. 12.3. Excerpt from the DSD request description of Goal C3

REQUEST:

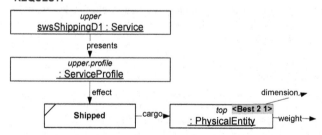

Fig. 12.4. Excerpt from the DSD request description of Goal D1

be shipped encodes that the best two effects described by this set should be provided (the two corresponds to the first parameter in the directive "<Best 2 1>"). The matcher thus binds the corresponding variable in the offer description with a set of two corresponding instances instead of a single value. For automated service invocation such a binding will either result in two invocations of the picked shipping offer (one for each package) or a single invocation with two package specifications sent to the service - depending on the interface of the service described in its grounding. Allthough Goal D1 could be successfully modelled the work on iteration directives is an ongoing effort. Thus not all possible cases of usage are currently supported by our implementation and a full discussion of the complete semantics is beyond the scope of this work.

All shipping services of the scenario return the actual pickup time as well as the price of the shipping operation within the response of the final invocation. The scenario did not require to make use of this information. However, it is possible to specify this fact in the offer descriptions and to mark corresponding concepts in the request as *request out variables*, thereby declaring that this information is required by the requester as output of a service invocation. In this case the matchmaker ensures that the information indeed is provided by the offers at hand and links the request out variable to the corresponding concept in the offer. After the service invocation the DIANE middleware extracts the values from the response and forwards it to the requester. This way requirements on the output of an operation can be specified in a request and are guaranteed by the middleware.

12.2.3 Offer descriptions for the second scenario

The second scenario contains three descriptions of imaginary online shops that sell electronic products. A concrete list of 19 available products is given statically in the scenario description but a listing of available products by product type (like a list of all offered notebooks) can also be obtained by calling a specific operation at the service's endpoints. Solutions were supposed to indicate how they would address a more realistic situation with hundreds or thousands of available products which change dynamically.

We think it is unrealistic to assume that extensive catalogue data can be included in offer descriptions which are published to a service repository. Among the reasons are the dynamicity of a large catalogue which would require an enormous number of updates, the sheer size of service descriptions that enlist thousands of products but also privacy issues that keep providers from revealing too much information about their current stock. We deal with these issues in more detail in [KKR07c] and address the situation in the context of the SWS-Challenge by using *dynamic offer descriptions*.

Dynamic product listings

Figure 12.5 shows the relevant excerpts from the offer descriptions of the Hawker vending service (all grounding information has been omitted). Without the listing of the products little information can be included in the static offer description. Basically the offer simply states, that Hawker sells products given it's GTIN number (a fictionary identifier used in the scenario) as input. One could use regular estimation operations to inquire about the available products. For performance reasons and since an offer like hawker is not very meaningful we created a special operation: Concepts tagged as *dynamic sets* may have an associated estimation operation that will be evaluated right at the beginning of the matchmaking process. Recall from the discussion about pickup times above that the matchmaker may have to determine appropriate

OFFER:

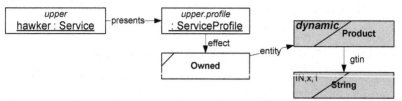

Fig. 12.5. Excerpt from the DSD description for the Hawker vending service.

values for inputs of estimation (and execution) operations if these are not provided in the request. To be sure that all input values of an operation have been determined already a complete traversal of the descriptions at hand is necessary. Since at the beginning of the matchmaking process it is not known whether all necessary input values have been determined by the matchmaker already, the corresponding operation must not have any specific IN variables. Instead the corresponding concept description from the request will be given as input. In the case of Hawker, Hawker's grounding simply extracts the type of Product seeked by the requester and then invokes Hawker's endpoint to list the available products of this type. The returned xml listing will be converted to a list of DSD based instances (using mapping information from Hawker's grounding) and Hawker's offer will be annotated with the retrieved instances, thus providing a concrete up-to-date listing of the available products. The matchmaking will then be performed based on that listing. By changing it's grounding and using additional information from the provided request concept beside the type of product requested, Hawker may finetune the procedure in order to avoid to return too long product listings.

12.2.4 Request descriptions for the second scenario

Figure 12.6 shows excerpts of the description corresponding to Goal C4 of the second scenario. The request asks to buy an Apple notebook, a webcam and a notebook sleeve with certain properties. The requests of the second scenario are more complex than those of the first scenario. In this section we will discuss the features of the requests that were not used within the first scenario in a similar way already.

Competing Request Preferences

Goal C4 states a price limit for the overall purchase but prefers better notebooks as long as that limit is satisfied. Additionally it defines a ranking of preferences to detail what constitutes a better product: more processor power is most important and more RAM is more important than a bigger harddisc.

DSD is very well suited to capture finegrained and competing preferences using fuzzy sets. Preference for more processor power, more memory, a larger harddisc and a higher resolution of the webcam are encoded using fuzzy direct conditions in the corresponding sets of the request description in the same way as preference for lower shipping prices was encoded in the first scenario. The processor speed may serve as an example. The fuzzy direct condition "$\sim== [2000, 5000]$ 5000" in the value set of the processor speed attribute is used to build a fuzzy set of Double values. The requested value is 5000, but values from the range

REQUEST:

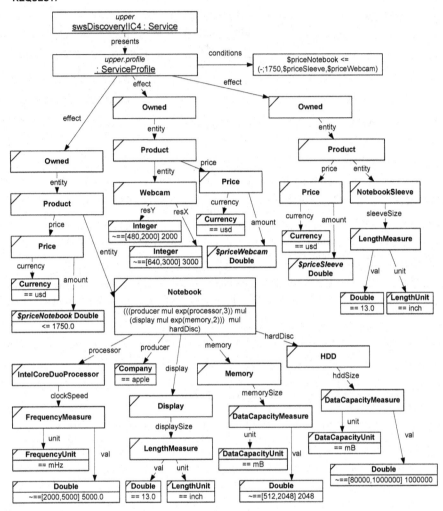

Fig. 12.6. Excerpt from the DSD description for Goal C4 showing preferences.

[2000, 5000] are included fuzzily with linearly increasing degree of membership and preference. This encodes that the requester requires the processor speed to be at least 2000 mHz and prefers faster processors. Typically some notebooks may have a bigger harddisc while others may have more processor power. To rank notebooks in such a situation the importance of each attribute must be captured. In DSD this is done using fuzzy *connecting strategies*. To determine the degree of match of two DSD concepts (either two sets or a set and an instance) the types are compared, any direct conditions (like "== usd") are applied and the degree of match of every property is determined. By default the degree of match of the two concepts is then computed as the product of the type match value, the match value that results from applying the direct conditions and the product of the matching results from the property conditions. The way how the results from the property conditions are combined may be changed by specifying a custom *connecting strategy*. In the Notebook set in Figure 12.6 you can see a formula that corresponds to $producer \times processor^3 \times display \times memory^2 \times hardDisc$. Thus the results from the referenced properties are not simply multiplied but the result of the memory and processor property condition are squared respectively cubed. Since all matching values are from the closed interval $[0, 1]$ a lower result from the processor or memory property will have a stronger reducing influence on the overall matching value than results from the hardDisc property, thereby encoding stronger preference for a fast processor and a lot of memory compared to a large hardDisc. More information on how to encode user preferences using fuzzy sets can be found in [KKRM05, KKRKS07a]. Despite the fact that most preferences could be encoded very intuitively, one goal posed difficulties. Goal B2 of the second scenario prefers black notebooks compared to white ones, but prefers to buy the white one if it is significantly (more than $100) less expensive than the black one. Such a rule-based preference does not map very well to the fuzzy set-based preference mechanism of DSD. Since the price limit was set to $1800 a price difference of $100 results in a difference of the matchvalue of roughly 0.055 (100/1800). Therefore the preference values for the color were chosen to reflect exactly this difference: black [1] and white [0,944]. A weighted sum of $0.5price \times 0.5color$ however does not result in the desired behaviour. The problem is that any black notebook regardless of the price or any product whatsoever that does not cost much would result in a matchvalue of at least 0.5. Therefore the connecting strategy was extended to $min(color, price, 0.5 \times price + 0.5 \times color)$. However, this way the matchvalue was soon dominated by the matchvalue for the price and the weighted sum didn't influence the outcome any more. To resolve this issue, the influence of the weighted sum was strengthened using a polynom yielding: $min(entity, price, (0.5 \times price + 0.5 \times entity)^5)$. This way the desired behavior could be successfully achieved.

Simple service composition

Beside competing request preferences and dynamic product listings the second scenario introduces some simple form of service composition in four different flavors. The above shown Goal C4 is the most complex one combining unrelated composition with global conditions and preferences as will be discussed in the following.

Unrelated composition

As can be seen, the request asks for three different products. This can be expressed by simply asking for multiple effects to be provided. Therefore Figure 12.6 shows three Owned effect sets, each corresponding to one article. The DSD matchmaker will use a multi-phased approach to match such requests. In a first phase offers are matched with regard to whether they are able to provide at least a subset of the requested effects. In a second phase offers are combined in a way that each combination (called *effect coverage*) provides each effect and each effect only once. In a third phase the matchvalue for complete effect coverages is determined and the best combination is picked. This algorithm has been introduced in [KKRKS07b]. Thus DSD is well capable of solving unrelated composition problems.

Unrelated composition with global condition

Goal C4 also states an overall price limit of $1750 for the complete purchase. This can be expressed in DSD by using the multi attribute conditions that were introduced in Section 12.2.1.

The condition shown in Figure 12.6 reads as $\$priceNotebook \leq 1750 - \$priceSleeve - \$priceWebcam$ and encodes the given requirement ($priceNotebook, $priceSleeve and $priceWebcam reference the value of the sets which are labeled accordingly). This way the goal could be expressed and solved but the same limitations that were discussed in Section 12.2.1 apply. Our algorithm is correct but currently not complete. Goal C4 needs to be solved by composing different properly configured services. The right services need to be chosen on a global level and the right products need to be purchased from each of these services. Our current matchmaking algorithm splits a request for multiple products into a a set of single requests, one for each product to be purchased. When determining the configuration of a service (i.e. choosing a product), it performs a local optimization with respect to the requirements of the desired product at hand instead of a global optimization with respect to the total set of requested products. Depending on the available products and the concrete global request at hand it may happen that after the first product is chosen, too little money remains to add the other two products. In this case the matchmaking will fail and no product will be purchased. A backtracking mechanism could ensure completeness in such cases. Backtracking, however, could result in an exhaustive search of the configuration space of the services at hand, which is not feasible anymore. Therefore, a more intelligent solution is needed. For many cases the problem at hand could likely be overcome with techniques from constraint optimization problem solving. Furthermore, a solution to a similar problem was presented in [KKRKS07b]. We are therefore optimistic to be able to solve the issue in our future work.

Unrelated composition with global condition and preference

Preferences have been discussed above already and the combination with composition does not add any difficulties in the setting of our solution.

Correlated composition

Goal C2 requests a notebook and a compatible docking station. Thus the two requested products are correlated and cannot be handled seperately. DSD is capable to express such correlations and to correctly compose and configure multiple offers accordingly [KKRKS07b]. Unfortunately, we were nevertheless unable to solve goal C2 correctly. Compatibility of docking stations and notebooks in the scenario is given by a property of each docking station that holds a list of the GTINs of the compatible notebooks. To ensure whether a notebook is compatible to a docking station one has to check whether the notebook's GTIN is contained in the docking stations compatibility list. Currently the DIANE framework lacks sufficient support for matching of list-based attributes to handle this case.

12.2.5 Service interactions

In this section we provide details about how DIANE performs the necessary interactions with a service endpoint to facilitate automated service consumption. We first deal with how estimation operations are integrated into the matchmaking process and then describe how the actual invocations of the services are carried out.

Integrating service interactions into the matchmaking

As mentioned in Section 12.1 our matchmaker follows a multi-phased approach [KKRKS07b]. The main idea behind this decision is to reduce the number of offers remaining in the matchmaking process before the most expensive matchmaking tasks are performed. The basic idea

```
supports = anonymous SOAPServiceGrounding at upper.grounding [
        // THE ORDER OPERATION
        soapOperations += anonymous SOAPExecuteOperation at upper.grounding [
                soapAction = "order",
                xmlTemplatePath = "bargainerOrderProductsTemplate.xml",
                endpoint = "http://sws-challenge.org/shops/Bargainer",
                mappingIN += anonymous XmlDsdMapping at upper.grounding [
                        // omitted due to space limitations
                ]
        ],
        // THE DYNAMIC OFFER COMPLECTION OPERATION
        soapOperations += anonymous SOAPOfferCompletionOperation at upper.grounding [
                setReference = $products,
                soapAction = "list",
                xmlTemplatePath = "bargainerListProductsTemplate.xml",
                endpoint = "http://sws-challenge.org/shops/Bargainer",
                mappingIN += anonymous XmlDsdMapping at upper.grounding [
                        // omitted due to space limitations
                ],
                mappingOUT += anonymous XmlDsdMapping at upper.grounding [
                        // omitted due to space limitations
                ],
                ...
        ]
        ...
],
```

Fig. 12.7. Excerpt from the grounding of Bargainer's offer description

of the matchmaking algorithm is to traverse the request description tree and to match each concept r_i from the request with the corresponding concept o_i from the offer. As mentioned before the matchvalue of r_i and o_i is thereby built by comparing the types of the concept, applying any direct conditions and then combining the match values retrieved from recursively comparing the properties (property conditions) of r_i and o_i. This structured approach to matchmaking allows to collect precise information about which parts of an offer did not match with the request. In a first run not only obviously unsuitable offers are filtered, but also information about whether a particular estimation operation should be executed is collected. This is the case when a concept from an offer that is declared as estimation out variable was neither a perfect match nor a definite fail using static information alone.

Thus after a first run only the estimation operations that offer information about such concepts will be executed [KKR07c]. When matching those goals of the shipping scenario for instance, which do not specify a price limit, the corresponding price information will not be gathered, since it has no influence on the outcome of the matchmaking. Similarly when matching Goal C3 of the shipping scenario with the available offers, the actual price of the Weasel offer will not be inquired since it is already known after the first matching run that Weasel does not ship to the United Kingdom and is therefore unsuitable anyway.

After the estimation operations are executed, the information returned by the service endpoints will be used to update the offer descriptions and another matchmaking run will be performed, yielding the most accurate and up to date results possible.

Performing service invocations

The information that is necessary to automatically invoke a service (regardless whether this is in the context of an estimation or execution operation) is specified in the grounding part of an offer description. Figure 12.7 shows excerpts from the grounding specification of the Bargainer service. Two SOAP operations are defined, the first used to execute the service, the other one used to complete the service description (i.e. to gather the dynamic product listings). Both

```
mappingIN += anonymous XmlDsdMapping at upper.grounding [
        variable = $products,
        dataNodePath = "ProductCategory",
        converterClassName = "org.swschallenge.shops.ProductCategoryConverter",
        converterMethodName = "convert"
],
mappingOUT += anonymous XmlDsdMapping at upper.grounding [
        variable = $products,
        dataNodePath = "/ProductList/Product",
        // gtin
        attributeMappings += anonymous XmlDsdAttributeMapping at upper.grounding [
                attributePath = "gtin",
                subNodePath = "productID"
        ],
        // mapping for Notebooks and NotebookDescriptions
        attributeMappings += anonymous XmlDsdAttributeMapping at upper.grounding [
                subNodePath = "self::node()[productCategory=\"Notebook\"]",
                className = "dsd.schema.domain.computer.Notebook",
                attributePath = "entity",
                attributeMappings += anonymous XmlDsdAttributeMapping at upper.grounding [
                subNodePath = "name",
                attributePath = "deviceSpecs"
        ],
        // elements of ProductDescription
        // macs are produced by apple
        attributeMappings += anonymous XmlDsdAttributeMapping at upper.grounding [
                subNodePath = "prodDescription[contains(brand,\"Mac\")]",
                attributePath = "producer",
                converterClassName = "[...]util.converter.InstanceNameConverter",
                converterMethodName = "getInstance",
                constantValue = "dsd.instance.domain.economy.Company.apple"
        ],
        ...
```

Fig. 12.8. Mapping definitions from the grounding of Bargainer's offer description

specify the SOAP action header to use (`soapAction`) and the endpoint to call (`endpoint`). The `setReference` property of the `SOAPOfferCompletionOperation` is used to map the operation to the dynamic set it belongs to. To lower ontological DSD data to XML messages to be sent to a service and to lift XML data extracted from the service's response to ontological DSD data, DSD follows a pragmatic approach that was introduced in [KKR06b]. For each operation an empty XML message template has to be deployed together with the service description at the DIANE middleware. The `xmlTemplatePath` property of the specified operations in Figure 12.7 points to that file. Mappings have to be specified in the grounding that define how to fill the template with the values from the properly configured offer description.

Figure 12.8 shows excerpts from the mapping definitions from the Bargainer offer's grounding used for the `SOAPOfferCompletionOperation`. `mappingIN` definitions are used to create the inputs of an operation, thus lowering from DSD data to XML. The shown example specifies the variable from the offer's description to use (`variable`) and an XPath expression that identifies the XML node in the message template to fill with data from that variable (`dataNodePath`). Depending on the type of the variable standard serialization is available, but in the case at hand a custom Java class is specified and used to deliver the proper product type in Bargainer's classification for a given product (`converterClassName` and `converterMethodName`). This class has to be deployed at the DIANE middleware and will be instantiated using reflections.

Once the given XML template is properly filled the correct message will automatically be sent to the corresponding endpoint. The reply needs to be interpreted to make the results of the service invocations available to the middleware, either to return them to the service requestor or to use them during the matchmaking process.

This is accomplished by `mappingOUT` definitions that are used to process the outputs of an operation, in this case by lifting the XML listing of available products to DSD instances.

They work similar to `mappingIN` definitions but in the example in Figure 12.8 illustrate some more features. As shown in the example, mappings can be specified in a nested way (which allows to handle nested lists). The `subNodePath` and `attributePath` properties identify an attribute of the variable and a descendent node of the XML node used by the parent mapping definition. If the `subNodePath` XPath expression evaluates to an empty list the mapping is not executed which allows to specify different mappings e.g. for different types of products (like notebooks, docking stations, etc.). In Figure 12.8 this is used to set the producer of a product to the instance `apple` if and only if the brand node in the given XML contains the string "Mac". The name of the instance to instantiate is provided as static value in the mapping and a converter class is used to retrieve a complex entity instance by its name. The lightweight mapping mechanism described above was sufficient powerful and flexible enough to not only cover the automated invocations in the shipping discovery scenario but also to handle the dynamic product listing of the second scenario.

12.3 Discussion and Summary

We have described how DSD and the DIANE middleware has been used to solve nearly all parts of the SWS-Challenge discovery goals. In this final section we will briefly discuss the lessons learned and the strengths and weaknesses of the DIANE approach in a structured way.

12.3.1 Domain ontologies

The scenarios did not require very heavy-weighted ontologies with rules and restrictions. Thus our lightweight ontology language was very well suited to describe all aspects of the domains at hand and we did not encounter any difficulties there. In particular the temporal semantics could be addressed easily by creating special DateTime instances that directly capture the temporal semantics of *now* or *today* by accessing the local system time.

12.3.2 Offer descriptions

Most aspects of the offers like the operation range of the shippers, the restrictions on package size or weight or the rates on request of the Muller shipping offer could be easily modelled in DSD. The main limitation with regard to the offers was the lack of direct support for rules. In the first scenario rules were needed to compute shipping prices and expected shipping times in dependency of certain attributes of the shipment. We circumvent this limitation by delegating the evaluation of rules to external entities (in our solution we used web services, but we could have used local method calls or any other mean, too). The integration of this delegation could be easily done since DSD already supported to gather additional information during the matchmaking (estimation operations). Some constraints on the possible collection time in the shipping scenario required to pose conditions on arithmetic combinations of different properties of a service description. Originally DSD was lacking support for such conditions but this feature (multi attribute conditions) has been added to DSD. However, as discussed in Section 12.2 this feature is problematic in combination with optimal offer configuration (which can not be achieved efficiently anymore). This is one of the fields of future work.

12.3.3 Request descriptions

Most aspects of the goal descriptions could be easily expressed in DSD. Shipping discovery based on destination, weight, price, temporal requirements or any combination could be directly solved. The same is true for the product purchasing scenario goals. DSD proved very capable of expressing fine-grained user preferences in requests via fuzzy sets to enable powerful ranking of services. Modelling of those preferences was very straightforward and intuitive except for one case where preferences were given based on rules (see Section 12.2.4). The composition goals of both scenarios could be expressed (except for Goal C2 which will be discussed below). In the second scenario we chose to ask for multiple effects in the request. In the one composition goal of the first scenario we chose to use iteration directives that change the set-based semantics of that request. Although the iteration directives were sufficient for the problem at hand, their implementation within the DSD Middleware as proof of concept is currently still incomplete and needs to be completed. This is subject of ongoing work.

12.3.4 Reasoning and matchmaking

DSD does not rely on standard logic for matchmaking but uses a custom set-based reasoning operation *subset*. This allows to express request preferences using fuzzy sets and in particular acknowledges the fact that offers usually need to be configured and should be configured in an optimal way. Thus DSD matchmaking does not only check whether an offer instance is suitable for a request instance, but also determines the best configuration of an offer. DSD has been designed to do this efficiently without iterating over all possible configurations, largely by allowing for local optimizations in many cases. This interferes with the multi attribute conditions that have been introduced to capture certain restriction on pickup times in the first scenario (see Section 12.2.1) and global restrictions on the price of a complete purchase in the second scenario (see Section 12.2.4). Due to performance considerations our current matchmaking implementation does not guaranteed anymore that the determined configuration is optimal or that an existing valid composition is found if offers or requests use multi attribute conditions. To improve on this issue is ongoing work.

Finally, DSD allows to use lists as properties of a concept. Unfortunately the current matchmaking implementation does not completely support such properties. This prevented us from solving Goal C2 of the second scenario (where compatibility of notebooks and docking stations is given as a list property of the docking stations that lists the compatible notebooks). To add the necessary support for matchmaking of list-based properties is future work, too.

12.3.5 Service interactions

DSD and DIANE have been designed to support fully automated invocation of services, thus the need to execute service operations (estimation or execution operations) did not pose severe difficulties to our approach. The pragmatic approach to mapping between XML and DSD data has proven to be sufficiently flexible and powerful to cover the scenarios. The practical experience however has shown that it is quite cumbersome and in particular error-prone to define these mappings without appropriate tool support. This has highlighted once more that powerful editing tools (which DIANE is currently still lacking) are an essential prerequisite for more widespread or daily use of any semantic web service technology.

Regarding estimation operations we believe that these are a particular strength of our approach. In [KKR07c] we argue that the ability to include dynamic information into the matchmaking is essential for any service matchmaking framework. Unfortunately however, this can easily compromise the efficiency of any matchmaking algorithm since the matchmaking time will quickly be dominated by the time spend to call external webservice's endpoints to gather that dynamic information. It is thus a key strength of DIANE that its structured graph-matching approach to service matchmaking allows to precisely determine which parts of an offer description matched how well – an important difference to the related work. This knowledge can then easily be used to inquire precisely only that dynamic information which will influence the outcome of the matchmaking.

12.3.6 Difficulty to switch from one problem level to another

It was one of the assumptions of the SWS-Challenge that the advantage of using semantic technology compared to traditional programming should be proven by showing that semantic based approaches would cope more easily with changes in the scenarios.

In our experience quite a bit of effort was involved in building a first running solution to the challenge. This is mainly due to two reasons. First, DIANE - as a research prototype - is partly lacking the tool support that one would wish to have (this is particularly true for the grounding definitions). Second, some scenarios required to add new features to the DIANE framework. However, to add these features (like multi attribute conditions) to the framework is a one time effort related to the development of the language and framework and should pay off when more scenarios become available that make use of these feature but do not require new ones.

Aside of these issues we do not feel that a lot of effort was necessary to switch from one problem level to another one. In particular little effort was needed to move from the first scenario to the second one. This is due to the fact that DIANE uses a generic set-based and not a domain-dependent rule-based approach to matchmaking. The principle behind DSD is to describe what offers can provide, what requests are seeking and have the matchmaking done by generic domain-independent matchmaking rules. Thus, when switching from the first scenario to the second scenario, we had to create the needed domain ontologies (describing IT hardware) and we had to describe the offers and requests. However, we did not have to specify matchmaking rules since these remain the same for all scenarios.

References

KKR06a. Ulrich Küster and Birgitta König-Ries. Discovery and mediation using DIANE service descriptions. In *Third Workshop of the Semantic Web Service Challenge 2006 - Challenge on Automating Web Services Mediation, Choreography and Discovery*, Athens, GA, USA, November 2006.

KKR06b. Ulrich Küster and Birgitta König-Ries. Dynamic binding for BPEL processes - a lightweight approach to integrate semantics into web services. In *Second International Workshop on Engineering Service-Oriented Applications: Design and Composition (WESOA06) at 4th International Conference on Service Oriented Computing (ICSOC06)*, Chicago, Illinois, USA, December 2006.

KKR07a. Ulrich Küster and Birgitta König-Ries. Semantic service discovery with DIANE service descriptions. In *Proceedings of the International Workshop on Service Composition & SWS Challenge at the 2007 IEEE/WIC/ACM International Conference on Web Intelligence (WI 2007)*, Silicon Valley, USA, November 2007.

KKR07b.   Ulrich Küster and Birgitta König-Ries. Service discovery using DIANE ser-
            vice descriptions - a solution to the SWS-Challenge discovery scenarios. In
            *Fourth Workshop of the Semantic Web Service Challenge - Challenge on Au-
            tomating Web Services Mediation, Choreography and Discovery*, Innsbruck,
            Austria, June 2007.
KKR07c.   Ulrich Küster and Birgitta König-Ries. Supporting dynamics in service descrip-
            tions - the key to automatic service usage. In *Proceedings of the Fifth Interna-
            tional Conference on Service Oriented Computing (ICSOC07)*, Vienna, Austria,
            September 2007.
KKRK06.   Ulrich Küster, Birgitta König-Ries, and Michael Klein. Discovery and media-
            tion using DIANE service descriptions. In *Second Workshop of the Semantic
            Web Service Challenge 2006 - Challenge on Automating Web Services Media-
            tion, Choreography and Discovery*, Budva, Montenegro, June 2006.
KKRKS07a.   Ulrich Küster, Birgitta König-Ries, Michael Klein, and Mirco Stern. DIANE
            - a matchmaking-centered framework for automated service discovery, com-
            position, binding and invocation on the web. *International Journal of Elec-
            tronic Commerce (IJEC)*, 12 - Special Issue on Semantic Matchmaking and Re-
            trieval(2), 2007.
KKRKS07b.   Ulrich Küster, Birgitta König-Ries, Michael Klein, and Mirco Stern. DIANE -
            an integrated approach to automated service discovery, matchmaking and com-
            position. In *Proceedings of the 16th International World Wide Web Conference
            (WWW2007)*, Banff, Alberta, Canada, May 2007.
KKRM05.   Michael Klein, Birgitta König-Ries, and Michael Müssig. What is needed for
            semantic service descriptions - a proposal for suitable language constructs. *In-
            ternational Journal on Web and Grid Services (IJWGS)*, 1(3/4):328–364, 2005.

An Approach to Discovery with miAamics and jABC

Christian Kubczak[1], Tiziana Margaria[2], Bernhard Steffen[3], Christian Winkler[2], and Hardi Hungar[4]

[1] Chair of Software Engineering, Technical University of Dortmund, Germany
   christian.kubczak@cs.uni-dortmund.de
[2] Chair of Service and Software Engineering, University of Potsdam, Germany
   {margaria,winkler}@cs.uni-potsdam.de
[3] Chair of Programming Systems, Technical University of Dortmund, Germany
   steffen@cs.uni-dortmund.de
[4] OFFIS, Oldenburg, Germany hungar@offis.de

Summary. We present a hybrid approach to service discovery that uses miAamics, a rule-based selection engine, as a matchmaker within the jABC, a framework for service-oriented process modelling, execution, and evolution. This approach aims at tailoring the service discovery process in such a way that different users with different technical and domain competence can efficiently participate at their level of expertise. We shape the collaboration between business experts and IT team following the well-known 80/20 principle: more than 80% of the discovery management, control, and use should not require any special IT knowledge. In particular, the specification of the set of weighted rules, which is miAamics' way of describing the aspect-oriented relevance of data/products/offers, can in our experience be dealt with by business experts without IT knowledge after a short training. Entering the predicates that describe the individual preferences of a user for a certain selection process can easily be done simply by clicking at certain preference criteria: this is so intuitive that it does not even require an explanation.

13.1 The miAamics Framework

In this chapter we address the SWS discovery scenario described in Chap. 2 using as a reasoning engine miAamics, a framework for rule-based evaluation originally developed for efficient and scalable personalization purposes[5]. miAamics was developed in 2000-2001 at METAFrame Technologies GmbH to address the needs of scalable real-time personalization in large scale CRM applications [9]. The underlying technology is being patented. A later redesign of the framework in a Java environment has made it widely portable [3]. We show in this chapter how we use miAamics at the core of a service discovery process that is itself implemented in the jABC framework, the same framework we used previously for the SWS mediation scenario. The jABC is described in detail in the context of the mediation scenario in Chapter 5. Here we concentrate on the miAamics technology and on the service discovery process we realized in jABC that embeds miAamics as core reasoning engine.

---

[5] Preliminary aspects of this work have been presented in [4].

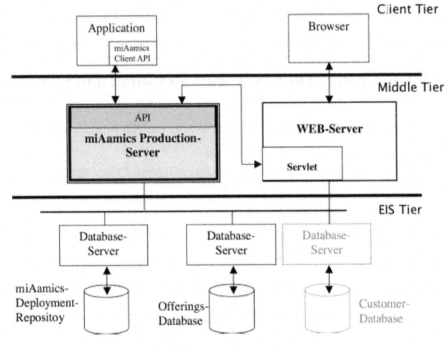

Fig. 13.1. miAamics' architecture

Seen from an abstract point of view, miAamics can be described as a rule based and situation aware matcher, that optimally matches profiles of requests to profiles of offers. It is situation aware in the sense that dynamic context information can also be taken into consideration via a context profile, which has a direct impact on determining which offers fit and their ranking.

miAamics solves the matching task by calculating an ordering of all possible vendors sorted by how well they match the given criteria. Provided a proper configuration, it can be ensured that highest ranked solutions in the resulting set of ordered offers are *optimal* in the sense that no other solution satisfies the specified constraints better.

13.1.1 miAamics' Architecture

Fig. 13.1 sketches miAamics' overall architecture. The miAamics production server performs at runtime the match of requests and offers. The criteria for the match are defined by users by means of an application whose use is shown in Fig. 13.4. They are stored in a repository of rules and strategies called Deployment repository. At runtime, a client, typically a browser, as in the case of the SWS Challenge scenarios, provides a request. This is passed by the web server to the miAamics production server, which determines according to the current evaluation criteria (the evaluation strategy now active in the deployment repository) which abstract profiles of offers fit best for the abstract profile of the request. The Web server then returns from the offer database a concrete offer with that profile.

The information evaluation flow is depicted in Fig. 13.2:

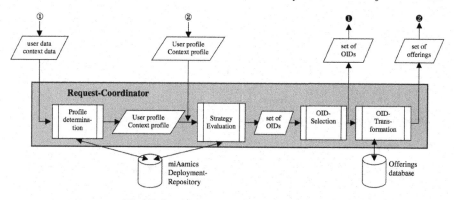

Fig. 13.2. miAamics information evaluation

- concrete data provening from the SWS Challenge testbed concerning a user request (in our case, it is a shipment request) and concrete situation data (if available, in our case there is no situation description so this is empty), are evaluated to determine the abstract profile of the (situated) request for miAamics.
- Alternatively, the user and context profile can be directly input by some external application that directly works at the ontology level
- The strategy evaluation in the production server determines the matching offer IDs (OIDs), which are an abstract description of the offers in terms of a profile.
- For matches embedded in external applications, these abstract descriptors are returned,
- for a concrete application, like in our case, the OIDs are resolved in the set of concrete offers corresponding to that profile, and usually one of them is returned. Note that since all the offers match that profile, they are equivalent, and thus it is legitimate to randomly select one of them.

In the discovery scenario described by the SWS Challenge, the best ranked proposal for an abstract description of a shipping request indeed resulted in the suggestion of a vendor which is able to fulfill this task and respects all the constraints specified in the request.

13.1.2 miAamics Evaluation Engine

The rule evaluation structure of the production server is the central component of the matchmaking. It is provided with ontological information based on attributes, categories, and rules, which we describe in the following.

The miAamics *evaluation engine* uses formulas reminiscent of event-condition-action rules to specify sets of business *rules* called *strategies*. This corresponds to the top layer of the miAamics knowledge representation structure shown in Fig. 13.3. Single incoming requests are evaluated with respect to the currently enforced strategy. We can define multiple strategies in miAamics, but only one at a time is active and used for request evaluation. Rules consist of premises based on request and/or situation data, and conclusions based on product or better offer data, respectively; i.e. they define functions of the kind

$$f(request, situation) \rightarrow \{offer\}$$

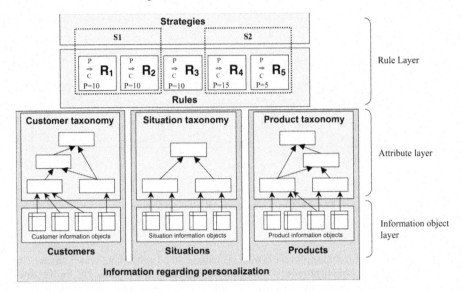

Fig. 13.3. Structure of the miAamics ontology

These functions are associated to numerical values that indicate on an integer scala the weight of the rule, called priorities in Fig. 13.4.

The SWS challenge discovery scenario

- does not consider situations, even though they would also make sense here, e.g. making the transport offers depend on daytime or week days, and it
- does not consider preferences: it asks for the set of suitable shippers for a given request, rather than for the best shipper according to some additional (likely non-functional) preference criteria.

Our solution therefore does not make use of situation information. It still considers preferences since they are naturally built-in the system, due to their relevance in real-life service selection scenarios. We show here how to express preferences, and in Chap. 16 we compare the miAamics way of defining and evaluating preferences with the Diane approach, that is capable of handling preferences too.

miAamics' evaluation is global to the strategy: whenever a request arrives, all rules of the current strategy are considered. In case their left hand sides match the request's profile, the rules' weights are added to the current weight of the proposed offers (in this case the shipper services), in order to compute the overall ranking of all offers available. This globality of evaluation is a central asset of miAamics: in other rule based systems, policies for rule selection and rule triggering play a major role in complicating the evaluation mechanism and making it intransparent to the user. It is in fact customary for example to take the first applicable rule and ignore the subsequent ones. This leads to a hidden priority expression, that is encoded implicitly in the ordering of the rules: changing the order of the rules affects the results. Other systems request disjointness of premises: it must be ensured somehow that only one rule is eligible to fire. This introduces dependencies between the rules: if a new rule is introduced, it can impact the definition of any other rule, since any overlap must be detected

and eliminated, usually by rule splitting. The result is a collection of rules with very complicated logical expressions in their premises, that hamper understandability and maintainability
by domain experts.

With our design choice, rules can overlap. Thus they remain "local" in their scope, simple
in their formulation, and understandable by the domain expert that just wants to capture this
little portion of business knowledge. They all are evaluated, if more than one are applicable,
their effects are collected and cumulated in a way understandable to the rule designer, who
can inspect their effects in a result chart. This guarantees complete transparency of the results
to the user as well as full diagnostic information for adjustments or revisions.

Since evaluation can be time expensive for scenarios with many criteria, offers, and rules,
the evaluation can be also sped up by pre-computing the effects of the evaluation in an optimized data structure (called RES, Rule Evaluation Structure), which is consulted at runtime,
bypassing the case by case evaluation of rules. This leads to a highly performant and scalable
selection process.

In the following, we first sketch the miAamics modelling style and its own terminology,
then we establish a relation between this style and terminology and Description Logic, a well
established modelling style for knowledge expression and ontologies in the Semantic Web
community.

13.1.3 Modelling in miAamics

We use in this case study a simple ontology to express the domain of discourse of the business
(and therefore of the rules): following the structure of miAamics's knowledge base depicted in
Fig. 13.3, for the discovery problem we define a taxonomy[6] based on abstract *attributes* that
are meaningful for the business expert. For instance, shippers that take 'heavy packages'
are defined by an attribute 'shipping heavy packages' whereby the 'maximum weight' data
field of the shipper profile can exceed e.g. 70 lbs. The corresponding definition of the attribute
is

$$\text{'shipping heavy packages: (maximum weight} \geq 70 \text{ lbs)'}$$

Attributes are thus technically predicates. They directly base on the concrete profile vocabulary
of the shippers, but rules are often more abstract, and refer to coarser concepts that combine
different attributes. These coarser concepts, called in miAamics *categories*, are technically
simply predicates over the set of attributes. Thus they can be logically combined, and they form
a hierarchy, often called *taxonomy*, reflecting an *is-a* relationship. In fact, our work is based
on these kinds of taxonomies rather than on the more general ontologies, whose additional
structure for knowledge expression seems to add in practice more complication than benefit
for an end user.

miAamics *rules* do not refer directly to the possibly huge number of involved entities
typically contained in a data base, but to the above-mentioned taxonomies, through the categories and attributes. In the Information object layer we have the connection between database
attributes (fields like "age", "price") and taxonomy attributes (predicates that refer to the information objects over those fields, like "age $\leq$ 40". This separation of the production database
(containing in our example the concrete shipper offers) from the matching process has two
reasons:

- Performance: the run-time critical matching process fully works on main memory.

---

[6] Under taxonomy we understand an ontology where the concepts are related only by an *is-a*
relation and where the resulting concept graph is acyclic, i.e. a DAG.

- Agility: it is possible to freely and dynamically exchange the data in the database, as long as the conceptual structure defined by the taxonomy is maintained. E.g., new shippers can be added at any time, as long as their characteristics can still be expressed in the existing taxonomy.

The production database is only used after the matching process, to retrieve concrete instances (like shippers' profiles and data) of the computed abstract descriptions in terms of taxonomy concepts.

As an efficient matching engine, miAamics brokers between input and output taxonomy-based profiles. It is thus an ideal backbone service for a specific personalization or evaluation task. The frontend, such as a graphical user interface to submit a query or display results, is independent of miAamics. It can for instance be reused from preexisting non-personalized versions of the application or the website. Also in this Service Discovery scenario, the match-making technology is completely embedded within the jABC.

13.1.4 Embedding in Description Logics

The style of domain modeling adopted in miAamics can directly be related to Description Logics (DL) [1]. In DL, the knowledge base description K is split into the

- *terminological box* T (TBox) describing concepts that apply for classes of individuals and the
- *assertional box* A (ABox) describing properties of the individuals that populate the described space.

TBox concepts C are defined by concept descriptions D (e.g. $c \sqsubseteq d$ with $c \in C$ and $d \in D$). In miAamics, the TBox directly corresponds to the taxonomies the matching algorithm is based upon: our attributes and categories correspond in fact to basic concepts and compound concepts in DL's TBox.

The ABox, which corresponds to miAamics' information objects, is only relevant when concrete instances need to be retrieved from the production database.

E.g. the attribute *Parent* (corresponding to a DL TBox concept) could be defined in terms of database information objects as People (member of the (ABox)) with children:

- Parent: People.childCount > 0

Categories in miAamics correspond to concepts (thus members of the DL (TBox) defined in terms of other concepts. In miAamics they are defined in terms of attributes and other categories, forming hierarchies of concepts. For instance, the category *Mothers* could be defined as the set of female parents:

- Mothers: Female AND Parent

by using the attributes *Female* and *Parent*. This is also directly expressible in DL.

miAamics' rules, which are based on predicate logic, define mappings of the kind $f(request, situation) \rightarrow \{offer\}$ simply via implication.

Due to its original application domain in online marketing, in miAamics rules allow premises to refer to categories and attributes of type request and situation only, and consequences to refer only to offers. Additionally it is enforced that these three types of attributes and categories are disjoint: they give rise to three distinct taxonomies.

All this can be directly expressed also in DL, e.g., by adding attributes that tell which concepts refer to requests, situations, and offers respectively. In particular, since the mapping expressed by the rules is an implication between concepts, it directly corresponds to implication in DL.

The main difference of miAamics to the typical DL-based scenarios is due to its weighting-based evaluation of strategies: all rules are weighted, they are always evaluated, and the resulting offers are ranked according to the sum of weights of all matching rules proposing this offer. This allows for a convenient, multi-faceted and modular specification.

It should be noted, however, that the restrictions on the rule format mentioned above are technically not necessary: they are imposed only for convenience of the users, as user guidance, like typing in a programming language, and they could easily be omitted or adapted for an application domain with a different structuring profile.

13.2 Rule Based Discovery for the Discovery Scenario

Setting up the miAamics configuration for a concrete scenario means creating a taxonomy for this domain. This expresses the knowledge base for the subsequent evaluation, therefore this task is central to get the desired evaluation results. As is well-known, creating such a configuration needs some care. In the following we present the most relevant basic steps concerning the knowledge expression for the SWS Challenge discovery scenario.

13.2.1 Domain Model: Choosing the Vocabulary

First we need to establish a domain vocabulary to be used as concepts in miAamics's taxonomies and rules. To this aim, we analyzed the textual descriptions provided both in the scenario Wiki and in the WSDL files of the single shippers. We identified relevant data sets for the discovery problem's inputs (the queries) and outputs (the shippers) and established a domain-specific terminology at the miAamics' attribute level.

The shipping constraints are taken from those textual descriptions too. For example, two constraints for the shipping vendors are:

- Packages weighing 50 lbs or less are shipped
- Collection is possible after 6.00 a.m.

To formalize those constraints, shippers' profiles have to contain (at least) the following data fields

- Maximum package weight (lbs)
- Collection start time (24h)
- Collection end time (24h)

that are then used to define the corresponding attributes. The elements of the profiles correspond to miAamics' information objects: they contain the concrete data items that are going to be evaluated and thus determine which attributes hold for which offers.

With this information we identify the domain specific concepts to be specified in the taxonomy by attributes and categories. We discovered for example that it is important in this scenario to characterize which shippers ship lightweight packages only. This is a relevant attribute in the taxonomy (ships lightweight only) and is defined by the constraint

- Maximum package weight (lbs) < 51

This way we identified and formalized the necessary information in order to obtain a complete classification of input and output data for the discovery.

13.2.2 Discretization and Preprocessing

The boolean abstraction intrinsic with miAamics' technology, that bases on attributes that are evaluable predicates over the information objects, brings two limitations when dealing with concrete data values:

1. miAamics's discrimination power is defined by the granularity level of the attributes, and
2. it cannot compute/compare numerical values. Thus the results of computations must be either modelled by rules, or one has to resort to an adequate preprocess, external to miAamics.

During the modelling of the SWS Challenge scenario we used both discretization and preprocessing. E.g., for modelling the weight of packages it seemed adequate to simply consider the few weight intervals referred to in pricing schemes. This was sufficient for the required classification, and it is quite intuitive. Doing the same for price calculations/comparisons would, however, either lead to

- a huge rule sets, with all the implied disadvantages, or
- it would be very imprecise, and therefore lead to unsatisfactory proposals.

In such cases it is therefore advantageous to resort to a hybrid approach: the computational part is done in a preprocess, whose aggregated results are then handed over to miAamics for determining a globally satisfying proposal that considers all the influencing facets. This gives one the option to play with the trade-off between general programming, that requires IT experts, and a much simpler, highly efficient way of combining many factors of influence expressed in simple rules, to a global optimum.

In the SWS discovery scenario, our preprocess also takes care of the user interaction (i.e. specifying the shipping request), invoking the Web service of a shipper, to query missing data not provided by the textual description (e.g. destination countries, shipping rates, sometimes provided only on demand). As described in [6], the preprocessing involves substantial orchestration, done in the jABC. This preprocessing updates the shipper's record accordingly at the backend of miAamics.

This is the typical usage pattern of miAamics, which is an embedded matchmaking component. It serves as engine to efficiently evaluate given rule sets. It communicates with the web or with the environment via an adequate user interface component or a communication service that fits the special needs of the scenario (e.g. display results, data preparation).

While we will describe the orchestration-based preprocessing in Sect. 13.3, we explain now how to comfortably interface miAamics with a user-level expression of the knowledge.

13.2.3 Automatic Generation of Comprehensive Taxonomies

Though they already consist of discrete values, some data domains that have to be covered by miAamics' rules are quite huge. Considering the destination countries in the given scenario explains the problem. Since we must define a complete taxonomy for the rule evaluation structure, we must create rules for all possible package destinations. The official list of countries of the United Nations[7] contains more than 240 entries. This means that the same number of shipping request attributes (e.g. premise: package shall be shipped to the US), shipping

---

[7] Countries or areas, codes and abbreviations in the United Nations Statistics Division (http://unstats.un.org/unsd/methods/m49/m49alpha.htm)

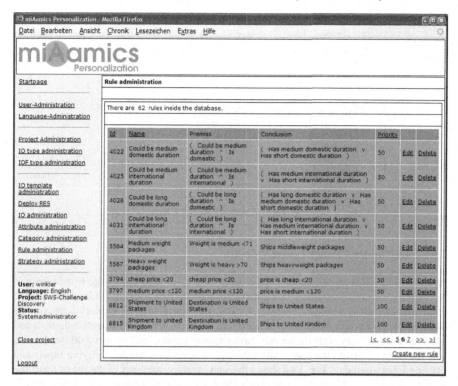

Fig. 13.4. miAamics Web Configuration Interface

offer attributes (e.g. conclusion: ships to North-America) and matching rules (e.g. shipment to the US holds if the aforementioned premise and conclusion hold) have to be created for the miAamics rule set, and that those rules have to be added to all strategies that consider shipment destinations. Of course, doing this manually would be a really cumbersome and error-prone task. Instead it is possible to populate miAamics' rule set in different ways. The underlying data structure used by miAamics to manage its rules and knowledge base is a relational database, hence it is possible to populate this database with concepts and rules in several ways. For the given example, we used jABC's DBSchema plug-in [10] to generate the attributes and rules for each country, based on the official database provided by the UN.

Other methods that allow us to import external data and create corresponding attributes and rules in miAamics are currently analyzed or already under development. For example we intend to import user profiles from FOAF[8] profiles, as well as profiles and concepts from existing ontologies provided in other modeling languages (like OWL[9]).

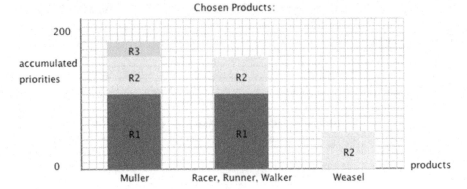

Fig. 13.5. miAamics Result Chart

13.2.4 miAamics Configuration Web-UI

Apart from these automated imports, the common way to provide knowledge to miAamics is to configure miAamics manually. A comfortable web interface offers capabilities to enter the configuration data as attributes, categories, rules, and strategies in miAamics' database. The web interface offers direct access to the backend database to configure *requests*, *situations* and *offers*. In the discovery scenario we only have shipping requests and shipper's offers.

The Web-UI assists the user while entering configuration data by verifying inputs and offering input assistance. Fig. 13.4 shows the web interface with part of the list of matching rules for the discovery scenario. As shown in the figure and already mentioned in Sect. 13.1.2, rules consist of a premise, a conclusion, a rating value (named *priority*) that allows one to provide the rules with a weight, and a name describing the rule.

Additionally to manually entering configuration data, other import methods exists to automatically import information of different formats, for example from plain text files, Excel, or other ontology definition languages like OWL.

13.2.5 Analyzing Evaluation Results

Depending on the amount of attributes and the complexity of rules used for an evaluation, miAamics results can often be quite surprising and hard to comprehend. To analyze the evaluation results, the miAamics' *Result Monitor* offers a graphical representation of the evaluation results as a bar chart. Fig. 13.5 shows such a bar chart for (*goal C3 of discovery scenario 1*):

> For all shipping requests, the packages are always sent from the Moon company in the US. The destination of the example shipment is a client in *Bristol* (UK). A single package of the dimension 10/2/3 (l/w/h in inch) and a weight of 20 lbs shall be shipped for less than 120$.

The constraints in the example request can be broken down to three major classes of constraints, as the sender's address is not significant in this example (but it is necessary for a

---

[8] The Friend-of-a-Friend project (http://www.foaf-project.org)

[9] Web Ontology Language, W3C Recommendation (http://www.w3.org/TR/owl-features/)

comprehensive discovery scenario in the SWSC) and the package dimension is just used to determine a *dimensional weight*, that might override the given weight - an issue for the pre-calculation steps. Thus only the constraints concerning the destination, weight, and price of the shipment need to be considered in order to solve the (simple) example request. This gives rise to the following classes of rules:

R1: Rules handling the ability to ship to a specific destination. For each possible destination there is a rule that 'fires' whenever this destination is requested, with the effect that the weights of the shippers shipping to this destination are increased by the rule's weight.

R2: Rules handling the ability to ship a package of specific weight. These rules are set up to distinguish the shipping weight limitations of the considered shippers. A rule for shipping medium weight packages could have the premise **package weight is** $\leq$ **100 lbs** and the conclusion **shipper's weight limit is** $\geq$ **100 lbs**. When it fires, it increases the (priority) weights of all shippers being at least able to handle packages weighting 100 lbs by the rule's (priority) weight.

R3: The third type of rules handles shipping costs. These rules are set up to distinguish expensive shipments from cheap ones. For the given request e.g. it would be necessary to have a rule that selects offers that cost less than 120$. This rule fires whenever a cheap shipping is requested (i.e. the price limit for the request is $\leq$ 120$), with the effect that the (priority) weights of the shippers offering shipment for less than 120$ are increased by the rule's weight.

For the SWS discovery example, we considered the following weighting scheme: Rules of class R1 got a rating (priority) of 100, R2 rules of 50, and R3 rules of 20. In the special case, where only one rule per class can fire, a total rating of 170 would indicate that all requirements are satisfied. Obviously, an offer that fulfills all criteria must have a sum of 170 rating points.

Fig. 13.5 shows the evaluation results for the example scenario. *Muller*'s offer is the best. It got 170 points showing that this offer fulfills all constraints specified in the example request. The bar also shows the fractions of the single rules that build the complete result. The second bar represents the second best offers. Those three shippers got 150 points, meaning that their offers are too expensive (exceed the 120$ limit). Finally, the last bar shows that this shipper does not ship to the required destination (R1 rule missing) and the offer is not within the price limitation.

Thus there is a solution for the example shipping request: the *Muller* service. However, we also see that whenever this shipper is prohibited for some other reason, there is no equivalent alternative and one needs at least to relax the price limitation.

13.3 The Discovery Application in the jABC

As described earlier in Sect. 13.2, miAamics is just the matchmaking engine of the full discovery solution presented by our group. It is embedded as a service in a jABC application in order to provide the service match and selection technology. As already done for Mediation [8, 5], we use the jABC environment [2, 7] to design a discovery application in a model driven fashion. The jABC framework is described in details in Chap. 5. In the discovery scenario, a similar application that we describe in detail in this Section uses miAamics as an embedded rule evaluation service. The full solution is supported by some additional services that, e.g., provide the user interaction, and select and invoke the Web service discovered with the miAamics technology. Also the error and exception handling is controlled via the jABC, but, in favour of readability, it is hidden here in the hierarchical structure of our process graphs.

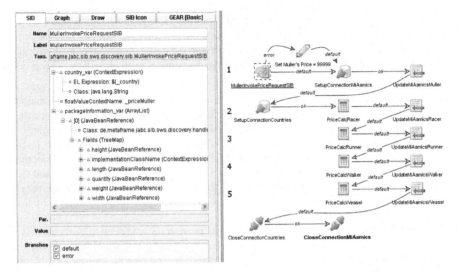

Fig. 13.6. The Muller Service in the jABC: a jETI SIB and its use

13.3.1 Modelling the Shippers

Fig. 13.6 shows how the Muller Web service is imported via jETI as a SIB in the jABC. On the left, we see the invocation of the SIB to enquiry the price quote in the Discovery SLG (see also Sect. 13.3.4 for a detailed description of this flow). On the left we see the interna of the SIB, according to the definition of a SIB given in Chap. 5. Also here, the SIB has a name, a label that is displayed for this instance in the SLG, taxonomy information (in this view, just its collocation as a Java class), and the rich data types of the SIB as Java class, that are automatically extracted by jETI from the WSDL interface description. These data types are the same we use as Information Objects for the miAmics model: on these we base the definition of attributes and categories, and thus also the rules. For each parameter we can in this SIB inspector also read or set the values. The SIB has only the two standard branches: whenever the execution of this SIB (requesting Muller for a quote) is executed and it terminates correctly the default branch is taken, while in case of abnormal execution the error branch is taken. In this case we decided not to stop the flow, but just to set the quote to an extremely high price, that rules out this shipper from the competition for this shipment.

13.3.2 Discovery Solution Main Model

Fig. 13.7 shows the main jABC service logic graph (SLG), expressing the orchestration of the discovery solution. Like for the mediation scenario, we graphically compose the business logic of this application by means of reusable Service Independent Building blocks (SIBs) that can be local or remote components and services.

The main SLG makes use of several standard SIBs that come with the jABC's default SIB palettes. The first two SIBs for example are used to simply store information to the SLG's shared memory that is used to exchange data between the SIBs during execution. Furthermore, database access SIBs are used to realize access to both the miAamics backend database and the *countries* database mentioned in Sect. 13.2.3. Besides standard SIBs, in the main model

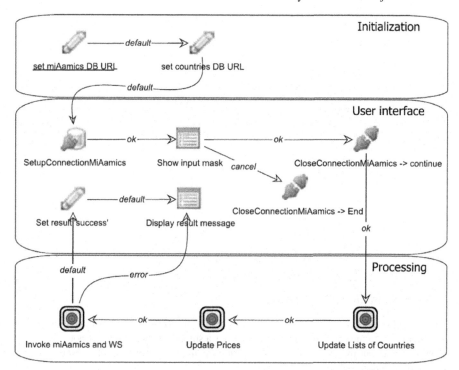

Fig. 13.7. Discovery Application: the main model

we use an additional SIB that was implemented specifically for the discovery scenario: a SIB displaying an input mask. This mask provides the user with some options to specify a shipment request based on the attributes defined in miAamics in the fashion already described. For instance the user could specify a package shipment request that

- concerns a **lightweight package** ($\leq$ 50 lbs),
- ships to a **destination location inside the USA,**
- and shall be shipped by a **cheap shipper** ($\leq$ 20$).

Here, the first two attributes select suitable shipper services, while the third indicates a preference criterium, often called a non-functional property.

Of course it would also be possible to let the user enter concrete values and then automatically evaluate which miAamics attributes hold for these values. E.g. the attribute **lightweight package** ($\leq$ 50 lbs) holds if the user enters a weight value of say 40 lbs. For simplicity reasons we chose here to directly work with miAamics' attributes in this case study. The complete information gathered from the user via the input mask is stored to the SLG's shared memory for later use.

The actual processing steps of the SLG make use of jABC's hierarchy feature. The three SIBs at the bottom row of Fig. 13.7 are *Graph-SIBs* that represent sub-models within the current model, each performing a self-contained subtask of the complete workflow.

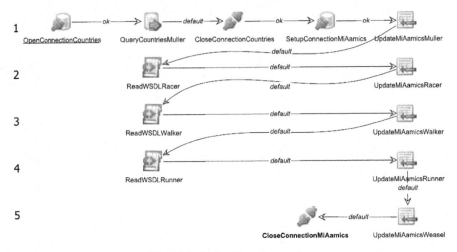

Fig. 13.8. Setting lists of countries

13.3.3 Setting Lists of Countries

The first sub-model (Fig. 13.8) updates the destination information of the shippers in its corresponding miAamics profile. The list of countries a shipper ships to is in fact not fixed in the given scenario, but may be retrieved from various sources, like for example a Web service's WSDL description.

Once again this model is mainly composed of SIBs from jABC's standard libraries, except for the one that updates a value for a given shipper's profile in the miAamics backend database. In Fig. 13.8, three different ways of obtaining the destination information are modelled:

1. For the first shipper (row 1), the destination information is given as the list of continents it ships to. The aforementioned countries database is therefore used to determine the concrete list of countries for this shipper. This is once again done with the help of DBSchema SIBs for database access.
2. Three shippers include a list of countries in their WSDL descriptions of their shipping services. A standard SIB that takes the WSDL's URL and a XPath expression is used to extract this information (rows 2-4).
3. The last shipper (row 5) only ships to a fixed list of countries that is specified directly in the SIB that updates the miAamics database. Of course it is not necessary to update the database entry for this shipper, but we decided to model also this case according to the standard pattern, for uniformity reasons.

Fig. 13.8 shows the flexibility of the presented approach. Adding additional shippers or changing the destination information (or their sources) can simply be done by graphically modifying or extending the model.

The effect on the underlying database of executing this model is immediately visible to miAamics, which thus automatically always refers to the most current information.

13.3.4 Calculating Shipping Prices

Calculating the shipping prices follows the same pattern as for the list of destinations. Again the concrete values have to be obtained from different sources. In one case, a Web service

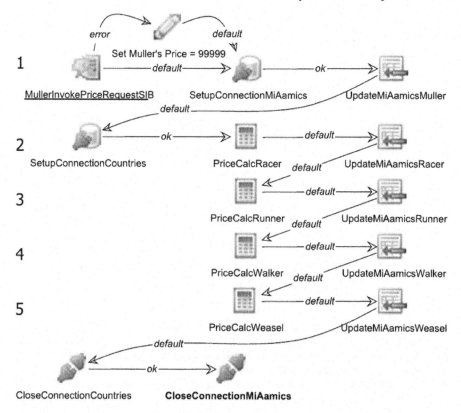

Fig. 13.9. Price calculation

invocation returns the price, while in other cases the concrete costs have to be calculated based on the package's dimension, weight, and destination.

The sub-model shown in Fig. 13.9 demonstrates the workflow. Again the different methods to obtain the concrete values are modeled using different SIBs, and additional methods are possible and feasible.

For the first shipper (row 1) a Web service has to be invoked that returns the shipping price for a single request. A corresponding Web service SIB was generated using the jETI framework in the same fashion as for the services in the mediation scenario (Chap. 5). In the case of any anomaly occurring during service invocation, the price for this shipper is set so high that this shipper is excluded from the further selection process.

For the remaining four shippers (rows 2-4) the prices simply depend on the destination continent. Thus it was sufficient to extend the aforementioned countries database to store the shipping fees for all shippers, and to implement a SIB that calculates the prices according to this information.

13.3.5 Evaluation and Invocation

The final major step – and the last sub-graph of the main model – concerns the miAamics-based selection and invocation of the best shipping Web service. The first SIB in Fig. 13.10

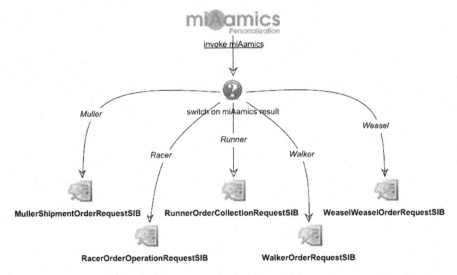

Fig. 13.10. miAamics and Web service invocation

implements a call to the miAamics evaluation API. Using the existing RES structure, built according to the rules and strategy defined before, and using the current values of the active database, miAamics determines the best shippers as described in Sect. 13.2.5. The process ends invoking a concrete shipping service from the selected result set.

Concretely, the miAamics SIB that performs the invocation to miAamics is implemented to accept a list of miAamics attributes that describe the (shipping) request and to provide a taxonomy-based specification of the set of optimal shipping offers. It is thus a profile-to-profile matcher, held on purpose very generic, so that it can be used in any miAamics project. The same applies also to the switching SIB, which can be re-used in potentially all other scenarios where a miAamics evaluation is the basis for selecting a single result. The required Web service SIBs are again generated from the WSDL descriptions provided by the SWSC organizers for the shipping services.

The main workflow ends displaying a message that summarizes the result of the Web service invocation.

13.4 Conclusion and Perspectives

We have presented a hybrid approach to discovery based on the combination of miAamcis, a rule-based selection engine, and the jABC, a framework for service-oriented process modelling, execution, and evolution. This approach aims at tailoring the discovery process in a way that different roles with different competence can efficiently participate at their level of expertise. Following the well-known 80/20 principle, more than 80% of the discovery management, control, and use should not require any special IT knowledge. In particular, the specification of the set of weighted rules, miAamics' way of describing the aspect-oriented relevance of data/products/offers can, in our experience, be dealt with by business experts without IT knowledge after a short training, while entering the predicates describing the individual preference of a user for a certain selection process, can easily be done simply by clicking at certain preferences, which is so intuitive that it does not even require an explanation. We consider this of major importance for practicality and acceptance.

As mentioned in Sect. 13.2 it is a matter of design and effort to decide how much to model in the miAamics ontology, to be evaluated with rules and policies, and what to deal with externally, via dedicated pre- or post-processing SIBs that enrich the overall process. Depending on the complexity of the criteria (e.g. computing VAT and sale taxes, which exceed the profile of the logic underlying the rules), the process option may be advantageous, since it allows generic programs as filters.

From the joint jABC/miAamics point of view, it is important that we offer a variety of integrated possibilities. It is in fact well possible that established strategies may need to be adapted, but for fear of disruption specific filters that express only the desired difference of behavior are quickly added as post-process SIBs for experimentation before integrating them as rules in the rule set. Conversely, criteria underlying rules and rule sets may need to be refined and become more and more complex, and eventually need to be extracted in a separate processing unit. For instance, when evolving from boolean decisions to complex classifications according to elaborate computations.

Key benefit of the miAamics tool is its performance and scalability. miAamics was originally developed to match huge amounts of offers to a big number of user profiles maintaining real-time demands in online applications (e.g. web shops). As miAamics calculates a matching solely based on the configured ontologies, computation time never depends on the number of instances populating those ontologies. Once the rule evaluation structure is calculated it is in fact even possible to add additional offers without recomputing RES, unless additional criteria (attributes, categories or rules) have to be considered.

In the SWSC discovery scenario, scalability was not yet an issue, neither concerning the shippers, nor the structure of constraints, nor the number of users. However, as soon as at least one of these three dimensions of complexity grow, performance will become an important issue. We are convinced that all three dimensions will become rather large in practice, in particular, because we think that the success of a provider of a discovery solution will grow with his coverage of possible selections.

References

1. F. Baader and W. Nutt. *The Description Logic Handbook, Theory, Implementation, and Applications*, chapter Basic Description Logics, pages 47–100. Cambridge University Press, 2nd edition, 2002.
2. S. Jörges, C. Kubczak, R. Nagel, T. Margaria, and B. Steffen. Model-driven development with the jABC. In *Proc. HVC'06 IBM Haifa Verification Conference*. Springer Verlag, October 23-26 2006.
3. C. Kubczak. Entwicklung einer verteilten Umgebung zur Personalisierung von Web-Applikationen. Master's thesis, Universität Dortmund, March 2005.
4. C. Kubczak, T. Margaria, C. Winkler, and B. Steffen. An approach to discovery with miaamics and jabc. In *Worksh. on Service Composition & SWS Challenge, part of WI-IAT07, the IEEE/ WIC/ ACM Int. Conf. on Web Intelligence*, pages 157 – 160. IEEE CS Press, ISBN-10: 0-7695-3028-1, November 2007.
5. C. Kubczak, B. Steffen, and T. Margaria. The jABC approach to mediation and choreography. In *2nd Semantic Web Service Challenge Workshop*, June 15-16 2006.

6. T. Margaria. The semantic web services challenge: Tackling complexity at the orchestration level. In *Invited paper ICECCS 2008 (13th IEEE Intern. Conf. on Engineering of Complex Computer Systems)*. IEEE CS Press, April 2008.

7. T. Margaria and B. Steffen. Service engineering: Linking business and IT, cover feature. *IEEE Computing*, pages 53–63, October 2006.

8. T. Margaria, C. Winkler, C. Kubczak, B.Steffen, M. Brambilla, S. Ceri, D. Cerizza, E. Della Valle, F. Facca, and C. Tziviskou. The SWS mediator with WebML/Webratio and jABC/jETI: A comparison. In *Proc. ICEIS'07, 9th Int. Conf. on Enterprise Information Systems*, June 2007.

9. miAamics GmbH: Technische Einführung in die miAamics-Personalisierungssuite. Dortmund (Germany), 2000-2001.

10. C. Winkler. Entwicklung eines jABC-Plugins zum Design von JDBC-kompatiblen Datenbankschemata. Master's thesis, Universität Dortmund, March 2006.

Part IV

Discovery Solutions Comparisons

Service Discovery with SWE-ET and DIANE - An In-depth Comparison By Means of a Common Scenario

Ulrich Küster[1], Andrea Turati[2], Birgitta König-Ries[1], Dario Cerizza[2], Emanuele Della Valle[2], and Federico M. Facca[3]

[1] Institute of Computer Science, Friedrich-Schiller-University Jena, 07743 Jena, Germany,
`ukuester|koenig@informatik.uni-jena.de`
[2] CEFRIEL, Via Fucini 2, 20133 Milano, Italy, `firstname.lastname@cefriel.it`
[3] Dipartimento di Elettronica e Informazione, Politecnico di Milano, 20133 Milano, Italy,
`firstname.lastname@elet.polimi.it`

Summary. Semantic service discovery and matchmaking has received increased attention within the last years. Various approaches have been proposed but agreed upon criteria how to objectively evaluate and compare these approaches are widely lacking. In this paper we present an in-depth comparison of two solutions to the discovery problems defined by the SWS-Challenge. By means of this common and independently developed scenario we can develop a much better understanding for the applied technologies in general, but also and in particular for the trade-offs involved in the different approaches.

14.1 Introduction

This chapter presents a comparative evaluation of the solutions to the SWS-Challenge's discovery scenario by the team from Politecnico Milano and CEFRIEL on the one hand (see Chapter 11) and the one by the University of Jena on the other hand (see Chapter 12). We will describe the various aspects of these approaches in a structured way and elaborate on the trade-offs involved in each technology.

The solution by the University of Jena is based on its DIANE-framework[4] while the other one is named SWE-ET[5] (Semantic Web Engineering – Environment and Tools) and combines CEFRIEL's Glue discovery engine[6] with the WebRatio framework[7] from Politecnico Milano. We adopt a structured approach to compare both solutions along several dimensions in the following sections. Table 14.1 shows a compact representation of the comparison result.

---

[4] http://hnsp.inf-bb.uni-jena.de/DIANE
[5] http://sweet.cefriel.it/
[6] http://glue.cefriel.it/
[7] http://www.webratio.com/

Feature	DIANE	SWE-ET
Ontologies	DE and DSD (custom formalism)	F-logic
Services and goals	configurable set of possible effects fuzzy set of acceptable effects	WSMO service capabilities WSMO goal capabilities
Ontology alignment	viewed as complementary and not covered	handled combined with the functional matchmaking
Functional matchmaking	set-based: subset value of configured offer in fuzzy request	rule-based: matching rules coded into wg-mediator
Preferences and ranking	preferences supported through fuzzy requests (integrated into matchmaking)	limited ranking support in Glue, selection done by the user through WebRatio interface
Dynamic descriptions	integrated into matchmaking	integrated into the discovery process through WebRatio
Invocation	automated by framework	automated through WebRatio

Table 14.1. Overview of comparison between DIANE and SWE-ET

14.2 Formalism Used to Model Ontologies

The goal of the DIANE project is to create a framework that is able to completely automate the whole process of service usage. Thus an ontology language was needed that on the one hand was expressive enough to precisely capture the necessary aspects of service offers and requests but on the other hand was as restricted as possible to ease the matchmaking process and maintain efficient processability. Therefore the approach followed by DIANE is to not use one of the logics commonly employed for semantic service descriptions, but to define its own language specifically tailored towards the use case at hand. Consequently DIANE uses its own ontology language, called DE (*DIANE Elements*) and DSD (*DIANE Service Descriptions*) which has been introduced in [KKRM05]. Ontologies are very lightweight and easy to use and the description elements of DSD used for ontologies can best be characterized as a small subset of F-logic [KLW95] without rules and quantifiers.

In contrast Glue – the discovery engine used in SWE-ET – is directly based on F-logic. This was motivated by the desire to create a discovery engine compliant with WSMO [dBBD+05]. At the time development on Glue started, tools for translating WSML (which is the official language of WSMO) into reasoner-specific formats were missing and WSML itself was a work-in-progress. However, after an analysis of the existent formalisms and their relations with WSML, it was decided to implement Glue on an F-logic reasoner, which supports rules and datatypes.

Thus the Glue approach models ontologies using F-Logic and can benefit from the entailed expressivity: F-logic allows to represent classes, instances, relationships among classes and instances, formulas that use logic operators and quantifiers, rules, and so on. F-logic provides a second-order, object-oriented-style syntax for a first-order logical language. In other words, as described in [KL89], F-logic has an appearance of a higher-order-logic, but, unlike it, is tractable and has a natural direct first-order semantics. In addition, sound and complete proof procedures for F-logic exist.

To address the SWS-Challenge's scenarios, both teams modeled necessary domain ontologies to capture required concepts like date and time, weight and dimensions, prices, locations, shipment etc. Despite the much bigger expressivity of the full F-logic approach taken by Glue, the modelled ontologies look fairly similar since the current scenarios did not require to use complex rules and restrictions in the ontologies.

14.3 Formalism Used to Model Services and Goals

While the underlying ontologies are rather simple, DSD supports more complex and expressive modeling operators to be used in request and offer descriptions. DSD takes a set-based approach to service modeling. Service offers are described as the set of effects they can provide wheras service requests are described as the set of effects that are acceptable for the requester. The default semantics of DSD defines that one effect out of the request effect set is requested and one effect out of the offer effect set will be provided by a service invocation. DSD sets are defined by defining direct conditions on a set and recursively defining the sets describing the attributes of that type as appropriate. Requests may use fuzzy instead of crisp sets to encode preference for certain effects – the higher the fuzzy membership of an effect in the fuzzy request set, the higher the preference of the requester for that particular effect.

Figure 14.1 illustrates the set-based modelling of services within DIANE. It shows an excerpt (hard disc and processor requirements have been omitted) from the definition of the product to be purchased within Goal A1 of the hardware purchasing scenario in an intuitive graphical notation.

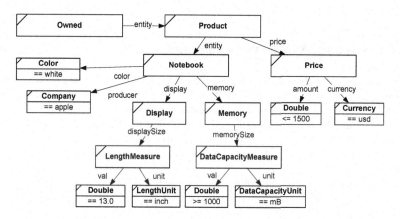

Fig. 14.1. Exerpts from the DSD request description of Goal A1

In Glue, Web services and goal descriptions are represented in F-logic, like ontologies. To model requests a shipping goal class was designed, capturing the desired capabilities as post-conditions following the WSMO modeling approach [dBBD+05]. Likewise, the semantics of the offer descriptions were captured by a Web service class for shipment. The restrictions that must hold in order to invoke a service were modelled as assumption and the result provided by an invocation as post-conditions. As explained in [DCC05], Glue refines the WSMO discovery conceptual model by making the notion of class of goals and class of Web service description explicit and by making a clear separation between instances and classes of goals and Web services.

Listing 14.1 shows the Glue goal instance description corresponding to the DSD description from Figure 14.1. It asks for a white "Mac Book" notebook with a maximum price of 1500,00 dollars, equipped with an Intel Duo Core processor of 2.0 GHz, 1 GB of RAM and 100 GB of hard disk. Note that some domain knowledge (e.g. that the given price is a maximum price and not a precise price requirement) is not formalized in the displayed goal but in the matchmaking rules.

```
1   goalInstanceA1:goalClass_Purchase[
2     capability−>_#:capabilityGoal_Purchase[
3       postcondition−>_#:requestsPurchaseService[
4         requestedProduct−>>{
5           _#:notebook[
6             hasPrice−>1500.0,
7             hasName−>'Mac Book 13'',
8             hasProc−>_#:proc[hasType−>intelCoreDuo,
9                              hasCapacityMHz−>2024],
10            hasMemory−>_#:memory[hasDimensionMB−>1024],
11            hasHDD−>_#:hdd[hasCapacityMB−>100000],
12            hasColor−>'white'
13          ]
14        }
15      ]
16    ]
17  ].
```

Listing 14.1. A goal instance of the class for the purchase scenario.

14.4 Goals and Web services alignment

Mediating between goals and Web services potentially requires two tasks. On the one hand, the supply (as expressed by the available offers) has to be compared with the demand (as specified in the goal) in terms of provided and requested functionality. This is usually referred to as matchmaking and will be covered in the following section. On the other hand, goals and Web services are specified by different entities and might thus be expressed using different ontologies. In this case, a schema alignment or ontology matching has to be performed additionally to the functional matching.

Glue covers both aspects combined. As described in [DCC05], at set-up-time a developer (different from both users and providers) creates wg-mediators, which are responsible for connecting specific goal classes to specific Web service classes and thus represent the core of the matchmaking. In this setting, goals and Web services can be very different and may refer to different ontologies. The heterogeneity of goals and Web services is solved by writing appropriate rules into the mediators. These rules perform the functional matchmaking (details below) but can be written in a way to also cover necessary ontology alignment (e.g. by comparing an attribute named "hddsize" in the goal instance with an attribute named "disc_capacity" in the Web service instance).

DIANE assumes that providers and requesters use the same ontology. Depending on the scenario, that may be an unrealistic assumption but ontology mediation is viewed as a problem orthogonal to the problem of functional matchmaking between service offers and requesters. The ontology mediation problem could be solved in a preprocessing step by writing translators which map a description expressed in one ontology to one expressed in another ontology analogously to the oo-mediators in the WSMO framework.

Handling functional matchmaking and ontology alignment combined as in the Glue approach eases the necessary ontology alignment, since only those aspects of an ontology need to be translated which are known to be needed during the functional matchmaking. Furthermore, if the translation is a lossy process, an integrated approach will be less likely to combine critical flaws. On the other hand, seperating concerns generally promotes reuse. If ontology mediation is treated seperately from the functional matchmaking, it is easier to change one aspect but reuse a solution for the other one. Thus, the advantageous approach to the problem depends on the use case.

14.5 The Process of Functional Matchmaking

14.5.1 Reasoning

DSD defines a special custom reasoning operation *subset* that solves the problem of service matchmaking. For a list of given DSD offer descriptions O and a given DSD request r, a matchmaker has to answer two questions for each $o \in O$: What is the subset value of o's effect sets in r's fuzzy effect sets (how well is o contained in what r requests) and which configuration of o yields the best such value? The DIANE matchmaker answers this question by traversing the request and recursively comparing the request sets with the corresponding sets from the offer. During the traversal the offer is optimally configured with respect to the request. Thus $subset(O, r)$ returns a list of altered offers O', sorted by the fuzzy subset value of each $o'_i \in O'$ wrt. r (called *match value*) and each $o'_i \in O'$ corresponds to exactly one $o_j \in O$ where o'_i differs from o_j exactly by the fact that all input variables in o_j have been filled with a concrete instance value. Therefore, in the DIANE approach the DSD matcher does not only passively select the most appropriate offer but also actively configures and optimizes each offer where possible. The expressivity of DSD has been tailored with the goal to support efficient computability of *subset*. For further information on matchmaking of DSD descriptions please refer to Chapter 12).

In contrast to DSD, which defines a custom reasoning operation, Glue can exploit standard reasoning tools available for F-logic. Flora-2[8] – a plug-in of the XSB inference engine[9] based on Prolog – was chosen as inference engine. The language of Flora-2 is a dialect of F-logic with numerous extensions, including HiLog and Transaction Logic. In Glue, discovery returns all the Web service descriptions that match the request at predefined levels. The level is computed by evaluating a wg-mediator (a WSMO entity that is in charge of mediating between Web service and goal), that basically specifies a set of F-logic rules specific to match instances of particular Web services classes with an instance of a particular goal class. Given a goal instance, in order to identify all instances of the Web service classes that match it, each rule is applied on a Web service description at a time, resulting in a value that states whether the rule is satisfied or not. Depending on what rules are satisfied, a discrete value stating the level of match is returned.

14.5.2 Specification of Matchmaking Rules

The DIANE matchmaker uses a set of high-level generic matchmaking rules that specify how to compute the subset value of two fuzzy DSD sets. It distinguishes between sets of complex and primitive types. Sets describing instances of a complex type (like `Product` or

---

[8] http://flora.sourceforge.net/
[9] http://xsb.sourceforge.net/

Notebook in Figure 14.1) are matched by comparing the *type* of the set with respect to a subtype relationship (e.g. Computer versus Notebook) and combining this value with the ones retrieved from recursively comparing the sets describing the attributes of the complex instances (e.g. color, producer, display, memory, ... for notebooks). Sets describing primitive types (like Double or DateTime) are matched by checking type compatibility and comparing any direct conditions (like ">= 1000") specified on those sets in the request and the offer.

The general matchmaking rules how to compare service descriptions by recursively comparing DSD sets are thus generic and domain independent. Domain-specific knowledge and matchmaking rules are encoded in the definitions of the fuzzy request sets. An example for such domain specific knowledge in the hardware purchasing scenario would be that the price of a computer should be low while its memory size should be large. Given a requested price, lower values are acceptable, but higher ones are not. Given a requested memory size, the opposite is the case. In DSD, this is expressed in corresponding direct conditions posed in the request on the primitive sets for the price value set (e.g. "<= 1500") and the memory size value attribute (e.g. ">= 1000"). Thus, DIANE uses a combination of fixed generic matchmaking rules which can be customized by specifying conditions on request sets using a set of available operators.

As mentioned before, matchmaking in Glue is performed via wg-mediators. Basically a wg-mediator contains a set of rules and there is complete flexibility in implementing a wg-mediator: the number of rules as well as their extent depend on the developer's preferences. Usually there is an entry rule that is the one that has to be invoked in order to get the references to all Web services matching the goal. That rule calls the others in turn. Usually, each of the other rules is responsible to check if a single aspect of the goal is satisfied by the current Web service.

```
1   matchProcessor(Req_proc,Pro_proc,ProcessorPower) :-
2     Req_proc:proc , Pro_proc:proc ,
3     ( // MATCH THE TYPE:
4       // No processor type specified in the goal
5       Req_proc[tnot hasType->_]
6     ;
7     ( // No processor type specified in the service description
8       Pro_proc[tnot hasType->_]
9     ;
10    (
11      // Otherwise (processor type specified in both goal and service description)
12      Req_proc[hasType->T],
13      Pro_proc[hasType->T]
14    )
15    )
16  ),
17  ( // MATCH THE CAPACITY:
18    ( // No processor capacity specified in the goal
19      Req_proc[tnot hasCapacityMHz->_],
20      ProcessorPower is 0
21    )
22    ;
23    (
24      ( // No processor capacity specified in the service description
25      Pro_proc[tnot hasCapacityMHz->_],
26      ProcessorPower is 0
27    )
28    ;
29    ( // Otherwise (processor capacity specified in both goal and service description)
30      Req_proc[hasCapacityMHz->Req_capacity],
31      Pro_proc[hasCapacityMHz->Pro_capacity],
32      Pro_capacity >= Req_capacity,
```

```
33          ProcessorPower is Pro_capacity
34        )
35      )
36    )
37  .
```

Listing 14.2. The rule to check the processor of a notebook.

The rules can be divided in generic rules and domain-specific rules. The generic rules are very frequent and apply to general concepts (for example, the rule that calculates the intersection between two time intervals). Such rules are related to generic concepts, so they can be moved into the ontologies in which the generic concepts are defined (in the example, the temporal ontology). In this way, if a wg-mediator imports such ontologies it can use the previously defined generic rules. All other rules that are domain-specific and consider specific aspects of a goal have to be included into the wg-mediator. For example, Listing 14.2 shows a domain-specific rule that compares the processor of the required notebook with the processor of an available notebook. In particular, it compares both the type and the power (if such data are available).

14.5.3 Matchmaking Conclusions

Both, the flexible Glue approach and the more rigid DIANE approach have use-case dependent advantages and disadvantages. Glue supports arbitrarily complex rules in the wg-mediators. This flexibility allows to support pretty much any matchmaking use-case. The flip side of this flexibility is, that for every attribute to be compared in a scenario, a specific rule needs to be specified in the wg-mediator. Glue's wg-mediators can thus become very lengthy when a use case involves comparing objects with many attributes like in the hardware purchasing scenario. Furthermore, whenever the structure of an attribute changes, the wg-mediator rules have to be adapted.

DIANE, on the other hand, allows expression of conditions in a very intuitive and compact way as long as they fit into the structure of the DSD descriptions and can be expressed using the available operators. Describing the hardware purchasing scenario in DSD therefore involved less effort than in Glue. The downside of the DIANE approach is that those aspects which cannot be expressed directly using the available DSD operators generally cannot be added as easily as in the Glue approach. In such cases one has to either use a workaround or extend the DSD language and matchmaking algorithm. In the shipping scenario, for instance, the rule-based computation of the shipping prices based on the weight and destination of the parcel had to be delegated to external Web services created only for this purpose.

An imaginary extension of the hardware purchasing scenario may further illustrate the issue. Currently all prices in that scenario are specified in US dollars. Assume now, that different vendors specify their prices in different currencies. In Glue one would adapt the wg-mediator and change the rule that compares the prices to check the currency and convert the amounts properly before comparing them. In DSD, prices are complex objects with properties `currency` and `amount`. The amount and the currency property are matched independently during the recursive matching of the attributes of the price sets. Thus, regardless of the amounts given, a price stated in Euro will never match a price stated in US dollars because the currency attribute will not match. To deal with this, one could create different request descriptions, one specifying a price condition in Euros and another one specifying the same condition in US dollars. Unfortunately this is not a good option if many currencies are involved. To really solve the problem, one would have to change the matchmaking algorithm's behaviour for measures,

244   Ulrich Küster, Andrea Turati et al.

times or prices which can be specified in different unit systems. Afterwards, DIANE would natively support the desired behaviour, but this change would require to change the code of the matchmaker's implementation. For a general case like this one this is a suitable option, but for cases which are more specific to a single use-case, this is not desireable.

14.6 Preferences and Ranking

Regarding selection the views taken by SWE-ET and DIANE are quite different. In the SWE-ET framework, discovery and selection are viewed as separate tasks. Glue as a discovery engine is able to discover a set of Web services that satisfy a request as represented by a goal. Selection is viewed as an additional step that follows the discovery and is responsible for choosing a single Web service to be invoked, starting from the set of Web services returned by discovery. In the philosophy of SWE-ET, selection should be left in charge of the user, which is the only entity that can take such a decision. For this reason, only limited support for preferences and ranking was implemented in Glue so far. Glue only supports the user's decision by applying ranking of the results corresponding to the above mentioned match levels. In a wg-mediator it is possible to define several levels of matching on the basis of the rules that a Web service satisfies with respect to the goal. For example, if a Web service matches all the rules (each of them checking a specific aspect of the goal) then we assign the ranking level 1 to it, otherwise if it satisfies a subset of such rules we assign it the ranking level 2, if it satisfies a smaller subset of rules we assign it the ranking level 3, and so on. In particular, into the wg-mediator we declare which are the rules that have to be satisfied in order to assign a specific ranking level to a Web service instance, so that we can assign a different importance to different rules. In this way we obtain discrete levels of ranking. Listing 14.3 shows that in the purchase scenario we defined two levels of ranking in which the first one checks all product features as well as the price while the second one checks only the product features and sets price to a standard value.

```
1   discovery_Rank1_Purchase(GoalInstance,WSDInstance, ...) :−
2      ...
3      matchProductFeatures(RequestedProduct,ProvidedProduct,ProcessorPower),
4      checkContainmentOfPrice(RequestedProduct,ProvidedProduct,Price).
5
6   discovery_Rank2_Purchase(GoalInstance,WSDInstance, ...) :−
7      ...
8      matchProductFeatures(RequestedProduct,ProvidedProduct,ProcessorPower),
9      //checkContainmentOfPrice(RequestedProduct,ProvidedProduct,Price)
10     Price is 0.
```

Listing 14.3. The two ranking levels for the purchase scenario.

In contrast DIANE is aiming at completely automating the whole process of service usage. This is only possible if selection is performed by the matchmaking process, too. This in turn is feasible only if it is possible to precisely capture user preferences within service requests and efficiently use that additional information during matchmaking. The first is achieved through DSD's fuzzy elements, the latter through the application of the specifically tailored subset operation used for matchmaking (see Chapter 16). Thus DSD is able to provide a more fine-grained matching compared to Glue at the price of restricted expressivity and limited compatibility to other semantic service frameworks.

Furthermore, in Glue the preferences are coded into wg-mediators directly. For example, the fact that a user who wants to buy a notebook usually prefers to have a larger hard disk at a lower price is coded into the rules of the wg-mediator (see listing 14.4).

```
1   // Matching rules for Price
2   checkContainmentOfPrice(RequestedProduct,ProvidedProduct,Cost) :-
3       RequestedProduct[hasPrice->MaxPrice],
4       ProvidedProduct[hasPrice->Cost],
5       Cost =< MaxPrice.
6
7   // Matching rules for Hard disk
8   matchHDD(Req_hdd, Pro_hdd) :-
9       Req_hdd:hdd , Pro_hdd:hdd ,
10      Req_hdd[hasCapacityMB->Req_capacity],
11      Pro_hdd[hasCapacityMB->Pro_capacity],
12      Pro_capacity >= Req_capacity.
```

Listing 14.4. Glue rules that compare prizes and hdd sizes of a request and an offer.

In contrast, in DIANE such preferences are expressed in the requests, which are written by the requesters (see Figure 14.1). This is advantageous in cases where the user preferences are not as stable and obvious as with prices and hard disk sizes. Most users, for instance, will prefer a more powerful processor. Thus, a corresponding preference has been coded into the corresponding wg-mediator in the Glue solution. However, more powerful processory typically consume more energy. Users which are more concerned about battery runtime than computing power do not necessarily accept stronger processors. In such cases, DIANE is more flexible than Glue since it allows users to specify the preferences in the request while in Glue users cannot modify the preferences written in the wg-mediators.

14.7 Dynamic Aspects of Service Descriptions

Some services required to collect dynamic information from the service endpoint to perform the matchmaking. One of the shipping services for instance, Muller, required to inquire the price of a shipping operation dynamically by calling a particular Web service endpoint.

Such requirements have been directly built into the DSD description language. For service consumption, DSD supports a simple choreography to interact with services where an arbitrary number of *estimation operations* is followed by a single execution operation. Estimation operations must not have effects on the real world and can thus be used to gather dynamic information from a service provider. Service providers can tag certain concepts in their descriptions to declare that further information about those parts of the description are available through particular estimation operations. If necessary the DSD matcher will initiate a call of the associated operation and then dynamically complement the description at hand with the retrieved information. This procedure was flexible enough to support all dynamic aspects contained in the scenarios (see Chapter 12).

Originally, Glue was not able to deal with dynamic aspects. In order to overcome this limitation, Glue has been extended. This extension has had a minimal impact on the SWE-ET infrastructure. It has been sufficient to add new features to the execution semantics at the end of the entire discovery process, in order to perform the negotiation.

Before publishing a Web service into Glue, in the case that the service includes special parameters that need to be negotiated (e.g. shipping price), its description has to be annotated with special tags, which point out what parameters are "dynamic" (see Chapter 11).

At the first step of the discovery, Glue deals only with the static descriptions of services, ignoring the parameters that have been tagged as "dynamic". Into the result set of the services returned after the first step of the discovery, Glue identifies those services whose description contains some dynamic parameters. For each of those identified services, Glue starts a negotiation by delegating it to WebRatio[10]. In other words, Glue is responsible for handling service descriptions and starting the negotiation process whenever is necessary to get the value of a parameter dynamically; while WebRatio is responsible for handling the actual invocation (including the grounding toward SOAP messages). After negotiation, WebRatio returns the actual value for the parameter, so that Glue can temporarily update the service description by adding that value and, finally, evaluates whether the updated instance of service satisfies the goal (by applying the appropriate rules and accepts or rejects the service correspondingly).

14.8 Invocation

Automated invocation of offers is directly supported by DIANE. In case of the before mentioned estimation steps the corresponding invocations can be initiated by the matcher directly and can be performed interweaved with the matchmaking process. Regarding the final execution of the service, the matcher – as outlined in Section 14.5 – outputs a list of readily configured offers, i.e. offers where all necessary input values have been set. The remaining task performed by the invocation agent is to perform the necessary lowering to create an appropriate XML message to send to the offer implementation and perform lifting on the returned response message. This is done using simple declarative mapping rules that map between DSD concepts and XML data [KKR06].

In the SWE-ET approach matchmaking and invocation are performed using different technologies. Invocation of a Web service is not directly executed by Glue, but is left to the application in which Glue is integrated – in the case of phase-III of the SWS-Challenge an external invocation component implemented within the WebRatio framework. This approach is described in [ZVM$^+$07].

14.9 Conclusions

Overall, we found that the discovery performed by SWE-ET and DIANE is not as different as it looks at the first glance. The main difference between SWE-ET and DIANE is how and where the matchmaking rules are specified and how the approaches deal with the fact that matchmaking needs to support a certain flexibility beyond identifying perfect matches.

DIANE uses a set of generic matchmaking rules that are completely domain-independent. The set of acceptable offers are described by the requester within the request. Preferences and flexibility are integrated in the request, a request could state for instance, that the display size of an acceptable notebook display must be precisely 13 inch, but that for the hard disc size any size above 100 GB is ok. Many scenarios can be formalized in DIANE very easily since only the preferences in the request need to be specified, but no domain-specific matchmaking rules are necessary beyond these preferences. On the other hand it can be very difficult to accommodate matchmaking requirements that do not fit well into the structure of the DIANE matchmaking rules.

Glue, in contrast, uses domain specific wg-mediators that contain the rules that determine whether a goal matches a request. Glue's wg-mediator support great flexibility and can - unlike DIANE - accommodate arbitrary matchmaking rules and requirements. On the other hand

---

[10] Negotiation denotes the action of contacting a service in order to get the actual value of a parameter. However, recently we prefer to use the more appropriate term of "data fetching".

a new wg-mediator needs to be written, when switching to a new scenario. Also, since preferences are encoded in the wg-mediator and not in the request, the mediator has to be changed if the user's preferences change.

Overall, DIANE presupposes the structure of the descriptions and the matchmaking to a larger extent than Glue. This results in a reduced effort to describe a new scenario but also reduces the flexibility to express arbitrary requirements. In contrast, Glue does not presuppose any structure of the descriptions which results in a higher description effort for some scenarios, but also in greater flexibility to express arbitrary requirements.

In general we found, that it really depends on the specific use case at hand which of these contrary approaches to service matchmaking is advantageous. For the SWS-Challenge scenarios, it seems that Glue would be the preferred choice for the shipping discovery scenario. This scenario involves rule-based price and shipping time restrictions which can be modelled much easier in Glue than in DSD and it does not involve to check many attributes, thus leading to simple and short wg-mediators. For the hardware purchasing scenario it seems that DSD would be the preferred choice. This scenario deals with a high number of attributes and benefits from the better support for user preferences in DIANE.

References

dBBD+05.   Jos de Bruijn, Christoph Bussler, John Domingue, Dieter Fensel, Martin Hepp, Uwe Keller, Michael Kifer, Birgitta König-Ries, Jacek Kopecky, Ruben Lara, Holger Lausen, Eyal Oren, Axel Polleres, Dumitru Roman, James Scicluna, and Michael Stollberg. Web service modeling ontology (wsmo). W3C Member Submission 3 June 2005, 2005.

DCC05.   Emanuele Della Valle, Dario Cerizza, and Irene Celino. The mediators centric approach to automatic web service discovery of glue. In *MEDIATE2005*, volume 168 of *CEUR Workshop Proceedings*, pages 35–50. CEUR-WS.org, 2005.

KKR06.   Ulrich Küster and Birgitta König-Ries. Dynamic binding for BPEL processes - a lightweight approach fo integrate semantics into web services. In *Second International Workshop on Engineering Service-Oriented Applications: Design and Composition (WESOA06) at ICSOC06*, Chicago, Illinois, USA, December 2006.

KKRM05.   Michael Klein, Birgitta König-Ries, and Michael Müssig. What is needed for semantic service descriptions - a proposal for suitable language constructs. *International Journal on Web and Grid Services (IJWGS)*, 1(3/4):328–364, 2005.

KL89.   M. Kifer and G. Lausen. F-logic: A higher-order language for reasoning about objects, inheritance, and scheme. In *Proc. ACM SIGMOD Conf.*, page 134, Portland, OR, May-June 1989.

KLW95.   Michael Kifer, Georg Lausen, and James Wu. Logical foundations of object-oriented and frame-based languages. *J. ACM*, 42(4):741–843, 1995.

ZVM+07.   Maciej Zaremba, Tomas Vitvar, Matthew Moran, Marco Brambilla, Stefano Ceri, Dario Cerizza, Emanuele Della Valle, Federico M. Facca, and Christina Tziviskou. Towards semantic interoperabilty: In-depth comparison of two approaches to solve mediation tasks. In *Comparative Evaluation of Semantic Web Service Frameworks Special Session at ICEIS 2007*, 2007.

15

Comparison: Discovery on WSMOLX and miAamics/jABC

Christian Kubczak[1], Tomas Vitvar[4], Christian Winkler[2], Raluca Zaharia[3], and Maciej Zaremba[3]

[1] Chair of Software Engineering, Technical University of Dortmund, Germany,
`christian.kubczak@cs.uni-dortmund.de`
[2] Chair of Service and Software Engineering, University of Potsdam, Germany,
`winkler@cs.uni-potsdam.de`
[3] Digital Enterprise Research Institute, National University of Ireland, Galway, Ireland,
`firstname.lastname@deri.org`
[4] The Semantics Technology Institute Innsbruck, University of Innsbruck, Austria,
`tomas.vitvar@sti2.at`

15.1 Introduction

This chapter compares the solutions to the SWS-Challenge discovery problems provided by DERI Galway and the joint solution from the Technical University of Dortmund and University of Postdam. The two approaches are described in depth in Chapters 10 and 13. The discovery scenario raises problems associated with making service discovery an automated process. It requires fine-grained specifications of search requests and service functionality including support for fetching dynamic information during the discovery process (e.g., shipment price). Both teams utilize semantics to describe services, service requests and data models in order to enable search at the required fine-grained level of detail.

The DERI solution is based on the Semantic Web services framework described in Chapter 10, including a conceptual model for Semantic Web services (Web Service Modeling Ontology, WSMO[1]), a language for service modeling (Web Service Modeling Language, WSML[2]), a middleware system (Web Service Execution Environment, WSMX[3]) and a modelling framework (Web Service Modelling Toolkit, WSMT[5]). In order to model the scenario, WSMO has been used for modeling of goals, services (i.e. required and offered capabilities) and ontologies (i.e. information models on which services and goals are defined), all expressed in the WSML ontology language. WSMO Mediators were not utilized since a common domain shipment ontology was used in both the goal and service descriptions.

The Dortmund-Postdam solution combines a model-driven design approach using the jABC platform [4], also used for the Mediation approach and described in depth in Chapter 5, extended with miAamics for the matchmaking involved in the service discovery scenario, as described in Chapter 13. miAamics was originally developed to personalize web applications. jABC is used here for the orchestration surrounding the pure discovery problem. Workflow for the discovery application is modelled graphically what provides the user interface to specify a

---

[5] `http://sourceforge.net/projects/wsmt`

shipment request, enquires and calculates some data for the shipment offers, necessary before miAamics' matching algorithm is invoked, and it finally invokes the selected shipper service. To match the shipment request with the best offer, miAamics acts as an embedded a rule-based matching service: it determines the best matching offers for the given request, based on a configuration reflecting the request, the situation (in this scenario, this is void) and the collection of available shipment offers.

In this chapter we compare the similarities and differences of the provided solutions along several structural dimensions, including data modeling, execution environments, service matching, service selection and tool support. We also look at the changes required in the solutions once the discovery requirements change.

15.2 WSMOLX – miAamics/jABC Comparison

Both technologies have successfully addressed the SWS-Challenge discovery scenarios. This section describes the similarities and differences of the two approaches, WSMOLX and miAamics/jABC, with respect to the discovery scenario.

Underlying technologies criteria will focus on the properties (e.g. language, expressiveness, runtime environment) of underlying technologies utilized by each solution. *Service description* will concentrate on the elements and conceptual model of service description. *Goal description* will refer to the elements and conceptual model of service discovery and execution request. *Data model* will cover the design and development of the ontologies capturing the domain of interests which is referred by service descriptions and requests. *Matchmaking* will look at the process of matching between semantic descriptions of services to a given request. *Selection* will focus on the problem of selecting a best service to execute out of several candidate services that can satisfy the client's functional requirements. *Web service invocation* will describe the service invocation techniques. *Execution monitoring* will focus on monitoring during the runtime phase (discovery, selection, invocation, etc.). Finally, *tool support* will investigate the level of maturity of each of solutions' tools. The essence of the comparison is summarized in Table 15.1.

Table 15.1: Comparison of the presented solutions.

Feature	miAamics/jABC	WSMOLX
Underlying technologies	jABC modeling framework, miAamics rule based matcher	WSMO - conceptual framework, WSML - ontology language, WSMX - execution environment
Service descriptions	SLG: preprocessing (for arithmetic calculations), matchmaking, invocation, boolean rules, discretization of continuous values into rules	Service capability (pre- and postconditions), execution and data-fetching interfaces, support for rules returning numerical values; arithmetical (e.g., $+, -, /, *$) and custom-made (e.g. *ceil, floor*) built-in support in service description
		continued on next page

continued from previous page		
Feature	**miAamics/jABC**	**WSMOLX**
Goal description	Boolean rules and strategies with priorities, rules specified on intervals of continues numerical data	Postconditions (hard constrains) - references to boolean rules and arithmetic rules (e.g., calculating price), non-functional properties (NFP) - preferences
Data model	Attributes and categories designed using web UI and automatic importers/generators	Ontologies created both from analyzing messages and internal data requirements of shippers services
Matchmaking	Rule evaluation; addition of weights attached to rules; profile-oriented; global evaluation of all rules; rules cover single aspects/criteria; pre-matchmaking step for arithmetic operations	Rule evaluation - IRIS (Datalog reasoner, Logic Programming); hard constraints - "must have" requirements and constraints over service functionality; preferences refer to variables bound in postcondition evaluation
Selection	Best from ordered set of suitable offers - highest sum of executed weighted rules	Based on ranking (LowerBetter, HigherBetter) following preferences modelled in NFP of the WSMO Goal, ranking applied on the concrete offerings of the candidate services.
Web service invocation	Implicitly in generated SIBs, SIBs are also used in matchmaking pre-processing step for calculating arithmetic values, Web service invocation - arithmetic services, price quotation and package shipping ordering	Invoker handling all communication with external services using grounding information provided in SWS descriptions, direct support for arithmetic operations and built-ins in IRIS reasoner; Web service invocation - price quotation and package shipping ordering
Execution monitoring	jABC tracer for orchestration, miAamics' results profiler for the pure matchmaking;	WSMX execution presented as components' events flow on Java SWING-based panel
Tool support	jABC framework, extensible by plug-ins; miAamics evaluation engine and web-UI; importers	Ontology, goals, services and mediators, WSMT and WSMO Studio as modeling tools

15.2.1 Underlying technologies

The Web Services Modeling Ontology (WSMO) framework consists of four top elements, namely WSMO Goals, Web services, Ontologies and Mediators. Discovery for the SWS-Challenge shipment scenario is accomplished by Instance-level Discovery Engine [5], a WSMX component that performs fine-grained service instance discovery determining dynamic parameters of service offerings by employing input-dependent rules and undertaking communication with the *safe methods* of the service during the discovery process. Other WSMX components include Choreography, Data and Process Mediator, Selection, Communication Manager and others [3]).

The realization of the discovery service in miAamics/jABC is modeled as a service logic graph described in detail in Chapter 13. It is organized in three sections: *preprocessing* , *matchmaking* and *invocation.*

- In case some values have to be calculated or queried in advance of each request, the *preprocessing* section provides the miAamics configuration database with these data. It also provides a user interface that asks for the specification of the current request.
- In the *matchmaking* section, the miAamics personalization framework is used as an embedded reasoning engine for selecting an appropriate shipping service for the specified request. miAamics is a rule based and situation aware matcher that in the given scenario matches abstract profiles of *shipping requests* to profiles of *shipment offers.*
- As final step, in the *invocation* section, depending on miAamics' evaluation result, the workflow invokes the selected Web service and initiates the shipment. For service invocation, which plays a role in all three sections, jABC is extended by the jETI framework [6, 7, 8] also described in Chapter 5. jETI provides access to remote services and supports the modeling process in jABC by providing generated SIBs for remote service invocation.

Both solutions employ rules and ontologies for modelling service functionality and goals.

The WSMOLX approach describes its elements (ontologies, goals, services) in WSML-Flight, a language which provides Datalog expressivity extended with inequality and stratified negation. Datalog falls under the Logic Programming (LP) paradigm, assuming a closed world, contrary to the open world assumption in Description Logics. It can give different reasoning results as LP facts that cannot be proven are considered to be false.

miAamics, as described in Chapter 13 is based on selective filtering of the current collection of offers according to rules. There are therefore no unproven facts, nor unknown ones, hence there are no issues of reasoning with unknowns, which make the difference between a closed or an open world assumption.

The closed world assumption of LP did not influence the matchmaking process in the WSMOLX shipment discovery approach, as all the information required during the evaluation was either available in service descriptions or was dynamically fetched from the services and there was no unknown information about service advertised functionality.

15.2.2 Service descriptions

A WSMO Web service is described using ontology elements and in principle consists of two main parts, namely: capability (preconditions, postconditions, assumptions and effects) and interface (choreography describing a public process and orchestration representing an internal process). Inside the WSMX framework, WSMO elements expressed in WSML are handled using wsmo4j[6], a Java model which provides a unified parsing mechanism, supports various

---

[6] http://wsmo4j.sourceforge.net

serializations and deserializations of the WSML variants and, most importantly, facilitates the manipulation of such elements by the components (e.g., reasoner) and other involved applications. Logical rules have been used quite extensively in order to explicitly describe various criteria of different shippers (e.g., *isShipped* rule in 15.1).

Listing 15.1 shows a snippet of Muller shipment service description modelled in WSML. '?' followed by an identifier represents a variable, which at runtime will be bound to instances that satisfy some condition. The *memberOf* keyword indicates that a variable or an instance belongs to an ontology concept, while *hasValue* specifies the value that an attribute has (if inside a condition) or will be assigned (in the actions part of a rule). Axiom *isShippedDef*, referred by the Goal (line 12 in Listing 15.4, checks whether a service can be used for the given shipment request. At the execution phase an internal ontology will be created and it will contain initially the data provided with the Goal, i.e the instances from Listing 15.4. This ontology is further referred as the knowledge base (KB) and service capability reasoning is performed against this ontology. The execution model requires that on a set of instances all rules and axioms are evaluated in parallel and the updates are executed in parallel as well, with the resulting instances added to the KB. The condition (lines 6-10) is evaluated by IRIS reasoner, meaning that binding instances for the variables are retrieved from the KB. The shipment order details are provided with the Goal (e.g. the *?weight* of the *?package* – line 27 on Listing 15.4). Considering provided goal C3 (Listing 15.4), the condition on the weight (line 10 in Listing 15.1) will evaluate to true and the relation *isShippedContinents* (line 9) will also evaluate to true for specified target shipment city (Bristol – line 42 on Listing 15.4). For the example shipment order specified in goal C3, the overall result of the *isShipped* rule will evaluate to true.

```
1   /* general abstract definition of the axiom in the common ontology */
2   relation isShipped(ofType sop#ShipmentOrderReq)
3
4   /* specification of the axiom in the Mueller ontology */
5   axiom isShippedDef definedBy
6     ?sOrder[sop#to hasValue ?temp, sop#package hasValue ?p]
7     memberOf sop#ShipmentOrderReq and
8     ?temp[so#address hasValue ?to] and ?to[so#city hasValue ?city] and
9     isShippedContinents(?city, so#Europe, so#Asia, so#NorthAmerica, so#Africa) and
10    ( (?p [so#weight hasValue ?weight] memberOf so#Package) and (?weight =< 50) )
11    implies
12    sop#isShipped(?sOrder).
```

Listing 15.1. isShipped Rule in Service Description

In miAamics, a service like the Muller shipper is just a record in the underlying database. It is seen at the miAamics modelling level as a collection of boolean predicates (called attributes in miAmics terminology) that abstract the concrete values in the database to logical properties for the miAamics evaluation engine.

The available services and their representations are stored in the miAamics configuration database for matchmaking. The available information that describes the services (i.e. SWSC Wiki and provided WSDL files) is analyzed to extract domain knowledge that is then expressed in terms of miAamics' (shipment-) *offers*. Offers are characterized by attributes that are defined following the challenge's requirements. The user can decide to group attributes into categories to alleviate definition of rules based on multiple attributes. The result is a collection of attributes (and categories respectively) describing an abstract set of services that fulfill certain criteria (e.g. "cheap service"). Each attribute comprises a criterion that is used to evaluate whether or not an attribute corresponds to a concrete offer (see Tab. 15.3 for examples). This way, a real service specification is characterized as the set of attributes it fulfills.

The granularity of the defined attributes (on quantitative fields) determines the discrimination power of the matchmaking algorithm for arithmetical purposes. Hence attributes have to be selected carefully.

The grounding of the concrete services in miAamics happens by means of the *information objects*: they specify for the service instances (here, the different shippers) the values that are used to determine the service profile in terms of the set of satisfied attributes (e.g. shipping to a specific country). Some of those values are calculated in the preprocessing step and automatically provided to the database, while others are entered manually using miAamics' web UI or importers that automatically generate the configuration from existing ontologies.

Type	Information object properties					
Request	*Data field*	Src_country	Dst_country	Price_limit	Weight	...
	Value	USA	UK	120$	20 lbs	...
Offer	*Data field*	Shipper_name	Ships_to	Price	Weight_limit	...
	Value	Muller	USA,UK,...	100$	50 lbs	...

Table 15.2. miAamics' Information Objects for Requests and Offers

Tables 15.2, 15.3 and 15.4 show a concise example of miAamics' configuration. Tab. 15.2 shows the information objects for the instantiation of a concrete request (for a shipment from the USA to UK, up to 120$ and a package weight of 20 lbs and an example for the offering services' grounding. It shows that Muller ships to USA and UK. Details of package dimension are omitted in the table for limited space. Requests are usually not stored in miAamics' configuration but passed to the evaluation engine on invocation.

Type	Attribute name	Rule	holds?
Request	Destination_is_UK	Dst_country == 'UK'	yes
	Ship_for_lessThan_120$	Price_limit ≤ 120$	yes
	Ship_for_lessThan_50$	Price_limit ≤ 50$	no
	Weight_moreThan_50	Weight ≥ 50 lbs	no
Offer	Ships_to_UK	Ships_to *contains* 'UK'	yes
	Price_lessThan_120$	Price ≤ 120$	yes
	Price_lessThan_50$	Price ≤ 50$	no
	Weight_limit_moreThan_50	Weight_limit ≥ 50 lbs	no

Table 15.3. miAamics' Attribute Definition and Evaluation

Table 15.3 shows examples of the attribute's definition for both requests and offers. The last column in this table shows the evaluation of each attribute for the corresponding instances in the example of Table 15.2.

Finally, Table 15.4 shows a very simple example of rule definition for miAamics. In this case, rules evaluate single attributes. In Chapter 13 a general case is discussed, which uses here taxonomies of attributes and categories, which are logical expressions over attributes and other categories. Rule's premises refer to requests (and situations, which are not used in the Discovery scenario) and rule's conclusions specify offer's attributes. Again the last column shows whether or not each rule is fulfilled for the given example. The third rule is not fulfilled, as the corresponding conclusion attribute does not hold for the example shipper. If a *strategy* for selection is based on destination only, it will comprise the first rule only and other rules will be ignored. Hence shipper 'Muller' would be returned as a valid shipper with a weight of 100. However, a strategy that considers destination and prices and would comprise all rules would return 'Muller' as a valid result with a weight of 120 (the sum of weights of all the applicable rules).

The example configuration in Tables 15.2-15.4 also considers package weights. Hence, the rule base is strong enough to select a shipper based on the destination, shipping costs and weight limits. However the package weight given in the example request is that small, that the rules related weight do not have any effect on the result.

Rule name	Premise (Request attribute)	Conclusion (Offer attribute)	Rule weight	fulfilled?
USA_delivery	Destination_is_UK	Ships_To_UK	100	yes
Cost_limit_120$	Ship_for_lessThan_120$	Price_lessThan_120$	20	yes
Cost_limit_50$	Ship_for_lessThan_50$	Price_lessThan_50$	20	no
Weight_limit_50	Weight_moreThan_50	Weight_limit _moreThan_50	20	no

Table 15.4. miAamics' Rule Definition, and Evaluation for Muller

Input dependent price calculation

The input dependent price calculation approach in WSMO is presented in Listing 15.2. If the service provider can offer information of its pricing strategy then suitable rules reflecting this information (e.g., calculating price) but also depending on the user input data can be specified in the service description like in case of *shippingEuropeDef* of the Walker service. If the location condition (*cityIsOnContinent(?city, so#Europe)*) in line 13 is satisfied, then the price can be generated following the rate for Europe, i.e. a flat fee of 41 plus 5.5 per each lb (line 15). Such policies are specified as WSML arithmetic rules that calculate the price of the shipping package. *builtin#ceil()* is a custom made built-in in IRIS that rounds down the package weight to the nearest integral value. Once the *?price* is calculated, it is added as an attribute value to a new instance *priceQuoteEurope* in line 8. This instance is added to the KB during the reasoning process and is helpful in the evaluation of Goal hard constraints on price and in service ranking.

```
1   /* Walker service — example of user input dependent rule generating price
2       for target country in Europe following provided service description:
3       Rates(flat fee/each lb): Europe(41/5.5), ...
4   */
5
6   axiom shippingEuropeDef
7     definedBy
8       priceQuoteEurope[sop#price hasValue ?price] memberOf sop#PriceQuoteResp
9       :—
10      ?shipmentOrderReq[sop#to hasValue ?temp] memberOf sop#ShipmentOrderReq and
11      ?temp[so#address hasValue ?to] and
12      ?to[so#city hasValue ?city] and
13      so#cityIsOnContinent(?city, so#Europe) and
14      ?package [so#weight hasValue ?weight] memberOf so#Package and
```

```
15    builtin#ceil( ?weight, ?c) and (?price = ( (?c * 5.5) + 41) ).
```

Listing 15.2. Walker Input Dependent Price Generating Rule

As shown in Chapter 13, part of the orchestration around the pure service discovery takes care of all the computations and invocations. Decision procedures were not embedded in mi-Aamics in order to keep it simple and extremely efficient. Any computation is performed outside of the matchmaker, in this case before the matchmaking, in an orchestration modelled in jABC that makes use of external services invoked via SIBs. This way, it is possible to resort to any available decision procedure, instead of being bound to the capability of the single reasoner.

Price by enquiry

Another situation presented in Listing 15.3 is when the service provider cannot or does not want to offer its pricing strategy and price can be provided on request only. In this case a data fetching interface is utilized as in case of the Muller shipment service. The condition of the transition rule selects shipment order request instances from the KB (line 13) and also checks whether the price can be provided for the given request (the *isShipped* relation in line 14). If the condition evaluates to true, the shipment request instance will be lowered and sent to a WSDL service where its concept, ShipmentOrderReq, is grounded as input (line 7). The data fetching operation will be invoked only if the service is able to handle given request (i.e. it covers the source and target country, the package weight is within the limits handled by the service, etc.). As a result of data-fetching interface invocation, an instance of *PriceQuoteResp* is received from the service and a further reasoning can be performed on the price, similar to the Walker case.

The data fetching interface, shown in Listing 15.3, is used for specifying the interaction with the service for dynamically obtaining the shipping price for the given request. In general, the interface can be concretely defined by a WSMO choreography expressed in ontologized Abstract State Machines (ASM) [9] (lines 4-18). The data-fetching choreography specifies access to auxiliary information that has to be dynamically obtained during discovery process in order to provide up-to-date information on service functionality. In the ASM, an ontology constitutes the underlying knowledge representation and transition rules are specified in terms of logic formulas. Again, in general a WSMO choreography is specified as a set of transition rules and KB changes (*add, delete, update* on incoming, outgoing and internal data). Additionally, *grounding* information specifies a link to the WSDL of utilized Web services. If an instance belonging to a grounded concept can be bound to a variable in the condition of a transition rule, it results in firing of the rule what entails communication with the service (*in* – incoming service to the WSDL, *out* – outgoing messages from the WSDL). For more complex choreographies controlled state ASMs can be used to ensure ordered transitions between available states and to avoid multiple executions of the same states. The results of executing the data-fetching choreography (i.e. determining the shipment price) are integrated into the reasoning context. Once the service has been selected for the execution phase there is a separate choreography which will consume the service functionality.

In this case, as shown in the following listing, the situation is very simple: there is exactly one partner (no choreography), the partner performs exactly one action, therefor the ASM has exactly one transition, and the transition is expressed very concretely as *add the price quote* to the knowledge base.

```
1    /* Muller Service interface – dynamic fetching of shipment price */
```

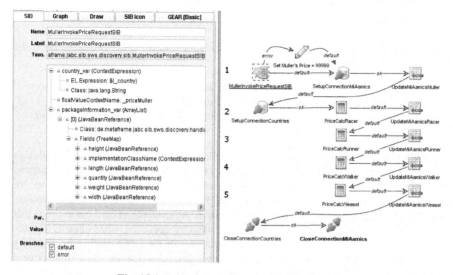

Fig. 15.1. Price Calculation in miAamics/jABC

```
2
3    interface datafetching#WSMullerGetPriceInterface
4       choreography WSMullerGetPriceChoreography
5       stateSignature WSMullerGetPriceStateSignature
6
7       in sop#ShipmentOrderReq withGrounding { wsdl grounding... } //input message
8       out sop#PriceQuoteResp //dynamically obtained price quotation
9
10      transitionRules WSMullerGetPriceTransitionRules
11
12      forall{?shipmentOrderReq} with
13         (?shipmentOrderReq memberOf sop#ShipmentOrderReq
14         and sop#isShipped(?shipmentOrderReq)
15         ) do
16         add(_#1 memberOf sop#PriceQuoteResp)
17
18      endForall
```

Listing 15.3. Muller Shipment Price Data Fetching Interface

A nice correspondence can be drawn with the jABC solution as shown in Fig. 15.1 (see also Chapter 13 Sect. 3.4 for a more comprehensive explanation), for the first shipper (row 1) (Muller) a Web service that returns the shipping price for a single request is invoked. This is then written to the Context (and thus communicated to miAamics): it is exactly one transition in the Kripke Transition System that underlies the Service Logic Graph, and it has the same abstraction as the little one-transition ASM of the WSMO solution.

In the miAamics case, a corresponding Web service SIB was generated using the jETI framework in the same fashion as for the services in the mediation scenario and (Chap. 5). In the case of any anomaly occurring during service invocation, that makes this shipper de facto unavailable, the price for this shipper is set so high that this shipper is excluded from the further selection process.

15.2.3 Goal descriptions

The same example of shipment scenario goal is used for comparing our two approaches. We use Goal C3 that reads as a following:

> For all shipping requests, the packages are always sent from the Moon company in the US. The destination of the example shipment is a client in Bristol (UK). A single package of the dimension 10/2/3 (l/w/h in inch) and a weight of 20 lbs shall be shipped for less than 120$.

WSMO Goal C3 is shown in Listing 15.4. Similar to a WSMO Service, WSMO Goals also contain the capability and interface parts, however a Goal's capability specifies some requested functionality and the interface will define how the Goal can interact with a potential service that can provide the requested functionality. WSMO Goal C3 specifies the hard constraints over the service to be discovered in its postcondition. An example of hard constraint is that the service must cost less than 120$. This is specified by $?price < 120$ in line 12. $?price$ here is a price quote that is either dynamically fetched from the service during the discovery process (Listing 15.3) or is generated by input-dependent rules (Listing 15.2). Another hard constraint is expressed by $isShipped(request\#shipmentOrderReq)$. This imposes a hard requirement on the service that it must be able to handle the package shipment to the specified location.

Additionally, preferences on service ranking are specified in the Goal's non-functional properties (line 3). Such preferences are used for ranking and selecting the most suitable service out of several services that satisfied the hard constraints. Preferences are specified in terms of the variables which appear in post-conditions (e.g. ?price, ?deliveryTime) and are bound to real data / values during the reasoning process. Following the preferences with actual variable bindings, the candidate services can be appropriately ordered. For the preference $?price - LowerBetter$ in the WSMO Goal, the returned services will be sorted by their shipping price from lowest to highest. The ordering direction can be $LowerBetter$ or $HigherBetter$.

```
1    capability GoalC3Capability
2    nfp
3        _"rankingcriteria" hasValue "?price−LowerBetter"
4    endnfp
5
6    /* Goal C3 -- goal based on destination, weight and price
7       with preference on lowest price */
8
9    postcondition
10   definedBy
11   ?x[sop#price hasValue ?price] memberOf sop#PriceQuoteResp and
12   sop#isShipped(request#shipmentOrderReq) and ?price < 120.
13
14   ontology goalRequestOnto
15
16   instance request#shipmentOrderReq memberOf sop#ShipmentOrderReq
17       sop#from hasValue MoonContactInfo
18       sop#shipmentDate hasValue shipmentDate1
19       sop#package hasValue package
20       sop#to hasValue SmithersContactInfo
21
22   instance package memberOf so#Package
23       so#quantity hasValue 1
24       so#length hasValue 10.0
25       so#width hasValue 2.0
26       so#height hasValue 3.0
```

```
27    so#weight hasValue 20.0
28
29    instance shipmentDate1 memberOf so#ShipmentDate
30       so#earliest hasValue "2008−07−11T15:00:00.046Z"
31       so#latest hasValue "2008−07−15T15:00:00.046Z"
32
33    instance MoonContactInfo memberOf so#ContactInfo
34       so#company hasValue "Moon Company"
35       so#lastname hasValue "Moon"
36       so#city hasValue so#MoonCity
37       ...
38
39    instance SmithersContactInfo memberOf so#ContactInfo
40       so#company hasValue "Computer Systems and Co"
41       so#lastname hasValue "Smithers"
42       so#city hasValue so#Bristol
43       ..
```

Listing 15.4. WSMO Goal C3 with Hard Constraints, Preferences and Input Ontology

To discover candidate shipping services, miAamics needs a set of *rules* that define the requests. Such rules are defined on attributes and categories respectively. Attributes are used to build an abstract description of the concrete instances of requests, situations and offers and might be grouped into categories. The evaluation is solely executed on attributes (and categories) and hence is not affected by concrete instances (or their number, respectively). In fact it can be executed without knowing the concrete service instances, and only on the abstract profiles - one could say, on the ontological level.

Rules define a matchmaking on premises (here the shipping requests defined by corresponding attributes) and conclusions (the candidate shipping services, defined by attributes respectively) and are rated with a weight that expresses their importance. Rules express aspects of the decision space, therefore it is usual that multiple rules apply to a single request. In this case, weights for the matching services are added and define a cumulative rating for the quality of the offer. Heavier rules "count" more in the evaluation. *Strategies* define sets of rules that are considered together for the given request. As has been described in detail in Chapter 13, with the same set of rules it is possible to define different strategies, that differ in the criteria considered (roughly, each rule expresses a selection criterion) and in their importance, which is expressed in miAamics through the weights. E.g. a strategy for discovery based on "destination only" would yield different results than a strategy for "destination and price", that combines location based rules with those that consider shipping prizes. Tables 15.2-15.4 in Sect. 15.2.2 show a small example configuration for the aforementioned goal C3 that is sufficient for discovery based on destination, price and package weight.

A goal description in WSMO does not have a notion of a priority, instead it contains preferences which allow to order and then choose the best offer from the services that satisfy the hard constrains.

On the other hand, miAamics allows modelling priorities of rules in term of their weights, that express how relevant the rules are for the goal. There is no explicit notion of hard constraints. Since miAamics was designed as a personalization matchmaker, it is tailored to return the "best" option available. Application domains like personalization have inherently no hard constraints, because it is a key feature to be able to find the "niche" match, due to a sum of small indicators that overcomes obvious, flat rules like "Dortmund males are Borussia fans". The niche discovery feature allows for high precision, but it requires attention when designing strategies in case real hard constraints are present. Hard constraints must be given sufficiently high weights, so that their overruling by a collection of soft ones becomes unlikely. This can be proven in advance, by simple arithmetics. Alternatively, hard constraints can also be conjunctively added to every rule, so that only offers that satisfy them are returned.

Lack of hard constraints may also lead to cases where no offer is suitable, but some satisfy some (soft) constraints and are thus returned. This can be detected in the surrounding workflow, or by having a two-stage selection, where hard constraints are checked first (for this, weights are not checked), and only the fitting services are forwarded to a second stage for preference-based selection.

15.2.4 Data model

Both teams provided expressive data models reflecting domain specific knowledge and exchanged messages on the data schema and instance level. Both teams modelled the concepts, their attributes and relationships between concepts in rule-based languages. In both cases, mature tools exist to edit underlying data models. DERI uses the WSML-Flight variant in the shipment scenario, a fully-fledged ontology language with rule support. WSMT or WSMO Studio can be used to model the required WSMO elements.

miAamics uses a taxonomy that characterizes profiles of individuals (requests, situations and offers). This taxonomy comprises *attributes* and *categories*. Attributes define sets of individuals via properties (evaluable predicates) on single data fields of an individual while categories are used to combine multiple attributes to more specialized subsets of individuals. To set up the data model, miAamics' web configuration interface as well as importers that generate the configuration from existing ontologies or other sources were used.

Both teams modelled their ontologies following a bottom-up approach, creating the ontologies based on the XML Schema definitions of shipment Web services and the shipment domain. In miAamics a number of higher granularity rules have been modelled (e.g. cheap-price, high-price, fast-shipment) which are defined in terms of conditions over concept attributes. In WSMOLX the $isShipped$ relation has been modelled and specified in the service description, but also referred by the Goal. Evaluation of $isShipped$ during the discovery process allows to determine whether a service can be used for the given shipment request input data (shipment source and target addresses, package weight, etc.).

15.2.5 Matchmaking

The DERI submission directly supports a data-fetching service which was necessary in case of Muller service where the shipping price has to be dynamically obtained as shown on Listing 15.3. IRIS[7] interfaced via the WSML2Reasoner[8] framework is used for the reasoning over the semantic description of service functionality. IRIS is a Datalog reasoner with support for arithmetic expressions and custom built-ins. WSMX Discovery component did not have to resort to the external arithmetic services as the required calculations were carried out internally within the context of reasoning.

miAamics is a purely logical matchmaker. Hence prices for shipment offers are calculated in advance and provided to the miAamics configuration database as concrete values. This step is done in the surrounding discovery workflow that invokes miAamics for matchmaking. The same way, the problem of invoking a shipper's Web service to retrieve the actual price is handled. A generated SIB invokes the service and the result is updated in miAamics' database.

---

[7] http://iris-reasoner.org
[8] http://tools.deri.org/wsml2reasoner

These database updates are limited to the concrete offer instances and do not affect the attribute definitions that classify the offers and are the basis of the matchmaking algorithm. Hence it is not necessary to recalculate the rule evaluation structures after manipulating an offer.

After the precalculation steps miAamics is invoked for matchmaking. It calculates results by evaluation of all rules that compose the active strategy. A rule consists of a premise and a conclusion, and the rule is fulfilled if both the premise holds for a request (or situation) and the conclusion holds for an offer. The weights for multiple matching rules are added and that way an order of matching results is formed. Finally the result is the set of offers with the highest accumulated weight. In case this set contains more than one offer, a randomly chosen one is returned, since they are all equivalently good for this strategy.

15.2.6 Selection

The Instance-based WSMX Service Discovery [5] component handles the service selection part. The goal can specify ranking criteria. The price is used in the shipment scenario to select the best service where multiple matching services which satisfy the Goal capability are discovered.

Invoking miAamics possibly returns a set of suitable offers that can accomplish the request. This set is ordered by the cumulated weight the offer received from the evaluation of all rules in the current strategy. The weight is the sum of weights of all rules that hold for the given request and the particular offer. Thus the offer with the maximum weight is selected which directly corresponds to a shipper's web service. If multiple offers have the same weight, one of them can be chosen randomly as they fit the request equally well.

15.2.7 Web service invocation

WSMX uses two dedicated components: Communication Manager for handling external communication with service requesters and Invoker for invoking involved services. Invoker manages XML $< - >$ WSML adaptation (performing lifting and lowering). Lifting is required when moving from syntactic data representation to rich, ontology model, while lowering does the opposite, namely it maps downwards to non-semantic data models (e.g. XML, EDI, RosettaNet).

A single SIB was generated by the jETI extension of jABC for each of the shippers' services. This is simply done by passing the URL of a service's WSDL description to the jETI plug in. The invocation of the corresponding service is an implicit part of the generated SIB that is used to build the discovery service SLG.

15.2.8 Execution monitoring

WSMX uses a Java SWING[9], a simple graphical monitoring facility to display WSMX components' progress of use-case executions. There is also a HTTP monitoring and management facility available which allows inspecting the state of the components and to access various statistics related to carried out service executions. A detailed log is kept of all internal operations performed in WSMX execution.

The execution of the discovery orchestration service can be monitored using jABC's Tracer plug in. It is an interpreter of the SLGs that model the orchestrations. It provides access

---

[9] http://java.sun.com/docs/books/tutorial/uiswing

to the current state of the execution (e.g. parameter values) and holds a history of all executed steps. The result of miAamics's evaluation can be analyzed by its *result monitor*, shown in Fig. 13.5 of chapter 13. It provides a graphical representation of the evaluation results with a profile of all offers matching at least one rule, and their total weights. Additionally some statistical information is available (e.g. the number of considered rules, the execution time of the evaluation).

15.2.9 Tool support

There is already sufficient support for editing WSMO elements in WSMT and WSMO Studio. However, there is currently only basic support for editing processes in the form of ontologized ASMs and no support for simulation and model testing. The tools utilized throughout the development lifecycle of the WSMOLX submission are being actively developed (WSMO editor, Data Mediation, WSMX etc.). Modeling aspects involved in the discovery scenario (e.g. WSMO ontology editing) are already supported by quite advanced and user-friendly functionality.

As explained in Chap. 5, jABC is an extensible framework that supports graphical modelling for different domains. Up to now many plug-ins already exist, making jABC a flexible, comfortable and mature tool. Moreover additional plug-ins are permanently developed depending on the user's needs, further extending the tool's capabilities. miAamics has proven its maturity in its original domain, the efficient personalization of web applications. But the SWS scenario shows that it can also be used for other domains. Therefore it was necessary to extend miAamics' configuration facilities to support automatic generation of huge numbers of attributes and rules. This was easy to achieve as the configuration is stored in a relational database that can also be accessed by other applications.

15.3 Coping with the scenario changes

The WSMX framework proved to be generic as only modifications of the WSMO Goals were necessary in order to correctly handle the newly introduced changes to the scenario. Discovery based on the location was successfully resolved using the common *isShipped* relation (see Listing 15.1). Additional criteria imposed on the service such as weight and price have also been evaluated to level 2 in the SWS-Challenge results. No changes in the WSMX code or in the service descriptions were required.

Coping with changes in advanced discovery scenarios that introduce more complex selection constraints needs the formulation of corresponding strategies in miAamics. In addition to the location based attributes and rules that are used in the simple discovery scenarios, attributes and rules that consider weights, prices, etc. are added and used to create advanced strategies. In those strategies, the rules already defined for simple strategies are reused. For example the strategy "Destination and Weight" combines rules defined for the "Destination only" strategy with rules that consider weight limits. All necessary changes can be done using miAamics' Web UI or its import functionality. Changes in the surrounding jABC workflow that invokes miAamics and the shipping services were not necessary.

15.4 Conclusions

In this chapter we have presented a comparison of the WSMOLX and miAamics/jABC solutions to semantic discovery in context of SWS Challenge. Both approaches were able to cater to a fine granularity of client requests and service functionality descriptions. Fine granularity of service search request aims to reduce manual work required in determining the actual functionality of services to a minimum. The combination of semantics with the dynamic data-fetching mechanism brings significant benefits to the runtime service late-binding, facilitating the volatile and frequently-changing nature of services in SOA.

For the future work, both teams plan to evaluate their frameworks with a large number of services from different domains to examine the scalability of the advantages obtained through using semantic descriptions with the data-fetch mechanism over purely informal and static service descriptions. We hope for the future SWS-Challenge scenarios that will allow to evaluate performance and scalability against large number of services.

References

1. Roman, D., Keller, U., Lausen, H., de Bruijn, J., Lara, R., Stollberg, M., Polleres, A., Feier, C., Bussler, C., Fensel, D.: Web Service Modeling Ontology. Applied Ontologies **1**(1) (2005) 77 – 106
2. de Bruijn, J., Lausen, H., Polleres, A., Fensel, D.: The Web Service Modeling Language: An Overview. In: Proc. of the European Semantic Web Conference. (2006)
3. Vitvar, T., Mocan, A., Kerrigan, M., Zaremba, M., Zaremba, M., Moran, M., Cimpian, E., Haselwanter, T., Fensel, D.: Semantically-enabled service oriented architecture: Concepts, technology and application. In Service Oriented Computing and Applications, Springer London **1**(2) (2007)
4. Jörges, S., Kubczak, C., Nagel, R., Margaria, T., Steffen, B.: Model-driven development with the jABC. In: HVC - IBM Haifa Verification Conference. LNCS 4383, Haifa, Israel, IBM, Springer Verlag (2006)
5. Zaremba, M., Vitvar, T., Moran, M.: Towards Optimized Data Fetching for Service Discovery. In: In Proceedings of the Fifth IEEE European Conference on Web Services (ECOWS), IEEE Computer Society. (2007)
6. Braun, V., Margaria, T., Weise, C.: Integrating tools in the ETI platform. Int. Journal on Software Tools for Technology Transfer (STTT) **1**(2) (1997) 31–48
7. Steffen, B., Margaria, T., Nagel, R.: Remote Integration and Coordination of Verification Tools in jETI. In: Proc. ECBS 2005, 12th IEEE Int. Conf. on the Engineering of Computer Based Systems, Greenbelt (USA), IEEE Computer Soc. Press (2005) 431–436
8. Margaria, T., Kubzcak, C., Steffen, B.: Bio-jETI: a Service Integration, Design, and Provisioning Platform for Orchestrated Bioinformatics Processes. In: Supplement dedicated to Network Tools and Applications in Biology 2007 Workshop (NETTAB 2007). Number 9 (Suppl 4):S12 in BioMed Central (BMC) Bioinformatics (2008) Published online 2008 April 25.
9. Roman, D., Scicluna, J.: Ontology-based Choreography of WSMO Services. Wsmo final draft v0.3, DERI (2006) Available at: http://www.wsmo.org/TR/d14/v0.3/.

Comparison: Handling Preferences with DIANE and miAamics

Ulrich Küster[1], Birgitta König-Ries[1], Tiziana Margaria[2], and Bernhard Steffen[3]

[1] Institute for Computer Science, University Jena, Germany,
{ukuester,koenig}@informatik.uni-jena.de
[2] Chair of Service and Software Engineering, University of Potsdam, Germany,
margaria@cs.uni-potsdam.de
[3] Chair of Programming Systems, Technical University of Dortmund, Germany,
steffen@cs.uni-dortmund.de

Summary. In this chapter we compare the DIANE and miAamics solutions to service discovery along a specific feature supported by those solutions: *preferences*. Although quite different in their theoretical and technical background, both techniques have in fact the ability to express user preferences, that are used internally to rank the evaluation results. These preferences are used here to incorporate functional aspects as defined by the SWS Challenge tasks, but they can also be used to express non-functional properties like quality aspects. Here we take a closer look at how preferences are realized in the two different approaches and we briefly compare their profiles.

16.1 Realizing Preferences with miAamics

The complete solution of the discovery scenario using as evaluation engine the miAamics personalization framework is described in detail in Chapter 13. miAamics' weight mechanism can be used to define user preferences on the evaluation. This is the particular aspect central to the comparison with the DIANE solution.

Creating a domain model in miAamics is mainly a matter of creating sets of *attributes* that define profiles of customers, situations, and offers. miAamics can be seen as a situation aware matcher that matches profiles of customers to profiles of offers, taking into account profiles of situations where required. Evaluation goals are defined by *strategies*, i.e. sets of *rules* that use the aforementioned attributes. The miAamics evaluation engine calculates results concerning a given strategy by evaluating all the rules pertaining to this strategy and adding up the weights of the applicable rules.

miAamics' rules define mappings of the shape

$$Rulename: \quad f(request, situation) \rightarrow \{offer\}$$

hence the premises refer to customer and situation attributes while conclusions must refer only to attributes of offers. Rules are labelled with a name and a kind of numerical rating, in miAamics' terms *weight*. The following rules are examples for rules defined for the discovery scenario. Once again the premises regard to customer attributes that in the discovery scenario describe shipping requests, while the conclusions are defined by (shipment-) offer attributes.

1. Shipment to USA: Destination location is in USA → Ships to USA
2. Cheap shipment: Costs must be < $50 → Ships for less than $50
3. Express delivery: Has to be delivered within 24 hrs → Guarantees delivery within 24 hrs
4. Normal delivery: Has to be delivered within 48 hrs → Guarantees delivery within 48 hrs

Given a set of rules, it is now possible to define strategies. Strategies define which rules are considered for an evaluation and with which weight. If a rule is included in several strategies, it can be associated in different strategies with different numerical ratings, as shown in Table 16.1. The evaluation algorithm rates all offers by adding up the weights of the fulfilled rules. Thus the results can be ordered by their total weight, that reflects the quality of the solution for that strategy, as a sort of rank.

Following the scenario description, as a very simple example Strategy A in Table 16.1 only considers the first rule, *Shipment to USA*. In this case, the evaluation result for requests that have a USA destination address will only return shipment services that ship to the requested country (USA). As Rule 1 is the only rule considered, all the fulfilling offers have weight 100. Since they all fulfill the strategy's constraints equally well, but a single offer is at the end selected, this happens by random choice among them.

Rule No.	Strategy A	Strategy B	Strategy C
1	100	100	100
2	*(not used)*	40	50
3	*(not used)*	25	20
4	*(not used)*	25	20

Table 16.1. Different rules and weights in different strategies

Functional and non-functional preferences using weights

In the more realistic scenarios, a customer specifies several quality criteria in his requests. (Situated) quality criteria are expressed in miAamics via rules, so more refined strategies include several rules. The rule base described above considers also criteria as the shipping price and time for delivery, besides the destination country. Both strategies B and C in Table 16.1 include all four rules, but with different weights. Taking a look at the weights defined for the rules in a single strategy, it is possible to describe in detail and intuitively how this strategy sets the user preferences for the request evaluation. In both strategies, the functional aspect is covered by Rule 1: that is the essential criterion to determine if a shipper is eligible. The other rules express preference criteria.

Strategy B ensures that a delivery to the requested country is possible because the value for this Rule (100) cannot be surpassed by the total weight of other rules (90). So, no shipper is ever going to be selected that does not ship to the USA - the central selection criterion. Furthermore, Strategy B privileges offers that can guarantee a delivery within 24 hours over cheap ones. If a shipment within 24 hours is offered (Rule 3), Rule 4 is also fulfilled, since a shipment within 24 hours is also within 48 hours. Thus a sum of 50 points is achieved in this case while cheap offers can only gain 40 additional points. Cheap and fast shippers can get the sum of the points, 90.

For a different customer profile preferences can be set in a different way via a different strategy, using for example the same rules but with adjusted weights. For example, if it is more important to chose the cheapest offer than to deliver a package within short time, weights could be defined as shown in Strategy C. Once again, delivery to the selected country is ensured, but this time cheap offers are preferred (50). Delivery time is still considered: cheap and quick shippers will be preferred (become a higher rating) over those that are simply cheap.

This example covers both functional and nonfunctional criteria. The design of the weights is sensitive, since it determines the relative relevance of the rules (and the criteria they express) in the overall selection strategy.

16.2 Realizing Preferences with DIANE

DIANE uses a set-based modeling approach for service discovery. Service providers usually do not offer a single service instance, but are able to provide a family of similar services, e.g. shipping to a multitude of locations. Thus, they describe their offer as the set of services they can potentially provide. The shipping services of the SWS-Challenge, for instance, provide shipping of packages that adhere to certain weight and size restrictions within given sets of countries.

Requesters with a certain need, on the other hand, may have a perfect service in mind, but usually accept quite different services based on the available offers. While a fast, reliable, and cheap shipping offer would obviously be a perfect choice, in reality a fast but expensive shipping offer might be as acceptable as a slower but also less expensive one. Therefore, service requests in DIANE describe the set of service instances which are acceptable to the requester. In order to express preferences among services, requesters may use fuzzy instead of crisp sets. A higher degree of membership in the fuzzy request sets corresponds to a higher preference for that particular service. For further information about service modeling and how services are matched in DIANE we refer to Chapter 12. In the following we detail how user preferences are expressed in the DIANE context by the examples of the SWS-Challenge discovery scenarios.

16.2.1 Basic Preferences

Within the SWS-Challenge, preferences were mainly used in the hardware purchasing scenario. Goal B1 for instance requires to purchase a notebook with certain properties (e.g. at least 60 GB harddisc size) and states that price matters most, thus cheaper offers should be preferred if the other requirements are met. Such basic preferences are captured by *direct conditions* on request attributes, in this case on the price of the product. A crisp condition like "<= 2000" on the price attribute of a product requires the price of that product to be less than 2000 but does not encode preference for lower prices. These are expressed using fuzzy conditions like "~==[0, 2000] 0". This expression requests the price to be zero, but accepts values from the interval [0, 2000] with linearly decreasing preference. Similarly an expression like "~== 2007-11-11T11:11" on the pickup time asks for pickup at the specified time, but accepts a default deviation of up to three days – again, with linearly decreasing preference.

16.2.2 Advanced Preferences

Fuzzy direct conditions are sufficient to express preferences on single attributes. However, most realistic scenarios involve preferences on multiple attributes with conflicting optimization goals, like preferences for a low price and a high-quality configuration at the same time. In such cases the different goals have to be balanced according to the user's preferences. In DIANE, this is achieved with *connecting strategies*. During the matchmaking, complex types are compared by recursively comparing their attributes and combining the retrieved values. The matchvalue of a particular notebook with respect to a notebook purchasing request, for instance, is obtained by combining the matchvalues obtained from comparing the attributes of the notebook (price, HDD size, RAM size, processor type, ...) with the corresponding requirements from the request. The resulting values are normalized to the interval $[0, 1]$ and by default combined by multiplying them. To emphasize particular conditions compared to others, a requester specifies a custom connection strategy, basically a function which maps the set of attribute matchvalues to the interval $[0, 1]$. Available base functions are product, weighted sum, min and max as well as the exponential function. Goal C4, for instance, specifies that the processor power of the notebook is most important and that more RAM is more important than a bigger hard disc. This is captured by the connecting strategy $processor^3 \times memory^2 \times hardDisc$ which penalizes lower values for the processor power most, and lower values for the memory size more than those for the hard disc size.

16.2.3 Practicalities

The definition of appropriate preferences is not always trivial (see Section 16.3) and requires a certain knowledge about DSD. DIANE thus supports the separation of concerns via parameterized *request templates*. Any concept in a DSD request can be replaced by a request input variable, thus parameterizing the request. This way, trained domain experts can create one or more DSD request corresponding to different preference profiles. In the shipping example, for instance, different request templates might correspond to requests prioritizing fast shipment, inexpensive shipment or precisely matching pickup times. End users can then select the most appropriate request template according to their needs and use them by simply providing values for the required input variables, i.e. the cargo to be shipped and the locations for the pickup and the delivery. This way, technical details of DSD can be hidden behind simple user interfaces, making dealing with DSD directly unnecessary for end users.

16.3 Challenging Example: Goal B2

Balancing preference criteria with different nature is not always easy in both approaches. Despite the fact that most preferences could be encoded very intuitively, one goal posed difficulties. Goal B2 of the second scenario prefers black notebooks compared to white ones, but prefers to buy the white one if it is significantly (more than $100) less expensive than the black one. Such a rule-based preference, combining a constant part (the color) and a variable part (price difference) does not map well neither to the fuzzy set-based preference mechanism of DIANE nor to miAamics.

Since the price limit was set to $1800 a price difference of $100 results in a difference of the matchvalue in DIANE of roughly 0.055 ($100/1800$). Therefore the preference values for the color were chosen to reflect exactly this difference: black [1] and white [0,944]. A weighted sum of $0.5 \times price + 0.5 \times color$ however does not result in the desired behavior. The problem is that any black notebook regardless of the price or any product whatsoever that does not cost much would result in a matchvalue of at least 0.5. Therefore the connecting strategy was extended to $min(color, price, 0.5 \times price + 0.5 \times color)$. However, this way the matchvalue was soon dominated by the matchvalue for the price and the weighted sum did not influence the outcome any more. To resolve this issue, the influence of the weighted sum was strengthened using a polynome yielding: $min(color, price, (0.5 \times price + 0.5 \times color)^5)$. This way the desired behavior could be successfully achieved.

Using miAamics, just expressing the goal is not a big problem. Defining price rules for each \$100 interval with a weight of e.g. 50 and an additional rule for black devices with a weight that is less than the 50 points of the price rules would roughly lead to the desired behavior. But this example also shows the drawbacks of the miAamics solution. Since miAamics is based on boolean rules, conditions on numerical values, e.g. the price, need to be discretized. This can lead to a huge amount of rules. Moreover, within a discretization interval for a criterion (here price), offers are indistinguishable for that criterion. As a consequence, two black notebooks priced \$900 and \$999 could not be differentiated in this example, while the DIANE solution would prefer the cheaper one. Furthermore the behavior is as desired only if the price of a black notebook is close to the upper bound of a price interval. For example a white notebook for \$899 would beat a black one for \$900 though it is not *significantly* cheaper. This is due to the fact that the white notebook falls in another price interval than the black one. This problem can only be reduced by choosing smaller price intervals and thus creating more rules - which can happen using our automatic rule generation facilities.

16.4 Comparison

The discovery approaches are different in four dimensions:

1. selection mechanism (underlying technology)
2. mode of use (pragmatics)
3. profile of users (who can do what when)
4. performance

16.4.1 Selection mechanism (underlying technology)

DIANE builds on arithmetics. In particular, it allows one to automatically weight and compare numerical parameters, and to specify a prioritized selection of data/products/offers based on those comparisons. E.g., price differences may be transformed into preference values, which may then be put into the context of other preference values, e.g. for timeliness, quality assurance, or color in a preference-based fashion. This is typically done by building a product of powers of the involved preference values: the higher the power of a value the greater its impact. This method also allows one to indirectly code a priority scheme between preference values if desired.

In contrast, miAamics is based on predicate logics: simple if-then rules describe single *aspects* of when a certain data/product/offer fits. The overall selection is then based on large sets of such rules, each weighted according to the relevance/significance of the modeled aspect. If various rules propose the same data/product/offer, the weights for these data/products/offers are added, and the data/products/offers with the highest such sums are the winners. This way of aspect-oriented modeling is highly compositional: to add a new aspect, one simply needs to add the according rules, weighted reflecting the according relevance/significance. Preference can be modeled indirectly using the weights, e.g. giving the pricing aspect a higher weight than the sum of the weights of competing aspects. Numerical values can be treated based on adequate discretization.

16.4.2 Mode of use (pragmatics)

Both approaches are based on ontologies/taxonomies, but their mode of operation is quite different:

DIANE is based on complex ad hoc queries, which describe the overall pattern of selection (see above): a user describes his desires and preferences according to DIANE's selection mechanism in a monolithic fashion. The resulting expression needs to be fully evaluated at runtime according to the current state of the environment (data bases etc.).

In contrast, miAamics' specification of selection is decomposed in two parts:

- the specification of the set of weighted rules describing the aspect-oriented relevance of data/products/offers. In our experience, these rules can be dealt with be business experts without IT knowledge after a short training.
- predicates describing the individual preference of a user for a certain selection process. These predicates may describe the user's price, quality, or color sensitivity, which may occur in the rules' 'if' part, thus steering which of the rules defined in in the first part are fired and which not. Setting these predicates, which means setting the profile of selection, can easily be done simply by clicking at certain preferences. This is so intuitive that it does not even require an explanation.

16.4.3 Profile of users (who can do what when?)

The correct conceptualization of a problem domain and the design of strategies or queries that appropriately capture an end user's preferences and desires is often a non-trivial task. Therefore, both approaches allow to distinguish two profiles of users:

- The *domain expert* conceptualizes the problem domain and develops appropriate parameterized query templates (in case of DIANE) respectively an aspect-oriented weighted rule scheme together with a set of strategies (in case of miAmics).
- The *end user* only selects and customizes the request by choosing appropriate parameter values for one of the predefined query templates (DIANE) respectivly by selecting some predicates for preference (miAmics).

In particular the latter role is open to a very wide public. Almost all internet users will be able to perform this kind of selection without requiring even an explanation. But also the first role does not require extensive IT knowledge. Both approaches envision domain experts with some basic training in the employed technology as the optimal clientele for the task. In some cases, in particular when the preferences are inherently complex, DSD might require a better mathematical understanding from the user than miAmics.

16.4.4 Performance

The runtime complexity of evaluating a DIANE request with respect to a single offer is roughly linear in the size of the request (i.e. the number of attributes). Thus, large requests together with large numbers of offers may pose a performance problem in a context, where thousands of users operate in parallel.

In contrast, miAamics technology comes with a compilation process, which transforms large sets of weighted rules into simple evaluation structures. This guarantees an extremely fast selection (orders of magnitude faster than the DIANE selection), and therefore scalability.

16.4.5 Summary

Overall, miAamics and DIANE were designed with very different goals: miAamics was designed with a focus on ease of use and scalability whereas DIANE was designed with a focus on expressivity and precision. This corresponds to the fact that miAamics is based on boolean rules and DIANE on arithmetics and fuzzy set theory. Consequently, DIANE is more flexible for specification, in particular considering the treatment of continous numerical values, that needs to be discretized in miAamics. On the other hand, miAamics restricted expressivity makes the specification of rules very easy and allows to achieve superior runtime performance. Thus the two technologies have complementary profiles, and therefore their own right of existence.

Part V

Lessons Learned

17

Status, Perspectives, and Lessons Learned

Charles Petrie[1], Ulrich Küster[2], Tiziana Margaria[3], Michal Zaremba[4], Holger Lausen[4], and Srdjan Komazec[4]

[1] Computer Science Dept. University of Stanford, Gates Building, Stanford, CA 94305-9020, USA petrie@stanford.edu
[2] Institute for Computer Science, Friedrich-Schiller-University Jena, 07743 Jena, Germany ulrich.kuester@uni-jena.de
[3] Chair of Service and Software Engineering, Institute for Informatics University of Potsdam, 14482 Potsdam, Germany margaria@cs.uni-potsdam.de
[4] Semantic Technology Institute Innsbruck, University of Innsbruck, Technikerstr. 21, 6020 Innsbruck, Austria,
holger.lausen,michal.zaremba,srdjan.komazec@sti2.at

Summary. We describe in this chapter our understanding of the SWS Challenge, and how to improve it, after approximately the first year of major startup efforts.

17.1 Introduction to Lessons Learned

As described in the Introduction to this book, the "year" covered actually spans a greater length of calendar time. But the phrase "first year" accurately describes our steep learning curve in developing and refining this challenge. We briefly summarize here the reflections and lessons learned over this first year of activity. They concern our *methodology*, the *infrastructure*, and the *scenarios*. We include some perspectives on the Challenge, some of the outstanding issues to be addressed, and plans for future developments.

In this chapter, we go into more detail some of the issues that were mentioned in Introduction. We begin with a discussion of one of the most important and difficult aspects of the SWS Challenge: the evaluation methodology.

17.2 Methodology

For the most part, our experience has validated the methodology though we have learned much: i.e., Our experience has largely validated the methodology: we refined the methodology but slightly over the course of a year, learning much in the course of discussions at the workshops and within the organizer team [5].

Each team selects one or more scenarios (see the Chapter on scenarios) and attempts to correctly access and select web services from the testbed. Most scenarios involve actually

---

[5] In 2008, we refined the methodology more. See the Challenge wiki for the latest developments.

invoking the web services, though some discovery scenarios require only selection of the right services. Where the services are invoked, teams should notify the manager of the testbed (Srdjan Komazec at the time of publication) that they think they have a scenario solution. The manager then verifies the correct exchange of messages. When a team has a solution, they submit a paper on their solution to the next workshop, and upload useful information about their technology on the Challenge wiki.

Workshop Activities.

At a workshop, each team presents their claims in a paper, and then we evaluate the claims by having the workshop participants mutually examine the code of the submission. In the case of a discovery solution, we ask for a demonstration of a correct selection of services. In all cases, we look at the code sufficiently to be collectively persuaded that the solution actually works as claimed. In addition, we may examine code changes to solutions to "surprise" problems, about which we say more below.

Initially, we thought that we would need to divide up into teams to examine the submissions but we found that the whole workshop could collectively examine each submission and that everyone wanted to do so. We suspect that since the evaluations are developed by the collective consensus of the whole workshop, they are better than they would have been had they been reached by smaller groups. In particular, we have found that expertise in understanding different technologies varies among the workshop participants and different people can examine different technologies more critically than others.

When the workshop participants are convinced that the particular team being evaluated really has solved a particular scenario problem, then that team receives a check mark on that problem, which is published on the Challenge public wiki. The team is entitled to claim a solution to this problem in their papers and to link to the evaluation matrix from their team web site with the appropriate claims. Since the problems are complex and there are frequently important caveats about the solution, these are published as footnotes on the evaluation matrix.

Comparison Criteria.

As discussed in the Introduction chapter, an important aspect of the Challenge is to evaluate what we might call here, for ease of discussion, the *malleability* of the tested technology: how easy is it to "bend" the software solution into a somewhat different solution.

This is a very important and difficult issue. While we do not have a good definition for "semantic" technologies, there is a, as yet largely unstated, hypothesis that such technologies will prove to be good for software engineering of net-based, distributed, interacting complex software systems, such as industrial manufacturing order and supply chains, especially those based upon web services, which can be well-defined[6].

Semantic technology in the context of web serices may be minimally described as technology that enhances the service descriptions by annotations that more precisely describe the service behavior beyond the signature information[1].

We can speculate here that software technologies called "semantic" are often those that use some set of terms defined in an "ontology" in such a way that these terms can be re-used in different applications in a consistent way. An "ontology" is some description of the terms of discourse that restricts their use. Many semantic technologies use some form of computational logic in describing and using the fundamental terms so that applications can most generally

---

[6] $http://tinyurl.com/webservdef$

compute with the term definitions for different purposes. However, for a large class of application, equivalent expressive power of re-use might be obtained by models less generally expressive than even Descriptive Logic. Fortunately, these speculations are not critical to the discussion here: the Semantic Web Services Challenge does not depend upon any particular definition of "semantic" technology.

The reason is that the Challenge is open to all technologies. We simply evaluate whether the technologies can solve the problem and provide some indication of their malleability. Our job is to certify functionality and we can avoid, at least for now, definitions of semantics.

However, the issue of malleability is important: to the extent that any participant team claims to have a technology that is an improvement over conventional programming technologies, it should be able to facilitate changes in a given solution. Web services permit various software components to be composed into different applications. As stated in the Dagstuhl definition[2], this is done by using a description of those components in presented in some widely-parsed format (such as XML[7]) and reachable via some standard Internet protocol (such as HTTP[8]). As companies (and in the future, individuals) produce such applications with distributed services, the resulting applications become more difficult to maintain. Making changes in these increasingly complex applications is a fundamental software engineering challenge. Particularly technologies that claim to provide semantic annotations of web services claim to facilitate such maintenance.

The issue of malleability is as difficult to evaluate as it is important.

We initially tried to rank the submissions in difficulty of moving from one problem level or sub-level to another by trying to determine whether code was changed that would necessitate a re-compilation and linking, or whether there was only a change to the declaration of objects upon which the code acted. Further, we wanted to distinguish between whether the current declarations had to be altered, or whether new declarations were simply added. We found that these distinctions could not be made objectively. For example, if someone is writing in Lisp, there is no objective difference between declarations and code. XML schemas and Java present similar though less extreme problems.

We tried making a collective consensus on simply whether code or declarations have been changed as a measure of difficulty in moving from one level solution to another. This has been particularly challenging especially in approaches where solutions are synthesized by arranging software components in a graph with a GUI. This can be considered as declarative input to a code synthesis engine, and the code of the engine itself never changes. Deciding whether this is programming or declaration, perhaps based upon whether the graph is interpreted or compiled, only hightened the nature of the subjectivity in deciding the difference between declarations and code. There was no firm ground in this case for reaching consensus.

In trying to determine code changes, we required a code freeze prior to each workshop and then released problem variations. Then at the workshop, we examined the new solutions to see how much work was required to go from the original to the new. In order to encourage teams to finish their original solutions sooner than later, we allowed all teams to freeze their code and work on the problem variations as soon as they had verified their first solution. However, in addition to the subjective evaluation of the work required to change a solution, this freeze made a lot of work for the testbed manager as well as the teams. We also did not have a mechanism for keeping the problem variations secret from new participants. So each variation because a public problem to solve next time.

---

[7] $http://www.w3.org/XML/$
[8] $http://www.w3.org/Protocols/$

Because of all these issues, at the last Stanford workshop (2007) we introduced a "surprise" problem. We did not require a code freeze but rather asked participants to work overnight to solve a new problem variation, the details of which would be kept secret from future new participants. The idea was that the participants either would or would not be able to successfully modify their solutions. If they were successful, they got a plus mark in addition to their check mark, indicatiing that their solution was indeed malleable.

We found that this approach also had problems. One operational problem is that people simply did not look forward to staying up all night to work on a problem.

Our approach in the future will be to require a single code freeze deadline for everyone who intends to have their malleability evaluated. These participants will then receive the details of a surprise problem only after they commit to working on it and being evaluated. Then their solution to the surprise problem will be evaluated at the workshop. We will have to experiment to find the right timeframe at which to release the problem so that everyone has enough time to work on the problem before traveling to the workshop, but the timeframe is short enough to differentiate between at least some technologies.

The more serious problem, which we still have to address, is that a good Java programmer is capable of solving such a surprise problem by re-writing the application from scratch even with no particularly sophisticated software engineering approach. At the Stanford 2007 workshop, we gave the participants a surprise problem, related to one of the existing solved problems. One participant, representing the University of Jena, was able to program it from scratch in Java and present a verifiable solution in about two hours. Again, we will be experimenting with determining the right qualities of the surprise problem.

Our working hypothesis is that it should require a modification of the existing problem such that it would be much more difficult to re-write it from scratch than to modify the existing definition. Where possible, we want to have a surprise problem that requires a technology to only restate the "goal" that the software application should achieve, or the constraints under which it should do so, so as to test and validate the advantages of technologies that automate the application synthesis.

Another of our working hypotheses is that we should build up a giant macro scenario out of our individual scenarios. This is intended to be a complex multiple customer/manufacturer/-multiple supplier/multiple shipper problems with complex product configuration constraints and goals. The hypothesis is that a problem change with such a complex scenario will differentiate software technologies and reveal advantages of a subset in modifying such a complex application.

Open Approach.

One of the major successes of our methodology has been the open approach. First, participants are asked to submit new scenarios (including web services) and these are constantly being evaluated and added to our problem suite. Second, all solutions are documented and participants are encouraged to "steal" from each other. One of the teams that has solved the most problems uses one approach to solve the mediation problem and another to solve the discovery problem. This team is composed of people from two different institutions who have developed a successful synthesis of technologies.

This is exactly the sort of outcome we hoped for: understanding of which approaches worked best for what kind of problems and cooperation among researchers at different institutions.

However, it must be reported that the online documentation of solutions has been difficult to obtain from the participants in a form that is readily useful to other participants. This is an issue that we continue to address in the future.

17.3 Infrastructure and Support

In the beginnning of the Challenge, we agreed on one fundamental principle: "No Participation without Invocation", meaning that we require solution claims to be verified on our testbed by actual invocation of web services. (We allow workshop participants to simply present relevant non-solution papers without an evaluation.) However this principle brought some well underestimated effort for both the organizers as well as the participants. On the other hand the challenge greatly profited by enforcing by having real web services available, documented and running at all times: it meant that we could not hush up a problem that occurred, but had to solve it.

Web Service Infrastructure.

We have started with three Web Services simulating a client trying to purchase goods using the RosettaNet protocol and its counterpart, the Moon legacy system. Taking into account different versions of services and the mediation systems that have been implemented to test the system we are operating at present around 20 different Web Services. Over time, five different developers have been involved for different aspects of the execution platform. All services have now been migrated to the axis2 engine for Web Services.

The complexity of the messages used has revealed several bugs in the implementation of the axis2 engine, which caused major resource expense just on the underlying technologies and not purely on "business" problem. However, we consider it a benefit of the Challenge that we are able to expose the deficiencies of the current state-of-the-art middleware tools, and work with the developers to fix them.

In fact it turns out that a variety of skills is required to master such a testbed. First, in-depth knowledge of WSDL and XML schemas is required to design proper service description utilizing the maximum of the descriptive power of the standards. Most obviously some knowledge on a web service engine (such as axis2) and the underlying application server (such as tomcat) is required as well as a fair amount of database design and web application programming skills. It also turned out to be necessary to understand a good deal about the Internet Protocol and firewalls in order to help participants to manage their invocations. And, last but not least, such an infrastructure requires some monitoring facilities that guarantee a 24/7 live system, which is not the usual approach in a university respectively research environment.

Effectively it demonstrated that in spite of the fact that Web Services are an established technology, current tools are only able to hide a small degree of the underlying complexity. As soon as we reached some case on the boundary conditions, understanding of underlying protocols and standards was essential and many problems occurred, especially with propagation of errors through layers of middleware.

Problem Description.

Besides the technical challenge we realized another important point: We decided to not formalize the problems using a logical formalism, but rather to describe them using natural language documentation. Having to communicate with developers as well as participants, we conclude that only having text-based documentation (in addition to the WSDL) as a common model is difficult. We realized that a fair amount of the solution to the problems is its formal description. In fact, had we had such descriptions from the start we could have saved several iterations of discussion with developers.

However, it is important that we do not impose a formalism on any of the participants. And we do not have the resources to provide a formal description of the problems in any case. So for now, we simply try to improve the description of the problems so that they are as consistent and unambiguous as possible.

Finding some middle ground for problem description between formalism and openness, as well as finding resources for the problem maintenance (which includes the requisite web services), is an ongoing issue for the Challenge.

Collaboration Infrastructure.

Having effective means to share information between the organizers and the participants is another important aspect for a successful challenge. We have started with a set of static web pages, however it was soon clear that this is suboptimal. A Wiki that enables corrections and improvements on the documentation in a collaborative fashion turned out to be much more adequate. While this improved the efficiency of the discussions around the different problems sets, it turned out not to be enough to share descriptions of the solutions between participants.

Similar to the problems, also the solutions come with a fair amount of complexity. In order for a team to participate, we required to publish the declarative parts of the teams solution on the Semantic Web Challenge Portal. A Wiki did not provide sufficient means to share such complex structures, so in addition we created FTP accounts. However this turned out to be suboptimal: while it enabled understanding and verification of a particular solution, the link between a solution's description in the papers submitted to the workshops, to the related discussion on the Wiki, and finally to the relevant parts of a solution's declarative description is still insufficiently integrated. We assume that this is one of the reasons why so far participants only share to a very limited amount of their formalizations. We hope to improve this in the future.

Evaluation and Debug Infrastructure.

Another aspect of involving real Web services is the possibility of automatically verifing a solution by issuing a set of different messages and monitor the subsequent message exchanges. This is a useful feature, since it makes the challenge more scalable with respect to the number of participants - it essentially enables to automatically verify solutions. Moreover it allows for teams to participate not only during workshops, but also at any other time by just exposing their Web Services. Other people interested in the claims of a team can just use the online portal to start a test set against a particular solution and verify its coverage.

Currently, the messages are independently verified by the testbed manager. We are building (and have prototyped) an automatic verification system based upon a standard and correct message exchange and comparing that to the exchange performed by a participant team. Determining that a team has selected the correct service in the discovery scenarios is rather trivial but we are considering more rigorous forms of verification for these as well.

Another aspect is to offer some form of debugging support. Already with six teams it was quite often necessary to examine the application server's log, be it to determine a typo in the endpoint addresses used in a mediator implementation, or to identify an invalid message.[9] Over time we added different views to the online portal that allows to examine parts of the message exchange and in particular the status of the systems involved.

---

[9] Making error logs available to the participants proved essential in 2008 and has been done.

17.4 Use of Industrial Standards

We have tried to make the scenarios industrially relevant by using standards in use in industry, starting with the WSDL. This effort shows up particularly in the mediation type of scenarios. As of now there are three levels related to the data and process mediation scenarios. The first, original scenario involves the mediation between Blue and Moon, within a stable (static) scenario: the protocols, the messages, and the data formats are known and fixed.

Data and process mediation scenarios have been based completely on the RosettaNet protocol. RosettaNet Partner Interface Processes (PIPs) allow trading partners to connect electronically to process transactions and move information within their extended supply chains. The first impression of the RosettaNet specification is its completeness, but once we started to work on scenario definition and implementation, we realized that several aspects of the specification should be improved to allow for automation of the RosettaNet processes.

We can give a couple of examples: The same fields in the schema of one message are defined differently in the schema of another message (even within the same PIP). There are various possible interpretation for particular fields in the messages, causing ambiguities: two teams working on the integration solution might actually use the same field differently. Various cases allow for free interpretation, e.g. having an address defined on the order level and on the line item level caused a confusion about which one should be used. Regarding the practical problems, potential RosettaNet messages are extremely large (e.g. even to confirm a message, the whole initial message must be included with it), but the schema requires that at the same time the whole message with many empty fields is sent. This is a problem with industrial standards that are essential the union of the interests of many stakeholders. In addition, there are no formal semantics, so processes defined by UML specification can be interpreted differently by various teams.

Within the Mediation type of scenarios is also the set of Payment problems. These aim at covering yet another aspect of the comprehensive SWS problem landscape: overcoming problems of web service orchestrations. Positioned as a mediation type of scenario, it very directly challenges the orchestration problem-solving capability of technologies used by participants.

This is a payment scenario and, again, we wanted to use industrial standards. Unfortunately, RossettaNet used in the mediation type of scenarios doesn't provide support for communication with financial institutions (e.g. banks) in order to conclude purchase order with a payment. After some time spent in research it was identified that the gap between RossettaNet-enabled systems and financial institutions could be bridged with a solution relying on ISO 20022 UNIversal Financial Industry (UNIFI) message scheme standard[10]. It is supported by major players in financial market (e.g. SWIFT[11] and TWIST[12]) and it provides a common development platform for exchanging and processing financial messages encoded in a standardized XML.

The standard covers a wide range of possible cases found in the respective domains (such as Cash management, Payments Clearing and Settlement, Securities management, Trade Services, etc). Among them, especially interesting for the scenario, was the Payments Initiation[13] case describing set of messages used to initiate and manage funds transfer between debtor (or customer) and creditor (or seller). This scenario uses slightly simplified versions of the original message specifications. All message definitions are given as appropriate XML schemas.

---

[10] http://www.iso20022.org
[11] http://www.swift.com
[12] http://www.twiststandards.org
[13] http://www.iso20022.org/index.cfm?item_id=59950

We continue to consider the extent to which we can incorporate such industrial standards, and which ones to use.

17.5 Evolution and Future Plans

The Challenge has been continuous through 2008 and future reports will describe those developments. The initiative is now going beyond its initial boundaries and at least three new teams have been added, with one additional technical approach by an existing team in 2008. The W3C Semantic Web Service Testbed Incubator Group initiated by Challenge organizers has issued a report on evaluation methodology[14].

The Challenge is now quite a growing and still naturally mutating "organism". Many of the initial assumptions about how the challenge should be run and structured have been verified while some have been modified during its execution. In this last section we would like to mention just a few new ideas for the future Challenge evolution.

Scenario Development.

The Challenge needs more new interesting scenarios. While the initial scenarios have been provided by several of the authors of this chapter, this is not scalable, and currently we have already new scenario problems created by the larger SWS Challenge community. We are open for new proposals of interesting use cases, which could be hosted by the Challenge testbed system and against which participants could test their execution engines.

These plans are also related with providing an easier process for submitting new problems. Currently we maintain a wiki infrastructure where all the scenarios are stored. Together with the growth of the community, we should have a more formal process of how we incorporate new use cases, how we make sure that they fit the interests of participants (a formal approval process), and how to implement and test the web services of the new problems.[15]

More Automatic Verification.

During previous workshops we used the whole workshop to evaluate solutions of all the teams. This may not scale as the number of teams participating in the challenge is growing. What is even more important is the lesson we learned during the Athens meeting, that teams may have different understanding of passing/not passing the same tests. The Challenge requires an improved integrated testbed allowing for automation of the verification process. The set of the automated tests would decide on behalf of organizers if the team accomplished the given level of problems, as the automated script would be run against proposed solution (e.g. a message unknown to participants would be send to their mediators to make sure that the solution is not hardcoded and can actually handle any valid message). This functionality is currently in development and is limited only by our resources[16].

---

[14] W3C SWS Challenge Testbed Incubator Methodology Report 31 March 2008:
$http://www.w3.org/2005/Incubator/swsc/XGR - SWSC - 20080331/$
[15] A new proposal for an extensive new scenario was presented in the 2008 Tenerife workshop and is in the process of being evaluated by the organizers.
[16] The STI Innsbruck provides most of the computer and staffing resources on a volunteer basis.

We need to document the verification procedure better on the wiki for the benefit of new participants. And we need to evolve a better procedure for testing the discovery scenarios where the only message that can be tested is a message to the selected service. This could of course be done manually, and so is no proof of the technology. Currently, the Challenge group is persuaded by live demos and code inspection.

Mashups and other Extensions.

There has been the idea of integrating different problems to allow "mashups" - combining content from more than one source into an integrated experience. Currently the scenarios are pretty separated and we proved during our past meeting the teams can accomplish one problem without even touching the other one. Given this independence, it would be interesting, to split the existing problems into micro-problems (and to host only micro-problems on the Challenge server), but to allow to mashup them freely to create even new scenarios, not envisioned by the creators of the mashups. However, so far we have not figured out a method of doing this.

It's clear that scenario descriptions could be to some extent formally decomposed. Typically the scenario consists of:

- the set of running, publicly accessible Web services with clear interface definitions provided in the form of WSDL files,
- the set of XML Schemas that govern message structure and content,
- the set of sample messages that a solution should be capable to deal with, and
- natural language description of the problem that should be solved.

The question is how to further formalize these characteristics so as to permit mashups and perhaps address some of the Challenge issues identified in this chapter.

Finally, we are looking at ways to import external web services into the testbed so that we can evaluate the technologies within the scope of a much larger suite of services. This is also likely to offer a test of various registry technologies, especially if the other participates are able to select among alternatives. We especially want to identify what parts of industrial web service issues that are not covered by existing scenarios. The development of any formal process for accepting and approving new scenarios to be established on the basis of outcomes of W3C Testbed Incubator should take into account coverage of possible SWS applications.

Cooperation with the S3 Contest.

We are interested in working with the "S3 Contest" (described in the Introduction chapter) in developing a common suite of test services that can be used in both evaluation workshops. Our methodology will remain distinct as we evaluate functionality, rather than performance. This is an important distinction. The S3 Contest assumes that certain semantic technologies are important and seeks to improve the breed with a contest involving speed and accuracy.

The SWS Challenge makes no such assumption. Rather we seek to understand what technologies, possibly semantic, are important software engineering technologies, and for what classes of applications. Semantic Web Service technologies promise to deliver long expected automation of overall Web service consumption thus minimizing the need for manual intervention during typical lifecycle steps (i.e. discovery, negotiation, selection, mediation, composition, choreography, orchestration and invocation). We want to test this promise.

17.6 Conclusions

This Challenge has exposed the fact that using web services is still hard, with or without semantics. We can only hope that the middleware tools will soon be mature. Otherwise, it will be not only too hard to participate in the Challenge, but web services would prove to be too difficult an area to which to apply semantic technologies.

A move to less mature alternatives to WSDL- type web services is not likely to help. First, WSDL is embedded now in industry. Second, as any similar alternative (with XML descriptions of the services) mature, the associated tools will go though similar maturity problems, unless they take advantage of the current tools, in which case WSDL is just as good. However, we remain open to the possibilities of other types of web services that fit the Dagstuhl definition. And we look for new tools and infrastructure that can make using web services easier for our participants.

This Challenge has exposed the fact that academic claims of being able to solve problems should be viewed very critically until they are verified by a methodology similar to that of the Challenge. Every participant has found that solving even the simplest Challenge problem has been far more difficult than anticipated, no one has solved all of the problems, and at least one participant worked for an extended period of time without solving a single problem. At least one semantically-oriented team has not attempted to solve other problems after seeing the effort required to solve the first "simple" problem.

Certainly a good bit of this difficulty comes from the immaturity of the WSDL stack. But the Challenge has exposed fundamental problems with some of the approaches. And it is clear that some of the technologies that have continued to participate have become increasingly semantic in the technologies deployed at each workshop, which we hope is beneficial.

But it is important that unless technologies are tested and evaluated by an initiative such as this Challenge, then claims made purely on paper should be taken with a grain of salt.

As discussed above, the Challenge has not yet proven that "semantics" is a superior software engineering technology, and indeed it is an open question of the right methodology for testing the malleability of any software technology. In the end, a "semantic" technology may only be some very declarative coding methodology that makes changes very easy to manage and which will allow processes composed of web services to scale, for some large and important class of industrial problems. Indeed, we may be surprised in the future to find that some scripting language, say PERL, can be used to compose web services as well as any more advanced technique. We do not expect that this is the case, only that we will find out whether it is,

As we move to more complex scenarios intended to reveal the advantages of semantic approaches, we continue to scientifically validate claims and investigate what technologies are good for managing services, the data they consume, and the processes that are composed of such services to solve industry-relevant problems. While in this process of discovery, The Challenge participants will continue to develop a level of understanding for each others technologies that would not have been possible without the common problem set and come to much a more precise understanding of the practically relevant tradeoffs between the approaches.

Index